Revolutionary Imaginings in the 1790s

Revolutionary Imaginings in the 1790s

Charlotte Smith, Mary Robinson, Elizabeth Inchbald

Amy Garnai
Tel Aviv University

First published 2009 by
PALGRAVE MACMILLAN

Palgrave Macmillan in the UK is an imprint of Macmillan Publishers Limited, registered in England, company number 785998, of Houndmills, Basingstoke, Hampshire RG21 6XS.

Palgrave Macmillan in the US is a division of St Martin's Press LLC, 175 Fifth Avenue, New York, NY 10010.

Palgrave Macmillan is the global academic imprint of the above companies and has companies and representatives throughout the world.

Palgrave® and Macmillan® are registered trademarks in the United States, the United Kingdom, Europe and other countries

ISBN-13: 978–0–230–57516–5   hardback

This book is printed on paper suitable for recycling and made from fully managed and sustained forest sources. Logging, pulping and manufacturing processes are expected to conform to the environmental regulations of the country of origin.

A catalogue record for this book is available from the British Library.

A catalogue record for this book is available from the Library of Congress.

10   9   8   7   6   5   4   3   2   1
18   17   16   15   14   13   12   11   10   09

Printed and bound in Great Britain by
CPI Antony Rowe, Chippenham and Eastbourne

For Nati, Erez and Anat

Contents

Acknowledgements

This book could not have been written without the assistance of many people and institutions and I am happy to have the opportunity to acknowledge them now. My first debt is to Robert Griffin, who was a generous, rigorous and inspirational dissertation advisor and who continued to read my work and offer his judicious guidance and criticism long after his duties as supervisor were over. His belief in this project was crucial at so many stages and I am deeply thankful for his support.

I am grateful to Harriet Guest for inviting me to the Centre for Eighteenth-Century Studies at the University of York, and to the British Academy for granting me a British Academy/ESRC Visiting Fellowship that made the visit possible. My semester at York was a moving and unforgettable experience: the pleasure of working at the beautiful King's Manor, in an office with a view of York Minster and within earshot of the hourly tolling of its bells, was matched by the kindness and hospitality of my hosts, and together created the ideal environment for research and writing. Thanks to the members of the Centre for their questions and comments on a shorter version of Chapter 1, "Precarious Bread", which I had the opportunity to present at a CECS research seminar. A special debt of gratitude goes to Jane Moody for reading an additional portion of the manuscript and for her helpful comments and conversation. Thanks also to Elizabeth Edwards, Mette Herder, Jordan Vibert and Alex Watson for helping to make my stay so enjoyable.

I want to thank the staffs of the British Library, the Huntington Library, the Bodleian Library and the National Art Library at the Victoria and Albert Museum for their assistance in making my visits fruitful and enjoyable. I also want to thank the Huntington Library for a short-term fellowship that allowed me to work in their wonderful collection. I am grateful to the Huntington Library, to the Bodleian Library and to the Trustees of the Victoria and Albert Museum for granting me permission to quote from their manuscript collections.

Working on a regular basis so far from the archives, there were also bound to be situations where I was in need of materials at times when it was impossible to travel to consult them. I am grateful to Natasha Tessone, Stefania Tutino and Galia Benziman for providing me with copies of texts when I was unable to access them myself. Special thanks to Julie Shaffer for sending me a copy of Charlotte Smith's *Letters of a Solitary Wanderer*, Vols. IV and V these many years ago.

At Palgrave Macmillan, I wish to thank Paula Kennedy for her original support of the manuscript and Steven Hall for patiently guiding me along

Acknowledgements ix

the way. I am also indebted to the anonymous reader for Palgrave Macmillan, for the insightful, penetrating comments and suggestions for revision which enabled me to write a better book.

Closer to home, I want to acknowledge the Department of English and American Studies at Tel Aviv University and the department's Cohen-Porter Fund. I would like in particular to thank Hedda Ben-Bassat, Elana Gomel, Milette Shamir and Hana Wirth-Nesher for their crucial help and encouragement at various stages of this project, from their initial support in providing me with funding for research trips and participation in international conferences and later on, in the transition from graduate student to faculty member.

My sisters, Anne Steiner and Bonnie Zinner, have always been there for me. Their ability to listen, to advise and to cheer me up when necessary has been an invaluable source of support.

The excitement that accompanies the completion of a first book is tempered in this case by the knowledge that my parents, Albert and Sara Bagon, are no longer here to see its publication. The lessons I learned from them of perseverance and hard work, and the belief they always had in me, have unfailingly accompanied me through the many years of the preparation of this project.

The book could never have been written without the love, encouragement and unwavering support of Nati, Erez and Anat Garnai; it is to them that I dedicate it now in its final form.

* * *

A slightly different version of *The Emigrants* section of Chapter 1 was previously published in *Eighteenth-Century Women* (2003); a shorter version of the Marie Antoinette section in Chapter 4 previously appeared in *Women's Writing* (2005); the section on *Every One Has His Fault* in Chapter 6 was previously published in *SEL: Studies in English Literature 1500–1900* (2007). I am grateful to the editors of these journals for permission to reproduce this material here.

Introduction

> But republican principles, whether true or only specious, appeal
> to some of the most favourite prejudices of the mind, the love of
> equality and the love of independence.
>
> William Godwin, Essay against re-opening
the war with France (1793)[1]

This book attempts to recover a particular historical moment and a scene of cultural production within it. Specifically, I examine the writings of Charlotte Smith (1749–1806), Mary Robinson (1758–1800) and Elizabeth Inchbald (1753–1821) and their response to the French Revolution and its aftermath. Smith, Robinson and Inchbald addressed the Revolution and its implications for British society in their novels, drama and poetry, and in doing so, took part in the ongoing debate over these issues that permeated print culture in general, and which found expression in newspapers, periodicals, diaries, journals and letters, as well as in literature. These texts provide access to the cultural climate of the 1790s, including the pressure exerted by a dominant conservative public opinion and its accompanying backlash on supporters of the original ideals and values of the Revolution.

In participating in the Revolution debate, Smith, Robinson and Inchbald consciously and willingly intervened in the public sphere of politics. The nature of this intervention, indeed, the terminology "public sphere" acknowledges Jürgen Habermas's conception of an inclusive space of political vitality and openness that first developed in the eighteenth century in which opinions were exchanged, debated and disseminated, a realm of public debate nurtured by the expanding presence of an increasingly influential and critical print culture, a sphere consisting of "the public of private people making use of their reason ... a sphere of criticism of public authority [. . .]."[2] As has been widely noted, Habermas's formulation excludes women from this site of discourse, for example in his claim that their participation was limited to a kind of literary readership that was separate, both legally and factually, from a "political public sphere."[3] Anne Mellor succinctly summarizes the response to this view, noting that women writers, on the contrary, "participated in the *same* formation of public opinion as did their male peers ... in the very public sphere theorized by Habermas himself."[4] As Mellor writes, "We know of more than 900 female poets, at least 500 female novelists, and numerous other female playwrights, travel writers, historians, philosophers, and political writers who published at least one volume in this period. Their writings received exceptionally wide attention and distribution through the literary reviews, the many new ladies magazines, and the fast-growing circulating libraries."[5]

Habermas's representation of an expanding sphere of public debate but also, more crucially, the critical response to his omission of gender from the equation, provide a useful context for understanding the work of women writers during the 1790s. This is a context whose tensions – the acknowledgement of a cultural dynamic yet also the need to continually re-establish the place of women within it – are apparent both in the anxious contemporary reception of these writers' work but also in more recent historiographical concerns and omissions as well. For although women's writing during the revolutionary decade has recently been receiving a generous amount of critical attention in the field of literary studies, more historically focused studies of the period marginalize, if not erase women's participation in the debate. Seminal works on the 1790s, such as E.P. Thompson's *The Making of the English Working Class* and Albert Goodwin's *The Friends of Liberty*, acknowledge only the most conspicuous interventions – the careers and writing of Mary Wollstonecraft and Hannah More – when they admit a female presence at all.[6] The numerous *other* female voices that took part in the debate and that, in their aggregate, constitute a historical phenomenon of women's political engagement, are absent from the discussion. At least as far as Thompson is concerned, this omission may be due to his marginalization of William Godwin and of Godwin's contribution to the political debate during the revolutionary decade. As Mark Philp explains, Thompson saw the Godwinian moment as one of "intellectual extremism" but also as "simply a part of the larger middle class reaction to the French Revolution: a reaction that was at first favourable, but which deserted the cause *en masse* after the September Massacres of 1792."[7] William Godwin is in fact an important figure in my discussion, personally connected to the three writers on whom I focus (an issue to which I will shortly return) and one whose ideas, and in particular his attack on oppressive social systems, were disseminated in their writings.[8]

The view which holds that the middle-class, intellectual support of the French Revolution in Britain had begun to waver by 1792, and had virtually disappeared by mid-decade, is necessarily complicated by the writings of Godwin, as well as by the writers whom I discuss in this study. Indeed, one of my main aims in this book is to show how a later pro-Revolution stand *was* conspicuously evident, specifically in the writings of Smith, Robinson and Inchbald, even in the final years of the decade. Moreover, the category of class is doubly important here: the middle class to which these writers belonged was, for them, informed by the ever-present threat of economic need (although, by the 1790s, for Inchbald this is more a memory of financial vulnerability) and a middle-class status was one to which they tenaciously held.[9] Political writing (and support of revolutionary values) was, then, both a means of making a living, and, paradoxically, one that endangered that living at the same time.

The political outspokenness that informs the writings of Smith, Robinson and Inchbald is present in the work of other prominent women writers of the 1790s, such as, most notably, Mary Wollstonecraft, Helen Maria Williams, Anna Barbauld, Mary Hays and Eliza Fenwick. This was an engagement which, although nuanced in varying degrees, represents, as Barbara Taylor writes, "the first coterie of women intellectuals to intervene in British reform politics; an involvement . . . in the major political controversy of the day [that] was an unprecedented development."[10] In her book, *Mary Wollstonecraft and the Feminist Imagination*, Taylor notes the shared concerns – reform politics – as well as the unconventional personal lives of the women writers in this cultural milieu, including the "vulnerability to male absence or delinquency,"[11] a characterization particularly appropriate for the subjects of this study: Smith and Robinson were both separated from their husbands, while Inchbald had been a widow since the age of twenty-six. In addition to Wollstonecraft, Taylor singles out for particular attention the lives and works of Anna Barbauld and Mary Hays – using the case of Barbauld to show that a reformist positioning was not always accompanied by the support for a feminist agenda and that of Hays in order to examine the career and beliefs of Wollstonecraft's closest associate, a writer who at times carried Wollstonecraftian values to even more controversial extremes.[12]

Taylor's book is only one example of how the field of literary studies has played a crucial role in the recovery of women's presence within the Revolution debate.[13] At the same time, in viewing her map of the female literary landscape of the 1790s, we must also be aware of the fact that every literary history is based on principles of selection and inclusion.[14] Thus, while her discussion provides me with a useful point of entry by delineating a specific scene of politically-informed literary production, it examines but one strain of women's writing at the close of the eighteenth century and is not the only lens through which we can locate a female response to the issues raised by the Revolution. To cite just one other possible emphasis, Claudia Johnson discusses the female literary response to the political upheavals of the 1790s through the topic of sentimentality – "politics made intimate"[15] – and the way it engaged with, and reacted to, issues raised in Burke's *Reflections on the Revolution in France*. In doing so, Johnson foregrounds (besides Wollstonecraft) a different group of writers than does Taylor, focusing on Ann Radcliffe and Frances Burney, as well as on a post-1790s response by Jane Austen, to expose the political anxieties and awareness that underlie the engagement with sentimentality and the affective response. Furthermore, it is important to remember that women's political writing was not limited to the pro-Revolution side of the ideological divide: a reading of the works of Hannah More, Elizabeth Hamilton and Jane West (along with many others) exhibits the fact that a female literary intervention into the public sphere of politics occurred on both sides of the Revolution controversy.[16]

I must now address my own principles of inclusion, and the motivations behind my selection of Smith, Robinson and Inchbald as the subjects of this study. What are the shared interests and common concerns that emerge in their writing and that can help illuminate this particular cultural moment? Why should they be discussed together? The quotation from Godwin's *Essay Against Re-Opening the War with France*, cited at the beginning of these pages, provides a good point of departure: for one, it is the "love of equality" and the "love of independence" – ideals that were nurtured by "republicanism" but also, in a wider sense, by the original revolutionary agenda itself – that found prominent expression in the works of these authors and indeed can be claimed to characterize their writing in general. The pervasiveness of revolutionary and politically-based themes can be found not only in their works published in the early 1790s, such as Robinson's poetic tribute to the Revolution, *Ainsi Va Le Monde* (1790) or Smith's radical novel *Desmond* (1792) but also, as previously noted, in their later writings, in which they acknowledge the failure of the Revolution, but also continue to valorize independence, equality and the hope for a better, more just world and, significantly, continue to link those values to the vanished possibilities of the original revolutionary project. Texts such as Smith's *The Young Philosopher* (1798), Robinson's *Walsingham* (1797), and Inchbald's *Nature and Art* (1796) present a strikingly bleak view of contemporary Britain, and it is precisely the way in which these novels encapsulate the Godwinian understanding of "what it is like to be terrorized within existing society" (to use Marilyn Butler's phrase)[17] that collectively characterizes them, and at the same time differentiates them in an important way from the social critiques that at times appear in loyalist fiction. For example, while a heroine of a novel by Jane West or Elizabeth Hamilton may struggle against the pressures and dangers of society, the threat is embodied in a villainous character who is an outsider promoting a "Jacobin" system of values; that is to say, the danger appears in an individual identified with a specific political worldview, but who is not aligned with, nor is representative of society itself or its governing institutions.[18] As we will see, for Smith, Robinson and Inchbald, existence itself (especially for an idealistic character) is continually threatened by the forces of class, patriarchy and the world as it is.

The original reception of the writings of Smith, Robinson and Inchbald exhibits an anxious acknowledgement of their participation in the Revolution debate and, in two instances at least, presents them together as a kind of collective representation of the subversive potential inherent in

women's politically-informed writing. Let us look first at Thomas J. Mathias's polemical poem *The Pursuits of Literature* which, with its extended notes
and commentary surveying the British literary landscape, first appeared in
1794 and went through multiple editions well into the nineteenth century.
In a note added to the fourth edition, Mathias asserts:

> Put for almost any modern novel, Mrs. Charlotte Smith, Mrs. Inchbald,
> Mrs. Mary Robinson, Mrs. &c. &c. though all of them are very ingenious
> ladies, yet they are too frequently *whining* or *frisking in novels,* till our girls'
> heads turn wild with impossible adventures, and are now and then tainted
> with democracy, and sometimes with infidelity and loose principles.[19]

In grouping together "Mrs. Charlotte Smith, Mrs. Inchbald, Mrs. Mary Robinson" and then turning this particularization into an abstraction as "Mrs. &c.",
Mathias doubly empowers these women by foregrounding their specificity
and, at the same time, by having them appear metonymically for all women
writers.

This comment appeared only in 1797, in the fourth edition of the *Pursuits,*
indicating the resilience of the radical reputation that Smith, Robinson and
Inchbald had earned through their earlier works.[20] The note is also a telling
example of the intensification of the attacks on the progressive intellectual
community in its wider context. As the reactionary backlash became more
and more entrenched, the *Pursuits* appeared in its later editions increasingly
as a "pursuit" of the radical intelligentsia rather than of literature per se. That
this work has in fact become a tool of surveillance is evident in another new
addition to the 1797 edition. In his advertisement, Mathias states that his
poem was written:

> upon no private motive whatsoever; but simply and solely as the conduct
> of the persons mentioned or alluded to, or the manner of their composi-
> tions, or the principles of their writings tend to influence and affect the
> learning, the government, the religion, the public morality, the public
> happiness, and the public security of this nation.[21]

Motivated, then, by the desire to expose the political "principles" present in
contemporary literature, Mathias readily qualifies his aesthetic appraisal of
the works of Smith, Robinson and Inchbald (and the "ingeniousness" of their
authors) with the "democratic" tendencies that feature within them. With his
emphasis on how literature influences "the public morality, the public happiness, and the public security of this nation" Mathias's perception reiterates
what for him is the danger, and thus, by extension, the power of politically-
motivated writing, of women's contributions to it, and – specifically here –
of the work of Smith, Robinson and Inchbald.[22]

These three writers are once more grouped together as a subversive cultural force in a review of William Godwin's novel *St. Leon* (1799) that appeared in two installments in *The Anti-Jacobin Review* in January–February 1800. To the remark that Godwin, as in "all works of this nature" makes "the defender of religion, of morality, and of government, use arguments proportioned to his, or her, own powers of refutation", the reviewer, William Heath,[23] then adds a note: "See, as proof of this, certain novels entitled – 'Man As He Is – Man As He Is Not,' by we don't know whom – 'Desmond,' by Charlotte Smith, the trash of Mrs. Robinson, – and above all that most impudent, malignant, and audacious heap of absurdity by Mrs. Inchbald, called 'Nature and Art.' "[24] It is difficult to determine whether Heath was genuinely unsure of the identity, or the gender, of Robert Bage, the author of *Man As He Is* (1792) and *Man As He Is Not*, also entitled *Hermsprong* (1796). Nonetheless, the fact that he specifically mentions by name three women authors, reinforces Emily de Montluzin's observation that "it was . . . the works of the feminist writers of the 1790s that Heath most often singled out for condemnation."[25] And, like Mathias, it is one that he finds particularly dangerous: "the majority of readers, heedlessly receive [their works] as truths, and treat the salutary lessons, which they formerly learned, as nurses' tales, or mothers' prejudices."[26] The remarks of Mathias and Heath – both prominent members of the *Anti-Jacobin* circle – point, then, not only to the recognition of the ideological provenance of the writing of Smith, Robinson and Inchbald, but also to how they signal together a kind of representativeness of a radical, female cultural engagement.[27]

The alignment of Smith, Robinson and Inchbald with a progressive, oppositional positioning is underscored in a number of wider cultural contexts that anchor my discussion. Prominent among these is the "Revolution debate" – the discursive engagement in 1790s Britain surrounding the French Revolution and the cause of domestic reform. Smith, Robinson and Inchbald consciously participate in the debate by staking their position through themes, tropes and vocabulary that reference the text that had initiated the discussion and set its terms – Edmund Burke's *Reflections on the Revolution in France* (1790).[28] In this work, considered by many as the founding text of modern conservatism,[29] Burke defends precedence and tradition and the "entailed inheritance"[30] that, for him, ensured the continuity of ordered civilization. The *Reflections* positions these principles as the alternative to chaos, and to what Burke envisioned as the destructive effect of the French Revolution on British society in particular. As Marilyn Butler has written:

> Burke celebrates . . . the aristocratic concepts of paternalism, loyalty, chivalry, the hereditary principle, bonding to the land through ownership of it. . . . [He] correctly analyses what has in fact has taken place, a bourgeois revolution. He responds with a vision of the ideal society which keeps the bourgeoisie in their place, and makes the great social institutions – the

Church, the Law, even the family – validate the aristocracy as the class of government, and the protectors of the world as we know it.[31]

Butler's synopsis succinctly points to those elements of the Burkean world-view with which Smith, Robinson and Inchbald consistently engage. Repeated portrayals of the injustice of primogeniture, for example, under-score their attacks on the hereditary system of power while justifying the defense of natural rights and the sovereignty of the people. Critiques of those "great social institutions" of the Church, Law and family, to use But-ler's formulation, appear in their insistent representations of institutional tyranny, aristocratic inadequacy, legal and domestic failure, economic and social defeat.

Burke articulated what was at the time a minority opinion among the intel-lectual elites, most of whom were sympathetic to the French Revolution in its early stages. However, as the events in France became more and more violent and especially following the September massacres of 1792, public opinion changed and many of the Revolution's early supporters shifted their position. (As mentioned earlier, E.P. Thompson saw the September massacres as the moment when the middle class deserted the cause almost entirely.) Increas-ingly anxious over the events occurring across the Channel, the government clamped down on the reform movements at home. Although especially fear-ful of working-class insurrection, the promotion of reform by a broader base, and by upper-class sympathizers and activists as well, was a serious cause of alarm and led to repressive legislation that targeted reformers across the social spectrum.

This reactionary backlash of the mid to late 1790s is a second cultural con-text that underlies my study. The 1794 Treason Trials and the 1795 Gagging Acts in particular, appear throughout this book as a kind of elusive yet omi-nous backdrop against which the later literary texts of Smith, Robinson and Inchbald were produced and circulated. Anti-reformist prosecution had, to be sure, begun earlier in the decade; the royal proclamation against seditious writings, declared in May of 1792, had already intensified the legal harass-ment of radicals.[32] In December of that year, Thomas Paine, who had fled from Britain to France, was tried *in absentia* following the publication of the second part of *The Rights of Man*. However, the trials of 1794 – first in Scotland and then in England – brought to the forefront of public consciousness the concerted campaign to quash the popular reform movement (working-class activists as well as intellectuals) while calling attention to the ubiquitous methods of surveillance employed in the attempt to do so. The Scottish tri-als ended in the conviction and deportation of three prominent activists. In London, while over thirty members of the reform societies were arrested, only Thomas Hardy, John Horne Tooke and John Thelwall, were eventually brought to trial, where they were later acquitted by the jury. Others, including the novelist and playwright Thomas Holcroft, were released without having to stand trial.

Holcroft was not the only writer to feature in the proceedings. The fact that Paine and the radical American writer Joel Barlow were repeatedly mentioned by the prosecution and referred to as "literary representatives"[33] emphasizes the way literature and literariness were perceived as having a potent agency in the cultural climate in which Smith, Robinson and Inchbald wrote their own reformist works. The fate of the original preface to Godwin's novel *Things As They Are, or the Adventures of Caleb Williams* illustrates this interconnectedness from the author's perspective: the preface was suppressed when the novel was published in May 1794, the month of the first arrests in the London trials. Godwin would later inform his readers that it had been "withdrawn ... in compliance with the alarms of booksellers .... Terror was the order of the day; and it was feared that even the humble novelist might be shown to be constructively a traitor."[34] Smith, Robinson and Inchbald were less conspicuous radical figures than Godwin, but in their works as well we will see paratextual and editorial references to the charged political times in which they wrote – in a note, a preface, the occasional qualification, the anxious revision.

The act of writing itself would come to the forefront of legal attention in the final months of 1795 with the passing of the Treasonable Practices Bill and Seditious Meetings Bill, often referred to together as the "Two Acts", or the "Gagging Acts." Precipitated by the stoning of the King's carriage while on its way to the opening of Parliament, the new laws further restricted anti-government speech and writing. Not only plotting to overthrow or kill the King, but any attempt to pressure him to change his "measures or counsels ... [or] to intimidate Parliament ... by overt act, or by speech or by writing" or to incite against the government and constitution was now considered a high misdemeanor. Meetings of over fifty people convened for public discussion and debate were subjected to strict discretionary control and prior approval by the authorities. The right to petition was severely curtailed.[35] Significantly, as John Barrell has shown, literary production also had a crucial role in the developments leading up to this legislation, with the performance of Thomas Otway's play *Venice Preserved* at Drury Lane the same night of the attack on the King's carriage. The play (originally written in 1682) tells the story of a group of republican conspirators plotting against the Senate of Venice and contains a number of stirring speeches that praise the rebel cause. Its production and the events surrounding its performance that night in the theatre – the hissing and cheering of various speeches and the disruptive atmosphere in general – were singled out as an "essential part of the republican plot" of the present time and a key factor in what was conceived as a concerted plan to overthrow the King.[36] The play was withdrawn from the stage the following day and it would be seven years before it would be performed again.

Politics and literature were also interconnected through the social networks in which like-minded men and women, many of whom were writers and artists, exchanged ideas and opinions. The social milieu surrounding William Godwin was one such network, with which Smith, Robinson and Inchbald were associated in varying and distinct yet also similar ways. Smith's connection with Godwin appears mostly through the giving and receiving of social visits during her extended stays in London at the end of the decade although she was also involved with him in a specific, shared literary endeavor when she wrote the prologue to his play, *Antonio* (1800). Robinson had two periods of intense contact with Godwin, preceding and following his marriage with Wollstonecraft and, in the final months of her life, a serious quarrel with him that caused her much anxiety. Inchbald's friendship with Godwin, unlike that of Smith and Robinson, was more consistently sustained, and began in the early 1790s. They regularly read and commented on each other's work, often attended the theatre together, and, apparently, even spoke of marriage.[37] Inchbald quarreled with Godwin after his marriage to Mary Wollstonecraft, and although they remained in intermittent contact until a year before Inchbald's death, their friendship had lost its earlier intensity.

The importance of the association of these writers with William Godwin, however, lies in much more than this specific documentation of personal experience (the major elements of which will be discussed later in this book). For it also exhibits their participation in the wider circle of radical sociability, in particular as it existed in the final years of the 1790s in London. My understanding of what is sometimes called the "Godwin circle" is indebted to the work of Mark Philp, and to his representation of the intellectual, oppositional activity of the late 1790s as an important cultural phenomenon. Philp has shown how the Godwin community is both a marker of a counter-culture that values "talents, merit and virtue" over wealth and breeding, as well as exemplifying an emergent social class "filled by professional and semi-professional men and women ... who shared a class interest in broad political reforms." For many of those associated with this milieu, it provided them with their "major, often sole, source of emotional, social and intellectual experience."[38] Philp's acknowledgement of the distinct but related categories of "counter-culture" and "emergent social class" aptly reflects the lives and work of Smith, Robinson and Inchbald individually while illuminating the broad cultural dynamic which they both articulate and experience. The notion of "counter-culture" appears through the idealized meritocratic, oppositional social vision that is expressed in their literary texts and in the willing ideological identification that informs membership in the "Godwin circle." The issue of class is evident in the way they themselves negotiate the fluctuating realities of their own class membership and their status as middle-class working women.

The connection of Smith, Robinson and Inchbald with Godwin finds expression not only in a context of radical sociability but also in their acknowledgement of his philosophical ideas and, specifically for my discussion, through their engagement with the notion of truth, as it was presented in Godwin's *Enquiry Concerning Political Justice* (1793). Truth was a central tenet of Godwin's ideological and philosophical project. It was, for him, the basis for human action; humans act upon the "truths of morality and justice … infinite, omnipresent and eternal."[39] The engagement with truth appears as a kind of ongoing refrain throughout my discussion of the works of Smith, Robinson and Inchbald, who employ the term to consciously reference a topical political concern and to stake an ideological position (although Inchbald is actually quite skeptical as to the efficacy of truth itself). While the word is no longer loaded with cultural currency in our own time, "truth" was indeed a "keyword" in the final years of the eighteenth century, in the sense of what Raymond Williams has described as the vocabulary we use to discuss and define our central experiences, "significant binding words in certain activities and their interpretation … significant, indicative words in certain forms of thought."[40] For Smith, Robinson and Inchbald the repeated invocation of "truth" carries with it important cultural and ideological baggage.

As I argue for the way that these three writers can be grouped together as a marker of a particular cultural discourse, what emerges in the pages that follow is also the recognition of difference. First, it is important to note that they were not, insofar as their personal lives are concerned, a "group" at all. Although associated with the same social circle, it is difficult to determine the full extent of the relations among the three. Godwin's diary records his meetings with them, sometimes on consecutive, or even the same days (for example, he called on both Smith and Robinson on 1 March 1800)[41] but provides no evidence of his seeing them *together*. As for the women themselves, Smith and Inchbald seem to have been in contact in particular in the latter part of 1797. While no correspondence between them survives, Smith mentions having written to Inchbald in a letter to her publishers; she also alludes to a conversation they had had regarding their financial agreements concerning the publication of their novels.[42] Later that year Inchbald refers to Smith in a letter written to Godwin following the death of Mary Wollstonecraft. Responding to his report of the tragic news (and referring to a previous altercation) Inchbald writes that she had spoken well of Godwin's late wife: "Let Charlotte Smith be my witness, who received [Wollstonecraft's] character from me, such as I gave of her to everybody."[43]

I have found no evidence for any contact between Mary Robinson and either Smith or Inchbald. Smith mentions Robinson disparagingly, in connection with the appearance of her (Smith's) portrait in the publication of the 1797 *Elegiac Sonnets*.[44] Robinson's own gesture to Smith, the "Sonnet to Mrs. Charlotte Smith, on Hearing That Her Son Was Wounded at the Siege of Dunkirk", was published in the *Oracle* on 17 September 1793, under the name of Oberon (one of the many pseudonyms she used when publishing in the newspapers) and Smith is referred to there as "Britain's genius."[45] Even if the poem had appeared under her own name, it is hard to say whether

Smith would have acknowledged it. Both she and Inchbald, notwithstanding their otherwise progressive opinions, were keen to distance themselves from Robinson's notoriety as Perdita, the former mistress of the Prince of Wales. Social reputations had to be maintained; sexual transgressions among peers and associates were, thus, difficult to forgive.

Charlotte Smith, Mary Robinson and Elizabeth Inchbald were all prolific writers. Smith wrote ten novels, the ninety-two sonnets that appeared in the ever expanding editions of her *Elegiac Sonnets*, two extended blank-verse poems, *The Emigrants* (1793) and *Beachy Head* (1806), numerous other shorter poems and a play, *What Is She?* (1799).[46] Robinson wrote six novels, and "literally countless" poems, many of which still remain uncollected,[47] a play, *Nobody* (1794), and the political tracts *Impartial Reflections on the Present Situation of the Queen of France* (1791) and *Letter to the Women of England* (1799). Inchbald wrote twenty plays, two novels, as well as theatre criticism – 125 prefaces to Longman's *The British Theatre* (1806–9). In light of the sheer quantity of this writing, it would be virtually impossible in terms of space (especially in a project that encompasses multiple authors) to discuss all the works of these writers in which a revolutionary awareness is exposed. Consequently, I have had to be selective. Thus, I have omitted from my discussion Smith's *The Old Manor House* (1793) and *Marchmont* (1796), Robinson's *The Natural Daughter* (1799) and Inchbald's *Next-Door Neighbours* (1791), works that also prominently engage with the issues raised by the French Revolution. There are various reasons for these omissions, and the choice of certain texts over others: with Smith, I have chosen works which directly acknowledge the Revolution and its aftermath, or in the case, of *The Letters of a Solitary Wanderer*, point to a generic development that emerges from the relation to it, the breakdown of epistolarity; with Robinson, I have chosen *Walsingham* over *The Natural Daughter* for the way in which, to my mind, the former novel more strikingly displays the wider manifestations of cultural crisis; with Inchbald, I have selected original plays rather than adapted translations.

My decision to focus on a limited number of texts results from a methodological aim – the desire to engage in extended close readings of the selected works, rather than to present a more inclusive survey that would point to the presence, indeed the ubiquity, of certain themes but would limit the ability to explore them in some detail. Surveys of the literature of the 1790s are, to be sure, indispensable in recovering the wealth of writing during this period, and direct us to the presence of issues and themes (in previously obscure works) of which we might otherwise be unaware. However, a survey approach limits the ability to discuss at length the cultural awareness that permeates individual texts, and in particular the more discrete observations and articulations that expand our view of the dynamics of an ongoing political consciousness and the poetics of its representation.[48] By closely examining specific texts, I want to acknowledge not only a profound political engagement, but also the literary value of previously neglected writing.

The six chapters of this book examine the work of Smith, Robinson and Inchbald, by highlighting this political awareness and the different ways it is expressed. Two chapters are devoted to each author: with Smith and Robinson, I focus on the early and later parts of the 1790s respectively, and with Inchbald, I discuss separately her novels and drama. I will be especially attentive to the anxious contemporaneousness within the works as they respond to the changing fortunes of the Revolution and of the reform movement in Britain. Generally we will see that whereas Smith and Robinson both distance themselves from, and qualify their support of, the French Revolution during the period of the Terror and the guillotining of Marie Antoinette (in *The Banished Man* and *Monody to the Memory of the Late Queen of France*, respectively) this is precisely the time when Inchbald (if we rely on the evidence of her early draft of *Nature and Art*) appears most resolutely radical. Moreover, certain thematic elements receive particular emphasis in my discussion of each author: with Smith I focus on the preoccupation with exile and displacement as signifiers of her response to the failure of revolutionary ideals; my discussion of Robinson stresses the concern with victimization and vulnerability as factors that shape, but also limit her identification with a radical worldview; regarding Inchbald, I center on the tension between ideology and caution as an ongoing feature that characterizes her writings. Nonetheless, alongside these varying focuses, what emerges from my readings is a view of a sustained literary response to, and ultimately support of, the French Revolution and of the political and cultural worldview which that support implies, one that is idealistically and ideologically inclined but also always cognizant of the practical realities that inform that positioning – both in terms of the failure of the Revolution itself and the pressures exerted on the presentation of a progressive worldview within an increasingly repressive cultural climate.

Indeed, recognizing these pressures, Charlotte Smith, in the preface to *Desmond*, her radical novel of the French Revolution, calls attention to a contemporary reality but then challenges it: "But women, it is said have no business with politics. – Why not?"[49] This project explores the way three women writers embrace the business of politics and as they do so, provide an emphatic answer to the question.

1

Precarious Bread: Charlotte Smith I

Charlotte Smith's literary work of the 1790s exhibits the pressures exerted on a woman writing during a time of political upheaval. The tensions that inform her presentation of a progressive agenda are apparent both in the display of her politics within her work and the way either explicitly or implicitly, it calls attention to the concerns of the revolutionary decade. Smith herself alludes to the pressures informing artistic endeavor in a poem published in the *European Magazine* in November 1792. Written for "one of the Brighthelmstone Players, under some embarrassment", and entitled simply "Occasional Address", Smith portrays the tenuous existence of a theatre troupe, with its continual struggle for artistic and economic survival. Indeed, the wandering life of the actors was one with which she could strongly identify:

> But pinion'd here, alas! *I* cannot fly,
> The hapless, unplum'd, lingering straggler, I!
> Unless the healing pity you bestow
> Shall imp my shatter'd wings, and let me go!
> Hard is *his* fate – whom evil stars have led
> To seek in scenic art precarious bread,
> While still, thro' wild vicissitudes afloat,
> An hero now, and now a *Sans Culotte*![1]

Smith introduces here a notion of impaired movement which nevertheless strives to proceed, its ineffectuality informed still by the spirit of artistic energy. And yet, her depiction of the precarious vocation of the artist receives further significance when viewed in the context of the conspicuous political engagement present throughout her work, one that she consistently sustained even as she recognized the ways it reinforced the pressures exerted on her literary career. Smith's reference to the "*sans culotte*" encapsulates this awareness, calling attention to the "wild vicissitudes" – those dramatic political upheavals that are taking place even as she writes. (And such was the force of the events in France that, as she writes in a note following this passage, "at the time, little else was talked of.")[2]

Charlotte Smith was no stranger to fluctuations of fortune in her personal life as well. In this chapter and the one that follows I examine Smith's "precarious bread", a literary oeuvre that emerges from a life defined by continuous economic instability as well as in later years, by profound political disillusionment. Separated from an abusive husband and raising a large family alone, Smith (1749–1806) was constantly pressed by the need to ensure her family's financial survival – this was a lifetime struggle whose ongoing progress she openly shares with her readers in the prefaces and notes that accompany her literary texts and through thinly veiled autobiographical characters that appear within them. In her attempt to advance the settlement of her father-in-law's complicated, labyrinthine will and to ensure that her children received the inheritance that was provided for them, Smith was ever aware of the pervasiveness of institutionalized injustice and inequality and of how gender and declining status define her particular experience of dispossession, "helpless" as she calls herself, "from sex and situation."[3] This understanding of the interconnectedness of the political and the domestic spheres reverberates through Smith's works, not only in allusions to her own life story but also in her acknowledgement of the failed vision of social reform and with it the recognition that the French Revolution, in which she had invested so much hope, had been ultimately unable to bring about a better and more just society.

The works I discuss in this chapter – *Desmond* (1792), *The Emigrants* (1793) and *The Banished Man* (1794) – display a political awareness which in many ways is characterized by its immediacy, as an ongoing response to, and a barometer of, the tumultuous events of the first half of the revolutionary decade. Although this response seems at times equivocal (in particular in *The Banished Man*) Smith never rejects the values which the Revolution had originally embraced. Yet, delineating this political engagement is a task freighted with its own problematics: How should we account for what was clearly perceived as Smith's retraction of her support of the French Revolution? To what extent can we associate or dissociate the characters in her novels from an authorial viewpoint? How can we accommodate Smith's politics within the personal, authorial and economic concerns that emerge in many of her prefatory addresses to the public?

In attempting to confront these issues, I turn first to a review that appeared in 1798 in the inaugural edition of the conservative *Anti-Jacobin Review*. In his discussion of Smith's *The Young Philosopher* (1798), the critic, Robert Bisset, constructs a trajectory of her politics:

> [Smith] has repeatedly changed from monarchist to democrat; from democrat to monarchist. In her "Desmond" she had adopted all the ideals of the

French revolutionists, and in her "Banished Man", when her daughter was married to an emigrant, she became eager for the nobility as they subsisted under the old government of France; ... since that time she has become a ranker democrat than ever. As in "Desmond", her chief object was to praise the new order of France; in "Marchmont" to disparise the existing establishment in England; so in "The Young Philosopher" she continues to abuse England, and attempts to prove, as she cannot say much for the happiness of France, that the only place of comfortable abode is America.[4]

Bisset identifies *The Banished Man* as a crucial moment in Smith's political thinking, as the turning point in which she disavows her original sympathy for and support of the Revolution. At the same time, his argument is also aimed at challenging her integrity: thus, while his comment that Smith "became eager for the nobility" suggests an identification with the French aristocracy and its values, his use of the term "repeatedly", and his claim that "she [had] become a ranker democrat than ever," deny her any sustained political thought or, it is implied, ideological seriousness of purpose.

I will suggest an alternative trajectory, one which privileges the continuity of Smith's progressive, reformist thinking, even as she signals her disappointment in the failure of the promise that the Revolution had seemed to embody. Thus, what has often been mistakenly perceived as Smith's disavowal of revolutionary principles is, rather, a dual project which upholds those principles but at the same time mourns their loss.[5] The focus on disillusionment and regret displays itself both thematically and structurally in Smith's writings. As the revolutionary vision collapsed and any hope for the implementation of its principles became untenable, she emphasizes themes of displacement, alienation and exile; as Bisset suggests, her characters' desire to reside *outside* of Britain becomes a pressing, if not imperative, concern. Furthermore, as we shall see in this chapter and the next, the breakdown of epistolarity in the movement from *Desmond* to *The Letters of a Solitary Wanderer* – the two novels that frame my discussion – is indicative of how the portrayal of disunity may also be manifested in narrative structures, and literary form itself becomes a marker of cultural crisis.

I

In order to chart the movement through which political confidence is transformed into disillusionment, we must first look briefly at *Desmond*, the novel where Smith most forcefully defends the ideals of the French Revolution, and in which she earns her radical credentials. Published in June 1792, it served as the touchstone by which all her further writings were judged. *Desmond* is an epistolary novel that tells the story of the idealistic Lionel Desmond and Geraldine Verney, the married woman with whom he is in love. The novel begins when Desmond embarks on a journey to France, to observe first hand the Revolution and its aftermath and to distance himself from Geraldine, who is married to a man who loses his fortune through drinking and gambling. In France, Desmond is joined in his travels by the Marquis de Montfleuri, a French nobleman and a supporter of the Revolution, and their observations enable Smith to present a defense of the Revolution through the eyes of both a sympathetic English spectator and an enlightened French nobleman. During his travels, but unknown to the reader at the time, Desmond has an affair with Montfleuri's sister, Josephine de Boisbelle, another victim of a marriage to a worthless husband. The baby born as a result of this affair is brought by Desmond to Geraldine, who agrees to raise the infant together with her own children.

Gradually, the political arguments between the characters which have served as the main focus of the opening section of the novel are rewritten into the portrayal of domestic concerns. Geraldine's financial situation worsens, and she is eventually ordered by her husband to go to France to be the "guest" of a duke, one of his wealthy friends, and thus is literally sold into prostitution. Managing to fend off the duke's advances, Geraldine receives word that her husband, who has joined a band of anti-Revolution forces, is mortally wounded. Compelled by what she sees as her duty as a wife, she ventures through war-torn territory to join him. She soon encounters Desmond, who, without her knowledge has been following her trail, and together they make the dangerous trip to Verney's bedside, where they nurse him until his death, to which he goes repentant, subdued and reconciled. With Verney conveniently out of the way, Desmond can declare his love for Geraldine. The couple returns to England, where they are joined by Desmond's friend Montfleuri, who has married Geraldine's sister, Fanny. The novel concludes with these characters grouped together in a tableau of domestic peace and contentment, which is also one of political and intellectual enlightenment.

The radical agenda in *Desmond* is exhibited most prominently in the eponymous hero's consistent and energetic defense of the French Revolution, both in letters to his friend and mentor, Bethel, and in his discussions with reactionary Britons whom he meets in the course of his travels. An example of such a conversation appears at the outset of the novel, where Desmond asserts to a female acquaintance:

> I am glad that oppression is destroyed; that the power of injuring the many is taken from the few. – Dear Madam, are you aware of the evils which in consequence of the feudal system existed in France? . . . That these powers are annihilated, no generous mind can surely lament.[6]

Desmond repeatedly defends the Revolution in "real time", referring, as the novel progresses, to the contemporaneous publication of the two works that defined and demarcated the British reaction to the events in France, Edmund

Burke's *Reflections on the Revolution in France* (1790) and Thomas Paine's *The Rights of Man* (1791).[7] Her protagonist's comments regarding these texts signal Smith's own participation in the "Revolution debate": the *Reflections* is, for him, "an elaborate treatise in favour of despotism" (pp. 154–5) and the response to Paine is equally trenchant, acknowledging what Marilyn Butler calls the "brutal directness"[8] of Paine's prose:

> I am forcibly struck with truths that either were not seen before, or were (by men who did not wish to acknowledge them) carefully repressed. They are bluntly, sometimes coarsely delivered, but it is often impossible to refuse immediate assent to those which appear boldest. (p. 177)

Desmond's comments call attention to the impact of Paine's work, the reformist energy across social classes that it galvanized and the clear and accessible writing that caused the authorities so much anxiety.[9] Although the true extent of Paine's vision of society and his detailed and far-reaching program for social reform would only appear in *The Rights of Man Part II*, published shortly before *Desmond* in 1792, *Part I* (to which the characters refer in their discussions) was significant in itself in its strident attack on monarchy, aristocracy and the Church.

Smith's various references to and support of, specific issues raised in *The Rights of Man*, such as the attack on Burke's view of the events of the "Glorious Revolution" of 1688 as binding for posterity,[10] the corruption of the peerage system, the injustice of game laws, and above all Paine's criticism of economic inequality in general, serve to reinforce the ideological linkage of that text and her novel.[11] Through her repeated acknowledgements of social injustice, Smith establishes a parallel between the situation that existed in pre-Revolutionary France, which gave the nobility "every power to impoverish and depress the peasant and the farmer" (p. 37) and that of present-day England and its own victims of economic oppression – "a poor man, an ancient woman, a deserted child, who were found dead in such or such alley and street" (p. 181). This parallel indicates not only Smith's identification with Paine but also reflects her participation in the wider cultural conversation in which the events in France were prominently linked to the need for political and social reform on the other side of the Channel.

Smith's radical awareness manifests itself in *Desmond* through this recurrent contrast between the state of events in Britain and what appeared in 1790–2 as the promise embodied in the French experiment. At the same time, she also situates her novel within wider Enlightenment and radical traditions; we find repeated references to Voltaire, Rousseau, Locke, Joseph Priestley and especially to Milton throughout the text. Significantly, three citations of *Areopagitica* appear at moments of intense political discussion, enabling Smith to call the attention of her readers not only to the possibilities of the revolutionary moment, but also, in referencing Milton's text on censorship and the freedom of the press, to the tensions that inform its defense. Although the Revolution debate was still in full and energetic force, Paine had already been summoned to trial in June 1792 and the further publication of *The Rights of Man* banned one month earlier.

Alongside this more general political engagement, Smith also offers her own particular contribution to, and perspective on, the Revolution debate by including gender concerns in her political equation. Her recognition of the reality of gender inequalities qualifies to a certain extent the exuberance of the particular political moment in which she was writing. The story of Geraldine Verney, the married woman with whom Desmond is in love, and her misfortunes at the hands of her wastrel husband, exemplifies the dual focus in this novel, which in excoriating tyrannical power also extends its critique to the tyranny of domestic institutions and thus, to use Diana Bowstead's words, "ties[s] injustice in the government of nations to injustice in the government of families."[12] Smith's villains indeed move seamlessly between these two fronts. For example, the Duke to whom Geraldine is "sold" by her husband is described by Desmond as "a most inveterate enemy of the Revolution [who] execrated the struggle [the French] had so successfully made for their liberties" (pp. 245–6). Through Geraldine's story, with its entwining of personal and political concerns, Smith tempers the euphoria of the moment by presenting a critique of patriarchal power to remind her readers of the grim realities of women's experience.

As various critics have pointed out, Geraldine's acquiescence to her husband's imperious demands stands in marked contrast to the novel's privileging of the Revolution, with its concurrent legitimizing of the overthrow of all forms of tyranny.[13] Yet, while Geraldine's actions signal obedience and submission, her thoughts, paradoxically, convey the same radical sentiments as those of Desmond. Traveling through France, she asserts that "every principal, all that we owe to God, our fellow creatures and ourselves, is clearly on the [side of the Revolution]" (p. 312). She then adds:

> This [understanding] must be from conviction, for it cannot be from the prejudice of education. – *We* [her sister Fanny, and herself] were always brought up as if we were designed for wives of the Vicars of Bray. – My father, indeed, would not condescend to suppose that our sentiments were worth forming or consulting; and with all my respect for his memory, I cannot help recollecting that he was a very Turk in principle, and hardly allowed women any pretensions to souls, or thought them worth more care than he bestowed on his horses, which were to look sleek, and do their paces well. (p. 312)

Yet if Geraldine *thinks* this way, making explicit the connection between political and family-centered injustice, how are we to understand her actions, which exhibit behavior precisely the opposite of what she preaches? One way of reconciling this tension is suggested by Chris Jones, who explains the seeming incongruity of Geraldine's behavior in relation to the Revolution by viewing her as a parody heroine, a "Trojan horse" through which Smith could call her readers' attention to the constraints in which eighteenth-century women writers were forced to construct their heroines: "Smith could not offend the susceptibilities of her readers by making her heroine act as she herself had done in real life by separating from her husband, but she emphasizes the untenable rigour of the convention by presenting Geraldine's behaviour in exaggerated, even parodic, terms."[14] While this view provides a plausible explanation of Geraldine's enigmatic behavior, I believe that the main significance of her story lies in this very tension between her radical thinking and "traditional", submissive action. Smith's particularized enactment of the financially vulnerable woman and the terror and helplessness that motivate her behavior indicates her awareness of a form of tyranny so profound that it resists the liberating potential of the Revolution. Revolutionary values, Smith implies, are limited, if not totally ineffectual, in their ability to alleviate the oppressiveness of female experience.[15]

Geraldine's financial decline exemplifies what Edward Copeland has identified as the existential terror which defines the experience of unprovided women as it is represented in late eighteenth century writing, the recognition that this "was indeed a society in which a woman without access to cash might have no place at all."[16] And although the revolutionary novel would seem to anticipate a parallel liberation for her, Smith is unable to provide one that moves beyond the conventional – the freedom and financial security that await Geraldine after her husband's demise. A less contrived freedom for women from the exigencies of financial duress, and from the subjugation of patriarchy itself, remains elusively outside the purview of the narrative.

The place of women within the revolutionary scheme, as Smith perceives it, becomes even more ambivalent when we turn to the story of Josephine de Boisbelle, the woman with whom Desmond has a brief affair during his stay in France. Like Geraldine, Josephine is tied to an "ill-assorted marriage" (p. 77) with a dissolute husband; unlike her English counterpart, however, she follows through with her sexual desires in her husband's absence. While not exactly condemned for her actions – Montfleuri, Desmond's friend, takes responsibility for the encouragement of the affair, and the other approved characters regard her with what appears to be sincere enough sympathy[17] – Josephine is nonetheless marginalized within the action and silenced in the text; her daughter is taken from her to be raised by Geraldine, and her voice is not included among the multiple voices that participate in the exchanges that constitute the epistolary narrative. If, then, the story of Geraldine represents the limits of the revolutionary vision, that of Josephine seems to acknowledge additional tensions, resulting not only from a further representation of female vulnerability, but also, I suspect, from Smith's unwillingness to position the unconventional woman more centrally in the text. Despite the fact that she was prepared to present a forthright, even courageous radical intervention, the exhilaration of the moment was nonetheless tempered by the awareness of how far she could overstep conventional sexual and social boundaries. At the very moment when she is able to most fully envision the realization of the revolutionary agenda (and by publishing her novel, to overstep, herself, prevailing cultural conventions) Smith reminds us of the degree to which the range of women's experience could be given a voice – by a woman – in a radical text.

This troubling recognition of the place of women, then, does not diminish Smith's radicalism as it is conveyed in the novel as a whole, but at the same time, alerts us to the limitations, as she sees them, of the Revolution's liberating potential. The final grouping of Desmond, Geraldine and their circle depicted at the close of the novel underlines this duality. On the one hand, we are presented with an enlightened, tolerant and politically progressive community as the final word of the text. And when compared with the exiles and displacements which will feature so prominently within Smith's later work, and with her later politically non-conforming protagonists who are effectively forced to leave their inhospitable homeland, the location of this community is especially telling: to find the progressive ideal of "studies . . . amusements, rural improvements [and] domestic and social happiness" (p. 408) one needs to look no further than the English countryside. (Such is its availability that even the French Montfleuri seems content to remain in England.) At the same time, the very representation of this circle of sociability once more indicates Smith's reservations as to the efficacy of the revolutionary project as far as women are concerned. As Anne Mellor has noted, the female voice receives no presence at all in the conclusion of *Desmond*. It is only through Desmond's words that we perceive the harmonious resolution of events – not only Josephine, but Geraldine, and her heretofore outspoken sister, Fanny, are silent as the narrative draws to a close.[18]

The general sense of political possibility in *Desmond* is more prominently underscored in the novel's structure, in the vitality of its epistolary form and in the exhibition of what Janet Altman has termed "comic epistolary closure."[19] The forthcoming marriage of Desmond and Geraldine ensures that the letter writers have no need to write anymore; the enlightened, progressive community is intact. The energy of *Desmond's* epistolarity is also indicative of its particular historical positioning within the tradition of the novel of letters, especially as it appears in the late eighteenth century. As Nicola Watson has argued, the epistolary novels of the 1790s exhibit a particular valence in representing women's political awareness, in particular through the appropriation of Rousseau's *La Nouvelle Heloise* as a shorthand for female desire and its subversive revolutionary implications.[20] In her study of the convergence of the letter and the revolutionary narrative, Watson also identifies how the letter in the novel, as well as the letter as the novel, succumb to, and are transformed by, the cultural pressures of the period: "the rapid disintegration of the epistolary novel in the late 1780s and the 1790s, far from being the 'natural' consequences of the increasing sophistication of the novel ... was ... intimately bound up with the problematic political resonances of its narrative mode in the revolutionary and post-revolutionary period."[21] Watson locates *Desmond*, published just before the Terror would cause many of the strongest supporters of the Revolution to question and re-think its principles, as the last novelistic moment in which the yoking of the sentimental letter to the enthusiasm of revolutionary politics was possible.[22] My study of Charlotte Smith, bracketed by her two novels of letters – *Desmond* and *The Letters of a Solitary Wanderer* – reinforces this claim. As we will see in the next chapter, the later novel, with its tenuous epistolarity, illustrates how, as the decade progressed, and especially in the peak years of conservative reaction at its close, neither the letter in the novel, nor the letter as novel was able to sustain itself as an outlet for the expression of changing radical concerns.

Desmond's narrative form successfully articulates the enthusiasm of revo-lutionary politics despite the fact that epistolarity itself actually signals the distancing of the protagonists from the authorial voice. In her preface to the novel, Smith acknowledges this potential for multiple points of view, just as she affirms her identification with the radical position:

> In carrying on my story in [England and France], and at a period when their political situation (but particularly that of the latter) is the general topic of discourse in both; I have given to my imaginary characters the arguments I have heard on both sides; and if those in favour of one party have evidently the advantage, it is not owing to my partial representation but to the predominant power of truth and reason, which can neither be altered nor concealed. (p. 6)

Smith's remarks call our attention to the "advantage" held by those (mul-tiple) characters in her novel who promote the revolutionary cause. Yet Susan Lanser has argued that it is, rather, the predominance of *one* corre-spondent that more successfully conveys the spirit of authorial purpose: the "compositional surrogacy by which the reader might assume an ideologi-cal equivalence between the author and the fictional letter-writer seems best accomplished through an epistolary structure that is dominated by a sin-gle voice."[23] The multi-vocal epistolarity of *Desmond* would seem, then, to problematize my claim for an identification between Smith and the radical political views presented in the novel. However, in terms of the identification with a particular ideology, it is important to note that *all* the letter-writers in *Desmond* except Bethel unequivocally support the Revolution, and he is not so much against it as cautiously skeptical. Moreover, Smith is being some-what disingenuous in stating that she has her characters present arguments heard on "both sides." The anti-Revolution views, such as those articulated by the reactionary Lord Newminster and General Wallingford are relayed to the reader not directly, but "second-hand", through the reportage of Desmond and Bethel in their correspondence.

Smith's prefatory remarks, furthermore, affirm Lanser's claim for the preface in the late eighteenth century as a site in which women could assert an authorial presence and "proclaim confidence in their work."[24] By emphasizing the power of "truth", Smith rejects the possibility the epistolary narrative affords her of concealing, or blurring her own political agenda, using her preface instead to reinforce an authoritative, ideological point of view. In this sense, *Desmond* operates similarly to another radical novel of letters that appeared in 1792, Thomas Holcroft's *Anna St. Ives*, in which truth is likewise associated with an ideological worldview and promoted by an eponymous protagonist, and in which the reader is left with no doubt as to which of the correspondents' views are sanctioned with authorial approval. In contrast to *Desmond*, *Anna St. Ives* is dissociated from actual historical events (the letters are undated and there are no references to contemporary events). However, the novel's consistent endorsement of social equality and the preeminence of "truth" firmly locate it as a radical political intervention. And although these views are repeatedly and conspicuously presented through the letters of Anna and her lover, Frank Henley, Holcroft, in further contrast to Smith, allocates an epistolary presence to voices that argue against the approved political positioning. The final volumes of the novel are dominated by the long, intense letters of Coke Clifton, Anna's rejected suitor, who is a supporter of the social and cultural status quo.[25]

The degree to which Smith was identified with the radical position endorsed in *Desmond* is apparent in the novel's critical reception.[26] And while Smith's views were commended by the liberal periodicals – for example, the reviewer for the *European Magazine* writes that "our Authoress has certainly vindicated the cause of French liberty with much acuteness"[27] – her outspoken political stand was censured in other circles, in one instance at least, generating a rumor that she "was bribed to [writing the novel] by the democratic party."[28] In an act that conspicuously acknowledges the political resonance of *Desmond*, Smith was recognized on 18 November 1792, by the British Club, a group of radical Britons living in France, who raised their glasses in toast to "the Women of Great Britain, particularly those who have distinguished themselves by their writings in favor of the French Revolution, Mrs. (Charlotte) Smith, and Miss H.M. Williams."[29] This toast, one of thirteen given that night, was part of an event (a celebration of the victory of Revolutionary forces at Verdun) in which, as David V. Erdman relates, the members of the British Club also "sang, danced ... and signed a manifesto of solidarity to be read at the [National] Convention."[30] The fact that the signed manifesto, along with the other events of the evening, was later publicized both in France and Britain and, in fact, reported on by a British government spy, points to the dissemination of Smith's radical reputation throughout public and political circles.[31]

Among those toasted at the British Club, Smith is the only one who had earned her place with a work of imaginative prose.[32] *Desmond* signifies, thus, not only a particular moment of political engagement (and recognition) and not only that literary and ideological touchstone against which her later work would be identified and compared. It also represents the power of fiction itself and the strength with which it could intervene in, mediate, and shape the political discourse of its time.

II

On 3 November 1792, two weeks before the celebration at the British Club, Smith had written a letter to one of the men who would sign its manifesto, the American writer and political activist Joel Barlow, who was in France observing the progress of the Revolution. In that letter, she reiterates once more the political views that she had presented in *Desmond*, and which would be acknowledged two weeks later in the toast in Paris. At the same time, however, through her plea to Barlow to intervene on behalf of the French emigrants, Smith exhibits the sensitivity towards individual suffering regardless of political persuasion which would continue to define her writing throughout the rest of her life. Her own financial vulnerability and general feeling of disenfranchisement caused her to feel a profound sympathy for the emigrant exiles, and their plight was one, from her own experience, she felt deeply. Smith's understanding of the misery of the dispossessed permeates her reasoned and compassioned letter to Barlow:

> The magnitude of the Revolution is such as ought to make it embrace every great principle of Morals, & even in a Political light (with which, I am afraid Morals have but little to do), it seems to me wrong for the Nation entirely to exile and abandon these unfortunate Men. How really great would it be, could the Convention bring about a reconciliation.[33]

Loraine Fletcher focuses on this remark in order to posit the claim that Smith had undergone a change – what she terms a *"volte-face"* – in her political thinking, arguing that Smith's sympathy for the French exiles has tempered her support of the ideals of the Revolution.[34] However, a reading of a section of the letter to Barlow that Fletcher does *not* quote evinces the fact that the opposite was actually the case:

> I really pity the advocates for despotism. They are so terribly mortified at the late events in France; and, as they never had anything to say that had even the semblance of reason; and now are evidently on the wrong side of the question both in Theory and Practice it is really pitiable to hear the childish shifts and miserable evasions to which they are reduced.[35]

Smith prefaces this assertion by complimenting Barlow on his *Advice to the Privileged Orders* and *Letter to the National Convention*. These texts, both written in 1792, exhibit Barlow's radical ideas: *Advice* is addressed to the ruling classes throughout Europe, whom he urges to adopt revolutionary principles, while presenting an overall condemnation of such institutions as primogeniture, the Church and the military. His *Letter to the National Convention* addresses legislators in France and specifically critiques the 1791 French constitution that had been prepared by the now defunct National Assembly. Barlow argues against the retention of a limited monarchy (which was indeed abolished by the Convention in September 1792, in its very first session) while also calling for, among other things, the end to capital punishment, to imprisonment for debt and to the criterion of property ownership in determining the right of representation.[36] What was seen by many as the "dangerous" radicalism of these texts is underscored in the fact that they were singled out for particular attention at the 1794 Treason trials. Passages from *Advice to the Privileged Orders* for example, were read aloud by the prosecution at the trial of John Thelwall in order to link him together with Barlow as members of a radical conspiracy.[37]

Although Fletcher qualifies Smith's praise of Barlow as merely a "tactful" gesture,[38] the depth of Smith's identification with his ideas is apparent in the way that many of them resonate in her own writing. For example, Barlow's claim that primogeniture is "abominable" and "contrary to nature" is repeatedly illustrated in the portrayals of imperious, wasteful and inept eldest sons that appear in Smith's fiction. Likewise, his mistrust of English jurisprudence was an issue with which she could readily identify from her own battles with Chancery over her father-in-law's will, and his comments on that subject must have seemed particularly relevant to her: "the administration of justice (which ought to be as simple as possible) is so involved in perplexity, that none but men of professional skill can attempt to understand it."[39]

At the same time, Smith's compassion for the French emigrants, whose situation she describes to Barlow as being "more deplorable even than ... enemies seem to deserve"[40] underscores her sympathy for the plight of the uprooted and dispossessed and exhibits an identification with a human condition that moves beyond more immediate political concerns. Smith's use of poetry as a vehicle for expressing this position is in itself significant, especially when compared to *Desmond*. As Paula Backscheider has observed, by reading that novel, with its strict temporal contextualization, together with *The Emigrants*, we can view "Smith's sophisticated understanding and use of genre differences as she develops her own political and social critiques and agendas. While the poem strives for detachment and even transcendence, the [novel portrays] immersion in immediate reality."[41]

The recognition that exile is somehow an inseparable feature of human existence is played out at length, as we shall see, in *The Banished Man* and *The Young Philosopher*, yet receives its first major expression in Smith's work in *The*

Emigrants (1793), in which the visibility of the suffering of the French refugees enables her to extrapolate a specific situation into an all-encompassing depiction of rootlessness, alienation and loss. The year that had passed between the publication of *Desmond* and *The Emigrants* had been a pivotal one in determining the public response in England to the Revolution. The September massacres, the imprisonment of the royal couple and the execution of Louis XVI had stemmed the support of moderates in England towards the events in France and Smith's expression of sympathy towards the French émigrés could be seen as a marker of this shift in public opinion.[42] As a reviewer for the *Monthly Review* noted approvingly, in *The Emigrants* "Mrs. Smith has judiciously confined her attention to those particulars in the case of the emigrants, which have excited sympathy in the minds of the humane of all parties."[43] It appears that Smith had moved from the intense radical engagement of *Desmond* into an area which, in spite of its political nature, would appeal to a wide popular consensus.

The support of the French exiles was a cause that was adopted by prominent figures across the political spectrum, including writers such as Hannah More and Frances Burney.[44] More's *Prefatory Address to the Ladies &c of great Britain and Ireland in Behalf of the French Emigrant Clergy* was published in 1793 and appeared together with her *Remarks on the Speech of Mr. Dupont, on the Subjects of Religion and Public Education*, in which she presents a defense of religious principles that had come under revolutionary assault. More's appeal on behalf of the French clergy reflects the urgency of the situation, as she suggests to her readers practical steps, such as the "retrenching"[45] of excessive consumption, which will enable them to contribute towards the welfare of the exiles. By invoking "Christian charity" (p. 5) and centering her argument not on political grounds but on a transcendent religious faith, More stakes a position that could be perceived as distanced from the impropriety of a marked political intervention. Burney's pamphlet, *Brief Reflections Relative to the Emigrant French Clergy*, which also appeared in 1793, reflects the same sense of urgency, but addresses more specifically both the material exigencies informing the exiles' experience and the political developments that had created them. Burney repeatedly alludes to this political reality, mentioning, for example, the "sanguinary despots of the Convention", (p. 4) and the "succession of terrors" (p. 11) in France, while, like More, also enumerating the practical means by which her readers can aid the French priests. Because of this topical, political, awareness, there seems to be a greater anxiety in Burney's pamphlet, a "tension about male authority" as Claudia Johnson has put it,[46] which is immediately apparent in her long prefatory "apology" for her female "interference."

Yet despite these differences, the two texts are linked by a firm acknowledgement of a subject position in which More and Burney constantly emphasize the fact that they are speaking as members of a privileged class and a privileged nation, an awareness that mediates and facilitates their hesitant

entrance into the world of male politics. Thus, Burney can repeatedly emphasize "the abundance we have received" and the fact that she, and the audience
she is addressing are "flourishing and happy ourselves" (pp. 10–14). The very
titles of these pamphlets point to the perceived "otherness" of the exiles,
doubly distanced both from More and Burney and from the "Ladies" being
addressed.

Smith, in contrast, invariably links herself socially, politically and psy-
chologically to the emigrants, in a sustained thematic intertwining which
emphasizes participation rather than spectatorship and which carries the narrative movement of the poem. As Stuart Curran argues, through this linking
she creates "her own identity in the poem by absorbing their emptiness."[47]
The implications of Smith's and the exiles' shared consciousness are even
more striking as it emerges in a climate where national identity receives much
of its impetus from the distinction between Catholic and Protestant. This
religious tension was one of the sources of the continuing enmity between
Britain and France throughout the eighteenth century, and remained as a
stated or unstated presence, even when the distrust and suspicion reconfig-
ured themselves into a direct confrontation with the Revolution. As Linda
Colley has shown, the parameters of a British national identity were shaped
by Britons' perception of themselves as Protestants, and as such, differ-
entiated and privileged from their Catholic neighbors across the Channel:
"[Protestantism] meant much more ... than bombast, intolerance and chau-
vinism. It gave the majority of men and women a sense of their place in
history and a sense of worth ... It gave them identity."[48] In *The Emigrants*,
Smith creates a different movement towards identity through the commonality of suffering and loss, submerging differences such as Protestant and
Catholic, English and French, poet and subjects.

In the dedication, and throughout the poem, Smith presents a view that
works against a historical, prejudicial division between England and France,
and strives towards a conceptualization and understanding of a common,
shared humanity. In addressing William Cowper, to whom the poem is
dedicated, she writes:

> Your philanthropy, dear Sir, will induce you, I am persuaded, to join with
> me in hoping, that this painful exile may finally lead to the extirpation of
> that reciprocal hatred so unworthy of great and enlightened nations; that
> it may tend to humanize both countries, by convincing each, that good
> qualities exist in the other; and at length annihilate the prejudices that
> have so long existed to the injury of both.[49]

The focus on suffering and loss, together with the desire to promote a universal and enlightened vision of humanity redirects the political import of
The Emigrants, a fact that was noted, as we have seen, by the *Monthly Review*
and also acknowledged by Smith herself: as she writes to her friend Joseph

Cooper Walker, "[i]t is not a party book but a conciliatory book."[50] At the same time, amidst this identification with the French exiles emerges a view of the Revolution and its aftermath that is not exactly apolitical, and that will continue throughout all of her works that were written during and after the Terror – a condemnation of the cruelty and horror of Jacobin violence which nonetheless continues to assert the validity of the original principles under which the Revolution was conceived. She acknowledges the fact that many Britons had "confounded the original cause with the wretched catastrophes that have followed its ill management" (133–4) and it is this tension – manifested in both the way that the Revolutionary excess had obscured those principles, as well as in the inability of the public to differentiate between the two – which repeatedly informs her writing. To put it another way, in *The Emigrants* we see not a juxtaposition of "Revolution" and "exile" as two binary opposites in which identification with one would preclude sympathy for the other. Rather, the values of Revolutionary France would continue to exist as an ideal, even as their manifestation became increasingly colored with disappointment and regret.

The Emigrants is, most prominently, a narrative of exile peopled with homeless and powerless victims, unnamed and impersonalized, an appropriate representation of their disenfranchisement. From the outset of the poem, Smith connects the exile of her French subjects to her own experience of loss.[51] Thus, the opening description of the emigrants, who dread the break of day and the consciousness of their misery which it renews is almost immediately connected to Smith herself, and her own experience:

> From proud oppression, and from legal crimes
> (For such are in this Land, where the vain boast
> Of equal Law is mockery, while the cost
> Of seeking for redress is sure to plunge
> Th' already injur'd to more certain ruin
> And the wretch starves, before his Counsel pleads)
> How often do I half abjure Society,
> And sigh for some lone Cottage, deep embower'd
> In the green woods, that these steep chalky Hills
> Guard from the strong South West; where round their base
> The Beach wide flourishes, and the light Ash
> With slender leaf hides the thymy turf!
>
> (I, 35–47)

Smith's portrayal of suffering encompasses all the inhabitants of the Sussex seashore and countryside upon which she gazes, and qualifies her depiction of nature, beautifully detailed as it is, as unable to ameliorate the sorrows and cruelty that exist in the world.[52] The "solitary Shepherd shiv'ring" who "tends his dun discolored flock" (I, 299–300) is linked together with the French priest, mother and the other French exiles whom she describes, and whose past she attempts to imagine, as common victims of "wide extended misery" (I, 307). As such, they are portrayed in a state which is both moving and static. The emigrants remember their actions in their previous world, but on the beach at Brighthelmstone they can only think and reflect upon their fate. They "travel wide" (I, 297) but arrive nowhere. In essence, the most meaningful movement in the poem may be the movement through history, as seen at the end of Book I. There, Smith revisits scenes of war but also points to a tradition of "just compassion" (I, 361) as a desired historical legacy:

> Thus may'st thou Britain, triumph! – May thy foes
> By Reason's gen'rous potency subdued.
> Learn, that the God thou worshippest, delights
> In acts of pure humanity! – May thine
> Be still such bloodless laurels! Nobler far
> Than those acquir'd at Cressy or Poictiers.
> Or, of more recent growth, those well bestow'd
> On him who stood on Calpe's blazing height
> Amid the thunder of a warring world
> Illustrious rather from the crowds he sav'd
> From flood and fire, than from the ranks who fell
> Beneath his valour! – Actions such as these
> Like incense rising to the Throne of Heaven,
> Far better justify the pride, that swells
> In British bosoms, than the deafening roar
> Of victory from a thousand brazen throats,
> That tell with what success wide-wasting War
> Has by our brave Compatriots thinned the world.
>
> (I, 365–82)

In privileging "bloodless laurels" over the "deafening roar / Of victory" Smith's invocation of historical precedent, and her allusion to the British commander George Augustus Elliott and the siege of Gibraltar, 1779–83, is not elaborated upon; she assumes her readers' prior historical knowledge.[53] Her appeal on behalf of the humanitarian cause is, rather, motivated more forcefully by the detailed and expansive representations of violence repeated with alliterative force: the "warring world", "flood and fire", "wide-wasting War" and the "thousand ... throats" clamoring for triumph.

Book II of *The Emigrants* opens with another acknowledgement of a world ravaged by war, appearing in the epigraph from Virgil's *Georgics*.[54] Juxtaposed to this portrait of destruction is the inherent motivation of the georgic – the "plow", the "fields" and the "sickle." The use of the georgic connects

The Emigrants to Cowper, to whom Smith dedicated the poem, and to his own poem in blank verse, *The Task*, in which redemption is achieved through productive labor and cultivation of the land.[55] And yet, Cowper's conception of a virtuous retirement is not feasible for Smith, neither in her own life, with its endless economic struggle, nor in her poem, whose landscape of despair precludes the possibility of both interior growth and external physical cultivation. Compelled by the urgency of the emigrants' situation and the dramatic events of the Revolution itself, Smith cannot adopt the leisurely particularity of Cowper's contemplations of his garden nor his desultory digressions on matters of the world in general.

Book II exhibits an evident sense of despondency. It is April, but the rebirth and rejuvenation associated with the coming of spring are absent, and nature is viewed only as a backdrop to a catalogue of the horrors of war, as Smith again, links herself to the narrative of the exiles:

> Shuddering, I view the pictures they have drawn
> Of desolated countries, where the ground,
> Stripp'd of its unripe produce, was thick strewn
> With various Death – the war-horse falling there
> By famine, and his rider by the sword.
> The moping clouds sail'd heavy charg'd with rain,
> And bursting o'er the mountains ['] misty brow,
> Deluged, as with an inland sea, the vales;
> Where, thro' the sullen evening's lurid gloom,
> Rising, like columns of volcanic fire,
> The flames of burning villages illum'd
> The waste of water; and the wind that howl'd
> Along its troubled surface, brought the groans
> Of plundered peasants, and the frantic shrieks
> Of mothers for their children; while the brave,
> To pity still alive, listen'd aghast
> To these dire echoes, hopeless to prevent
> The evils they beheld, or check the rage,
> Which ever, as the people of one land
> Meet in contention, fires the human heart
> With savage thirst of kindred blood, and makes
> Man lose his nature; rendering him more fierce
> Than the gaunt monsters of the howling waste.
>   (II, 216–38)

The landscape of war is presented here in explicit and graphic detail but without the compensation of benevolent action that we saw in the earlier passage. This scene becomes a depressingly familiar one, as we find similar portrayals of violence, misery and destruction in many of Smith's later writings, for example, "The Story of Corisande" in *The Letters of a Solitary Wanderer* (1800), with its description of the aftermath of the massacre of the Huguenots – "streets [that] were strewn with the dying and the dead, and the pavement . . . slippery with blood", or the depiction of a contemporary scene in *Marchmont* (1796) – "a waggon-load of wounded soldiers from beyond sea – some without legs, and some without arms."[56] As Anne Mellor notes, *The Emigrants* is an attack (one of many in Smith's writings) on patriarchal militarism,[57] and the recognition of its pervasiveness (and its consequences) denies the possibility of the meaningful, compassionate conception of history that had concluded Book I. A personal narrative replaces the political one, yet the movement only leads to death:

> Ah! Yes, my friends
> Peace will at last be mine; for in the Grave
> Is Peace – and pass a few short years, perchance
> A few short months, and all the various pain
> I now endure shall be forgotten there.
> And no memorial shall remain of me,
> Save in your bosoms.
>
> (II., 371–6)

The merging of Smith with the emigrants is shown here in its ultimate expression – the final convergence of consciousness and memory into the figures of the French exiles.

At the same time, in this poem, as in all of her works, Smith never *does* manage to totally disappear from the text. Her repeated insertion of a knowing, explaining and qualifying authorial voice into the notes that accompany this poem reassert her presence even as it is absorbed into the emigrants' collective identity. The notes that accompany *The Emigrants* reinforce and clarify points made in the poem itself, establish historical background and acknowledge her literary sources. For example, after her description of a priest who is amazed at the compassion he receives in exile because "these strangers are, by his dark creed, / Condemned as Heretics" (I., 122–3), Smith adds in a note that "nothing is farther from [her] thoughts, then to reflect invidiously on the Emigrant clergy." Elsewhere, she follows comments in the poem about the current (1793) situation in France with notes that reiterate her understanding of the charged political climate in which she was writing. Thus, the lines "As now in Gallia; where Confusion, born / Of party rage and selfish love of rule, / Sully the noblest cause that ever warm'd / The heart of Patriot Virtue" (I, 343–6) are followed by a note stating tersely that "[t]his sentiment will probably *renew* against me the indignation of those, who have an interest in asserting that no such virtue any where exists."

   The need to clarify her politics points to Smith's anxiety in dealing with her subject matter, and, perhaps, with her own rethinking of her political stand, in which the justification of the original values of the Revolution – "the noblest cause that ever warm'd the heart of Patriot Virtue" – coexists with a rejection of its excesses and violence. And yet, Smith's self-consciousness in dealing with a political theme exhibits itself in another dimension of *The Emigrants* as well, and to examine this we must return to the epigraph from the *Georgics* which opens Book II of the poem. Although recent critical studies have comprehensively and forcefully discussed the use of Virgil's *Georgics* in late eighteenth and early nineteenth century writing, little attention has been given to Smith.[58] Ostensibly, Smith cites Book I of the *Georgics* in her epigraph in order to underscore her own portrayal of a world devastated by war, destruction and suffering. However, seen self-referentially, the use of the georgic may signal an additional preoccupation for her – the focus on labor as a means of survival. As Kurt Heinzelmann writes, "Authority in the *Georgics* is a function of labor. Most readers, from antiquity to the present, have agreed that Virgil's *Georgics* has a single locus of energy: everyday life, the daily struggle to survive."[59] Heinzelmann and other contemporary critics focus their attention on labor and the georgic through studies of various abstract poetic meditations on rural improvements, enclosures and the poet's view of his own literary project as labor or, to use Annabel Patterson's phrase, of "the mind at serious work."[60] And my use of the gendered pronoun is, indeed, intended. For these studies omit any reference to Smith (or, for that matter to any woman writer) for whom the serious work of the mind is often urgently, transparently connected to writing as vocation, as the means of earning a living. For Smith, the connection between labor and her poetic project are more than a theoretical contemplation (although she, too, is intensely interested in the political and economic changes occurring in the countryside)[61] but, rather, are linked primarily to her own struggle for economic survival. Throughout the poem, Smith intersperses allusions that foreground her pecuniary anxiety, including the opening lines of the preface, when she refers to "the heavy pressure of many sorrows" (132) that accompany her writing, a reference her contemporary readers would immediately have recognized as part of the ongoing narrative of her financial and legal troubles which she continually provided in each of her publications. Her use of the *Georgics* functions thus as a particularly telling reference, with its dual focus on the landscape and destructive potential of war, and the need for the individual to toil, labor and find a vocation within its purview. This dual focus would become, I want to claim, the central axis of Smith's career after 1793, as she sought to rearticulate her political beliefs within an increasingly hostile political climate. The desire to portray the devastation of war and the refusal to abandon politically committed writing were forced to coexist within the framework of labor, a cultural labor – writing – that was also an economic necessity.

III

Smith's positioning in *The Emigrants* is replicated in *The Banished Man* (1794), a text in which she repeatedly calls attention to the pressures that accompany literary work when it is produced as a result of financial necessity, and as it appears during times of war. These tensions are even more apparent when we view the novel within the context of the year of its publication. The spring of 1794 was the height of the Terror in France; across the Channel, in May of that year, and a little over two months before Smith had completed her final draft of *The Banished Man*, John Horne Tooke, John Thelwall, Thomas Hardy and other prominent radical activists were arrested for treason. A mob attacked Hardy's house following his arrest, and as a result of the shock sustained by these events, his wife died in childbirth. The potential for mob violence, the increased scrutiny and control over the press, the sense of "ballad and broadsheet vendors [running] through the streets with sheets headed 'TREASON! TREASON! TREASON!' " – this is the backdrop against which Smith was writing *The Banished Man*, – and is a crucial element in our understanding of her political positioning – and the strategies she employed in expressing it – throughout the novel.[62]

Although Smith does not mention the Trials in *The Banished Man* or in her other literary works, it is worth noting that she was acquainted with Thomas Erskine, the brilliant attorney who successfully defended Hardy, Thelwall and Tooke, and who represented her for a time in her legal battles with Chancery over her father-in-law's will. On 6 November 1794, she wrote to her publishers, Cadell and Davies, "Mr. Erskine . . . has engaged to undertake the cause of my injured children against their infamous Trustees as soon as the pressure of public business is a little over."[63] The trial of Thomas Hardy commenced on 28 October 1794 and ended twelve days later with his acquittal on 5 November – the day before Smith wrote this letter. The trial of Thelwall commenced on 1 December and concluded on 5 December. It is not difficult to guess, then, what "public business" Smith is referring to.

In Mark Philp's words, "this is not the atmosphere in which enthusiasm survives."[64] And thus we must ask: to what extent did Smith's enthusiasm survive in 1794, at the crucial juncture of the Trials and the Terror? In attempting to answer the question, it is necessary to keep in mind the distinction between the response to the violent turn that the Revolution itself had taken and the support for the cause of reform in Britain. These two scenes of political engagement, France and Britain, were, to be sure, linked together in the public – and government – consciousness, with the fear generated by the extreme scenes playing themselves out in France taking its toll, in a climate of increasing political and legal oppression, on the progressive domestic agendas that the Revolution had initially brought to the forefront of public debate. Indeed, the precise period in which Smith completed *The Banished Man*, the months following the arrest of the defendants of the Trials in May, but *before* their eventual acquittal in November–December, was also the very moment when the reformist community awaited the answer to how far a radical agenda would be legally tolerated. Against this backdrop, Smith seems to be asking if, and how, it were possible to continue to support the cause of reform and, in doing so, also attempting to differentiate between the original vision inspired by the French Revolution and its present day excesses.

Obviously, *The Banished Man* does not display the same unequivocal radicalism that was present in *Desmond*. The events occurring in France in 1794 had clearly left their mark on Smith's political thinking, and it is with genuine anger that she decries the excesses of the Terror. "Englishmen", she writes in the preface to the novel, "must contemplate with mingled horror and pity, a people driven by terror to commit enormities which in the course of a few months have been more destructive than the despotism of ages."[65] Her use of the phrase "in the course of a few months" is significant, however, in its refusal to deny the legitimacy of the ideals that the Revolution had embodied in its early stages. As we will see, the support of those values is repeatedly expressed in the novel, while their present inefficacy is but one of many losses – and *The Banished Man* is preoccupied with loss – which is mourned throughout the text.

This tension between ideological aspiration and misguided implementation is apparent elsewhere in the preface as well. Thus, Smith insists:

> [i]f I had been convinced I was in an error in regard to what I formerly wrote on the politics of France, I should without hesitation avow it. I still think, however, that no native could help *then* rejoicing at the probability there was that the French nation would obtain, with very little bloodshed, that degree of freedom which we have been taught to regard so highly. (p. x)

This admission of original support will receive textual substantiation only later in the novel – the entire opening sequence reflects a strictly anti-Revolution point of view, as we accompany D'Alonville, the second son of an aristocratic French family and a supporter of the *ancien régime*, and his struggle to rebuild his life. The novel commences when D'Alonville, having fled the revolutionary forces with his dying father, finds refuge in a German castle, which soon comes under siege. After his father's death, he continues his wanderings, first with the residents of the castle, who are likewise forced to escape, and later, alone, through a landscape of war and desolation. D'Alonville eventually meets Ellesmere, a young Englishman who continues to support the original principles of the Revolution and who becomes his close friend. Traveling together, the two friends meet other dispossessed wanderers, including the Polish rebel, Carlowitz and his daughter Alexina. Although Ellesmere falls in love with Alexina, the couple is soon parted when, accompanied by D'Alonville, he returns home to England, to his noble but financially declining family, whose preference for his older brother and distrust of foreigners align the young men in a shared sense of displacement. In England D'Alonville meets Angelina, with whom he falls in love, and her mother, Mrs Denzil, who is experiencing her own economic vulnerability and loss of social position and who supports her family by her writing.

After a brief stay in England, D'Alonville returns to France, where he attempts to join the anti-Revolution forces. He has further adventures, including a sojourn in a Gothic castle, and an arrest by revolutionary officials, at which time he meets his brother, a prominent adherent to the Revolution who had renounced his name and title, and who eventually becomes another victim of the Terror. Ultimately, D'Alonville is reunited with Ellesmere in England, where they marry Angelina and Alexina, respectively. However, England is inhospitable to them – Ellesmere's marriage to a Polish exile is viewed with contempt by his family in a sign of the xenophobia that is a by-product of the increasing conservative backlash. The suspicion towards foreigners is positioned as a parallel to the way in which economic tension also creates a sense of otherness. Angelina's family, particularly Mrs Denzil, are repeatedly reminded of the loss of their social status, most prominently when D'Alonville goes to work as a tutor at Rock March, the home of Lord Aberdore, a rich relation of Mrs Denzil, concealing the fact that he has married into her family. The vulnerability and powerlessness of his situation and that of the Denzils serves as the motivating factor for their desire to leave England. The novel concludes with Ellesmere and Alexina preparing to join D'Alonville, Angelina, Mrs Denzil and the rest of her family, who have settled in Italy. The theme of alienation that links the main characters of *The Banished Man* receives its ultimate expression as they anticipate their reunion in an exilic community in Verona, in which mutual love and affection mediates but cannot really mitigate their loss, whether of national identity, economic privilege, or both.

The Banished Man was generally received as a turning point in Smith's politics, and the opinions of D'Alonville – Smith's focalizer in the novel – were identified as those of Smith herself. (Recall Robert Bisset's remark, cited above, that she had displayed in the novel an "eager[ness] for the nobility.") Thus, the liberal *Analytical Review* sardonically writes,

> [Charlotte Smith] now, it seems, is grown more enlightened; and has discovered, that on account of various excesses and enormities, which have arisen in the course of this great effort for the recovery of freedom, the cause is to be abandoned. Accordingly, she makes her [amends] for her past political transgressions by writing a novel on contrary principles.[66]

Likewise, the conservative *British Critic* concludes its review of the novel by:

> congratulating the lovers of their king and the constitution, in the acquisition of an associate like Mrs. Charlotte Smith convinced by observation that the changes in France have only produced rapine and murder ... She

makes full atonement by the virtues of *The Banished Man* for the errors of *Desmond*. Such a convert, gained by fair conviction, is a valuable prize for the commonwealth.[67]

Alongside this recognition of what was perceived as a reversal in her politics, common to these reviews is their criticism of the self-referential portrayal of Mrs Denzil, a writer struggling under financial duress and the mother of Angelina, D'Alonville's love interest in the novel. This character is viewed as "as an opportunity of representing [Smith's] own misfortunes" and as a "private history [which] should not be introduced for public perusal."[68] Yet, as we will see, the novel's political narrative and its focus on authorship are intrinsically related in *The Banished Man*, and the relation of the two is central to an understanding of the supposed political change of heart that had so impressed Smith's original reviewers.

Although some modern critics such as Gary Kelly and M.O. Grenby share the opinion that *The Banished Man* represents a retraction of Smith's pro-Revolution views, other recent critical assessments stress its ongoing radical engagement.[69] My reading of *The Banished Man* concurs with this latter view yet places greater emphasis on Smith's self-consciousness and anxiety in articulating her political position. This anxiety appears primarily, I suggest, through the portrayal of authorship, as she acknowledges her own vulnerability in presenting a (now) unpopular point of view. I argue that what begins as an anti-Revolution focus in *The Banished Man* is gradually counterbalanced by the increasing presence afforded to both the defense of the original revolutionary values and to the critique of British society, as they are articulated by the character of Ellesmere, the secondary hero of the novel. The repeated expression of these concerns points to the way that this novel is not exactly a retreat from "past political transgressions" (as the *Analytical* had it) but rather a modified, disappointed and cautious re-working of that earlier ideological position.

Smith initially addresses the issue of authorship when she interrupts the narrative at the beginning of the second volume in order to insert a commentary, the "Avis au Lecteur", a meditation on the relevance of novel-writing during a time of cultural upheaval.[70] As a (displaced) second preface, the "Avis" begins, aptly enough, by quoting *Tristram Shandy*: " 'There was, an' please your honor,' said Corporal Trim, 'There was a certain king of Bohemia, who had seven castles' " (Vol. ii., p. iii).[71] The reference is to Trim's unsuccessful attempt to create a fiction, one which is repeatedly interrupted, and in fact confounded by Uncle Toby's efforts to ground the story in historical fact.[72] As Toby says, "they [his stories] are all true." The allusion to Sterne sets up the relationship between fiction and referentiality as the theme of this authorial digression, as Smith attempts to dissociate imaginative writing that is deliberately, identifiably fictive from the historical, political consciousness that invariably impinges upon it.

Smith uses the introductory gesture of the "Avis" with its Shandean pose and textual playfulness as, I suggest, an attempt to mask what is actually a serious, highly personal reflection on the social and economic pressures under which she was working in the charged political climate of 1794. For the "Avis", appearing shortly before the introduction of Ellesmere and the reformist narrative into the text, is virtually a catalogue of authorial anxieties. Smith admits of having nearly exhausted her repertoire of imaginative possibilities ("I have hardly a watch tower, a Gothic arch, a cedar parlour, or a long gallery, an illuminated window, or a ruined chapel left to help myself" (p. iv)), of her persistent fear of being accused of plagiarism,[73] and of the "same [financial] necessity" (p. xii) that motivates her authorship. Embedded within these various acknowledgements of the pressures that accompany her writing, the treatment of the novel's political topicality appears all the more anxious. Especially significant is the suggestion that *The Banished Man* has no pretensions of contemporary relevance. Smith wonders "how it were possible to adhere to le vrai in a work like this" (p. v) – a remark that belies the overt historical and political contextualization that the reader has already seen in the opening section of the book and will continue to observe in its continuation. This positioning, and what appears to be a deliberate effort at distancing her novel from urgent contemporary concerns, contradicts a remark in the opening preface, where Smith writes: "I have in the present work, aimed less at the wonderful and extraordinary, than at connecting by a chain of possible circumstances, events, some of which *have* happened, and all of which *might* have happened" (p. xi). The inconsistency of these authorial remarks – first, the claim for verisimilitude in the opening preface and then the recognition of the "impossibility" of adhering to it in the second one – emphasizes the pressures that accompany the presentation of a politically-informed narrative.[74]

Smith's anxiety is further evinced in her reflections on literary form. She desires to view *The Banished Man* as a Gothic novel (an identification that repeatedly appears in the metonymy of a castle) but in doing so to view the genre as merely "the immediate taste" (p. iii), devoid of political awareness. Yet as opposed to Smith's *stated* perception of the Gothic, readers and critics have always been conscious of the ways that the genre encodes a critique of patriarchy and institutional tyranny. At the end of the eighteenth century, the Gothic also signaled a specific engagement with the social and political upheaval of the French Revolution and served, in Ronald Paulson's words, as "a metaphor with which some contemporaries in England tried to understand what was happening across the channel in the 1790s."[75] In her illuminating discussion of the development of the Gothic novel, Margaret Doody calls attention to Smith's specific contribution to the genre, which is precisely her use of its images and themes to articulate a political and social awareness. As Doody writes, "In a highly original manner [Smith] relates individual difficulties, states of mind, and views to larger cultural conditions. Her insight into the significance of the Gothic is a result of this desire to connect. . . . [However] she possesses the limitations of her qualities which are intellectual rather than powerfully imaginative . . . In defining matters clearly and programmatically, she tidies away the nightmare."[76]

Doody's argument is important, as it exposes the political engagement in Smith's Gothic (despite Smith's own argument to the contrary) and the way that it is clearly available to readers of her novels. What is crucial here, it seems to me, is Smith's attempt to distance this political valence, to downplay the relevance of the Gothic, and thus to purposely de-politicize her novel. Accordingly, while she registers her unease with the limitations of the genre – "how it were possible to adhere to le vrai in a work like this" – she also, on another level, finds comfort in that very fictionality. This is ultimately, however, a futile, if not disingenuous gesture. For what after all, is a "work like this"? Not only is the Gothic all but absent from *The Banished Man*, when it *is* briefly invoked (during D'Alonville's nocturnal sojourn in the ruined castle of Vaudrecour) it is linked to a historical legacy of political oppression. For example, almost immediately after his arrival at the castle, D'Alonville stumbles upon a corpse. Continuing along he sees "one of those cages, in which it is said Louis the Eleventh was accustomed to confine the miserable objects of his revenge" (Vol. iii. p. 126).

The authorial self-reflexivity present in the "Avis au Lecteur" reappears with the introduction of Mrs Denzil into the narrative. The autobiographical parallel is made apparent through the story of a woman who must continually write in order to support her children, in the references to her constant legal battles for the money she is supposed to receive and in the general sense of alienation and displacement that marks her story. (The blurring of the boundaries between fact and fiction appears most strikingly in a textual inconsistency: the character is variously referred to as "Henrietta Denzil" (Vol. iii, p. 193) and as "*Charlotte* Denzil" (Vol. ii., p. 236.))[77] Amidst Mrs Denzil's description of her life as an over-worked, financially- pressed author, who "leaves her bed in a morning, when her health permits, to go to her desk, from whence she rises only to sit down to a dinner she cannot eat" (Vol. ii., pp. 223–4), there are also references to the political pressures that inform her (Mrs. Denzil's) writing, and thus obviously, to those which permeate the larger text (Smith's) that frames it. Smith alludes to these pressures by having Mrs Denzil quote her publisher:

> Must insist in having a hundred pages at least by Saturday night; also the Ode to Liberty mentioned by you as a close to the same: but I shall change the title of that, having promiss'd [sic] the trade that there shall be no liberty at all in the present work; without which asshurance [sic] they would not have delt [sic] for the same. (Vol. ii., p. 231)

Seen in relation to the wider contexts that I have been discussing, this passage is clearly significant, as it crucially aligns Mrs Denzil with the "Ode

to Liberty" and thus with pro-Revolution sentiments, but also with a pragmatic and cautious stance – "*no* liberty" – in the negotiation of an oppressive
political climate. As Harriet Guest has argued, this remark exemplifies how
Smith "repeatedly reminds her readers that she writes under the booksellers'
surveillance, that her novels are subject to censorship by the demands of the
marketplace."[78] Later, in narrating yet another litany of the economic and
political limitations under which she toils and which motivate her desire
to leave "this dear England of ours" (Vol. ii., p. 218) Mrs Denzil further
acknowledges the contemporary concerns and tensions of 1794:

> This land, that from her pushes all the rest; and ... [where] I have lost
> in it everything *but my head*, and should I now venture out of it I think
> I should be in danger of being deprived of that also, my sole remaining
> possession. (Vol. ii., p. 218)

The notion of "losing one's head" is one that is freighted with political
implications and a persistent sense of unease. This anxiety is underscored
later in the narrative, when, in what Margaret Doody has called the first
guillotine scene in English fiction, D'Alonville, who has been imprisoned
in a French jail, is forced to witness the execution of eleven of his fellow
prisoners.[79] Traversing both Britain and France, Smith's uneasiness was certainly justified by the events that were occurring in both countries. Linda
Colley has noted how the guillotining of Marie-Antoinette had a profound
effect on Britons in general, and on British women in particular. The fact
that such a prominent and visible woman was executed effectively caused all
women to feel anxious for their safety, and wonder (as Colley puts it): "If a
woman could be violently done to death after a rigged trial in which she was
accused among other crimes of child abuse, what else might happen to other
members of her sex?"[80] Mary Wollstonecraft's description of the mob's invasion of the Queen's rooms at the Tuilleries is an example of how even radical
writers portrayed that event in the terms of "a prolonged and public rape":

> The sanctuary of repose, the asylum of care and fatigue, the chaste temple
> of a woman, *I consider the Queen only as one*, the apartment where she
> consigns her senses to the bosom of sleep, folded in it's arms forgetful of
> the world, was violated with murderous fury.[81]

Accompanied by the guillotining of other prominent women, such as Manon
Roland and Olympe de Gouges, together with the absence of legislation for,
and eventually the negation of, rights for women in Republican France,[82]
the execution of Marie-Antoinette reinforced British women's understanding
that, amidst these unsettling affairs, their situation was infinitely preferable to that of women across the Channel. Yet, Mrs Denzil's musings here
illustrate the inability to acquiesce to this assumption of security. Although
Revolutionary France is no longer able to function as a viable alternative
for her, it is in *England* that she has lost "everything but [her] head." The
terror of the guillotine is compounded by its referentiality with the English

landscape and with what emerges as an all-encompassing sense of isolation and fear, one which can neither be ameliorated by the French ideal which has now gone terribly wrong, nor derive comfort from the identification with Englishness and national identity.

The refusal to unequivocally identify with, or to conform to, a limiting (and chauvinistic) sense of nationhood underscores the reformist social critique in *The Banished Man.* Yet before I return to this critique, it is worth noting one dimension of the novel in which Smith *does* resort to distinctions between England and France as she negotiates her controversial subject matter. For what she permits herself to criticize in England is off limits as far as her French characters are concerned and they are given far less leeway than the British in the nuancing of their political views. There is no differentiation between Girondins and Jacobins or any acknowledgement of even moderate support for the early stages of the Revolution. Thus, D'Alonville, the eponymous hero, is, of course, a firm opponent to the Revolution while his revolutionary brother, Du Bosse, who holds a high though unspecified position in the new order, is presented in consistently negative terms, even when he rescues D'Alonville from the guillotine, an action that eventually costs him his own life. The notice of Du Bosse's death that D'Alonville later reads in a public print states that it was occasioned by "the unpardonable crime of [his] having received his brother, an emigrant" (Vol. iv., p. 22). The value placed on domestic and filial affection, so prominent elsewhere in the text, is unable, in the story of the two brothers, to penetrate the ideological binary through which Smith sanctions approval of her French characters. Furthermore, and perhaps even more tellingly, throughout his adventures in France, D'Alonville is afraid above all of being taken for an adherent to the Revolution – the "evil he the most dreaded, [was] that of passing ... as one of the perpetrators of the miseries that desolated France" (Vol. iv., p. 19). This dread of misidentification may suggest Smith's own fears that she will be perceived in a similar fashion as well.

This rigid demarcation would seem to signal Smith's abandonment of any identification with the Revolution itself, which indeed appears to be the case as long as the action centers on France and the French characters. But to what extent does it reflect her position regarding the wider political landscape? We do not see a similar single-mindedness when she comes to address the ills of British society and, significantly, it is there that she continues to acknowledge and defend the ideals inspired by the original revolutionary moment. Along with Mrs Denzil (recall the "Ode to Liberty") the character of Ellesmere is Smith's vehicle for representing a progressive worldview coming to terms with the events in France yet continuing at the same time to advocate the cause of domestic reform. Introduced into the story shortly after the "Avis au Lecteur", his position is stated as follows:

> [Ellesmere] learned to feel veneration and esteem ... [... for D'Alonville ...] without, however, being influenced by [his] conversation ... or by the pity

he felt for [his] ruined fortunes, to alter his original opinions, as to the errors of the former government of [his] country, or the propriety of those reforms, which, had they been carried out by reason and justice, would have rendered France, under a limited monarchy, the most flourishing and happy nation of Europe. (Vol. ii., pp. 33–4)

This positioning exhibits the more varied perspective absent from the portrayal of the French characters. Moreover, if "Ellesmere seems to present [Smith's] own [political] views", as Chris Jones has suggested,[83] then the defense of a limited monarchy may imply a change in her own stand on the subject, or at least in the way she presents it. If we return to the November 1792 letter that she wrote to Joel Barlow on the subject of the emigrants, we can see there a clear opposition to the monarchy, alongside the expression of personal sympathy for Louis XVI:

To punish him [Louis XVI, or Louis Capet, as she calls him, using the radical appellation] for the past, seems as needless [*sic*] to make him an example for the future, for if no more Kings are suffer'd, it will avail nothing to shew the ill consequence of being a bad one by personal punishment inflicted on the unfortunate Man, who could not help being born the Grandson of Louis 15th.[84]

Ellesmere's expression of support for a limited monarchy is indicative of how the events of 1794 – the Terror as well as the onset of the conservative backlash in England – motivate a more nuanced presentation of a pro-Revolution agenda. It is difficult to say whether Ellesmere's position exactly parallels Smith's own re-thinking and modification of her stand regarding the monarchy in light of the sympathy she felt for Louis's plight and her horror at the violence in France, or if it simply reflects a tactical, textual strategy, exhibiting what Jones calls the "justifiable caution" with which she articulates a progressive viewpoint in *The Banished Man*[85] – indeed it is most probably a combination of the two. Furthermore, in examining this supposed reversal of Smith's views regarding the monarchy, we cannot ignore the public or private nature of the texts in which she presents her views. The letter to Joel Barlow was a private text, while *The Banished Man* was intended for a wide public audience. Albert Goodwin notes how, even in the less repressive climate of 1791, radical societies such as the Society for Constitutional Information were themselves quite cautious in dealing with this issue, taking care to "disavow Paine's republican principles [as expressed in *The Rights of Man*] ... and promoting a "guarded constitutionalism" instead.[86]

Nonetheless, a later passage reiterates the fact that Smith continues to valorize those very principles that had toppled Louis's reign:

An Englishman would perhaps have beheld [Revolutionary France] with different sensations [than those of D'Alonville] – an Englishman might have thought the experiment right; and that the attempt to shake off such burthens as the taille, the gabelle, the corves, and vassalage, was a glorious attempt, and failed only because the headlong vehemence of the French national character, and the impossibility of finding (in a very corrupt nation, and among men never educated in notions of real patriotism) a sufficient weight of abilities and integrity to guide the vessel in the revolutionary tempest, has occasioned it to fall into the hands of pirates, and utterly to destroy it. (Vol. iii., pp. 92–3)

Clearly, this is *not*, as Bisset would later claim, "eager[ness] for the nobility as they subsisted under the old government of France."[87]

This passage is filtered through the consciousness of D'Alonville upon his re-entry into France, where he has gone to join the anti-Revolution forces. The progressive narrative, then, is not located exclusively in one voice, but is, rather, disseminated more generally throughout the novel, appearing also in the character of Carlowitz, the Polish political exile whom Ellesmere and D'Alonville befriend and in the Rock March sequence that appears towards the conclusion of the novel. Carlowitz appears as an obvious allusion to the Polish freedom fighter Kosciusko[88] and, as Angela Keane writes, his arguments with D'Alonville are "an outlet for republican discourse that can no longer be articulated sympathetically through a French subject."[89] It is worth noting that, as an "umpire" in these political discussions, Ellesmere "seldom thought that the *bold assertions* of Carlowitz were carried too far" (Vol. iv., p. 74). The sequence at Rock March, the noble estate where D'Alonville goes to work as a tutor to distant relatives of Mrs Denzil, further reinforces the reformist inflection of *The Banished Man*. Smith now foregrounds a society in which imperious privilege prevails. Even D'Alonville, that staunch supporter of the old regime, cannot but note the contrast between the grandeur of the noble estate and the "meanest cottages of clay and thatch" (Vol. iv., p. 184) that surround it and reflect upon the "strange inequality of conditions" (Vol. iv., p. 185) that define the (British) social experience.

Thus, although we never discover what Carlowitz's "bold assertions" are, it no longer really matters. The conclusion of *The Banished Man* collapses the polarized political constructions that had featured earlier in the narrative, replacing them with a focus on exile and on a universalist purview; on the common experience of alienation that binds rather than the disparate political opinions that divide. D'Alonville's subordinate status in the great house together with the Denzils' increasing financial vulnerability create a parallel in which economic tension, loss of status and political exile are enmeshed together, establishing the shared sense of banishment as the final concern of the text. Ellesmere, earlier in the novel, had defined his support of the original principles of the Revolution in terms of national belonging, by asserting that "he had an heart attached to the true *English* principles, an heart detesting tyranny and injustice" (Vol. ii., p. 41). But now even he comes to the realization, after experiencing the effects of social ostracism following his marriage with a Polish woman, that these "true English principles" can exist only in a psychic space, rather than a geopolitical one. In his final narrative presence, in a letter to D'Alonville, he expresses views which seem to reflect those of Smith herself:

> We [Ellesmere and D'Alonville] differ still as to the commencement of a revolution, which, in its progress has baffled all the reasoning which we could derive from analogy, in reflecting on the past events of the world – ... *You* think that even in its first germinations it threatened to become the monster we now see, desolating and devouring France. I still think, that originating from acknowledged faults of your former government, the first design, aiming only at the correction of those faults, at a limited monarchy and a mixed government, was the most sublime and most worthy of a great people that ever was recorded in the annals of mankind. But wide as our sentiments are as to their origin, I believe we perfectly agree in our position of affairs at this moment. You, as a Frenchman, execrate the misery and devastation it has brought on the finest Kingdom of Europe. You lament as an individual the death of your dearest friends, the dispersion of your family, the ruin and beggary of many to whom you were attached. – I, as an Englishman, deplore the injury done to the cause of rational liberty throughout the world. I deplore, as a citizen of that world, the general devastation, the blood that has been shed in the field or on the scaffold, and the stupendous destruction that has overwhelmed a great nation. (Vol. iv., pp. 321–3)

Notice how Ellesmere defines himself first as an "Englishman" and then as a "citizen of [the] world"; when he concludes this letter by announcing his "intention to quit England" (Vol. iv., p. 326) we learn that he will soon become an exile as well. This blurring – and replacement – of affiliations encapsulates Smith's perception of how political, social and economic upheaval undercuts the valence of national identity. The portrayal of exile that we viewed in *The Emigrants* returns here with renewed force, lacking even the basis of landscape and history that the poem had provided, if not as a means of solace, than at least as touchstones of reference.[90]

To what extent can the community in Verona compensate for this sense of dispossession and ameliorate the exilic experience? Some critics have argued that because of the diverse national origins of its members and the climate of tolerance and benevolence that defines it, Verona functions as a privileged space, a "cosmopolitan fantasy" and an "ideal of cosmopolitan community."[91] However, I believe that D'Alonville's description of his happiness as "mixed and dashed" (Vol. iv., p. 339) and Ellesmere's admission that although he "love[s] England" (Vol. iv., p. 327) social alienation nonetheless compels him to leave it, qualify the celebratory aspect of this cosmopolitan vision and emphasize instead the way memory, longing and loss accompany and define this particular kind of citizenship of the world. Accordingly, I prefer to read the conclusion of *The Banished Man* more as the culmination of what Harriet Guest has called "the inverted national tale." Marking "the fragmentation of English culture under the pressure of an oppressive modernity", what ultimately emerges is the way English identity is displaced by "the atomized units of inward-looking domestic intimacy or individual isolation, of people bastilled by the social regulations of 'arbitrary power'."[92] Mrs Denzil's final cry, "Oh, for a cup of oblivion" (Vol. iv., p. 336) underscores this sense of displacement. For although Verona signifies a kind of consolatory alternative through the affective relations of its exile-residents, the cosmopolitan experience is informed by the pressures of cultural memory, incapable of mitigating the loss of what has been left behind by those who have been disenfranchised because of economics, society or ideology.

I want to conclude my discussion of *The Banished Man*, and this chapter, with a brief look at one additional passage from the novel that illustrates its timely political awareness. Ellesmere relates the story of his neighbor, a manufacturer of buttons, who had built a grand estate near his family's home. Upon his death, his property had been purchased by "a Mr. Darnly, who had just returned from a thirty years residence in India, with a great deal of money ... The neighbors venerated his riches, though acquired perhaps by means somewhat less innocent than those of its late possessor (Vol. iv., p. 38). In describing the "improvements" that had been made on the estate, Ellesmere remarks on how "instead of pictures of Price and Priestly, the aspiring Pagoda was represented on the painted sattin [sic] that covered the walls" (Vol. iv., p. 39).[93] The removal of these figures from public view literalizes the triumph of reactionary politics and, together with another image of *what has been replaced*, links together in broader terms the political negotiations of Charlotte Smith that I have been examining in this chapter. The previous owner, we are told, had "placed a bust of Franklin in his vestibule ... had Ludlow among his books, quoted Milton to his companions, and drank to the rights of man" (Vol. iv., pp. 37–8). These signposts of radicalism are, to be sure, otherwise absent from *The Banished Man*; the praise of Paine that we viewed in *Desmond* seems to belong to a distant and irretrievable cultural era, unmentionable. Yet, as we shall see in the following chapter, Smith *will* return to a more forthright endorsement of those very principles that seem displaced in her novel of 1794. Exuberance is now replaced by resignation, no one will drink to the rights of man, but the memory and aspirations of the cultural moment evoked by that very phrase will once more appear, unequivocally, in her writing.

2
"A Disciple of a Better System": Charlotte Smith II

If the previous chapter ended with Smith's radical awareness at its most oblique, and the "rights of man" seemingly distanced to an irretrievable past cultural moment, this chapter seeks to show how Smith returned to a more overt progressive positioning, even as the reactionary backlash of the final years of the eighteenth century became more and more profound. Beginning with a brief glance at two poems included in the second volume of her *Elegiac Sonnets* (1797) and moving on to her final novels, *The Young Philosopher* (1798) and *The Letters of a Solitary Wanderer* (1800–2) with their portrayal of the bleak social reality at the close of the revolutionary decade, I will show how Smith once more situates her political critique unequivocally on the radical side of the debate. At the same time, here, too, as in her earlier work, various textual and paratextual markers indicate the anxiety that invariably accompanies the presentation of a reformist narrative in a time of political oppression.

Mark Philp's depiction of the radical circle of sociability surrounding William Godwin as a community "held together by their discussions, their allegiance to the cause of progress and by their professional activities" and his portrayal of its eventual demise, informs my study of Smith's later works, as she, too, writes under the shadow of the "terror" of the *Anti-Jacobin Review* and the reactionary print culture that it represents.[1] Against this backdrop of failed possibilities, one of the main themes emerging from Smith's work is a deep disenchantment with British society, which receives fictional resolution in the portrayal of emigration and exile from England, such as we have seen in *The Banished Man*, and will view with further force in *The Young Philosopher*.[2] Indeed, recent critical studies focusing on Romantic-era conceptualizations of nationhood pay particular attention to Smith, and view her attitude to England as suggestive of a shifting concern with national identity – as a rejection of a past ideal of national belonging that is at the same time a celebration of cosmopolitanism, transatlantic possibility and citizenship of the world in general.[3] While Smith's work is conducive to the study and representation of Romantic border-crossings, I want instead to suggest in this chapter that her ideal of enlightened community references itself more pertinently to her own experience of, and participation in, a progressive circle of writers and thinkers in *Britain,* and particularly in London. Although this community was past its peak years of influence insofar as being able to harness its energy to an attainable agenda of reform, its availability certainly existed for Smith as a – perhaps utopian – intellectual and ideological option, as a desired ideal of belonging.

William Godwin's diary records fifty-eight meetings with Smith between the years 1796–1800. These meetings were usually for dinner, tea or supper – at Godwin's lodgings and at Smith's.[4] At times there were others present, such as Coleridge, Thomas Holcroft, John and Eliza Fenwick, the painter James Northcote, the translator George Dyson, the writers Harriet and Sophia Lee, Smith's son George. The recent discovery of previously unknown letters from Smith to Godwin provides more concrete evidence than has heretofore been established for the topics of conversation and the register of discourse that most certainly would have featured in these meetings, expanding our view of those social interactions that the Godwin diary simply records. As Pamela Clemit asserts, these letters attest to Smith's place within a "key literary-political grouping of the Romantic era"[5] while also exhibiting Smith's conscious foregrounding of her own ideological position in relation to the events of the time. Thus, Smith's comment in a letter dated 27 February 1800 regarding a friend who "is in such a rage ab[ou]t the writers of the Anti-Jacobin for January, that he is trying to find out who they are that he can wreck [*sic*] some sort of vengeance on them", underscores the centrality of that periodical in the assault on radical thought and evinces Smith's willing identification with the group under attack.[6] Another remark, in a letter written on 1 September 1797, further exhibits Smith's political self-positioning. Here, she writes to Godwin of a domestic matter, asking for his assistance in helping to find lodgings in his London neighborhood of Somers Town for her daughter Lucy and future son-in-law Thomas Newhouse and in the course of the letter relates other information pertaining to family concerns.[7] However, even in addressing these quotidian issues she employs the vocabulary of political engagement: Smith's son, Charles, a wounded war veteran is referred to as the "victim of our accursed systems", Newhouse is recommended as a "disciple of a better system ... there are few better Citoyens", and Godwin is informed that she is only now reading his political-philosophical text, *An Enquiry concerning Political Justice.*[8] Providing evidence of shared cultural and intellectual community, the sentiments exhibited in Smith's correspondence with Godwin receive further, *public,* acknowledgement in her literary works written during this period, with her critique of political and social systems articulated against the backdrop of increasing government and legal repression. Yet even as it was collapsing before her very eyes, it is this twilight moment of radical energy with which Smith – who views herself, too, as a disciple of a better system – identifies and that functions as the privileged point of reference in her later writings.

I

In June 1797, Smith finally published her expanded two-volume edition of the *Elegiac Sonnets, and other poems*.[9] She put much effort into this work, paying what she called "fastidious" attention to the preparation of the edition, as is evident in her repeated revision and corrections of the manuscript, in her treatment of the list of subscribers to the volumes and in her careful scrutiny of the engravings – including her portrait and its caption – that accompanied the poems.[10] In spite of this intense effort, the volume had fewer subscribers than her earlier subscription edition – *Elegiac Sonnets I* (1789) had 817 subscribers, but *Elegiac Sonnets II* had only 283.[11] Judith Stanton suggests that one possible reason for the decline in the number of subscribers may have been Smith's strong support of the French Revolution, and it is not difficult to imagine that there were those "persons of high fashion" who had subscribed to the earlier edition who might have been taken aback at Smith's strident, oppositional political criticism that had appeared in the intervening years.[12]

And yet, Smith's careful overseeing of the production of *Elegiac Sonnets II* and her strong hopes for its success did not translate into a preemptory caution, or self-censorship, in regard to the poems to be included in the edition; this is not a volume oblivious to social issues or devoid of political engagement. Alongside poems that deal with the themes traditionally associated with the *Elegiac Sonnets* – nature, reflection, isolation and mourning, or, in Jacqueline Labbe's words, "straying, exile, alienation, mystique",[13] Smith also addresses those topical, political matters that continued to interest her. Thus, for example, she writes of the tragic result of forced military conscription in "The Forest Boy", adapts a section of *The Emigrants* (now reworked from blank verse to rhyme) as "The Female Exile", and reflects upon upholding one's integrity in a corrupt society in "To A Young Man Entering the World." This last theme is also the subject of Sonnet LXXXII, "To the shade of Burns," a poem that at the same time calls attention to that tenuous artistic and like-minded political community – real or desired – to which Smith directs her gaze.

"To the shade of Burns" as its title indicates, is dedicated to the memory of the Scottish poet Robert Burns, who died in July 1796 at the age of 37. As in very many of Smith's poems, quotations from other poets are interspersed throughout the text, exhibiting, in Paula Backscheider's words, how "[Smith] enjoyed playing off the lines and rhythms of the great poets of her century ... placing herself beside these poets – in their tradition and, after a few editions of *Elegiac Sonnets*, on their level."[14] In this sonnet, Smith's poetic referencing extends beyond her near contemporaries, and thus lines from Pope ("Epitaph on Sir William Trumbull") and Milton (*Lycidas*) appear here to exhibit her recognition of how Burns, the "associate worthy of the illustrious dead"[15] is now ensconced with them – and with Smith herself – in a privileged literary tradition. In this specific sonnet, however, the imagining of literary community with Burns is apparent in another dimension as well. Smith's note to the poem conveys her sorrow over the death of the poet, urges those who have admired his work to "reliev[e] by their benevolence [his] unfortunate family" and connects his life immediately to her own situation as "the object of subscription."[16] What particularly interests Smith in this sonnet is the connection between artistic merit, ideological integrity and financial degradation, which together create a status – or state of being – she perceived herself as sharing with Burns. This linkage receives particular emphasis for Smith in their common oppositional stance:

> ... And even beneath the daily pressure, rude,
> Of labouring Poverty, thy generous blood,
> Fired with the love of freedom [.] – Not subdued
> Were thou by thy low fortune: But a time
> Like this we live in, when the abject chime
> Of echoing Parasite is best approved,
> Was not for thee [.]
>
> (p. 71, 4–10)

Praising Burns's integrity, Smith thus also calls attention to her own resistance to the pressures that accompany artistic endeavor as it is produced in times of economic vulnerability.

Smith's affinity to Burns is further underscored in the fact that he is mentioned elsewhere in her work as well. In her children's book, *Rural Walks: in Dialogues intended for the use of young persons* (1795), the young girl, Caroline, quotes from his poem "Man was Made to Mourn" and Mrs Woodfield, the mother/teacher figure, responds with his "To a Mountain Daisy". These references to Burns appear as Mrs Woodfield and the group of children meet an indigent old woman and contemplate the subject of old age, poverty and institutionalized social neglect. Smith has Caroline recite three *non-sequential* stanzas from the former poem, choosing those with a more explicit social commentary and with lines such as "Man's inhumanity to Man/Makes countless thousands mourn!" that foreground the common ideological ground of the two writers and reinforce for her readers her own critical position.[17] The acknowledgement of the price one pays for this oppositional worldview, expressed in Smith's "To the Shade of Burns", echoes Burns's own awareness of the issue in the "Mountain Daisy", a poem which contemplates the fate of the disempowered subject, and "suffering worth"[18] that is threatened by the implacable forces surrounding it. Consider, for example, his following lines, in which the place of a vulnerable authorial integrity is specifically addressed:

> Such is the fate of simple Bard,
> On Life's rough ocean luckless starr'd!
> Unskilful he to note the card
>   Of *prudent Lore*,
> Till billows rage, and gales blow hard,
>   And whelm him o'er![19]

Smith would have identified with this representation of the tenuous position of the author when "prudence" is ultimately neglected. Her own experience resonates in what is perhaps the most overtly political poem in *Elegiac Sonnets II*, "The Dead Beggar", subtitled "an elegy, addressed to a lady, who was affected at seeing the funeral of a nameless pauper, buried at the expence of the parish, in the church-yard at Brighthelmstone, in November 1792." In this poem the speaker consoles the spectator-mourner by contrasting the bleak world of the aged poor with the leveling eternity of the classless dead. The timeless theme is qualified, at the same time, by both the specific temporal context exhibited in the introductory lines, November 1792 (a subject to which I will return) and by the topical, controversial reference in the penultimate stanza:

> Rejoice, that tho' an outcast spurned by Fate,
> Thro' penury's rugged path his race he ran;
> In earth's cold bosom, equall'd with the great,
> Death vindicates the insulted rights of Man.
>   (17–20)

The "rights of man" is, of course, a loaded, politically fraught phrase, a fact that Smith herself acknowledged in the second edition of *Elegiac Sonnets II*, which was published in 1800. There she writes, in a note that accompanies the poem:

> I have been told that I have incurred blame for having used in this short composition, terms that have become obnoxious to certain persons. Such remarks are hardly worth notice; and it is very little my ambition to obtain the suffrage of those who suffer party prejudice to influence their taste; of those who desire that because they have themselves done it, every one else should be willing to sell their best birth-rights, the liberty of thought, and of expressing thought, for the *promise* of a mess of porridge. (p. 96)

These are among the most direct and unequivocal words that Smith writes on the subject of her political beliefs and on the repressive climate of the late 1790s with its attendant pressures exerted towards caution, prudence and the restraint of "liberty of thought." And these pressures are indeed apparent in the fact that although Smith asserts that "such [accusatory] remarks" are "hardly worth notice", she devotes a fairly long note to rebutting them.

Moreover, we must consider why Smith chose to include "November 1792" in the poem's subtitle in the first place, a date five years prior to the poem's first publication in *Elegiac Sonnets II* and not linked to any recognizable event within the text that would justify the mention of a particular month and year. November 1792 had been a politically charged time for Smith – after the initial euphoria over the Revolution, after the *in absentia* arrest of Paine, after the September massacres, but when she was still highly, radically engaged, corresponding with Joel Barlow and toasted at the British Club in Paris. This dating may function, then, as the means of anchoring the poem's narrative within the context of a past time in which it was still just possible for Smith to defend the "rights of man"; when a discourse of reform could be aspired to, and articulated in those terms.

Or so she hoped. The appearance of this note in 1800 (with its acknowledgement of the criticism she incurred) indicates her failure in attempting to distance the narrative time of the poem from that of its publication. The timeline of events – the beggar's funeral in 1792, which is observed and recorded in 1797 and then revisited and defended in 1800 – exhibits the pervasiveness of a reactionary political conformity, of the absence of "liberty of thought" and of how the attempt to obfuscate, if only briefly, the changes wrought in the intervening years had proved to be impossible.[20]

II

The ubiquity of the political reaction in the final years of the eighteenth century and the price paid by those who continued to adhere to a progressive, if not radical, political agenda is the main subject of Smith's 1798 novel, *The Young Philosopher*. There, she returns to the themes she had addressed in *The Banished Man* and specifically to the perception of the inhospitable nature of British society in which exile is viewed as an infinitely preferable option. In the years preceding the novel's publication, Smith had continued to respond to those issues in her prose writing and (as we have just seen) in her poetry, focusing increasingly on the institutionalized injustice that was, for her, an ever-present feature of British society. The terror evinced by the British legal system is omnipresent in her work, and in a telling parallel to the violence in France, she has a character in *Marchmont* say, "Robespierre and his agents are not more destructive and more cruel than English lawyers."[21]

The Young Philosopher, like *Desmond* and *The Banished Man*, is an overtly political novel, but one that was written with the additional perspective of time. As Loraine Fletcher notes, "the author has the advantage of hindsight, while the earlier political novels were written to the moment."[22] And this hindsight both sharpens and hardens Smith's gaze: by 1798, wherever she looks, she can see only disappointment, madness and ruin. Unlike *The Banished Man*, in *The Young Philosopher* Smith presents a consistent endorsement of idealized radical principles, one that is underpinned by the demarcation of positive and negative characters according to their political views. The novel relates the adventures of George Delmont, the "young philosopher", a second son (again) and an idealistic young farmer, and his group of friends. Throughout the novel, this little group is placed in opposition to and persecuted by the dominant social order, represented by, variously, Mrs Crewkherne, Delmont's aunt, a woman motivated by reactionary political beliefs, religious fanaticism and greed, Adolphus, his imperious and fiscally irresponsible elder brother, and a host of corrupt lawyers. Delmont falls in love with Medora Glenmorris, who has returned with her mother, Laura, to England from their home in America in order to secure the daughter's share of the family inheritance which Laura had lost when she married against her family's wishes. Glenmorris himself has remained in America, leaving his family under the care of his friend, Armitage, who is a writer and progressive political thinker, and a figure who is viewed with suspicion and unease by the community.

In spite of its title, *The Young Philosopher* is, above all, the story of the victimization of Laura and Medora Glenmorris, who, in their efforts to recover the inheritance, are subjected to a conspiracy that results in Medora's abduction by her parents' adversaries and Laura's madness in its aftermath. Indeed, Laura's adventures in the novel exhibit what is virtually a catalogue of female oppression. Volume II is an inset story, a first-person narration in which she relates the events of her youth and her earlier struggle against the forces of greed and tyrannical patriarchy. Even after she escapes her imprisonment by her family in order to marry the independent, free-thinking Glenmorris, she undergoes a series of ordeals in which, after Glenmorris is abducted by pirates, she is taken prisoner by his relations, loses her infant son in her ensuing imprisonment and narrowly escapes the advances of various "suitors" whom she meets in the Scottish highlands.

These events foreshadow a second set of adventures later in the novel, in which Laura attempts to find Medora. Her futile search for assistance underscores her isolation, and points to the political nature of her plight. The fact that she is married to Glenmorris, and associated with Armitage doubly disadvantages her – those acquaintances to whom she turns, instead of aiding her, reprimand her for the "predeliction of [herself] and Mr. Glenmorris for the manners and morality of modern Gallia" (p. 209), and thus call attention to her vulnerability both as a financially-pressed woman and as an adherent to a now unpopular political ideology. The sequence of events generated by the abduction of Medora culminates in Laura's decline into madness while wandering the inhospitable streets of London in search of her daughter, her arrival, unknowingly, at the home of her estranged mother, and her forced incarceration in a madhouse. Laura eventually manages to escape from the madhouse, just as Medora does from her captivity, and they are reunited with Glenmorris (who has now arrived from America) and Delmont. The novel concludes with the decision of the two couples to move to America, a move that acknowledges the hope invested in the American alternative but even more the traumatizing effects of life in Britain for those marginalized by class, gender and ideology.

Smith put much effort into the writing of *The Young Philosopher*. As far back as 1 May 1796 she wrote to her publishers Cadell and Davies that she was about to "begin a work of quite a different nature from any I have yet undertaken"[23] – and although this novel is not really so much a departure from her earlier works, Smith evidently perceived it as such. Evidence of her careful preparations for writing the novel appears in a letter to Cadell and Davies, where she asks them to pay for a "set of books" that are "necessary for the work [she is] about"[24] as well as in her reading of Godwin's *Political Justice*, as we learned from Smith's letter to Godwin from 1 September 1797. The date of this letter suggests that Smith might have been reading the second, revised edition of *Political Justice*; if so, she would have seen a version of the text which, like *The Young Philosopher*, is shaped by, and responds to, ongoing, contemporary political developments and anxieties. In 1796, Godwin's ideas are "more cautious and reactionary than in the first edition"; his account of, and prescription for, social change is influenced by the forces of reaction in Britain but also cognizant of the excesses of the Revolution itself.[25] For example when Armitage, Smith's Godwinian character, says that he holds "all wild schemes of universal equality . . . utterly impracticable",[26] he is echoing Godwin's own cautious response to and reaction against the *sans-culotte* and mob violence that had occurred in France.[27]

As we saw in the previous chapter, *The Young Philosopher* was reviewed by Robert Bisset in the inaugural edition of the *Anti-Jacobin Review* (1798).[28] A glance at the contents of this issue, in a journal that had been conceived as a mouthpiece for government support, provides access to the hostile reception in 1798 for progressive authors. Among other items, the volume also includes Bisset's review of Mary Robinson's *Walsingham*, a novel that, like *The Young Philosopher*, presents a highly critical view of present-day British society while at the same time expressing support for the original revolutionary agenda.[29] Bisset's treatment of Smith's and Robinson's novels reflects his uneasiness with the strident social criticism of the authors. Significantly, Smith and Robinson are censured for participating in political discourse and for the transgression of gender boundaries that their writing exhibits. As Bisset writes, "the best of our female novelists interferes not with church and state."[30]

This unease receives a visual representation in the periodical in James Gillray's plate, "The New Morality", in which *The Young Philosopher* and *Walsingham* are among the various radical works that lay scattered on the ground.[31] The drawing presents a world characterized by disorder and disruption in which human figures and texts merge together in an all-encompassing depiction of chaos. Three figures, representing "Justice", "Philanthropy" and "Sensibility" frown down from a pedestal on the scene below. The figure of "Sensibility" places her foot on a skull and at the same time weeps over a dead bird she is holding in one hand, while in the other she holds a book entitled simply "Rousseau".[32] Gillray does not separate the female-authored texts from those of male authors, rather, he obfuscates gender differences, defining at the same time, in the midst of this chaotic scene, a shared cultural engagement against which, by its very nature, the *Anti-Jacobin Review* places itself in opposition.

Bisset's review of *The Young Philosopher* acknowledges Smith's radical affiliation but qualifies it at the same time. Let us recall his trajectory of Smith's politics that I cited in the previous chapter in which Smith had been portrayed as repeatedly "chang[ing] from monarchist to democrat; from democrat to monarchist ... "[33] (In this novel, with the claim that she "continues to abuse England",[34] the change is, obviously, from 'monarchist to democrat' once again.) Bisset's view of an instability that marks Smith's politics contributes to the overall sense of scornful yet anxious aggressiveness that characterizes his commentary. A later remark further illustrates his anxiety:

> Mrs. Smith's exhortation to leave this country we shall answer by a common toast – "The land we live in, and may those who do not like it leave it." Should Mrs. Smith be pleased to be one of the number, the loss to this country, from the want of her political speculations, will not be considerable.[35]

Bisset's comments replicate Smith's awareness of exile as a desirable and preferable option for those who speak out against the political consensus just as his personal attack reinforces her own perception of "this land, that from her pushes all the rest."[36] Within a climate of aggressive and derisive intolerance (of which Bisset's review is indicative) and in seeing the hope that had been embodied in the French experiment in a rubble at her feet, Smith could in fact envision America as a "comfortable abode"; an alternative to tyranny, institutionalized injustice and political persecution.

Recent criticism of *The Young Philosopher* focuses on Smith's conception of an American utopia as the motivating force of the novel. For example, Angela Keane argues that the novel's American context represents "the most utopian ending of any of Smith's novels", and Leanne Maunu claims that "Smith essentially fashions America into a political and social utopia ... [a] utopic alternative to life within the British nation."[37] While I agree that the presence of an idealized American alternative appears as a point of reference to which the characters repeatedly direct their gaze, I want to argue that the novel's main narrative energy is located not in the movement towards America, but rather in the scathing indictment of British society, in particular its ruthlessness towards those who are marginalized by class, gender, an oppositional political worldview, or indeed a combination of the three. The American option functions, similarly to Verona in *The Banished Man*, primarily through contrast, as a worthy alternative to the ills of contemporary British society, signifying a refuge, though not a utopia, for the victims of its oppressiveness.

At the same time, the perception of the inhospitableness of British society in *The Young Philosopher*, unlike in *The Banished Man*, is clearly linked to an unequivocal identification with a pro-Revolution viewpoint. In shoring up this positioning, which carries with it repeated reflections on the abuse of power in Britain, Smith draws upon, and weaves through her narrative, arguments presented by prominent radical writers. Mary Wollstonecraft is alluded to in the portrayal of systematic female oppression which culminates in Delmont's reflections on the "wrongs of woman" (p. 290), Joel Barlow is acknowledged in the attack on British jurisprudence and on primogeniture in the representation of the imperious eldest son, and Rousseau resonates in the depiction of botany as an approved area of female education.[38] At the same time Smith rebuts the arguments of Burke in his *Reflections on the Revolution in France*, quite forthrightly, as we will see, in her representation of the Glenmorrises' (upper-class) adversaries as the true "swinish multitude." This repertoire of contemporary references marks *The Young Philosopher* not only as a critique of present-day British society, but one which valorizes a range of radical alternatives, which, although no longer potentially viable in Britain, still exhibit a specific ideological worldview as a discursive presence.[39]

This progressive positioning is not without its attendant anxiety, as evident in Smith's prefatory remarks to the novel:

> I will now content myself with declaring against the injustice of inferences, frequently drawn by the Reader, in regard to the Author of such books as these; I mean their appropriating to him or her as individuals, sentiments and opinions given to any of the characters intended to be described as amiable. There may be many traits, many ideas, and even many prejudices, which may be necessary to support or render these characters natural, that are by no means those of the composer of the book; I declare therefore against the conclusion, that *I* think either like Glenmorris or Armitage, or any other of my personages. (p. 5)

The attempt to dissociate the authorial voice from those characters who represent the Godwinian philosopher and the belief in gradual reform[40] is a particularly telling expression of political self-consciousness in the cultural climate of 1798; this is a far cry from the claim for "self-evident truth" that had been used to identify political views associated with author-character relations in *Desmond*. However, Smith's "success" in achieving that distancing – and the sincerity of her desire to do so – already appear questionable when viewed in light of an earlier statement that appears in the preface. There, she is anxious to defend herself from the charge of plagiarism in her portrayal of Laura Glenmorris's incarceration in a madhouse. As she explains:

> I may just mention, that the incident of a confinement in a mad house [*sic*] of one of my characters was designed before I saw the fragment of "The Wrongs of Woman," by a Writer whose talents I greatly honoured, and whose untimely death I deeply regret. (p. 5)

Smith's forthright praise of Mary Wollstonecraft comes shortly after the publication of Godwin's *Memoirs of the Author of the Vindication of the Rights of Woman*, in which his frank account of Wollstonecraft's life caused a public furor and created a backlash against her writing.[41] As Elizabeth Kraft notes, "Smith's endorsement of Wollstonecraft was therefore an act of integrity in the climate of 1798"[42] as it connects the two women not only through their common use of the metaphor of the madhouse to represent the vulnerability of women in society, but also, by extension, through their work as co-artists writing more generally about shared cultural concerns. Yet, even as it points to a radical affiliation, the fact that the reference to Wollstonecraft appears in the context of a defense against charges of plagiarism, and precedes a qualification of the political content of her novel, once more suggests Smith's persistent anxiety as a writer, one which manifests itself in the overlapping concerns of authorial integrity, political commitment and economic survival.

Smith's depiction of contemporary British society in *The Young Philosopher* stresses from the outset the vulnerability of those who are disenfranchised from its systems of power. Delmont's education and his philosophic retirement have been shaped by the powerlessness that he had seen around him as a boy, and depicted in yet another of Smith's catalogues of despair:

> Thus when he ... was springing forth on one of those rambles which were his principal enjoyment, he was often stopped on the way by some piteous story of hunger, of houseless poverty, of disasters from fire or flood, from sickness or shipwreck – a wounded soldier shewed him his mutilated limb – a sightless sailor recounted how he had lost his eyes by lightning from heaven, or by an explosion of powder – an old man, bent to the earth by years or calamity, related that he had been driven from his home by the magistrates or officers, who, when the son who used to support him had been forced to go for a soldier, would compel the decrepid [*sic*] father to return to a remote parish, whither his feeble limbs refused to convey him–a woman pale and emaciated presented herself, one infant hung on

her breast, two others following her; she was the widow of an Irish soldier, he was dead in the West Indies; she was refused relief in any parish here; she was begging her way to Ireland. (p. 21)

Smith's tight, rhythmic prose underscores her awareness of the unending cycle of economic terror and relentless persecution against which the action of *The Young Philosopher* is played out. This depiction of powerlessness functions as the counterpoint to the world of Delmont's brother Adolphus and his aunt Mrs Crewkherne, which is defined by its hostility to the socially vulnerable. The contrast between compassionate and antagonistic social behavior is underpinned in the characters' competing political and religious worldviews, as illustrated in Mrs Crewkherne's opinion of Armitage, whose friendship with Delmont particularly upsets her:

[Armitage] writes books – very bad books, I am afraid, from what some good friends of mine, and very good judges too, have told me – a person, Sir, who affirms that by works alone we are safe … who would dissolve all the chains of due subordination and obedience, and set the mechanic and the labourer a thinking when they ought to be working for their superiors; and who avail themselves of the foolish inexperience of wrong-headed youth, to teach them not to follow in the paths that have led up their progenitors to honours, and titles, and preferments, and fortune. (pp. 17–18)

Kraft notes that "Armitage's belief in the efficacy of works to attain salvation marks him as a Latitudinarian or broad churchman, who emphasizes the reasonableness of Christianity, as opposed to Mrs. Crewkherne, who has clear Methodist leanings."[43] Although Methodism was commonly associated with the lower social orders – and Mrs Crewkherne, on the contrary, is financially comfortable and zealously guards her own illustrious family lineage and inheritance – the adherence to its beliefs also reflected, together with the wider Evangelical revival of which it was a part, the sense of crisis brought on by the French Revolution and its aftermath. As Leonore Davidoff and Catherine Hill explain:

The nation, [the revivalists] believed, was suffering from moral degeneracy. Events in France were a warning of what was to come if individuals did not inspire a revolution in the "manners and morals" of the nation, a transformation that must begin with individual salvation.[44]

The religious enthusiasm of Mrs Crewkherne extends to her milieu of friends and associates, who together exhibit a religious fervor that is portrayed by Smith as profoundly cynical. They plot against Delmont and the Glenmorrises not only to prevent Medora from receiving her portion of her family's inheritance, but also because of their association with Armitage, who "had written in favour of the Americans; nay, who had aided and abetted ... the atrocious French Revolution" (p. 53). Interests of greed, religion and politics merge together to underscore the powerlessness of the individual in his or her struggle for social justice and the price exacted from those who continue to express their support for original revolutionary values.

Mrs Crewkherne's heightened political awareness is indicative of how Evangelism enabled women to exert a certain degree of cultural authority. As Davidoff and Hill have shown, religious activity allowed women a social and public voice, albeit within carefully constructed parameters. Mary Poovey notes this phenomenon as well: "Indeed, women can be seen as the prime beneficiaries of this [Evangelical] movement – it gave them a constructive vehicle for their talents."[45] However, Smith's depiction of Evangelical women displays this social energy as destructive rather than constructive, as reinforcing the powerlessness of *other* women, such as Laura Glenmorris, who do not share their religious fervor or political views. Religious zeal is, for Smith, an additional feature of the reactionary ideology harnessed by the privileged class in order to maintain and preserve its status in the face of political and cultural dissonance.

Smith's social and political critique is further illustrated in her representation of primogeniture as a signifier of an oppressive patriarchal system. Delmont's older brother Adolphus is depicted as a thoughtless wastrel, and his fiscal irresponsibility threatens to destroy Delmont's own happiness and financial security, as he is forced to mortgage his property in order to save his brother from insolvency. Smith describes Adolphus's point of view:

> He persisted, however, in considering George as one born only to promote his [Adolphus's] views and obey his mandates. Impressed with ideas of primogeniture at a very early age, he could never submit to any mention of equality even among brethren. Nothing, he said, was more infamous than the change made in that respect in France. (p. 19)

The yoking of primogeniture to the events in France immediately suggests an engagement with and rebuttal of Burke's *Reflections on the Revolution in France*. Burke based his objection to the revolution on an argument that valorized tradition, continuity and conservation of the values of the ancestral British past. This is, for him:

> an *entailed inheritance*, derived to us from our forefathers, and to be transmitted to our posterity; as an estate specially belonging to the people of this kingdom without any reference whatever to any other more general or prior right ... We have an inheritable crown; an inheritable peerage; and an house of commons and a people inheriting privileges, franchises, and liberties, from a long line of ancestors.[46]

Mary Wollstonecraft, in her response to Burke, *A Vindication of the Rights of Man* (1790), focuses on the injustice of a social system based on inherited privilege, and specifically on the laws of primogeniture:

> Property ... should be fluctuating, which would be the case, if it were more equally divided amongst all the children of a family; else it is an everlasting rampart, in consequence of a barbarous feudal institution, that enables the elder son to overpower talents and depress virtue.[47]

Smith appropriates this view of the elder son in her portrayal of Adolphus, whose tyranny both foregrounds George's powerlessness (he is away on an errand to help settle Adolphus's financial affairs when Medora is abducted, and thus is unable immediately to help) and hastens his desire to leave England and go with her to America after they are reunited. Even his attachment to his home, Upton, is "considerably embittered ... by the residence of his brother so near it" (p. 353), and thus proves a decisive factor in his decision to move to America. The fact that even the beloved landscape is now defined by embittered familial memory rewrites the consciousness of institutionalized, inherited oppression onto the very essence of the British experience.

Smith's engagement with Burke and Wollstonecraft has other resonances in *The Young Philosopher* as well. Prominent among them is the way that Burke's infamous "swinish multitude" remark is reversed by Laura Glenmorris.[48] Laura has just returned from a meeting with her lawyers and creditors, and, dismayed by their vulgarity, thinks to herself:

> Of people like these is made up the bulk of that world, to which prejudice and fear induce us to sacrifice real happiness. – It is this mob, which over-bears all retiring and simple virtues, and destroys all simple pleasures. – This affectation of the manners of upper life – how ridiculous! – and how very unlike are these people to those they would copy – Ah! It is not the *swinish multitude* ... that disgust one with the species. It is such people as these; people who hold the honest labourer and the industrious mechanic in contempt, yet are indeed poor in intellect and vulgar in all they do and say. (p. 197)

Smith's uneasiness regarding the aggressiveness of the nouveaux riches is accompanied by the anxiety of the financially distressed woman who has lost her own social rank. (At this point in the narrative, Laura has not received the money that her husband had sent from America, and her family in England is unwilling to acknowledge her – she is penniless and vulnerable.) This financial unease is inextricably linked to a political narrative, one that is emphasized through a reference to Burke's *Reflections*, one of the definitive political texts of the time. As E.P. Thompson has shown, Burke's "swinish multitude" remark inflamed popular political discourse, creating a host of angry satirical replies, with titles such as *Hog's Wash* and *Pig's Meat*.[49] (Interestingly, *Pig's Meat* lies not far from *The Young Philosopher* in the scattered radical writings strewn on the ground in Gillray's "The New Morality.") Thompson's discussion of the angry response to Burke stresses how the working class embraced the potential for freedom incipient in the early years of the French Revolution. Smith, writing in 1798, when, to use Thompson's phrase, the "reflex of despair"[50] had set in among the working classes, acknowledges the reality of their defeat, and that of progressive forces in general. The working class portrayed in *The Young Philosopher* are, as we have seen, the victims of war and poverty, and Laura herself will be driven literally insane by the "mob" of upwardly-mobile, socially intolerant merchants and lawyers who comply in the abduction of her daughter.

The ultimate confrontation between the progressive and reactionary forces in the novel occurs in the meeting between Armitage and Mrs Crewkherne, when the former goes to inquire as to the whereabouts of Medora. Armitage responds to Mrs Crewkherne's calling him, among other things, a "jacobin" (p. 244) by saying:

> as to my being a jacobin, which, I take for granted, includes everything you can imagine horrible, and to be a sort of constellation of terrible charges; I have only to say, that if you mean, among other heavy misdemeanors included under it, that I either approve, or ever did approve of the violence, cruelty, and perfidy, with which the French have polluted the cause of freedom, you are greatly mistaken; far from thinking that such measures are likely to establish liberty, and the general rights of mankind, I hold them to be exactly the means that will delay the period when rational freedom ... shall be established in the world. (...) but you must allow me to remark, that if the folly and wickedness, by which mankind have, in every age of the world, endeavoured to establish tenets, either of religion or government, were to prove the falsity of those tenets, there is no one system which would not be liable to the same objections as have been made to the revolution in France; that it has been the source of misery, of bloodshed, of crimes, from which reason and humanity recoil with terror and detestation. (p. 247)

In carefully distinguishing between "freedom", "liberty" and the "rights of mankind", on the one hand, and the "violence, cruelty and perfidy" which have "polluted" their acquisition, on the other, Armitage dissociates himself from the excesses of the Terror, while continuing to uphold the original ideals of the Revolution. As Leanne Maunu puts it, this conversation is "Smith's own opportunity to defend herself against charges of supporting the more recent violence of the Revolution [while] ... Armitage's praise for the Revolution lets Smith's readers know that Smith herself has not forsaken her values, even if she does not support the turn that the Revolution has taken."[51] Furthermore, in presenting those excesses as just another sequence of a repeated historical progression, Armitage denies the events in France the historical uniqueness, that apocalyptic valence, that so informed the reactionary backlash.

It is instructive to compare Armitage's response to Mrs Crewkherne with the comments of the *Anti-Jacobin Weekly*, appearing on 14 May 1798, less than one month before the publication of *The Young Philosopher*:

> It cannot be too much impressed upon Men's minds – it must be, and is impressed upon the mind of every Man who has thought anxiously and fearfully upon the times in which we live (and GOD knows, they are as such as to call forth all our anxieties and all our fears), that to maintain *at this day* the ORIGINAL PRINCIPLES of the FRENCH REVOLUTION – pretending *at this day* to separate those Principles from the Practice, is either gross hypocrisy, or a blindness approaching to infatuation. To maintain the principles, is to recommend the trial of them. The success of the experiment we have seen.[52]

Yet, Smith did in fact "maintain the principles." And I say "Smith" despite her remarks in the preface, where she had distanced herself from the character of Armitage. For his lengthy, uninterrupted speech on the distinction between revolutionary values and revolutionary violence indeed recalls and replicates previous remarks on the subject in her other works both by her approved characters, such as we saw in *The Banished Man*, and in her prefatorial remarks to *The Emigrants*, where she had decried those who "confounded the original cause [of the Revolution] with the wretched catastrophes that have followed."[53] This identification is further evinced here in Mrs. Crewkherne's inability to respond to Armitage's claims:

> Mrs. Crewkherne found that, repelled by *integrity* and *truth*, the shafts she had delighted to throw against Armitage would fail of every effect she intended. She was one of those worthy personages who are never wrong in their own opinion . . . but she felt, however willing to acknowledge it, all the power of *truth*. (p. 247)

The association of "truth" with the defense of the original values of the Revolution (expressed here, significantly, by the narrator) echoes the argument for "the predominant power of truth" that Smith had invoked in *Desmond* to justify an ideological positioning in 1792. And, keeping in mind her reading of *Political Justice* during the writing of *The Young Philosopher*, it once more suggests her alignment with William Godwin, who, even in the second, revised edition of that work continued to argue that "it is the property of truth to be fearless, and to prove victorious over every adversary."[54] Yet, as Smith knew well, the climate of 1798 was hostile to a defense of Revolutionary values, just as idealized truth was a fragile philosophical concept amidst the tumultuous political, social and legal events of the time. Therefore, Armitage's remarks may succeed in momentarily silencing his reactionary adversary but are ineffectual in motivating any kind of change in the existing alignment of power: he leaves Mrs Crewkherne's house without obtaining a more practical kind of truth – an answer as to the whereabouts of the missing girl.

The inability of Armitage (as well as of the other male characters) to alleviate the suffering of Medora and Laura Glenmorris points to Smith's specific concern in *The Young Philosopher* with the representation of female vulnerability, a theme whose ubiquitous presence in the novel signals, as Fletcher suggests, "in its frightened hierarchy and male domination the final triumph of political and sexual reaction in England in 1798."[55] While the terrors of female experience are conventionally depicted in the story of Medora, who, as a quintessential Smith heroine exerts fortitude in overcoming the obstacles with which society has presented her (including, in this novel, abduction and near rape) and in turn is rewarded with the ideal husband – gentle, adoring and politically progressive, she is essentially a foil for the true heroine of *The Young Philosopher*, Laura Glenmorris, whose first-person story comprises an entire volume of the novel, and whose decline into madness generates much of its narrative energy.

Smith's contemporary critics had confounded her portrayal of Laura with her other semi-autobiographical characters, such as Mrs Stafford in *Emmeline* and Mrs Denzil in *The Banished Man*, and Laura's tale of financial distress, legal troubles and abuse at the hands of avaricious lawyers reiterates a popular Smith theme.[56] However, in her portrayal of Laura and her subjection to a cycle of persecutions and incarcerations – she experiences, variously, parental tyranny, forced confinement, sexual aggression, financial vulnerability and eventually madness – Smith presents the older, experienced woman as a central figure in this novel, not as an autobiographical representation, but rather as her enactment of "everywoman." Laura's experience literalizes Wollstonecrafts's perception of the totality of female oppression, of a world which is, for women, "a vast prison."[57]

It should not be surprising then that, despite her reunion with Medora and with her husband, Laura continues to suffer the after effects of her harrowing ordeal. As she puts it:

> Oh ... let us not stay in a country to which we have both returned only to suffer; where we know and have experienced that the poor may, in some cases at least, be persecuted and oppressed with impunity ... I fear, I know not why, that the calm and contented state we then enjoyed [in America], we shall never recover. Oh! no! I feel that my mind is hurt, my temper embittered ... and here I shall be haunted by ... the dread of persecution ... while I stay in England I am sure I shall be incapable of happiness. (p. 350)

As noted earlier, the subsequent decision to return to America has been viewed in recent criticism of *The Young Philosopher* in the context of Smith's attempt to formulate alternative conceptions of national identity against the backdrop of the cultural crisis of the 1790s, perceiving what has been a cosmopolitan vision throughout her work as now a specifically American ideal.[58] These readings emphasize the movement of "away *to*" as opposed to "away *from*"; the journey to the New World is viewed as a process of rectification and recovery imbued by a new and meaningful sense of national belonging.

While indirectly acknowledging the corrective potential of America, Laura's remarks, and the conclusion of the novel in general, exhibit more forcefully, I believe, the trauma incurred in her British experience. Her companions, accordingly, agree to make the journey, not, it seems, because of their own desire to do so – in fact, Glenmorris, at first, "did not [even] assent to her reasons" (p. 350) – but rather in acquiescence to her wishes, out of solicitude for the precarious state of her health. In consenting to leave, they too, like her, focus more on the point of departure than on the point of destination: Delmont explains his decision to go to America by his aversion to the presence of his brother Adolphus in the vicinity of his home, and Glenmorris prefaces his own agreement with a recitation of the wrongs of Britain, and of a society in which "the miseries inflicted by the social compact greatly exceed the happiness derived from it," (p. 352). Glenmorris's earlier reflections following his return from America reinforce this sense of the inhospitableness of Britain and in doing so echo in the fictional text the demise of the Godwin circle and of the radical moment more generally: Thus, "[t]he charm [Glenmorris] had formerly found or imagined in society, such as is to be met with in a great city, had vanished; his friends were gone; some were dead, others disappeared from poverty or from weariness" (p. 299).

Above all, it is Laura's lingering madness that informs the conclusion of *The Young Philosopher*: "I fear ... we shall never recover." Thus, while America may signal the existence of a desirable alternative and a new, chosen national identity, it is more a default option; a "comfortable abode" but also a retreat into exile motivated by despair, disappointment and insanity. It cannot really be seen as utopian because it will not entirely erase, or subsume, the ravaging effects that Laura's experience has had on her. The characters' departure to an enlightened community, tempered by the vestiges of the terrors that marked their sojourn in Britain, signifies instead the irreversibility of social and political defeat.

III

In *The Letters of a Solitary Wanderer* Smith continues to delineate madness, trauma and their afterlife. Her final novel is actually a series of novellas grouped together in a loose epistolary form in which the eponymous hero, a melancholy man of means, tries to ameliorate his depressive state by recording in a series of letters to his friend his impressions of people he has met and stories he has heard. The novel has an uneven publication history. The five volumes of *The Letters of a Solitary Wanderer* appeared in two separate editions: Vols. I–III were published by Sampson Low in 1800, however, following his death, the manuscripts were auctioned off and the remaining two volumes were eventually published in 1802 by Longman and Rees. As Smith explains it, this development:

> occasions the book to appear under very aukward [*sic*] circumstances; and has prevented my concluding it, at least at present, according to my original agreement with Mr. Low, which was to furnish him with six volumes . . . As it is, the story of the *Solitary Wanderer* himself remains to be told; but the want of it does not affect any of the narratives except the last; and I have written much of it a second time, to disentangle it, as far as I could, from that which would have closed the work, had it been finished according to my first design, and with which I intended to connect it. (Vol. iv., p. iv.)

Smith does not really manage to "disentangle" the narrative, and although the wanderer in fact begins to play an integral part in the action in Volume V, we never learn his name or the reason for his prolonged melancholy, and it is tempting to imagine how he would have evolved according to Smith's original plan for the novel.[59]

Nonetheless, as they stand, the tales, taken together, present an all-encompassing portrayal of rootlessness and disenfranchisement, one that is played out in a variety of locales and historical and political moments – on the island of Jamaica during a slave uprising, in sixteenth-century France in the aftermath of the St Bartholomew's Eve massacre, during the political upheavals in Hungary and war-torn Ireland, as well as in a gothic mansion in contemporary England. Smith's aversion to violence and tyranny is underscored in this geographical and temporal diversity: war, destruction and uncertainty are everywhere, it seems, and life is a continual struggle to find the fortitude with which to face them. The terrors that Smith's characters experience in these novellas are so profound that even conventional closures such as marriage, or receiving a rightful but unexpected inheritance, cannot mitigate the traumas they have undergone.

The tenuous epistolarity of the novel exhibits another dimension of instability and uncertainty informing the text. The letter-writer is unnamed (and the recipient's name, merely "Harry" is mentioned only once, in Volume V) and the letters are for the most part undated. The *Solitary Wanderer* is what Janet Altman would term a "passive" epistolary novel, where the letter merely reports events and the writer and receiver play a passive role, and the actual writing in itself can have a therapeutic function.[60] Altman calls our attention, furthermore, to the two traditional modes of closure in an epistolary novel – comic closure, when the letter writer has no need to write anymore (the form which, it will be recalled, we saw in *Desmond*) and tragic closure, when the novel concludes because the letter writer cannot write anymore. As she puts it, "both comic and tragic closure in epistolary fiction point once again to those polar limits – total presence (reunion) and total absence (death) – that constitute the conditions obviating the letter."[61]

However, the *Solitary Wanderer* does not accord with Altman's paradigms, evincing neither the therapeutic possibilities which letter writing enables nor the closures that it offers. There is little emotional development on the part of the writer, and slight, if any, recovery from his melancholic condition. (His tentative attachment to Leonora, the heroine of the fifth volume, remains uncertain and undeveloped at the conclusion of the book.) There is no sense of either tragic or comic closure, only a promise of continued writing to come. It is instructive, then, to compare the epistolarity of the *Solitary Wanderer* with that of *Desmond*, for the structural cohesion and sense of historical accuracy that are conveyed through the letters of the earlier novel are conspicuously absent in the later work. This progression reinforces Nicola Watson's claim for "the rapid disintegration of the epistolary novel in the ... 1790s" as it illustrates the connection between the collapse of the radical narrative and the function of the letter itself as a marker of cultural dissonance.[62]

Alongside war-torn landscapes and epistolary unsettledness, it is also the solitary wanderer himself who provides *The Letters of a Solitary Wanderer* with its post-revolutionary cultural awareness. In spite of his almost complete effacement from the first three volumes, and his enigmatic presence in the final two, the wanderer informs the text with a sense of gloom, unease and longing. Adriana Craciun's and Kari Lokke's discussion of this character type in relation to Frances Burney's *The Wanderer* (1814) is appropriate for Smith's novel as well: "For Burney ... the act of wandering offers no liberation, no mystical transport, and no solace in nature, unlike the more familiar effects of wandering (and solitude) in the works of Wordsworth and Rousseau."[63] And although the title of Smith's novel evokes Rousseau's *Reveries of a Solitary Walker*, and the novel echoes the Rousseauvian text in its loose episodic structure and the wanderer's stated aversion to society, the alienation that Rousseau depicts is transcended through the privileging of nature and retrospection. Smith's wanderer is offered no similar transcendence. Although in many of her other works, a bleak reality is ameliorated by the experience in nature, this text repeatedly emphasizes oppression and exile instead. Thus, the wanderer can write to his friend that the study of botany "used to interest and soothe my mind beyond any other study; but now I am in a state of spirits when it would rather depress than charm them," (Vol. i., p. 9).[64]

In my discussion of the *Solitary Wanderer* I will focus on the opening tale, "The Story of Edouarda", in which the heroine is denied the rewards of personal happiness in general, and love and marriage specifically, for her fortitude. I have chosen this story, the most profoundly pessimistic of the novellas, for the way that it succinctly exhibits many of the concerns

that I have been acknowledging in this chapter, portraying institutionalized oppression and concluding in both exile and trauma, while at the same
time presenting a fleeting, if poignant reminder of the collapse of the revolutionary vision. The tale begins when Edouarda arrives at the mansion of
her father, Sir Mordaunt Falconberg, after having been forced to leave the
convent where she was brought up. Edouarda exemplifies a typical Smith
heroine in her intelligence, natural good sense and courage in facing the
obstacles that confront her, and yet in this narrative these obstacles are so
deeply rooted in the powerful institutions of religion and patriarchy that
Edouarda, from the beginning, has no chance of prevailing against them.
Upon arriving at the mansion, Palsgrave Abbey, Edouarda soon realizes that
Sir Mordaunt's actions are influenced by two Jesuit priests who are intent on
controlling not only his spiritual life, but his extensive financial holdings
as well. Through her portrayal of the priests, Smith presents a fiercely anti-
Catholic viewpoint in this story, one which is a departure from the earlier,
more tolerant approach exhibited in *The Emigrants*.

With her presence a threat to their schemes, the priests confine Edouarda
to a room in the mansion, and the knowledge of her arrival is kept from her
father, who is at this time almost virtually insane. Contriving to leave the
room and wander about the premises of the estate, she first meets a young
man, a Mr Hartington, who immediately falls in love with her (an attachment that will have fatal consequences) and then her brother, whom she
had assumed was dead, and who has returned to claim his name and inheritance. When exploring the rooms of the house, Edouarda discovers what
appears at first to be a ghost, but turns out to be her mother, who had been
imprisoned for sixteen years in a cell in the mansion. Indeed, the ghost who
is not a ghost exemplifies the Radcliffean understanding that characterizes
Smith's Gothic as well – that evil and fear are embodied in the malevolence
and greed of humans, rather than in the supernatural.[65] And in fact, these
qualities are shown in their full magnitude when the reunited members of
Edouarda's family recount their stories of abandonment and disenfranchisement. Sir Mordaunt's original misanthropy, amplified by his suspicions of
his wife's unfaithfulness and encouraged by the priests who were gaining
increasing power over his actions, had led to the forced interment of his
wife, and the disowning of his two younger children (his first son, whom
he had acknowledged, had died as a young man) a plot development that
recalls Ann Radcliffe's *Sicilian Romance* (1790) in its portrayal of the wife who
is effectively buried alive as the extreme manifestation of patriarchal power.
After Hartington unwittingly informs him of the presence of his daughter in
his house, Sir Mordaunt breaks into the room where they are meeting and
kills his son, whom he had mistaken as his daughter's lover. His wife dies
from the shock of the encounter, as does Sir Mordaunt himself. Edouarda,
traumatized by the event, receives the inheritance, only to leave England
forever, rejecting the proposal of marriage of her suitor, and other proposals

that follow, and settling in Lausanne, surrounded by her books and "one or two friends" (Vol. i., p. 307).

This story stands out among Smith's fiction for its totally pessimistic vision, displayed most prominently in its portrayal of interpersonal relationships as unable to transcend institutional tyranny. In *The Banished Man* and *The Young Philosopher*, we recall, and indeed in all her novels, Smith was able to present the formation of idealized relationships (and especially love relationships) as a corrective for social, political and economic evils, and the valence of these relationships tempers the despair that accompanies defeat in the public realm. However, the conclusion of Edouarda's story affords her no similar rewards. Regardless of the financial stability awarded to her, she remains alone by choice, stoically philosophical, rather than happy. Her inheritance serves only to help her "endure a life, from which her early misfortunes had taken every hope of domestic happiness in the bosom of a family of her own" (Vol. i., p. 307). The retreat to Switzerland offers none of those compensations that had previously accompanied Smith's various exilic conclusions – love, community and a sense of "citizenship of the world." "The Story of Edouarda" would seem, then, to carry to its extreme that less celebratory sense of exile that I have been stressing throughout my discussion of Smith.

It is telling that although Edouarda had had many offers of marriage, one of the reasons she rejected the possibility of marriage and a family was because "ideas of her father's malady, and the shocking catastrophe it had led to, were ever present to her. She could not bear to suppose that she might transmit such a deranged intellect to her posterity" (Vol. i., p. 307). Edouarda's thinking here coincides with eighteenth-century perceptions of mental illness. George Cheyne, in *The English Malady* (1733) cites "the ill State of Health and bad State of Humours of the Parents, which, possibly, *they* might have transmitted to them from theirs, and so on from many Generations backwards" as one of the causes of madness.[66] And indeed, insanity and its organic, inevitable, inescapable connection to patriarchal authority not only informs and defeats present aspirations in this text, but extends to futurity as well, enabling Smith to portray a world of horror, evil and hopelessness that transcends time and place even while asserting their existence in the real world of the narrative. This pessimistic vision is embedded in the portrayal of interpersonal relationships in general: every suggestion of a possibly meaningful relationship – Edouarda with her mother and brother, Edouarda with her suitor, Edouarda's mother with an Italian male friend (the friendship that caused her husband to question her faithfulness to him) – every possibility of love or friendship leads to tragedy and death. Even the introduction of a reference to a Miss Hervey, a friend of Edouarda's from the convent, appears, only to lead nowhere.

One dimension of this pessimism appears in the repeated convergence of sex and death in this text. Sir Mordaunt punishes his wife for her supposed betrayal by almost literally burying her alive in a cell in the mansion, with a memorial stone noting her death and prayers put up for her soul to signify the fact. Edouarda's suitor's passion for her leads to his revealing the secret of her presence to her father, an event which causes his violent outrage and the two deaths that occur as its result. Henry Falconberg discovers his real identity when his supposed sister in the Italian family in which he was raised is raped by a Dominican priest and then, after being stabbed by her husband for her suspected "unfaithfulness", exposes the truth of his parentage in her dying breath. Lady Falconberg equates death and sex in a linkage in which each reiterates for her the horror of the other. When relating her story to her children after their reunion, she recalls that, upon having the opportunity to be reconciled to her husband, she still saw her life-in-death situation as infinitely preferable. "So great was my abhorrence of his person, which I had never loved", she relates:

> that when, far from other motives than those of real affection, he once more approached me, mingling resentment and doubt even with his caresses, I would gladly have returned to my dungeon, or even have sought shelter in the grave, rather than have become, as I was however gradually compelled to do, the mere victim of his animal gratifications. (p. 262)

In Smith's novels the young heroines are always fortuitously (and conventionally) rescued from male aggression before an actual rape can take place, and as a result the possibility of a post-rape scenario is never explored.[67] The prevailing pessimism of "The Story of Edouarda" is reinforced in the way that Smith denies Lady Falconberg such a fortunate rescue from unwanted sex. Although, of course, she is neither young nor a virgin, her retelling of what she was "compelled to do" underscores this unrelenting portrayal of female victimization. In tentatively addressing the subject of forced sex *within* marriage, Smith presents a form of sexual aggression that cannot be rescued – as in her earlier novels – by the demands of the sentimental novel.

Lady Falconberg's death, after witnessing the killing of her son, is an extreme expression of the tragic possibilities resulting from female oppression. The appearance of Henry Falconberg further politicizes the narrative by explicitly representing the struggle of the individual against entrenched forms of authority. Henry repeatedly anticipates his own death throughout the story, and expresses his fight against the tyranny of his father and the priests in heroic language that recalls the rhetoric of revolutionary discourse and the ideals of the Revolution itself. "Wherefore shall we fear?", he asks Edouarda, "Let the guilty tremble, we are innocent; let the oppressor recoil, we are the oppressed" (p. 205). Henry's sentiments are echoed and reinforced by the narrator as well. "Never was he known to submit to injustice from the stronger without ... resistance, or to compel submission from the inferior by menaces or blows (and) ... with ... great personal courage, and that consciousness of acting right which alone gives consistency and value to character, Henry Falconberg seemed designed by Heaven for all that is good and great" (Vol. i., p. 218). Yet, his principles remain in the realm of an idealized vision, unable to withstand the prejudice, evil and insanity of patriarchal society. Appearing for less than half the narrative, Henry's presence in the text signals in his aspirations but also in the ineffectuality of his struggle both the promise and the failure of the revolutionary ideal.

The attempt to represent in imaginative writing the ongoing progression of the revolutionary vision is, as I have tried to show, a central concern of Smith's literary project. Yet despite her abhorrence of the violent events of the mid-1790s, as well as her ongoing anxiety of self-representation within an oppressive cultural climate, she never abandons the hope for a better world that the Revolution had seemed to embody and never manages, or, it seems, never really wants to completely dissociate herself from the topical political referencing that supports even her more abstract conceptualizations of peace and social equality. Thus, in "The Hungarian", Vol. IV of the *Solitary Wanderer*, the wanderer can look around and say: "To wish for peace, to desire that the waste of life may cease, and suffering humanity feel no longer the scourge of war, and its certain consequences, contagion and famine, is to be an *Atheist*; a *Jacobin*, I know not what!" (Vol. iv., p. 9). The "wish for peace" and the vocabulary in which it is expressed recalls Smith's use of that same vocabulary in the letters to William Godwin with which I opened this chapter, exhibiting here once more the political awareness that continues to permeate her novels, and that accompanies her in her daily life.

At the same time, Smith's solitary wanderer is also allusively grounded in a literary tradition, suggesting continuities present in literary history itself. Smith's protagonist writes to his friend at the close of Volume III: "you shall hear, when he has anything worth telling you, from your friend, who, in the words of Dr. Johnson, may well describe himself as 'A kind of Solitary Wanderer in the wild of life, without any direction or fixed point of view; a gloomy gazer on the world to which I have little relation'" (Vol. iii., pp. 380–1). Smith has appropriated this quotation from Boswell's *Life of Johnson*, from a December 1754 letter from Johnson to Thomas Warton, in which Johnson expresses his feelings following the death of his wife. Smith's use of the quotation is in perfect agreement with this context, in underscoring the isolation and loneliness resulting from emotional loss.[68] The reference to Johnson also points to how the acts of reading and writing have an inherent significance for the wanderer – for, in the midst of his sadness he has linked Johnson to a promise to continue to write – and the way that they create a degree of meaning for him in an otherwise meaningless life. Moreover, the allusion to Johnson is emblematic of a persisting tension in Smith's oeuvre: the continual struggle to achieve a literariness in her project within the constraints of a bleak economic and political reality. The publishing history of *The Letters of a Solitary Wanderer*, as Smith relates it, encapsulates this awareness, as we imagine her running between the various publishers who held the copyright to her work, realigning her narrative to fit the limitations under which she was forced to write, but all the while maintaining reflexivity towards the inherited literary tradition.

I will conclude this chapter with a brief reference from the *Letters of a Solitary Wanderer* that exhibits once more this enmeshment of the literary and the political, the public and the personal. In Volume V of the novel, Smith presents the story of Leonora, one of the most thinly disguised of those autobiographical portraits that continually appear in her writing. Leonora, a young woman who was married off at an early age to a worthless, spendthrift husband, is retelling her story in writing. The text, written to a friend, is read by the wanderer and almost immediately causes him to fall in love with her. Significantly, Leonora begins her story with a political context – the contemplation of war:

> I believe if the real motives of those wars which have depopulated the world could be discerned, they would, whatever important causes have been assigned to them, be found to have originated in the pride or folly of some individual, unworthy to manage a village school, but to whom it has pleased heaven to entrust the government of the poor creatures of the earth. (Vol. v., pp. 170–1)

As Smith continues to delineate present social evils, this passage shows that her political views in 1802, if not exhibiting the exuberance of 1792, still retain, with yet another critique of Burke, much of their trenchancy; she remains, in spite of everything that has passed, a disciple of a better system.

Leonora immediately connects this political framing to a focus on her own subjectivity, when she continues, "but I am digressing from myself, who am, as you know, at least one of the heroines of my own tale (Vol. v., p. 171). And this is also, to be sure, Smith's "own tale." In a letter to her friend Sarah Farr Rose written in 1804, two years before her death, she could look back upon her life and describe it as a "long and uneasy pilgrimage" in which she was "oblig'd to wander as [she] could."[69] Smith and her literary representations – her characters, wanderers as well – signal the ways in which literature may be used not only to promote a radical political ideology, with its concurrent promise of personal liberty, but also, in what becomes the main focus of her later writing, to chart its defeat.

3
"Poetry [and] Politics": Mary Robinson I

The literary career of Mary Robinson (1758–1800),[1] like that of Charlotte Smith, is marked by an ongoing engagement with political and cultural concerns informed concurrently by the pressures of financial need, and her response to the French Revolution and its aftermath is likewise shaped by an identification with victimhood and vulnerability drawn from personal experience.[2] Robinson's identification with the Revolution is differently nuanced from Smith's, however, and emerges from the events of her unconventional life. As a young, married actress, she had become the mistress of the Prince of Wales and later of a series of prominent public figures, before settling into a long-term and equally unconventional (and conspicuous) relationship with Banastre Tarleton, a military hero from the American Revolutionary War and later MP. Even as she published six novels, several collections of poetry and various political and prose tracts, she could never escape from the burden of an unremitting social notoriety, especially during her early literary career, but also to a certain extent during her later years as well, when she moved in the progressive intellectual circles of London. Such was the strength of Robinson's understanding of social ostracism that alongside her support of the French Revolution, the focus on individual suffering and existential loss, especially during the Revolution's more contentious periods, often takes precedence over and in fact obscures, other, more abstract, ideological issues. Political awareness, individual experience and sympathy, and the various ways they converge in her writing thus serve to characterize, yet also complicate the perception of Robinson's revolutionary project.

The consciousness of marginality, and what Stuart Curran identifies as the predominant concern of Robinson's poetry, the "sudden and total displacement of the stabilities on which existences depend,"[3] plays a prominent role in Robinson's literary writing in general, in her portrayals of upheaval, victimization and rupture. This emphasis on displacement is apparent in the exilic identities of her eponymous heroes Hubert de Sevrac and Walsingham and in the recurring identification with such disparate figures as Thomas Chatterton and Marie Antoinette: the description of Chatterton as "exiled, poor and unpatronised, driven to wander"[4] exemplifies that state of being repeatedly portrayed by Robinson, just as her many allusions to him harness her concern with marginality to the very act of writing itself.

Robinson's own sense of vulnerability was underpinned by her celebrity status as "Perdita", the name used to identify her from the time she first caught the Prince's attention during her performance in *A Winter's Tale*. The intense, often malicious public scrutiny to which she was subjected is reflected not only in her choice of subject matter but also in the contemporary reception that accompanied the publication of her work, and which, especially in the early part of her literary career, was unable or unwilling to ignore the "Perdita" narrative. The review of *Ainsi Va Le Monde* (1790), Robinson's first published response to the French Revolution, in *The General Magazine*, exemplifies the nature of this early reception. The reviewer begins his remarks by acknowledging that "[t]hese verses, which the world owes to the pen of the celebrated Perdita, though the flash of a moment, are not a flash without fire." After praising Robinson's "refined sensibility", "richness of fancy", and "correctness of taste", he concludes this favorable discussion of the poem by commenting that "[w]e here take our leave of this effusion of a naturally generous mind, which, pity is it, *a passing cloud* should ever have shadowed."[5] This pattern of reception – with its foregrounding of the ubiquitous sexual narrative – extended well into the twentieth century; it was Robinson's status as "Perdita" which created an interest in her life and writing and invested them with cultural currency, with biographical studies plotting her life mainly around the axis of emotional engagement and the fluctuations of her relationships with the Prince and with Tarleton.[6] This kind of biographical/historical assessment has received a recent corrective with the publication of Paula Byrne's biography of Robinson. While chronicling a life of celebrity and meticulously recording the details of Robinson's conspicuous presence in the social world, Byrne also provides a serious discussion of her authorship, with extended analyses of her literary works and her place within, and contributions to, the literary community of the 1790s.

There was, however, another pattern of reception that accompanied the publication of Robinson's work in her own time as well. There, her support of radical issues *did* attract attention, enough so to warrant her inclusion among the "transgressive" women writers cited by the critics of the "Anti-Jacobin" circle. As we have already seen, Thomas J. Mathias, William Heath and Robert Bisset took anxious notice of Robinson's politics, with the former two linking her together with Charlotte Smith and Elizabeth Inchbald in a representation of what was for them a disconcerting and disruptive presence in the public sphere.[7] Writing in 1811, William Gifford, the author of the *Baeviad* (1791) and the *Maeviad* (1797), singles out Robinson for particular (retrospective) attention: "This wretched woman, indeed, in the wane of her beauty fell into merited poverty, exchanged poetry for politics, and wrote abusive trash against the government at the rate of two guineas a week."[8] Likewise, Richard

Polwhele includes Robinson in his famous polemic against women writers, noting that her novels contain "the doctrines of Philosophism [and thus] ... merit the severest censure."[9] And indeed, Robinson's presence in Polwhele's text suggests that during her own era she was both sexed and "unsex'd" at the same time.

The comments of Mathias, Heath, Bisset, Gifford and Polwhele are significant, as they point to a contemporary awareness of, and identification between, Robinson and a certain political stand. And yet, in dissociating Robinson's politics from her poetry, Gifford also expresses a critical view (shared by his "Anti-Jacobin" colleagues) that links her radicalism exclusively to her later novels. Thus, while for these observers Robinson's public presence was more than that of actress, mistress and celebrity, they ignore the political import of the texts that she wrote during the early 1790s, when she was conspicuously under the burden of celebrity status.

In this chapter and the one that follows I will trace Robinson's articulation of a radical worldview, one that emerges in the early stages of the French Revolution and which repeatedly posits its original values as a possible site of redemption. I will present my argument in the form of a historical trajectory in which Robinson's pro-Revolution stand commences with *Ainsi Va Le Monde* (1790), and thus originates in the early years of her literary career and extends to her poetry as well. In doing so, I will contest Gifford's claim for the exchange of "poetry for politics", for although he identifies an ideological awareness, he, as well as the other critics of the "Anti-Jacobin" milieu, appear seemingly oblivious to Robinson's earlier political interventions. In presenting a discussion that proceeds chronologically, I want not only to emphasize the continuity of Robinson's attention to the Revolution, but also to recuperate her early writings as sites of political valence.

At the same time, I am also aware of the problems that accompany this type of politically-focused argument insofar as Robinson specifically is concerned. On one level, my argument will have to accommodate the fact that an identification with victimhood at times displaces the adherence to a specific political agenda, such as in Robinson's support of and identification with Marie Antoinette. In presenting a literary and political progression that begins in 1790, I will need to confront those texts in which Robinson's defense of the Queen supersedes, and even conflicts with her earlier positioning in regard to revolutionary ideals.

On another level, the recognition of the various inconsistencies which characterize much of Robinson's work as well as what emerges at times as a slippery authorial presence would seem to preclude the claim for a kind of thematic, not to mention political, coherence. Anne Mellor, in presenting Robinson as a "script of female sexuality",[10] has argued that the different ways Robinson's subjectivity was constructed in contemporary narratives as well as her performative enactment of authorship indicate that "her identity – personal and authorial – can be nothing more nor less than the sum total of the scripts she performed both in public and in private, in her own narratives and in those of others."[11] Mellor's recognition of the fluidity of Robinson's authorial identity is underscored most forcefully in the ways that Robinson affixes her name to her published work. The fact that her writing was disseminated under various names and personae (Laura Maria, Oberon and Tabitha Bramble, among others) as well as anonymously, contributes to the sense of "performance" that accompanies her literary career, and complicates the attempt to locate the presence of a political awareness in its aggregate. Among two of her earlier politically-motivated texts, for example, *Ainsi Va Le Monde* was originally published under the name of "Laura Maria", and the 1791 tract, *Impartial Reflections on the Present Situation of the Queen of France*, by "A Friend to Humanity". While there may be particular reasons for this – "Laura Maria", for one, stresses her participation in the Della Cruscan exchange – the fact that the name "Mary Robinson" only later replaces the original notations of authorship in these two key texts underlines the elusiveness of that name and of whether it could be recognized, and then associated by Robinson's contemporaries with an *ongoing* ideological intervention on her part.[12]

The interplay between Robinson's political awareness and her constructions of literary history will play an important part in my discussion. For Robinson's work is replete with catalogues, surveys and references that place cultural production in opposition to the often hostile climate in which it is enacted and underline how, for her, political consciousness and literary practice mutually inform one another. Through a reading of *Ainsi Va Le Monde* (1790) and the Marie Antoinette texts (1791–3) in this chapter and *Sappho and Phaon* (1796), *Hubert de Sevrac* (1796) and *Walsingham* (1797) in the next, I hope to demonstrate that this convergence of concerns in Robinson's work – political awareness, literary self-consciousness and social ostracism – is informed by the presence of a sustained engagement with, and ultimately a defense of the French Revolution, and thus enables the presentation of yet another script among the many with which she may be associated.

I

One of the first and most prominent places where we can view Robinson's identification with radical ideology is in her poem *Ainsi Va Le Monde*, in which the desire for artistic community is articulated through the focus on the French Revolution and on its implications for literary endeavor. The poem inscribes the events in France and their ramifications in Britain as a prominent concern and sets up the ideal of a vigorous cultural production enabled by the energies inherent in the revolutionary moment. Published in June 1790, *Ainsi Va Le Monde* appeared as a response to Robert Merry's poem *The Laurel of Liberty*. Previously known for his participation (with Robinson, among others) in the Della Cruscan poetical exchanges of the late 1780s,

Merry establishes his radical credentials in *The Laurel to Liberty* by presenting an enthusiastic tribute to the French Revolution and to the universal equality it promised. He acknowledges his Della Cruscan past only to put it aside for the "nobler, grander"[13] theme of emerging liberty placed in contrast to the corrupt British system of political representation and the "insidious" (p. v) power of its ruling institutions.

Robinson's poem similarly valorizes the Revolution, but without rejecting the Della Cruscan moment in order to do so. Its echoes are at once apparent in the fact that, unlike Merry, who published his poem under his own name, she published hers under the pseudonym – "Laura Maria" – she had adopted for her participation in the Della Cruscan poetic exchanges. (*Ainsi Va Le Monde* was re-published under her own name in her 1791 *Poems*, and reprinted again in the posthumous *Poetical Works* (1806).) The Della Cruscan connection is further indicated in the poem's dedication "[a]s a Tribute of Esteem and Admiration to Robert Merry, Esq. Member of the Royal Academy at Florence, and Author of the Laurel of Liberty, and the Della Cruscan poems," a move that explicitly acknowledges the intensity of the poetical dialogue along with the act of writing itself as crucial features of the convention. As Jerome McGann explains, "the Della Cruscan movement came into such rapid cultural dominance during the 1790s ... because the writing explicitly encouraged further writing, whether response or elaboration."[14] A note affixed to the poem's appearance in Robinson's *Memoirs* emphasizes both the immediacy and the heightened sense of reciprocity that had informed its original moment of publication:

> In 1791, Mrs. Robinson produced her quarto poem, entitled *Ainsi Va Le Monde*. This work, containing three hundred and fifty lines, was written in twelve hours, as a reply to Mr. Merry's "Laurel of Liberty," which was sent to Mrs. Robinson on a Saturday; on the *Tuesday following* the answer was *composed and given to the public*.[15]

The manner in which this poetical exchange foregrounds both the addressee *and* the writer herself is underscored in another comment that appears in the *Memoirs*: "In the poem entitled "Ainsi Va Le Monde" Mrs. Robinson is at once the animated eulogist of Mr. Merry's talents, the dignified assertor of her own, and the graceful and intrepid champion of Freedom."[16] In my reading of *Ainsi Va Le Monde*, I will focus on Robinson's "championing of Freedom" as it signifies a heightened political awareness. At the same time, I want to suggest that the poem occupies a unique position within Robinson's writings as she appropriates the Della Cruscan concern with writing and literary production in order to articulate a political narrative.

The opening lines of *Ainsi Va Le Monde* exhibit the customary Della Cruscan features of the invocation of the dedicatee and a particularized, ornate description of nature. Thus the initial address to Merry, "O Thou, to whom superior worth's allied, / Thy country's honour – and the Muses' pride" (1–2) is elaborated in characteristic Della Cruscan style:

> Who deign'd to rove where twinkling glow-worms lead
> The tiny legions o'er the glitt'ring mead;
> Whose liquid notes in sweet meand'rings flow,
> Mild as the murmurs of the Bird of Woe.
>
> (9–12)

And yet, this acknowledgement (and reinscription) of Merry's poetic performance is almost immediately elided into a critique of the otherwise bleak state of contemporary poetry:

> Too long the Muse, in ancient garb array'd
> Has pin'd neglected in oblivion's shade;
> Driv'n from the sun-shine of poetic fame,
> Stripp'd of each charm she scarcely boasts a name.
>
> (31–4)

This state of emptiness, indicated in the Muse's "faded garland", "with'ring laurel", "sighs" and "tears" (38–40) is contrasted with the literature of the past, as Robinson at first mentions Milton, Shakespeare, Chatterton and Otway (42–4), and later in the poem Chaucer, Pope, Spenser, Dryden but also Merry himself (117–18).

Robinson's catalogue represents, with the exception of Merry, both the recognition of a traditional canon, and in its inclusion of Chatterton and Otway, a not uncommon eighteenth-century gesture which locates in these writers a literary worth that is yoked to the assumption of a national guilt for their tragic early deaths. Robinson repeatedly returns to Chatterton in her writings and he is mentioned, always in terms of his isolation and poverty, in *Angelina* (1796), *Walsingham* (1797), *The Natural Daughter* (1799) and *The Sylphid* (1800). Her "Monody to the Memory of Chatterton" (1791) illustrates more specifically her participation in the late eighteenth-century project that conferred on him a privileged status both as misunderstood outsider, and as "natural" and tragic genius.[17] Robinson's acknowledgment of "Chatterton oppress'd" (43) in *Ainsi Va Le Monde* sets up an affinity between her and her fellow Bristol poet, and with it, a subtext that articulates the linkage between victimization and literary endeavor, one which will become a recurring theme in her work.

The reference to Chatterton, in signifying an awareness of past injustices, at the same presents the current literary climate as one that is defined by "empty witlings" with their "puny jest" and "low buffoonery" (131–2). The degenerate state of contemporary cultural production is a major concern for

Robinson, yet in *Ainsi Va Le Monde* (almost uniquely in her writings) she can offer a specific corrective, one that appears with the repeated and renewed invocations to Merry. He is called upon to "cheer with smiles the Muse's glorious toil, / And plant perfection on her native soil" (59–60), a task will energize the entire literary landscape, as "the Arts, that thro' dark centuries have pin'd / Toil'd without fame, in sordid chains confin'd / Burst into light with renovated fire" (61–3). The next invocation, "Again to MERRY dedicate the line" (153), links him specifically to "Freedom" and its enabling possibilities which, for Robinson, have an all-encompassing effect on society that is equalizing, energizing and erotic. Connecting the "soldier" (167), the "poet" (170), the "peasant" (174), and the "throne" (174):

> Celestial Freedom warms the breast of man;
> Led by her daring hand, what pow'r can bind
> The boundless efforts of the lab'ring mind.
> The god-like fervour, thrilling thro' the heart
> Gives new creation to each vital part;
> Throbs rapture thro' each palpitating vein,
> Wings the rapt thought, and warms the fertile brain.
> (158–64)[18]

This abstract conceptualization is almost immediately localized with the address to "Enlightened Gallia!" (185). The thematic shift that occurs at this moment, slightly over half way through the poem, introduces the specific focus on the events occurring in France as a major concern in the work. Robinson presents her defense of the French Revolution through a particularized attention to historical detail and with a series of images which decry tyrannical abuses of power. For example, she inserts an extended description of the Marquise de Maintenon, the governess of the illegitimate children of Louis XIV, and later his secret wife, in order to expose the enmeshment of royal and religious misuse of privilege that had characterized the *ancien régime*:

> O, monstrous hypocrite! – who vainly strove
> By pious fraud, to win a people's love;
> Whose coffers groaned with reliques from the proud,
> The pompous off'rings of the venal crowd,
> The messy hetacombs of dire disgrace,
> To purchase titles, or secure a place. –
> And yet – so sacred was the matron's fame,
> Nor truth, nor virtue dar'd assail her name;
> None could approach but with obsequious breath,
> To *smile* was TREASON – and to *speak* was DEATH.
> (205–14)

The critique of arbitrary privilege, reinforced in the emphasis on "treason" and "death", continues in Robinson's description of the "black BASTILE" [*sic*] (233):

> Where recreant malice mock'd the suff'rer's sigh
> While regal lightnings darted from her eye. –
> Where deep mysterious whispers murmur'd round,
> And death stalk'd sullen o'er the treach'rous ground.
>
> (235–8)

At once the symbol of absolute power and of revolutionary triumph, Robinson's Bastille enacts the movement from tyranny to freedom as a progression from night to day, darkness to light, Gothic obscurity to Enlightenment. Thus, her depiction of its collapse emphasizes the awakening "from the torpid slumber of disgrace" (244) and the concurrent enabling of vision, as Freedom's "beaming eye" (241) surveys the "dread scene" (242), and "Heav'n's own breeze" (275) spreads "broad sun-shine in the caves of death" (276).

In locating the energizing potential that accompanies the destruction of tyrannical power, this movement also recalls Robinson's appeal to Merry earlier in the poem, in which his hoped-for rejuvenation of literature was envisioned in terms of a progression from darkness to light. This common imagery points to Robinson's awareness of the interconnectedness of "Art" and "Freedom", and the ways that they mutually inform each other. In 1790, this understanding is exhibited through the portrayal of the political events in France and the state of literature in Britain, in dual narratives of artistic and political progress that at once juxtapose the energy inherent in the revolutionary moment to the moribund state of current cultural production, but at the same time reveal its potential for reinvigoration.

This enabling potential is reiterated in the conclusion of *Ainsi Va Le Monde*, in the depiction of freedom opening "her radiant gates to *all mankind*" (302) which is then enjoined to a proscriptive vision of enlightened and benevolent leadership:

> Yet let Ambition hold a temp'rate sway,
> When Virtue rules – 'tis Rapture to obey;
> Man can but reign his transitory hour,
> And *love* may bind – when *fear* has lost its pow'r.
> Proud may he be who nobly acts his part,
> Who boasts the empire of each subject's heart,
> Whose worth, exulting millions shall approve,
> Whose richest treasure – IS A NATION'S LOVE.
>
> (311–18)

Up until this point, the political views that Robinson presents in the poem – praise for the Revolution accompanied by a critique of the cruelty and inequality of the *ancien régime* and embodied in the specific but also metonymic representation of the Bastille – seem to parallel the prevailing response among the liberal British public, which in 1790 had generally welcomed the Revolution (Burke is a notable exception) and where, as E.P. Thompson writes, "even traditionalists argued that France was coming belatedly into line with British notions of the 'mixed constitution.' "[19] The depiction of a benevolent monarchy which inspires a "rapturous" obedience would appear to coincide with this prevalent, mainstream (and obviously not overly radical) applauding of the events in France. Indeed, the review of *Ainsi Va Le Monde* in the *Critical Review* cites this passage as evidence of Robinson's "just and rational [. . .] political sentiments."[20]

However, in this passage Robinson also views "man" – that is to say, a king – as "transitory", and one whose authority is grounded in the conditional response of feeling. This more ambivalent representation, and its suggestion of a monarch /subject reciprocity, recalls the premise, articulated prominently by Richard Price in "A Discourse on the Love of our Country" (1789), that a lawful king is "one who owes his crown to the choice of the people"; the true base of a king's power is the public's approval.[21] This perception, linked together with the immediately preceding image of freedom embracing "all mankind", with its implication that the upheavals of liberty are not limited to France alone, is indicative of a sharper, more radical engagement at the core of *Ainsi Va Le Monde*. This is underscored in the concluding stanza of the poem, as an all-encompassing "freedom" transcends historical specificity and extends the purview to the realm of the mythic, concluding in a final, joyous representation of possibility:

> The tuneful sisters prompt the heavenly choir,
> Thy temple glitters with Promethean fire.
> The sacred Priestess in the centre stands,
> She strews the sapphire floor with flow'ry bands.
> See! From her shrine electric incense rise;
> Hark! "Freedom" echoes thro' the vaulted skies.
> The Goddess speaks! O mark the blest decree, –
> TYRANTS SHALL FALL – TRIUMPHANT MAN BE FREE!
>   (339–41)

This passage portrays a freedom that is celebratory, sensual and universal. It is articulated by a "Goddess" – as Anne Janowitz has suggested, Robinson herself[22] – who, after having established her poetic authority, assumes through the revolutionary rhetoric a political authority as well; the linkage between art and liberty emerges once more as the final word of the poem.

Robinson's vision, in which a mythically-proportioned freedom is linked to a narrative of contemporary political events, seems to have been particularly suggestive to Mary Wollstonecraft, who presents this final stanza in its entirety in her review of *Ainsi Va Le Monde* in the *Analytical Review*, in which she calls it an "Invocation to Freedom."[23]

Significantly, this same stanza is *completely* omitted from a later version of *Ainsi Va Le Monde* which was included in *The Poetical Works of the late Mrs. Mary Robinson* (1806), a collection edited by Robinson's daughter, Maria Elizabeth. Furthermore, in a series of anxious interventions, Maria Elizabeth also omits the various references to Robert Merry that appear throughout the poem. In calling attention to these omissions, Adriana Craciun shows how Maria Elizabeth's editorial work was an attempt to "distance Robinson from the radical politics of Merry and the Revolution, politics which she herself had embraced in her lifetime."[24] Thus, Robinson's framing of her literary catalogue "[f]rom Chaucer ... till MERRY'S lucid days" (118), is revised in the 1806 edition of the poem as "[f]rom Chaucer ... till these enlighten'd days" (118).[25] The displacement of Merry by an abstract concept of enlightenment is further reiterated in Maria Elizabeth's next editorial maneuver, which appears in a stanza that re-invokes Merry's poetic inspiration. The original stanza:

> Ah! Gentle Muse, from trivial follies turn,
> Where Patriot souls with god-like passions burn;
> Again to MERRY dedicate the line,
> So shall the envied boast of taste be thine
> So shall thy song to glorious themes aspire,
> "Warm'd with a spark" of his transcendent fire.
>
> (151–6)

is rewritten as:

> Ah! gentle muse, from trivial follies turn,
> Where Patriot souls with god-like passions burn;
> So shall thy song to glorious themes aspire,
> Rapt in the wonders of the Poet's lyre.
>
> (155–6)[26]

Merry's effacement from the text is completed by the replacement of Robinson's original dedication with two new prefatory comments: "Inscribed to a Friend" and "Written at the Beginning of the French Revolution."[27]

These erasures appear particularly significant in light of the fact that Robert Merry was a recognized radical presence throughout the 1790s. Robinson's repeated praise of Merry and of his correspondent poem in the dialogue, *The Laurel of Liberty*, implies an affinity with its political agenda, one which he outlines in the preface to his poem:

> In delivering the following Poem to the Public, I fear I shall displease many, who have pretended to think meanly of the late Revolution in France; and to treat it as an object of ridicule or contempt. I perhaps also by occasional forebodings may offend those, who look upon the present situation of Great-Britain with delight, and who are so charmed by apparent commercial prosperity, that they could view with happy indifference the encroachments of insidious power, and the gradual decay of the Constitution ... I would almost venture to affirm, that should the collected Tyrants of the World unite in a kind of political Crusade against the prevailing propensity of Europe, they would ultimately be defeated, for the progress of Opinion, like a rapid stream, though it may be checked, cannot be controuled. THE CAUSE OF FREEDOM IS THE CAUSE OF ALL MANKIND. (pp. v–vi)

A brief passage from the poem itself is representative of Merry's conception of this universalizing effect of the Revolution:

> That naught can *rightly* govern, but THE LAWS,
> Kings their *effect*, and Equity their *cause*;
> And that unless the gen'ral voice combin'd,
> Approve each law, – TIS TREASON TO MANKIND.
> (409–12)

In November 1792, two years after the publication of *The Laurel of Liberty*, Robert Merry experienced a much more literal relation to treason when he signed the British Club manifesto in Paris. (As will be recalled, at this same gathering Charlotte Smith was recognized and toasted for her contributions towards the revolutionary effort.) His speech given on that occasion was forwarded to the British Foreign Office and the period of his political persecutions began.[28] This conspicuous and controversial political stand, at a time when public opinion was shifting towards a condemnation of revolutionary violence, further radicalizes Merry's presence in *Ainsi Va Le Monde*. Consequently, Robinson's *own* politics, not least her vision of a new literary era heralded in by Merry himself, would have been reinforced to a later reader through that same retrospective gaze. Maria Elizabeth's attempt at an obfuscation of her mother's politics, and particularly the distancing achieved in the editorial reminder that the poem was "written at the beginning of the Revolution", acknowledges, then, the troubling progression of the Revolution itself, in which enlightened ideals of liberty succumbed to the violence

and oppression of the Terror. Yet even more pertinently it exposes the anxiety that informs the reactionary backlash in its aftermath, evinced here in
the attempt to impose a retroactive censorship on Robinson's poetic vision.
Merry's own career following his return from France encapsulates the full
power of the reaction: the threat of bankruptcy, his fears for his personal
safety, the constant surveillance of his movements, internal exile and his
eventual retreat to America illustrate the fate that awaited the victims of
Pitt's repressive policies.[29]

It is difficult to ascertain to what extent Maria Elizabeth's editorial interventions and a wide dissemination of the more politically neutral 1806 edition
of *Ainsi Va Le Monde* contributed to the neglect of this poem as a marker of
Robinson's earlier radicalism. Yet even before the revisions, the prominent
and influential conservative critics at work in the 1790s repeatedly exclude
the poem from what it perceives as Robinson's repertoire of subversive texts.
I will now suggest possible reasons for this exclusion: the position of *Ainsi
Va le Monde* as both a poem at the borders of the Della Cruscan exchange,
and as a *poem*, in a cultural climate which more readily identified women's
political consciousness with novels. Let us return, then, to Thomas J. Mathias,
who acknowledges Robinson as one of those politically-engaged women writers who, to use his words, "instruct or confuse us and themselves in the
labyrinth of politics, or turn us wild with Gallic frenzy."[30] And yet for Mathias, Robinson's political transgression is accompanied by a literary one – the
writing of Della Cruscan poetry. In an earlier section of *The Pursuits of Literature* he states: "[t]he author of the *Baviad* has taken some pleasant trouble off
my hands. The *Albums*, the *Laura Marias*, the *Jerninghams*, *Antony Pasquins*,
Mary Robinsons, *Piozziz and Bozzi'z*; the *Phillidas*, *Hypsipilas*, *vatum et plorabile
si quid*. Unfortunately there are too many left."[31] Mathias is referring to
William Gifford, whose *Baviad* and *Maeviad*, much like Mathias's *Pursuits*,
appeared in multiple editions at the end of the eighteenth and beginning of
the nineteenth centuries, and which, like his own text, surveys and critiques
the contemporary literary scene. Unlike Mathias, however, who discusses a
wide and heterogeneous range of genres and themes, Gifford is almost exclusively concerned with mounting an attack on Della Cruscan poetry, and it is
one so scathing that it is considered to have undone the movement.[32]

I wish now to sketch out some contexts of Della Cruscanism which are
crucial for an understanding of the afterlife of *Ainsi Va Le Monde* and for the
later perceptions of Robinson's literary project. Mainly, I want to claim that
while Gifford holds similar views as Mathias, he conceals or marginalizes the
political referentiality of his criticism, and thus constructs a critique of Della
Cruscanism that insistently dissociates the movement from the contemporary concerns that surround it. For example, while he introduces *The Laurel of
Liberty* as a "philosophical rhapsody on the French Revolution" his critique
of the poem focuses almost entirely on its imagery and diction.[33] Likewise,
he refers to *Ainsi Va Le Monde*, the response to Merry's poem, only implicitly,

writing that "there are various opinions concerning [the *Laurel*], and ... I do not choose perhaps to dispute with a lady of Mrs. R——'s critical abilities."[34] The fact that he does not elaborate on the connection and its shared thematics – an engagement with the French Revolution – carries with it an assumed obliviousness to the radical energy of both poems in the dialogue.

Gifford's attempt at distancing the putative theme of his text from urgent political concerns is later reinforced in the preface to the *Maeviad*, in his explanation of the delay in the publication of the work:

> When the MAEVIAD (so I call the present poem) was nearly brought to a conclusion, I laid it aside. The times seemed unfavorable to such productions. Events of *real importance* were momentarily claiming the attention of the public; and the still voice of the Muses was not likely to be listened to amidst the din of arms.[35] (emphasis added)

Nonetheless, Gifford's political affinities do ultimately exhibit themselves, and most strikingly so in the 1811 edition of *The Baviad and the Maeviad*, when the Revolution was safely distanced in the past and Merry and Robinson were long dead. There, we recall, he asserts that Robinson "exchanged poetry for politics, and wrote abusive trash against the government at the rate of two guineas a week."[36] This claim for "an exchange", and thus the acquisition of a *later* radicalism exposes Gifford's ideological leanings, but also reinforces yet again his earlier, ostensibly non-political reading of Della Cruscanism. The relegation of his own politics to the level of subtext further complicates the reception of *Ainsi Va Le Monde*. It appears that, on one hand, Gifford was intent on distancing his criticism from urgent political issues, from "events of real importance", and was genuinely unwilling to posit a connection between that poetic convention and any kind of ideological import. On the other hand, his politics *do* hover uneasily over his text, but only in the sense that they register an awareness which coincides with, but never really extends to the poetry itself. To put it another way, Gifford's recognition of Robinson's and Merry's political affiliation most certainly contributes to the general hostility towards the practitioners of Della Cruscanism that informs his criticism, but at the same time the status of *Ainsi Va Le Monde* as a radical poem has been emptied out by his apparent indifference to its political message. By acknowledging that message – with its radical ideological energy – Gifford would have conferred on Della Cruscan poetry more significance than he wanted it to have.

Gifford's "poetry / politics" binary illustrates the role of genre in dictating the poem's political reception. (But to be clear, for Gifford it is not "poetry" in the wider sense that is being distinguished here but Della Cruscanism.) His comment also recalls the view presented by Mathias, who had written in *The Pursuits of Literature* that Robinson (and her colleagues) were "too frequently whining or frisking in *novels*" (emphasis added).[37] This distinction is further reinforced by Richard Polwhele in his famous polemic against women writers (which, incidentally, was dedicated to Mathias) *The Unsex'd Females* (1798). There, Polwhele differentiates between Robinson's poetry, which, unlike Gifford, he praises, writing that it has a "peculiar delicacy" and her novels, which, and as we saw earlier, he subjects to the "severest censure."[38]

Many critics have argued that the form of the novel is conducive to the representation of a political viewpoint, specifically, in this historical juncture, in its thematic and structural development, and particularly for women writers.[39] The commentary of Gifford, Mathias and Polwhele provides contemporary evidence that reinforces this assessment, and of what Gary Kelly has called the "novelization of the Revolution," in which women writers appropriated the genre identified as being uniquely "theirs" in order to intervene in the public and political sphere.[40] However, in locating Robinson's political interventions exclusively in her novels, these evaluations exhibit how the consciousness of genre dictates a limited – and limiting – reading of a literary text. As the case of Robinson and *Ainsi Va Le Monde* makes clear, the prominence of novels as vehicles of political expression obscures the fact that other, less ostensibly "gendered" literary forms, and specifically here, a controversial Della Cruscan poetics – also expressed the same political awareness.[41]

There were, however, other readers, Robinson's contemporaries, who *were* keenly aware of this political engagement. Recall, for one, Mary Wollstonecraft, and her appellation of the poem as an "Invocation to Freedom." Moreover, Maria Elizabeth Robinson's efforts, in 1806, to realign the politics of the poem point to an anxious awareness of its radical implications, of its engagement with "events of real importance." Yet there have been few modern-day discussions of *Ainsi Va le Monde* as an example of radical, poetic energy,[42] and for the most part it seems that the vitality inherent in this literary moment has largely been ignored, then as now, the poem merely relegated to the status of an exception; viewed as an anomaly within the larger poetic convention with which it is associated rather than as a singular moment that articulates, at its borders, the exuberance of revolutionary awareness.

II

Between the years 1791–3 Robinson produced three texts which represent a further engagement with the progress of the French Revolution – the prose tract *Impartial Reflections on the Late Situation of the Queen of France* (1791) and the poems "Marie Antoinette's Lamentation" and "Monody to the Memory of the Late Queen of France", both written in 1793. In these works Robinson presents what is first an emotional and spirited defense of the Queen, and then an elegy on her death.

Above all, the Marie Antoinette texts exhibit Robinson's preoccupation with the plight of the French queen as a particularized, yet also emblematic study of victimization and loss, perhaps even as an aggrandized version of her own story. Both women experienced a subjection to public ridicule and scorn, which was based most prominently on a foregrounded and highly visible representation of their sexuality.[43] Robinson's view of her own such status is related in the *Memoirs:*

> The daily prints now indulged the malice of my enemies by the most scandalous paragraphs respecting the Prince of Wales and myself. I found it was now too late to stop the hourly abuse that was poured upon me from all quarters.[44]

Robinson is alluding not only to the frequent, and often malicious scrutiny with which the press followed her movements, but also to the obscene prints that had appeared during, and following her affair with the Prince of Wales. A prominent example of these prints is Gillray's "The Thunderer", in which Robinson is represented as sexually impaled upon a whirligig, while Banastre Tarleton and a beheaded Prince of Wales stand below. Although this print appeared in 1782, following Robinson's visit to France, it is nonetheless indicative of these blatant representations of her sexuality, and the way in which their dissemination throughout London caused, in Jan Fergus's and Janice Farrar Thaddeus's words, an "unimaginable torment [for] the genteelly nurtured Robinson."[45]

It was, indeed, such torment that motivated Robinson's visit to France in 1781. As stated in the *Memoirs*:

> To desert her country, to fly like a wretched fugitive, or to become a victim to the malice, and swell the triumph of her enemies, were the only alternatives that seemed to present themselves. Flight was humiliating and dreadful, but to remain in England was impracticable.[46]

Robinson's fascination with Marie Antoinette most certainly had its origins in the meeting that took place between the two women during this visit. The Queen's invitation to Robinson was preceded by the intense interest surrounding Robinson's stay in France and her widely-noted public presence as "la belle *Anglaise*",[47] an epithet which illustrates what Judith Pascoe calls the "seemingly reductive attention to particular physical attributes", but also calls attention to the more general reciprocity of mutual admiration that characterized the meeting.[48] Yet, at the same time, Robinson's status as *"Anglaise"* (the term repeatedly appears in the *Memoirs'* account of her visit to France) reflects a sense of otherness, and an exilic identity that at once recalls the acute persecution and victimization which had motivated her departure from England.

Ten years later, Robinson's experience in France would inform her view of the progress of the Revolution, in the intertwining of her own knowledge of exile with the memory of the young and beautiful Marie Antoinette on one hand, and with the abjection and misery of the Queen's present situation, on the other. In what follows, I argue that as the Marie Antoinette drama unfolded, this memory and identification are what shape Robinson's ideological positioning towards the Revolution. After first attempting to reconcile the support of its original values with a defense of the Queen's actions, Robinson eventually focuses almost exclusively on the personal story of sexual victimization, social ostracism and the fall from prominence, and such was the power of that story that it superseded other political concerns.

The first of the texts that I discuss, the *Impartial Reflections on the Present Situation of the Queen of France*, was written not long after the unsuccessful attempt of the royal family to flee to Varennes in June 1791, an event whose urgency and drama are apparent in the reference to the "present situation."[49] In this work, Robinson at first articulates a critique of tyranny in general and then resituates the Queen as another one of its victims. Thus, the images of "the petty tyrant who lords ... over his vassal" (p. 7), and "the possessor of a throne, who beholds millions groaning under the ponderous yoke of despotism" (p. 7), appear at the outset as signifiers of the sensitivity to oppression that characterizes the discussion as a whole, but also as a context for Robinson to stress the fact that she continues to endorse the original revolutionary agenda:

> The present situation of France awakens the feelings, and calls forth the attention of all nations: that the Revolution is the most glorious achievement in the annals of Europe, is universally felt and acknowledged. That "oppression often rouses distress to vengeance" is incontrovertible: that the seeds of liberty are implanted in every human heart, cherished in every climate, and form a part of our instinctive minds, even from the earliest infancy cannot be denied. Man is a Commoner of Nature, his soul is impregnated with the sprit of independence, and revolts at the attacks of oppression, in whatever garb or shape it may present itself. (pp. 8–9)

And yet, rather than aligning Marie Antoinette with the oppression of the *ancien régime*, Robinson introduces her into the text as the victim of the systems of power over which she ostensibly rules: the "Court", its "surrounding sycophants", its "needy dependants", the "united machinations of envy and distraction" (p. 14). This positioning enables her to configure the Queen's story within the ongoing revolutionary narrative, as illustrated in the following example: At the moment of liberation, when "the sun of truth ... dart[ed] through the cloud of superstition" (p. 16):

> the propagators of evil sought for safety in flight. Guilt has a thousand wings; they escaped; while the lovely victim of their infernal

machinations remained, exposed to all the horrors of mistaken vengeance. (p. 17)

Robinson thus acknowledges a double sense of victimhood, as she situates Marie Antoinette between the "evil" of the old regime and the "vengeance" of the new. This positioning reflects the tenuous status of the Revolution at this particular historical moment, in which its ideals are still upheld, yet its violent potential is, at the same time, conspicuously evident. For Robinson is indeed aware of the potential danger to the Queen, and how she would serve, up through her trial and execution, as the focus of the rage of the French public. In doing so, she addresses what we now understand to have been a wide, culturally symbolic victimization of Marie Antoinette. As Pierre Saint-Amand writes:

[The Queen] had become a myth, fabricated by the revolutionary mob. She was made to bear all the signs of a witch; she was about to be burned at the slanderer's stake. She was simultaneously guilty of infanticide, incest and bestiality ... All the stereotypes of persecution fell onto her head.[50]

Lynn Hunt recognizes in the mythic status of Marie Antoinette's victimization an anxiety surrounding gender roles during the Revolution in general, in which "queenship [was seen] as the most extreme form of women invading the public sphere."[51] Her death, then, was a necessary prerequisite for the establishment of a new, virtuous social order in which women would be "relegated to the realm of domesticity."[52]

Robinson's text attempts to erase this symbolic, disruptive potential. Her defense of the Queen focuses on personal attributes – "grace in her affability", "propriety in her pleasures", "delicacy in her vivacity" and the "warmth of her generosity" (pp. 18–19) – which reconstruct a specific individual presence rather than a symbolic one, and rewrite it in terms of traditional notions of eighteenth-century femininity. This portrayal repeatedly emphasizes the Queen's status as an obedient wife, whose actions are justified through the "criterion of conjugal virtue, to share the fate and follow the fortunes of a man ... to whom she was united by every bond human and divine" (p. 26). Thus, while Robinson in effect condemns the royal family's flight to Varennes, she absolves the Queen from any complicity in the event:

That [she] should *consent* to accompany her husband on his late flight, was more than reasonable, it was natural; duty claimed her *acquiescence*, and common sense must justify the propriety of her *obedience* ... Whatever criminality may be imputed to the event, certainly the Queen was not the aggressor. (pp. 25–6).

Furthermore, if the Queen hadn't consented to submit to the plan of escape, Robinson conjectures, she would have been "exposed to the frenzy of the multitude ... marked as the helpless victim of an enraged populace" (p. 27). Yet, notwithstanding Robinson's perspicuity in foreseeing the future treatment of Marie Antoinette, her repeated efforts to construct a narrative of vulnerability and victimization understate the Queen's role in revolutionary politics. Not only was an escape from France (to Austria, and her brother, the Emperor Leopold II) Marie Antoinette's "favored means of liberating the monarchy from its predicament", but she took an active role in the negotiations to restore royal authority once the family had been returned from Varennes as well.[53]

The way that Robinson's narrative absorbs this historical inaccuracy reflects other similar incongruities present in this text. Prominent among these is her linkage of Marie Antoinette's precarious situation following her return to Paris to another round of praise for the revolutionary effort, and, simultaneously, to her appeal to the National Assembly for the protection of the Queen:

> Events, at which nature shudders, might then [if the Queen had refused to accompany her husband] have tarnished the expanding glories of a nation just emancipated from the shackles of ignominious slavery; horrors might have been perpetrated which even the moderation, virtue, and discretion of the National Assembly could not have prevented. It is now in the power of that august Tribunal to prove, that *"the Days of Chivalry"* are not *"at an end"*. (p. 27)

In referring to the "days of chivalry" Robinson alludes here, of course, to Burke's *Reflections on the Revolution in France*, and his mourning of a lost world of inherited tradition and values.[54] Given the way in which his famous phrase resounds throughout the 1790s, Robinson's own invocation of the "days of chivalry" is remarkable in its ideological dissonance, as she recalls his scenario of the near rape of the Queen and at the same time constructs her own, all the while praising the struggle for emancipation which had so troubled him.[55]

At the same time, this appropriation of Burke also suggests how his representation of the events in the Queen's bedroom in October 1789 was, in Claudia Johnson's words, the "preeminent, publicly canvassed 'tale of sorrow'" that gripped the collective imagination of the English public.[56] As Johnson argues, more than simply exhibiting his interest in the situation of the Queen as a person, Burke's text was crucial in situating the ideal of "chivalric sentimentality" itself as the "affective front of ideology."[57] Thus, in spite of its (later) resonance, the Queen's story is essentially, for Burke, a rhetorical gesture which calls attention to his larger concern of valorizing "the social hierarchy ... law, tradition, precedent, prescription, and all that was venerable."[58]

Robinson's intertextualization acknowledges the affective potential of the chivalric, sentimental appeal, but, paradoxically, reverses it at the same time.

For her, unlike for Burke, the Queen is indeed the issue, and the past that she mourns is not a collective one, but one which exists in personal memory and in individual lives. In spite of its political contextualization, Marie Antoinette is for her essentially one particularized story of the fall from youth, beauty and power:

> Who can reflect on the present situation of the Queen without dropping a tear of pity, compare it [*sic*] to that which she enjoyed but a very few years since. She was then the idol of the French nation; universal adoration breathed around her, and called forth the splendors of her youthful mind ... What is she now? A forlorn and mournful Captive; immured within the walls of a palace, but a short time since the scene of domestic joy, and splendid festivity! Who can mark, unmoved, the hourly decay of exquisite beauty; the bloom of youth fading in the blast of detraction; that eye which beamed with benignity or glistened with the gem of sensibility, downcast, dejected and sunken ... now chill'd by the icy touch of neglect and scorn, and labouring under the agonizing pressure of impending despondency. (pp. 28–9)

That Robinson presents Marie Antoinette's story as the ultimate narrative of decline is evinced in her assumption that the power of that story will evoke a universal sentiment of pity. "There is not a doubt that all good men", she writes, "whatever their *political* sentiments may be, feel deeply interested in the fate of the captive Queen. Every *impartial* eye has a tear for her sufferings," (pp. 30–1). By concluding her text with this appeal to both reason *and* sentimentality, Robinson calls our attention to the unique convergence of her own concerns, which enabled her to support the Queen but also to reconcile that support with an adherence to the revolutionary agenda, in perhaps the last moment in which that dual project would be possible.

Robinson's later representations of Marie Antoinette's story, in contrast to the *Impartial Reflections*, are distanced from an account of revolutionary triumph. "Marie Antoinette's Lamentation" and "Monody to the Memory of the Late Queen of France" do not exhibit the ideological ambiguity that results from the attempt, which we have just viewed, to present those conflicting narratives within a shared space. The absence of support for the Revolution in these two poems might be explained by the fact that they were written against the backdrop of events whose particular violence occluded, even for many of its supporters, the Revolution's earlier promise. However, these poems also exhibit the awareness that as long as the Queen's plight was a part of the revolutionary drama, Robinson's view of the larger political picture was determined by and subordinated to the story of her continuing misfortunes.

And yet, while the Marie Antoinette poems exhibit the limits of Robinson's political vision, they also suggest the wider continuity of her thematic concerns. For, as in the *Impartial Reflections*, they indicate the prominence that she assigns not only to the individualized presence of Marie Antoinette but, just as urgently, to the repertoire of existential concerns which her story displayed: the fall from prominence, the experience of victimhood, the exigencies of exile. My interest in these poems lies, then, not only in their political import, but also in the way they exemplify Stuart Curran's understanding of the "displacement of ... stabilities", of a marginalized and ostracized mode of existence, as the common theme of Robinson's pathetic poetry. Although referring specifically to *Lyrical Tales* (1800), Curran's insight, which crucially locates revolutionary and counterrevolutionary warfare as a motivating force of these portrayals, applies to the Marie Antoinette poems as well, in which Robinson addresses perhaps the ultimate narrative of displacement of her era.[59]

"Marie Antoinette's Lamentation" positions the Queen almost exclusively within the realm of domesticity. The subheading of the poem – "Written in March, 1793" – immediately addresses her distressed domestic state, as it calls our attention to her recent widowhood (Louis XVI was guillotined in January 1793) and thus further intensifies her vulnerability as a grieving, devoted widow and, moreover, a persecuted mother. The use of the first-person narrative voice throughout the poem serves to reinforce this singular perspective, as it illustrates the urgency of her situation through the evocation of an ostensibly personal experience. At the same time, the "thrice grated window" (2), the "rabble's din" [and] "the tocsin's fateful sound" (55); the "iron lattice" (58) and the "tyrant jailor" (60) serve as constant reminders of the political referentiality of this portrait of individual distress and underscore the way the poem, like the *Impartial Reflections*, reflects the particular moment of its composition, no longer a plea for protection, but not yet the final expression of farewell and closure.

While Marie Antoinette's suffering is conceptualized in the "Lamentation" through the focus on motherhood, it is first presented as indelibly linked to memory and to personal loss:

> Why does remembrance picture to these eyes
> The jocund MORN OF LIFE, that once was mine?
> Alas! because, in sorrow doom'd to mourn,
> I ne'er shall see THAT BLISSFUL MORN RETURN!
> (15–18)[60]

These lines express a recurring theme in Robinson's writing, and their insertion here exhibits once more her preoccupation with this narrative of displacement and decline, its sheer magnitude reinforced by her own personal memory of the French queen.

Nonetheless, this gaze is then immediately turned outwards – as the Queen "behold[s her] darling INFANTS" (19), a move that at once effaces her youthful status as "an avatar of aristocratic frivolity",[61] and replaces it with the portrayal of "maternal sorrow" (28). Through this tableau of domestic solicitude, Robinson once more responds to those allegations surrounding Marie Antoinette's sexuality which had formed the centerpiece of her victimization. Although she is writing *before* her October trial, Robinson is alluding to, and providing a corrective for the stories that had proliferated of the Queen's transgressive sexual behavior, in which she was accused of having incestuous relations with, variously, her brother-in-law the Comte d'Artois, Louis XV (the king's grandfather) and even her own father, and which set the stage for the explicit charges of incest with her own son that were presented during the trial.[62]

The Marie Antoinette of the "Lamentation" seems to have reconciled herself to this victimization. Excluding the transitory passage marking the progression from a happy youth to a mournful present time, there is little temporal movement in the poem, besides the appeal to an abstract futurity for the safety of the children –"Oh! Give the tender BRANCHES TIME TO SHOOT!" (36), and a recognition of the eventuality of her own death: "Yet bear thy woes, my SOUL, with proud disdain; / Meet the keen lance of DEATH with stedfast [*sic*] eye" (61–2). And indeed, death appears in this text as a desired alternative to the "thousand ills" (67) that surround her:

> When will my SOUL, in sweet OBLIVION'S dream,
> Fade from this ORB, to some more peaceful shore?
> When will the CHERUB PITY break the snare,
> And snatch ONE VICTIM from the LAST DESPAIR?
> (75–8)

This final depiction of the Queen concludes the poem by locating her story within a wider conceptualization, in which she is "one victim" among countless others whose untold stories exhibit those same irreducible burdens of the human condition.

The "Monody to the Memory of the Late Queen of France", published on 2 December 1793, presents the final chapter of Marie Antoinette's story. The "Monody" begins with an implied continuity with the "Lamentation", signaled in the portrait of the Queen that appears as a frontispiece to the work. The portrait, drawn by the Marchioness de Marnesia, depicts the Queen in all the trappings of widowhood, her somber gaze directed towards an unknown point in the distance. The fact that Robinson attached an importance to the inclusion of this portrait is evident in the "Advertisement" to the work:

MRS. ROBINSON is extremely happy in having an opportunity of embellishing this Poem with so fine a Resemblance to the QUEEN OF FRANCE, taken from a Portrait by the MARCHIONESS DE MARNESIA, whose exquisitely beautiful Paintings are so much admired, and so justly celebrated.[63]

There is also, however, an inherent ambivalence in this presentation of the Queen. Robinson's acknowledgement of the skill of the Marchioness of Marnesia in creating "so fine a resemblance" and her pleasure in having the opportunity of "embellishing" her poem with the Marchioness's work calls our attention to Robinson's conscious promotion of both an implied association with an artist "so much admired", and of her own discerning artistic taste. The reviewer of the "Monody" for the *Monthly Review* affirms, but also rewrites this appraisal:

> To the ["Monody"] is prefixed an article of decoration, of which it stood in no need; – an elegant profile of the late "illfated queen," from a drawing by the Marchioness de Marnesia, exhibiting her as in her latter days, under the changes and ravages of misfortune.[64]

The erasure of the "ravages of misfortune" from Robinson's advertisement does not reflect a similar absence in the poem itself where Marie Antoinette's altered physical appearance receives substantial treatment. I dwell on the paratexts (the portrait and the advertisement) however, because they seem to me to be significant in setting up the concern with artistic production as an important issue in the poem. As I will show, Robinson views art as providing a degree of meaning in what is, for her, a world characterized by momentous and senseless loss.

The "Monody" is a long and diverse poem, in which Robinson presents another particularized depiction of the Queen, but one that is now totally situated within a purview of violence, chaos and ruin. Excepting a lone reference to a "TRIUMPH scarce [begun]" (232), the focus here is exclusively on the destructive outcome of the Revolution, which encompasses individuals, classes and nature itself. The images and inset stories that appear throughout the poem portray a world of ruin and exile, but also serve as a backdrop to the focus on the Queen and the colossal dimensions of her fall – "Hurl'd from the LOFTIEST height of human bliss, / To the WORST horrors of DESPAIR'S abyss" (45–6) – in what is now for us a familiar refrain. And the magnitude of this fall is reinforced by the all-encompassing chaos that surrounds it, manifested in both natural upheaval, as the "rich flow'ret" (65) precariously perched in nature, until, "from the flinty steep the waters flow / Pouring destruction o'er the vale below" (75–6) and in social rupture, where "EACH dreads his fellow, EACH his fellow braves! / While, in one horrid mass, ALL miseries blend" (102–3).

At the same time, Marie Antoinette's plight is repeatedly singled out amidst this portrayal of shared suffering. As opposed to the earlier erasure (in the

"Advertisement") of the physical manifestations of the Queen's ordeal, here they receive particular attention:

> Mark, in her alter'd and distracted mien,
> The fatal ensigns of the pangs within!
> See those fair tresses on her shoulders flow
> In silv'ry waves, that mock the ALPINE snow!
>
> . . . .
>
> Those eyes! Like SAPPHIRE gems were wont to shine;
> Bright beaming samples of their NATIVE MINE!
> WHAT ARE THEY NOW? clos'd in the sleep of DEATH!
> Their BLAZE extinguish'd by REBELLION'S breath!
>
> (141–54)

The reference to the "silv'ry waves" acknowledges the cultural value with which the Queen's hair had been invested, just as its changed color metonymically represents her fallen fortunes in general. As Saint-Amand writes, "[t]he hair that was celebrated all over Europe and fetishized as Marie Antoinette's most spectacular adornment, the same hair that started the fashion of 'the Queen's hair' color, had now become the mane of an aged woman."[65]

This transformation encapsulates what is, for Robinson, the unbearable tension inherent in the consciousness of past and present states of being, and which is reiterated in another evocation of past memory: "OH! I have seen her, like a SUN, sublime!" (159), at once recalling Burke's famous description of the Queen.[66] Unlike the allusion to Burke that we viewed in the *Impartial Reflections*, this appropriation is not accompanied by a parallel pro-Revolution narrative but, rather, by a description of pre-Revolution France in which its historic injustices are both distanced and minimized in relation to the current scene that Robinson surveys. Thus, while briefly acknowledging the "crimes LONG PAST" (247) of the old regime, she asks:

> Was it for THOSE, the last illustrious race
> Wash'd, with their blood, the page of dire disgrace!
> Was it for THOSE, an ALIEN'S heart was torn
> With taunting Insult's agonizing thorn!
>
> . . . .
>
> Was it for THOSE ill-fated LOUIS fell,
> 'Midst the vile clamours of the rabble's yell?
>
> (259–66)

The thrice-repeated "Was it for those?" insistently reinforces this disparity between cause and effect, past and present, as it registers Robinson's disillusionment and horror at the execution of the Queen and the political climate that enabled it.

Robinson's disillusionment with the Revolution is further evident in her portrayal of a heterogeneous community of victims whose suffering accompanies that of the Queen. These include wandering exiled priests, Marie Antoinette's fellow prison mates, a widowed mother weeping over her children and the detailed portrait of the "mountain PEASANT" (399) whose story rewrites old regime rural France in the terms of a pastoral idyll:

> NO MORE, amidst the simple village throng,
> He joins the sportive dance, the merry song!
> Now, torn from THOSE, he quits his native wood,
> Braves the dread front of WAR, and pants for blood!
> Now, to his REAP-HOOK, and his pastoral reed,
> The crimson'd PIKE and glitt'ring SWORD succeed!
> His russet garb, now chang'd for trappings vain;
> His rushy pillow, for the tented plain!
>
> .   .   .   .
>
> FANCY, with agonizing pow'r, displays
> The peaceful comforts of his HAPPIER DAYS!
> Shows, on the PALLET of his former rest,
> His INFANTS moaning on their MOTHER'S breast;
> Pinch'd by pale FAMINE, sinking to the grave;
> No FOOD to nourish, and no FRIEND to save!
> Ah! then he cries, half madd'ning with despair
> "IS THIS THE FREEDOM I was CALL'D TO SHARE?"
> (411–36)

Framed by the stories of Marie Antoinette and this peasant farmer, the totality of suffering and destruction that Robinson portrays would appear to preclude any acknowledgement, or even existence of her former pro-Revolution sentiments. The exuberant appeal, "TYRANTS SHALL FALL – TRIUMPHANT MAN BE FREE!" which had concluded *Ainsi Va Le Monde* seems to belong to a distant, irretrievable past, one which has been replaced by a comforting reliance on the values of continuity and tradition.

At the same time, however, I would argue that Robinson's valorization of tradition and continuity does not reflect an unequivocal endorsement of those values in the Burkean sense of the terms, just as her representation of equality is not limited to the commonality of suffering. The story of the peasant leads her to the expression of an abstract but desired ideal:

> YET, let REFLECTION'S eye discriminate
> The difference 'twixt the MIGHTY and the GREAT!

VIRTUE is still ILLUSTRIOUS, still sublime,
In EV'RY station, and in EV'RY clime!
TRUTH can derive no eminence from birth,
Rich in the proud supremacy of WORTH;
Its blest dominion vast and unconfin'd,
Its CROWN ETERNAL, and its THRONE THE MIND!
THEN, HEAV'N FORBID, that PREJUDICE should scan,
With jaundic'd eye, the dignities of man!

(451–60)

This articulation of an abstract realm of equality suggests that, notwithstanding her idealized view of the past, Robinson's abhorrence of the current state of events in France cannot be translated into an all-encompassing renunciation of the values which she had advanced in her earlier writings, addressing, rather, the excesses which have accompanied the project of their implementation. Thus, the claim:

That LIBERTY, immortal as the spheres,
Should steep her LAUREL in a nation's TEARS!
Oh, falsely nam'd!

(467–9)

reflects the ongoing promotion of the ideal of "liberty" in the abstract, while pointedly distancing the term from contemporary political reality.

At the same time, the yoking of "liberty" to its "laurel" immediately recalls Robert Merry's *The Laurel of Liberty*, and Robinson's response to that poem, *Ainsi Va Le Monde*. On one level, this allusion registers dissonance, as Robinson acknowledges and rewrites her ideological investment: the promise of the Revolution has now been reduced to falseness and tears. On another level, however, it exhibits the continuity of her engagement with an intrinsically related cultural concern. In *Ainsi Va Le Monde*, Robinson had envisioned the re-energized state of literature as a desired by-product of the vitality of the revolutionary moment. The "Monody" picks up the concern with artistic practice during a time of political upheaval and reconfigures it within this narrative of changed expectations:

Immortal GENIUS! let the votive line,
THE MUSES LAUREL, and her FAME, be THINE!
For THOU shalt LIVE, when PRIDE'S indignant eye,
Clos'd in eternal solitude, shall lie!
When THOSE, who flutter'd through their *little* day,
Shall, like their FOLLIES and their NAMES, decay;
When the faint mem'ry of INFERIOR souls,

Down the dark channel of OBLIVION rolls –
THOU SHALT SURVIVE!

.   .   .   .

Then, GENIUS, let the toilsome task be THINE,
To LABOUR in the dark precarious MINE;
And if, amidst the *chaos*, thou *shouldst* find
One great, one beauteous attribute of mind,
To twine round MERIT'S brow the wreath of FAME,
And give *Nobility* A LOFTIER NAME!

(509–32)

Robinson locates artistic merit, then, as a possible means of redemption "amidst the chaos", and its practitioners as a new "nobility" that will prevail in a time of cultural turmoil. Moreover, what is viewed here as the depersonalized, solitary and singular conceptualization – "Genius" – will return, in Robinson's later writing, to the formulation first presented in *Ainsi Va Le Monde*, to be articulated in terms of more specified catalogues of literary production. Although Robert Merry had proved unable to revitalize culture and will henceforth be absent from those catalogues, Robinson can yet salvage the ideal of a community of literary meritocracy from the ruins of the failed Revolutionary promise, providing at least the possibility of representation amidst the struggle for survival.

And Marie Antoinette's story *was* the ultimate enactment of this drama of survival. As we have seen, Robinson's engagement with that story takes place amidst a wide cultural fascination with the Queen, one which manifested itself in various ways, extending beyond revolutionary France and reflecting, especially for women, different cultural and social concerns. Earlier in this study, I referred to Linda Colley's perception of how the guillotining of Marie Antoinette caused a heightened sense of vulnerability among British women, and reinforced their own awareness of home, family and nationhood as a comforting parameter of safety.[67] Another aspect of this fascination is examined by Terry Castle: "Particularly among women in England, where sympathy for the *ancien régime* had long been a staple of popular romantic sensibility, Marie Antoinette was in fact a kind of cult figure – the object of a widespread and often curiously eroticized group fixation."[68] Although in many ways Robinson's textual engagement with the Queen reflects this same collective fascination, it does not opt into the comforting sense of patriotism and community that Colley and Castle describe. Rather, her Marie Antoinette texts are distinguished through their focus on victimization, exile, a shared sense of ostracism, and, not infrequently, by the expression of pro-Revolution values as well.

The contemporary critical reception of the "Monody" acknowledges the hold that Marie Antoinette's story had on the public imagination, with the reviews for the most part expressing a critical approbation that also locates the work within a larger, sympathetic, cultural response.[69] Only the liberal *Analytical Review* qualifies the sense of "catastrophe" and "outrage" which accompanies the attention given to the poem itself in the reviews,[70] and which characterizes the general reaction to the death of the French queen:

> Without strictly examining the accuracy of the portraits exhibited in this piece, or discussing the propriety of the sentiments which the writer expresses, as a poetical production, we do not hesitate to pronounce it a very successful exertion of those talents, to which we have already more than once paid the willing tribute of applause.[71]

This reviewer's comments, while praising Robinson's work, also suggest the impossibility of completely dissociating the poetical elements of the work from its ideological agenda. Yet, although the critic acknowledges a past history of reception in the *Analytical* (and privileges an aesthetic continuity in Robinson's work) he or she ignores the political *discontinuity* present in that same repertoire of Robinson's works that the periodical had, itself, reviewed.[72] Let us recall the review of *Ainsi Va Le Monde*, which the *Analytical* had foregrounded as an "invocation to liberty." The present critique of the "accuracy" and "propriety" of Robinson's portrayal of the political landscape is not accompanied by any kind of recognition of the shift from the ideological investment that was present in the earlier poem, confirming once more the inefficacy of *Ainsi Va Le Monde* in establishing for Robinson a radical name. Just as important, however, is the fact that the "Monody to the Memory of the Late Queen of France" will not convey a similar sense of incongruity in relation to the later political writings that follow it. For the defense of the original Revolutionary agenda *would* re-emerge in Robinson's writings, but at a distance from the imprisonment and execution of the Queen, and dissociated from the referentiality of her story. This later political stand would be informed by that same existential anxiety that had accompanied her defense of the Queen. As we will see in the following chapter, Robinson articulates her disillusionment with the actual progress of the Revolution and its implications for British society while concurrently expressing her support of freedom and resistance to tyranny through the idealization of the incipient revolutionary moment that had foregrounded those issues so prominently.

4
"The Best and the Wisest": Mary Robinson II

Mary Robinson's writings acknowledge in different ways the longing for community. Informed by the progress of the French Revolution and the cause of domestic reform, Robinson's reflections on, and desire for, community are expressed, variously, through her identification with the vulnerable and persecuted celebrity shared with Marie Antoinette, with the shared endeavor of women intellectuals and with the radical circles of London. Furthermore, this desire is invariably linked to artistic practice. We saw in the previous chapter how Robinson viewed the Revolution as an event that would usher in a literary revival; subsequently, its failure carried with it the consciousness of disappointment on the cultural front as well. Thus, in the "Monody to the Memory of the Late Queen of France", the artist is depicted as one who toils in isolation surrounded by the ruins of failed expectations and of the promise that the Revolution had embodied in its early years. In the years following the Queen's demise Robinson seeks to mitigate this sense of isolation through a vision of a select, progressive, and now oppositional community, the "best and the wisest" as she terms it in her novel *Walsingham*, who struggle to survive during a time of cultural repression.[1]

At the same time, the "Monody" also reminds us of how, for Robinson, the identification with the victimization of Marie Antoinette took precedence over other ideological concerns. Yet equally noteworthy is the manner in which Robinson returned to a conspicuous radical positioning once Marie Antoinette had exited the political stage. The Queen's experience, stirring as it was for her, did not preclude the later, renewed embrace of an idealistic revolutionary ideal. In fact, it is already evident just three months following the Queen's execution, when, on 23 January 1794, Robinson wrote a remarkable letter, which she signed as Tabitha Bramble, to Robert Dundas, the Lord Advocate for Scotland.[2] Robinson begins by praising "reformers contending for principles, & certain renovations which every body allows to be founded in Justice," and then asserts that, even within the current repressive climate, "such are the charms of Truth, there are many Friends of Liberty." In what becomes the main point of her letter, she decries the "sanguinary & harsh" sentences (fourteen years' transportation to Botany Bay) which had been handed out to three radical activists – William Skirving, Maurice Margarot and Thomas Muir – who had been convicted of sedition as a result of their participation in the Edinburgh "British Convention" of 1793 and in the events leading up to it.[3] Robinson's defense of the leaders of the Edinburgh political meeting which had consciously imitated the French National Convention, "dress[ing] itself up," in the words of John Barrell and Jon Mee, "as a legislative body, a revolutionary anti-parliament"[4] underscores her own reformist positioning. Her accusatory tone at the conclusion of the letter, in which Dundas is called "cruel" and "odious" and in which his violent assassination is anticipated, renders it very radical indeed.

Robinson's letter to Dundas is mediated through the pseudonym of Tabitha Bramble, the particular figure in her repertoire of authorial personae that consistently indicates an oppositional worldview.[5] And although her published works do not display the same direct radical intervention such as appears in the letter to Dundas, they continue to promote the "principles" and "renovations" of reform such as she had expressed to the Lord Advocate. This chapter will examine Robinson's radical positioning as it is evinced in three texts that appeared in the latter half of the revolutionary decade – the sonnet sequence *Sappho and Phaon* (1796) and the novels *Hubert de Sevrac* (1796) and *Walsingham* (1797). Each of these works exhibits a different dimension of her political engagement: *Sappho and Phaon* reflects upon literary production – and in particular, female artistic production – in a time of cultural change, *Hubert de Sevrac* revisits a historical legacy of oppression in order to justify anew the original agenda of the French Revolution and *Walsingham* examines more generally the cultural instability that characterizes the aftermath of the revolutionary moment and the repressive climate that defined it. I conclude the chapter with a brief discussion of Robinson's relations with William Godwin in the final years of the revolutionary decade – which were also the final years of her life – in order to show the convergence of radicalism and the desire for community as it displayed itself in her own life and through her own personal experience.

I

Sappho and Phaon is both a narrative of passionate and unremitting love and a study of literary history and practice. Alongside its referencing of her personal life and in particular her tempestuous relationship with Banastre Tarleton, which was now drawing to a close,[6] Robinson's sonnet sequence and its prefatory material also serve as a commentary on the wider literary and political landscape to which she turns her gaze. In doing so, the work is, as Jerome McGann argues, "a learned production fully aware of the major works serving the tradition it interprets"; a work with "serious and radical philosophical pretensions."[7]

Robinson's three prefaces – a general preface, a note "To the Reader" and an "Account of Sappho" – establish her authority on poetical matters and examine Sappho's life and work within different cultural contexts. In the opening preface Robinson addresses the development of the sonnet form and the representation of the Greek poet and her work at various historical moments, in Sappho's own time and through to her own. She cites Addison and Pope, and the near contemporary French account of Jean-Jacques Barthélemy in order to align her own work with a literary tradition but also (in a point to which I will return) to infuse it with a contemporary awareness. Likewise, in this passage she once more presents, as in *Ainsi Va Le Monde*, a catalogue of a valorized literary past, one which includes Milton, Spenser, Pope, Cowper, Collins and Waller, but *not* Robert Merry, whose absence is noteworthy in light of his conspicuous presence in the earlier poem. This erasure indicates Robinson's own move away from Della Cruscan poetry, but also, more pertinently for my argument here, denotes the inefficacy of the Merry / Revolution axis – that exuberant vision of culture and politics joining together in a common movement of progress.[8] In 1796, Merry was in the provinces, unable to make a living by his writing and persecuted for his opinions; the Revolution had ended in failure. However, Robinson's realization in *Sappho and Phaon* that neither the French Revolution nor Merry had revitalized literature is not accompanied by the abandonment of a belief in the role of the artist in society, but rather by the revision of how that role is enacted. What appears now is a perception of the relations between artistic production and political reality as oppositional and alienated rather than affirming and acquiescent. The artist, rather than being enabled by political events, strives to proceed even amidst their failure.

In her preface Robinson specifically addresses the marginalized status of the artist. Thus, accompanying her catalogue of literary greats is the understanding that they, and other worthy writers, had gone unrecognized during their lifetime:

> yet it is a melancholy truth, that here, where the attributes of genius have been diffused by the liberal hand of nature, almost to prodigality, there has not been, during a long series of years, the smallest mark of public distinction bestowed on literary talents. Many individuals, whose works are held in the highest estimation, now that their ashes sleep in the sepulchre, were, when living, suffered to languish, and even to perish, in obscure poverty: as if it were the peculiar fate of genius, to be neglected while existing, and only honoured when the consciousness of inspiration is vanished for ever.[9]

These remarks underscore once more the sense of alienation that is repeatedly depicted in Robinson's writings. Unlike, however, in *Ainsi Va Le Monde*, where "Chatterton oppress'd" and "famish'd Otway" receive a specific present and future corrective in the form of Robert Merry and the enabling possibilities of revolutionary energy, here the focus is on the tension between a more abstract ideal and a pervasive cultural and institutionalized oppression:

> It is the interest of the ignorant and powerful, to suppress the effusions of enlightened minds; when only monks could write, and nobles read, authority rose triumphant over right; and the slave, spell-bound in ignorance, hugged his fetters without repining. It was then that the best powers of reason lay buried like the gem in the dark mine; by a slow and tedious progress they have been drawn forth, and must, ere long, diffuse an universal lustre: for that era is rapidly advancing, when talents will tower like an unperishable column, while the globe will be strewed with the wrecks of superstition. (p. 148)

The fact that Robinson can yet envision an "era . . . when talents will tower like an unperishable column" points to her insistent belief in the power of literary merit to ultimately prevail amidst the bleak conditions in which it is enacted. And indeed, Sappho herself is central to this understanding. By representing her as, in McGann's words, both "the index of a current (inadequate) condition and the prophet of a future day," Robinson crucially acknowledges the "feminized sources of poetic power" of this hoped-for literary revitalization.[10] McGann's reading of this passage identifies Robinson herself and her contemporaries among these sources of power, emphasizing (for his specific discussion of Robinson as well as for his general argument for sensibility as a prominent cultural force) the recognition of how she and her " 'illustrious countrywomen' have entirely restructured the philosophy of literature in terms of the feelings and the passions."[11] Note, however, the ways in which Robinson's own perception of the place of women writers unfolds within a wider context of social ostracism:

> It is at once a melancholy truth, and a national disgrace, that this Island, so profusely favored by nature, should be marked, of all enlightened countries, as the most neglectful of literary merit! and I will venture to believe, that there are both POETS and PHILOSOPHERS, now living in Britain, who, had they been born in any *other* clime, would have been honoured with the proudest distinctions, and immortalized to the latest posterity. I cannot conclude these opinions without paying tribute to the talents of my illustrious countrywomen; who, unpatronized by courts, and unprotected by the powerful, persevere in the paths of literature, and ennoble themselves by the unperishable lustre of MENTAL PREEMINENCE! (p. 149)

The repetitive force of the negative adjectives "unpatronized" and "unprotected", appended to a more general depiction of neglect and disregard, illustrates Robinson's consciousness of the fact that this theoretical project takes place within a specific social reality. Thus, I would contend that while she provides women writers with weighty cultural baggage, and, furthermore, has them replace Merry as the purveyors of a new literary era, it is in a context that also displays their marginality within that culture.

This awareness of a tenuous cultural presence is underpinned by Robinson's appropriation of an important late eighteenth-century treatment of the Sapphic myth. Her inclusion in the "Account of Sappho" of a lengthy passage from Jean-Jacques Barthélemy's *Voyage du jeune Anacharsis en Grèce* (1788) identifies his work as an authoritative text, as she praises the "learned and enlightened" Barthélemy, and his "vindication ... of the Grecian poetess" (p. 153). In doing so, she acknowledges the prevalent perception of Sappho promoted by Barthélemy, among others, in which, as Joan DeJean writes, Sappho is "gradually being assigned an increasingly complex and detailed role in the political life of her day, a role that presents revealing parallels in the French political arena."[12] In this view, Sappho is invested with a subversive radical potential, in which she appears as "a political exile, a revolutionary who had fought ... to overthrow tyranny."[13]

Nonetheless, the passage that Robinson quotes from the *Voyage*, as well as her own fictive construction of Sappho in the sonnets themselves, are devoid of political engagement, concentrating, rather, on Sappho's heightened emotional state, and particularly her propensity to love "to excess, because it was impossible for her to love otherwise" (p. 154). Accordingly, in Sonnet XXX, named by Robinson as "Bids Farewell to Lesbos", Sappho's departure is described as follows:

> Oh! Bark propitious! bear me gently o'er,
> Breathe soft, ye winds; rise slow, O! swelling wave!
> Lesbos; these eyes shall meet thy sands no more:
> I fly, to seek my Lover, or my Grave!
>
> (11–14)

Here, at the moment when her exile commences, as throughout *Sappho and Phaon*, Robinson's Sappho is motivated exclusively by the energy and passions of heterosexual love. At the same time, the endorsement of Barthélemy implies an affinity with a wider repertoire of cultural resonances and tensions, one that manifests itself associatively throughout her own project in the convergence of politics, literature, exile and the recognition of marginality.[14]

In recognizing the interplay of these concerns, I cannot agree with the view put forward by Yopie Prins in which Robinson's Sappho is perceived as a marker of the disappearance of a female literary presence altogether. Prins focuses on the deployment of the persona of Sappho by Victorian women writers as one that consistently signals an awareness of the emptiness and depersonalization of the Greek poet, but also manifests itself in a "rhetoric of dispossession" that reflects the status of the authors themselves. In looking back on the "Romantic precursors" of Victorian women's engagement with Sappho, Prins argues that Mary Robinson's sonnet sequence embodies this same sense of displacement and loss, one which ultimately calls into question Robinson's own authorial presence. As Prins states it, "the effect of this self-reflexiveness is not to constitute a female subject as an ironically alienated other, but to make it disappear altogether; there is no 'I' to speak of."[15] While she cites Robinson's own argument for the importance of women's writing, she also claims that her poetry itself refutes this awareness; "women poets rise to authorship only by falling."[16] As opposed to Prins, I believe that rather than functioning as contradictory forces, the sonnets and the paratexts in *Sappho and Phaon* mutually inform one another. Sappho may very well be falling, but we must not forget that that fall had been prefaced here by the recognition of a female "persever[ance] in the paths of literature" and the "unperishable uster of MENTAL PREEMINENCE." Can *this* awareness lead exclusively to its own annihilation? Rather, I want to claim, it is the possibility of the fall together with the inexorable tension that exists in remaining nonetheless on the ground; it is the perseverance as much as the prospect that signals the concerns of Robinson's literary project.

II

Robinson's *Sappho and Phaon* acknowledges, through the reference to Barthélemy's *Voyage*, and its allusion to an ideological, exilic conception of the Greek poet, "one of the traditional stereotypes of the unnatural woman [...] the woman who attempts to play a political role."[17] Yet in 1796, Robinson's political awareness was apparent in other texts as well. For with her novel *Hubert de Sevrac*, published that same year, Robinson commenced those literary-political interventions through which she earned her radical reputation, those "doctrines of Philosophism" as Richard Polwhele had it, that he and his colleagues in the "Anti-Jacobin" circle associate with an unnatural, disconcerting, subversive female presence.[18]

   Hubert de Sevrac was published one month after *Sappho and Phaon*.[19] Despite the disparity between the two works – the one a sonnet sequence set in ancient Greece and the other a Gothic romance played out against the backdrop of the French Revolution – they share the common theme of the emotional and political manifestations of exile. Set in Italy and covering roughly the years 1792–4,[20] *Hubert de Sevrac* relates the story of an aristocratic French family fleeing the terror of the Revolution. We meet the de Sevracs – Hubert, his wife, Emily (a woman of Scottish descent) and their daughter Sabina, as they arrive in Italy in order to seek refuge in Montnoir, a castle belonging to Ravillon, the godson of Hubert's deceased father. The exigencies of exile are further complicated by family problems, since both Hubert and Emily had married against their parents' wishes, and as a result are left without recourse to financial or domestic assistance. It soon becomes apparent that the tense relationship between de Sevrac and Ravillon is motivated by issues of usurpation and inheritance – the latter is heir to the de Sevrac family fortune (Hubert having been disinherited following his marriage) but only during his lifetime, after which, the fortune will revert to Sabina. In order to ensure that the property remains in his family, he plans to marry her to his son, Arnaud. In addition to the repeated attempts to possess Sabina, which take place against the backdrop of the mysterious castle, Hubert and his family undergo other adventures: Hubert is arrested for murder, strange occurrences unfold at the castle, and a young English traveler, St Clair, joins the family and falls in love with Sabina, notwithstanding the fact that he is, unbeknownst to them (and to the reader) already married.

Leaving the castle as the result of Ravillon's and Arnaud's constant persecution, the de Sevracs find a brief respite of tranquility in a modest mountain retreat, but continue to be victimized by various agents of Ravillon. De Sevrac is once more accused of murder and the family resumes its wanderings, to avoid his arrest and the constant pursuit of Ravillon's associates. We gradually learn of Hubert's life prior to his marriage with Emily, including his involvement in various court intrigues and his rivalry with the cruel aristocrat, de Briancour, who is now also an exile in Italy, and whom the de Sevracs re-encounter in the course of their wanderings. Crucially, only at this point is it revealed that, with de Briancour's assistance, de Sevrac had some years earlier contrived to have a man (the father of a woman whom he had loved before he met Emily) interred in the Bastille through a *lettre de cachet*. In spite of Hubert's later attempts to release this man, de Briancourt exerts his influence over the King to have him remain in prison, as the result of a power struggle between de Sevrac and himself. After further adventures, news arrives that Ravillon is dying. On his deathbed he confesses his complicity in contriving the misfortunes of Hubert, and after his death his property is awarded to Sabina. During this time, Emily's mother passes away, and she inherits her own family fortune as well. Financially comfortable, the family moves to England where they are soon afterwards joined by St Clair (now conveniently a widower) yet not before Hubert can triumphantly claim that he is now "a convert to liberty [and] the friend of human kind!"[21]

In its maze of successive adventures, in the superficial treatment of its characters, and in the sheer improbability of many of its plot developments (it seems as if the Italian countryside is peopled almost exclusively with former acquaintances of the de Sevracs, just waiting to be recognized) *Hubert de Sevrac* is a complicated novel to follow, a fact that is underscored in contemporary critical reviews.[22] Nonetheless, the central thematic concern with the French Revolution affords Robinson the opportunity to rearticulate her support of the revolutionary effort and also to portray individual experience, and her characteristic preoccupations with exile, marginality, vulnerability and the fall from power, within that context. Despite the novel's formulaic nature and negative reception, the fact that a pro-Revolution stand was widely disseminated in print[23] is crucial for the perception of Robinson as a radical author. This was particularly so in 1796. The year following the legislation of the Two Acts had seen the intensification of cultural repression; it was, as E.P. Thompson describes it, a time characterized by "fear, spies, watchful magistrates with undefined powers, the occasional example."[24] This was not, to say the least, a climate conducive to a public defense of the French Revolution. Robinson's rambling plot may be linked, then, to her uneasiness in expressing that defense, and to a kind of wariness that is manifested not only in the novel's representation of censorship within the text, as William Brewer has argued,[25] but also in her management of the story line as a whole. The belated introduction of Hubert's complicity in the corrupt world of old regime France and the overall inconsistency that characterizes the place of the Revolution itself within the narrative exhibit the tension that accompanies Robinson's political positioning at the particular moment in which her book was written.

Hubert de Sevrac's revolutionary contexts are apparent from the opening pages of the novel, with the initial introduction of Hubert as he "commences his wandering journey" into exile:

> It was at that awful hour [the summer of 1792] that de Sevrac examined the retrospect of his prosperous days. All the phantoms of delight purchased by the sufferings of the people, all the irritated tribes of wretchedness, whose wants had hitherto been unregarded, now conspired to taunt his imagination. He probed his lacerated bosom; and he found, that though no act of oppression, immediately proceeding from himself, had contaminated its feelings, he had been accessory to crimes, and deserved to participate in their punishment. The scene of delusive grandeur was at an end; the splendid pageantry viewed through the medium of reflection faded into nothing; all of the deceptive had vanished; and the prospect before him and his companions was cold, desolate, melancholy and forlorn. (Vol. i., p. 8)

In opening her novel by foregrounding the crimes of the old regime through the consciousness of her eponymous protagonist, Robinson immediately presents a pro-Revolution discourse as an important narrative context. The fact that Hubert's complicity in those crimes is emphasized *at this point* as deriving solely from his aristocratic status enables Robinson to initially position her text in a progressive yet not overly threatening middle ground by articulating the awareness of a general class-based culpability and accountability for the injustices of pre-Revolution France, while also presenting a sympathetic portrayal of an aristocratic French exile. As the novel progresses, however, the emphasis shifts, first, when the political elements of the narrative are resituated in the background of what becomes mainly a series of adventures of an exiled family, and yet again when Robinson returns to an overt political positioning by concluding her novel with a clear defense of the Revolution.

Indeed, much of *Hubert de Sevrac* is concerned with detailing a particularized experience of exile and the need to exert fortitude in order to survive. For Robinson, this struggle for survival is never a simple one, and after having lived some weeks at Montnoir, Hubert's situation is described as follows:

> [His] was that mental malady which persuasion cannot eradicate, or affection cure. The memory of his father, the political affairs of his country, the solitude that fed his affliction, and the poverty that threatened his family, united in one terrible phalanx to overturn his reason ... he despised himself for the weakness of his nature. (Vol. i., p. 31)

Similarly to its place within Hubert's catalogue of afflictions, *ancien régime* France and the Revolution exist throughout most of the novel mainly in individual reflection, and in the occasional conversations of the characters, when they find the time to contemplate their own social and economic vulnerability or that of people whom they meet in the course of their travels. Unlike, for example, Charlotte Smith's *The Banished Man* (1794), in which action within and reaction to the Revolution motivate the plot, the Revolution exists in *Hubert de Sevrac* primarily as a focal point for retrospective analysis and justification of the original circumstances that brought it on. A characteristic instance of the invoking of the Revolution appears during a discussion of the behavior of one of the associates of Ravillon, the corrupt Abbot Palerma. Giovanni, a local peasant, explains to the de Sevracs that he had learned to condemn the nobility by viewing the Abbott's actions:

> "It is those who forbid us to speak" [he says] "that teach us how to think." ... "Alas!" exclaimed Mademoiselle de Sevrac, "these are scenes of which I had not the most faint idea! Little did I think, when I beheld the splendours of Versailles, the brilliant circle, the illumined ball room, and the sumptuous banquet! That the poor and houseless peasants were exposed to all the storms of Heaven, unpitied and defenceless! We never talked of them; the season, whose severity pinches the child of nature, was to us a season of festive luxury." (Vol. ii., pp. 82–4)

Sabina's argument (as well as Hubert's own reflections that were cited earlier) stress the economic inequalities that were present during the *ancien régime*. The actual events of the Revolution itself are marginalized in the novel, and there is little – if any – acknowledgement of people, places and events which would reinforce the contemporaneousness of these political discussions, or place them in a relation of cause and effect. That is to say, the "cause" – the focus on the social injustice of past times – is continually emphasized, while the "effect" – the Revolution itself and its various developments – is, after an auspicious beginning, markedly absent. Although Robinson begins her story by alluding to "that dreadful period, when the tumult of discontent perverted the cause of liberty" (Vol. i., p. 7), she never returns to elaborate upon the progress of the Revolution and the dramatic events that accompanied it. For example, although we are told of the conversations of Hubert and his companions "which naturally occurred on political subjects" (Vol. ii., p. 147), we never learn the content of those discussions. Certainly they would have included reactions to the guillotining of the French king and queen or to Robespierre's Terror, events which took place during the time period covered in *Hubert de Sevrac*. Yet these momentous occurrences are conspicuously absent from the text.

At the same time, this lack of particularity exposes other equally relevant tensions. Giovanni's reflection on censorship – "those who forbid us to speak" – references not only the Italian countryside of which he is an inhabitant but also the situation in England in 1796, when free speech had been severely curtailed, and, directly preceding one more discussion of *ancien régime* France, points perhaps to Robinson's unwillingness to articulate a fuller, more comprehensive discussion of *current* political developments. Sabina's rejoinder, "we never talked of them" (the "poor and houseless peasants") reminds us of other contemporary issues that continue to be silenced. Brewer cites this scene as an example of how "censorship and self-expression are central themes in [this] novel."[26] I would extend Brewer's argument to include not only incidents *within* the text, but also the movement of the narrative as a whole, pointing to how Robinson limits, and, in fact, cautiously censors, her own presentation of a pro-Revolution argument.

These omissions receive an indirect acknowledgement in Mary Wollstonecraft's discussion of *Hubert de Sevrac*. In her otherwise scathing review, she nonetheless approvingly notes that "the object of [*Hubert de Sevrac*] is apparently benevolent", as it aims to show that "the vices of the rich produce the crimes of the poor." At the same time, however, she ignores the way that the novel's political and historical contexts underline that awareness, writing that it has "no centre out of which [that moral] could naturally emanate."[27] Wollstonecraft appears oblivious to the fact that old regime France appears as the point of departure for discussions on inequality and social injustice (such as in Sabina's response to the peasant Giovanni) that explicitly vindicate the revolutionary effort, despite its inconsistent presence within the narrative itself.

An additional scene further illustrates this point. Hubert has noticed Sabina's melancholic state following the supposed death of her beloved St Clair, and he rebukes her for succumbing to despair. She immediately rejects this attempt to regulate her feelings by undermining his moral authority, which is flawed in her view by his affiliation with the old regime establishment: "And what is that, which can only derive happiness from the misery of millions? [she asks] Is it virtue?" (Vol. ii., pp. 148–9). Sabina then proceeds to present yet another extended critique of pre-Revolution France:

> Laws, that owned no code, but in the bosom of a despot, were the mere mockery of freedom . . . Time was, when the few were happy, and the millions wretched! When virtue, valour, genius, and humanity, bowed at the foot-stool of ignorance and pride! When palaces rung with festivity, and dungeons groaned with victims! When folly feasted to satiety, and honest labour starved! Malice or caprice, then, had power to scourge the suffering multitude, or awe them into silence. Who could redress them? – the throne was barricadoed [*sic*] by the nobles; and the bastille – (Vol. ii., p. 150)

"Here", the narrator intervenes, "Mademoiselle de Sevrac suddenly stopped" (Vol. ii., p. 151). Hubert realizes his error, and, moved by his daughter's vehement speech, reconciles her with a fatherly embrace.

Significant issues emerge here. First, note the way this scene moves from a personalized focus (the mourning of an ostensibly dead lover) to a political one (a justification of the original revolutionary effort) and then concludes with a return to domestic concerns. This movement is constantly repeated throughout the novel, as political references appear only to be submerged into yet another set of personal adventures. As one further indication of Robinson's anxiety in writing within a repressive political climate, it is significant that the conversation between Hubert and Sabina is cut off at the very moment when the Bastille is mentioned. Defending the Revolution even in general terms was a brave enough act in 1796, and the retreat from such a prominent image seems to reflect Robinson's awareness of her novel's uneasy contemporaneousness, as she hastily resituates the narrative at a comfortable distance from the Bastille's controversial walls.

That said, I am not suggesting that the emphasis on domestic issues depoliticizes *Hubert de Sevrac*. One of the prominent features of the eighteenth-century novel in general is, of course, the politicization of the domestic, and the representation of the family unit, especially by women writers, as a site through which to explore power relations and patriarchal structures.[28] In this context, Sabina's energetic rejection of her father's heritage and its system of values serves as a good example of the intertwining of the political and the personal. And yet, the wavering between overt and discreet political consciousness in this scene suggests how, throughout the novel, the re-shifting of narrative emphasis accumulatively obscures much of its pro-Revolution message. Wollstonecraft, as we have seen, misses that message almost entirely.

This scene, moreover, also points to the inconsistencies that characterize Robinson's construction of her protagonist. The succession of chaotic adventures to which Hubert is exposed shifts the focus on this character from a political one to an individual story and it is Sabina who, throughout the novel, carries the burden of defending the Revolution. In the conversation with Sabina quoted above he is essentially voiceless and, rather than refuting or concurring with her political claims, merely concedes that he "had no right to scrutinize [her] heart"(Vol. ii., p. 151). At the same time, even the minor presence allotted to Hubert's politics is marked with discontinuities, as Robinson belatedly confers upon him a more specific complicity in the corruption of the old regime, and a degree of personal as well as class-based culpability. This retroactive identification of Hubert's politics is enabled by the introduction of the incident of the *lettre de cachet* into the narrative. In marked contrast to the description that appears at the beginning of the novel, where, we recall, it is stated that his sense of guilt derives from "no act of oppression, immediately proceeding from himself", it now becomes clear that Hubert's participation in the machinations of French court life had been far from innocuous. His desire to marry Adelaide, a young woman of a different social class, had been confounded by family and social pressures and, in an attempt to prevail over these obstacles, Hubert had had her father arrested through a *lettre de cachet*.

As Mary Favret explains, the *lettre de cachet*, as an "emblem of secrecy and sequestration ... had a symbolic status which far exceeded its actual role in France."[29] Its presence in this text as a metonymic representation of the abuse of arbitrary privilege signals Hubert's complicity in the power and corruption of the *ancien régime*. Yet, his own confession of this involvement also enables Robinson to conclude her novel with a move, articulated through the consciousness of her protagonist, towards a more general justification of the Revolution. This movement culminates soon after the revelation of the *lettre de cachet* affair when Hubert chances to meet Adelaide's brother, de Fleury, who had fled France following his father's interment in the Bastille and his own subsequent challenge to de Briancourt (who was first Hubert's accomplice in the scheme, and later his rival). Witnessing de Fleury's death – he commits suicide shortly after relating his story of exile and defeat – Hubert thinks to himself:

> The scene of present horrors he at last beheld, as the mere effect of past enormities, among which the *lettre de cachet* was an evil of the greatest magnitude. Reflection told him that the rays of truth, which had been obscured by the intervening glooms of tyranny and superstition, were now collected in one glorious beam, to illumine the whole earth! (Vol. iv., p. 294)

This understanding sets the stage for Hubert's final exclamation, "Hubert de Sevrac is the convert of liberty! The friend of human kind!" (Vol. iv., p. 316). By concluding with this declaration, Robinson appears to be imposing an artificial closure upon the text, as if Hubert's realization is the result of a sustained process of deliberation, one that had been prepared for throughout the novel by parallel narrative developments. And yet, the very fact that one of the final actions in *Hubert de Sevrac* privileges a conversion to liberty, calls our attention to an ideological (if not aesthetic) logic, one which provides a final, conclusive endorsement of the Revolution.

This conclusion, with its emphasis on a direct affiliation between her protagonist and the revolutionary agenda, is indicative of Robinson's own political stand in the text. Clearly, she is vindicating the revolutionary effort, but in a way that repeatedly rehearses its original contexts rather than its later manifestations. Apart from the brief reference mentioned at the outset of the novel to the "dreadful period" in which violence "perverted the cause of universal liberty", *Hubert de Sevrac* could have been written immediately following *Ainsi Va Le Monde*, and Hubert's acknowledgement of the "glorious beam ... illumin[ing] the whole earth" indeed recaptures the darkness-to-light imagery of the earlier poem. By repeatedly emphasizing the original revolutionary moment and by skimming over the violent events of 1792–4 as if somehow they did not happen, Robinson can justify a political ideal without having to acknowledge its egregious excesses. In deliberately keeping to generalizations, she is also possibly attempting to sidestep the cultural terror at home, and the actualities of censorship and repression in Britain in 1796.

Just as her characters ignore the tumultuous developments of this immediate political moment, there is, likewise, no reference to Robinson's own earlier criticism of the Revolution, and no sense of self-consciousness that would attest to her cognizance of the fact that she is providing a disparate ideological viewpoint from the one presented three years before in the "Monody to the Memory to the Late Queen of France." Writing in 1796, after Marie Antoinette was long dead, she was once more able to portray the struggle for survival and the fight against injustice as complementary to, and enabled by, the Revolution. Tellingly, then, her protagonist's final identification as "a convert to liberty" functions not only as a point of novelistic closure, but also foregrounds Robinson's own renewed public allegiance to the Revolution's original values.

III

Robinson would return to address the French Revolution and its aftermath in the writings that followed *Hubert de Sevrac*. Prominent among these is her novel *Walsingham* (1797), in which the Revolution (or, more specifically, its original values) functions not only as an ideal, but, more importantly, one that receives its moral currency through an implicit contrast to contemporary British society. Set primarily in 1791–2, *Walsingham* tells the story of a young man, Walsingham Ainsforth, who seeks to find his place in the world. The novel is presented in loose epistolary form – three brief letters at the beginning of the novel, and two short ones at the end frame what is in effect one extended letter written by Walsingham to his friend, Rosanna. This structure recalls Charlotte Smith's *Letters of a Solitary Wanderer*, where, likewise, what begins as a novel of letters soon collapses into a single-voiced narrative account. Unlike in the *Solitary Wanderer*, however, there *is* a brief resumption of correspondence at the conclusion of *Walsingham*. Furthermore, this modified epistolarity does not suggest the (future) inadequacy of the genre for Robinson; she would return once more to a structured novel of letters in *The False Friend* (1799). Despite the decreasing importance of epistolary novels in general at the close of the 1790s, Robinson continued to privilege the sense of immediacy and the focus on heightened subjectivity afforded by the genre, and, in contrast to other writers of the period, would continue to use it to present, among her ongoing thematic concerns, a progressive political awareness.[30]

In his letter/narrative, Walsingham relates the story of his life, from the brief idyllic period of his infancy to the trials and tribulations that thereafter seem constantly to pursue him. The son of a poor Welsh curate, Walsingham is taken at a very early age (soon after his mother's death) to live with his aunt and uncle, the Aubreys, in their Gothic mansion, Glenowen. This blissful childhood period is brief, however, for upon the death of Sir Edward Aubrey and the birth of his child, Sir Sidney, that follows shortly after, Walsingham is removed from his privileged position in the family. The hostility which now informs his reception is the source of Walsingham's unremitting grief, and posits the theme of the inherent injustice of arbitrary, inherited privilege and power as the dominant concern of the text.

The adventures that Walsingham encounters are numerous and varied: he challenges Sir Sidney to a duel, following which he exiles himself from Glenowen; he is introduced, by Colonel Aubrey, the brother of Lady Aubrey's late husband, to fashionable society, where he becomes the victim of a gambling scam; he is mistakenly arrested at least three times, and he seduces and later betrays an innocent young woman, Amelia Woodford, who has fallen in love with him but who, as it turns out, unknown to Walsingham, had been engaged to none other than Colonel Aubrey himself. (Walsingham, for most of the novel, is in love with his childhood companion, Isabella.) Alongside these adventures, his experiences with dissipated society repeatedly reinforce his own profound sense of alienation and disenfranchisement. Eventually, events lead Walsingham back to Glenowen, where Lady Aubrey, and later Sir Sidney, have fallen ill. Following the deaths of the housekeeper, Mrs Blagden, and her son Edward (who, it transpires, is Walsingham's half-brother) Lady Aubrey reveals the secret surrounding the family: it turns out that Sidney is really a woman, but had been passed off as a man in order to ensure the family inheritance: the allocation of substantial sums and properties had been, in Sir Edward Aubrey's will, contingent to the birth of a *male* heir. It is revealed that Sidney herself had all the while been in love with Walsingham, and had repeatedly persuaded other women who had been attracted to him to distance themselves from the object of her affections. For himself, Walsingham immediately acknowledges his love for Sidney. At the same time, in his eagerness to give her a dose of medicine, he inadvertently gives her poison, and flees to the Continent, leaving her in a near-death state. Here, his long, four-volume letter ends. The two short letters that mark the conclusion of the novel inform us of Sidney's recovery and her marriage to Walsingham.

The reversal of gender, declared only at the very end of the novel, moves the implausibility that had characterized much of the plot to a new, even disconcerting level. However, as opposed to *Hubert de Sevrac*, where startling plot developments occur with no narrative preparation whatsoever, Robinson intersperses subtle hints throughout *Walsingham* that prepare the reader for the revelation that appears at its conclusion. For example, early in the novel Sidney exclaims, "It shall terminate, by Heavens! It shall terminate. The fatal secret shall be unfolded, and I will dissemble no longer" (p. 147). Thus, alongside improbable coincidences and adventures similar to those in *Hubert de Sevrac*, there *is* a more coherent management of narrative events in *Walsingham* than in the earlier text. It is clear that Sidney's gender reversal derives from a conscious authorial aim, as the ultimate manifestation of the worldview that Robinson displays.[31] This is a fragmented world in which the tyranny of inherited rank and privilege prevails and where the values of truth and social justice, imbued with a progressive revolutionary awareness, appear as a desired yet fleeting ideal.

Walsingham, much like *Hubert de Sevrac*, met with little critical approbation in the contemporary periodicals. *The Analytical Review*, for example, writes of its "defective and incongruous . . . parts" and its "incredible events", and the *Monthly Review* notes its "disgust" with the novel's "improbabilities and inconsistencies."[32] Significantly, only in the avowedly conservative periodicals – *The Anti-Jacobin Review* and *The British Critic* – does this negative assessment extend to include a discussion of the political worldview presented in *Walsingham*. Thus, in addition to noting its "perplexed and improbable" plot, Robert Bisset, the reviewer for the *Anti-Jacobin* asserts:

> [Robinson's] judgement [*sic*] is frequently distorted by very false notions of politics. Like Charlotte Smith, she has conceived a very high opinion of the wisdom of the French philosophers; and, like many other female writers, as well as superficial male writers, she considers the authority of those whom she admires as equivalent to argument.[33]

Bisset's grouping of Robinson together with Smith is not surprising. He reviews Smith's *The Young Philosopher* in the same issue of the journal, and, as we saw in an earlier chapter, both novels were represented there in Gillray's satirical print "The New Morality", as part of the radical, subversive literature that lay scattered on the ground.[34]

The fact that the political agenda in Robinson's novel was easily identified by the reactionary periodicals exhibits how, in Sharon Setzer's words, "English conservatives frequently connected the twin threats of gender and class crossing with . . . the invasive force of revolutionary ideology."[35] Setzer's work, as well as the assessment of the *Anti-Jacobin Review*, identifies the disruptive force of Sidney Aubrey's gender reversal as a response to the French Revolution. In the discussion that follows I will likewise focus on Robinson's portrayal of gender as a central element in her political critique, but one that is part of a wide-ranging, more general commentary on the social and political landscape of the revolutionary decade. Walsingham's Godwinian appeal to "sublime and immutable truth" (p. 94) at the outset of a novel that repeatedly portrays mistaken arrests, censorship and the immovable power of social and gender hegemonies, and his invocation of "GENIUS, TRUTH and NATURE!" (p. 496) at its conclusion, frame this work as an expression of a progressive yet recognizably tenuous cultural ideal at the very moment when the triumph of the reaction is imminent.

Current interest in the construction and performativity of gender perhaps explains why *Walsingham* has received substantially more critical attention than Robinson's other novels. In an argument that exemplifies this critical focus, Chris Cullens presents a reading of the novel that centers on issues of gender performance and their enactment within a larger context of social disruption. Thus, the transvestism at the center of the novel is indicative of a "world turned upside down" in which "[f]rom the hidden nucleus of Sidney's secret a virus of contagious destabilization seems to spread out, for the use of the transvestite motif in the novel is directly linked to the more general epistemological breakdown of social semantics portrayed in it."[36]

In addressing Robinson's central theme of destabilization, I first want to briefly discuss the two masquerade scenes in *Walsingham*, which allusively acknowledge the gender disguise yet also point to a wider cultural degeneracy in the world that the novel presents. The proximity of the masked balls – just a few weeks separate one masquerade from the next – registers the intensity of Robinson's critique, and is all the more noteworthy in light of the decline of masquerading as a preeminent social activity at the end of the eighteenth century. As Terry Castle has shown, following its heightened popularity throughout the eighteenth century, the masquerade experienced an abrupt decline at its close, and, "[b]y the time of the French Revolution, [it] had fallen quite precipitately out of fashion."[37] It would seem, then, that the characters in *Walsingham's* fictional world are engaged in what would already be an archaic, out-dated mode of entertainment, a fact of which Robinson, always acutely aware of fashion, would certainly have been aware.[38] Yet despite – or perhaps because of – its anachronistic status, the masquerade functions on a symbolic register to encapsulate the cultural instability at the heart of the text, with its emphasis on false perception, excess and a kind of destructive social chaos.

The masquerade as an emblematic moment of disruption is immediately clear to Walsingham himself. He perceives the first ball as "all ... bustle and confusion. The number of black dominos nearly presented a sombre similarity, which levelled all forms and features to one gloomy mass of insipidity," (p. 273). As Castle has noted, an abundance of guests attired in the domino – a plain black cloak or robe – imposes an "enigmatic uniformity" on the crowd, one which is, at the same time, "somewhat sinister [in its] power of effacement, its utter incommunativeness."[39] The fact that Walsingham (who is also dressed as a domino) concurrently perceives characters disguised as "Venus", "Diana", a "blue-eyed nun", "Zephyrus" and others (p. 273) adds a further degree of perplexity to this uniformity and contributes to the overall mayhem of the scene.

At the same time, the frolics of the masquerade are not very dissimilar to the other descriptions of social life that appear throughout *Walsingham*. This is truly a society in which frivolity, deception and disguise are ubiquitous, and in which empty conversation is not limited to the mindless chatter of masquerades. Walsingham's thoughts upon entering the faro room at Bath could easily serve to describe the masquerade itself:

> The spirit of mischief there revelled with renovated vigour. Gold flew round, like dust before the whirlwind; and dissipation reared her standard over the brow of reason, terribly triumphant. It was the pandemonium of licentiousness; every vice was tolerated, every mind contaminated by the force of pernicious example. (p. 180)

The comment of one Lady Fubsy, during a momentary lull in the conversation of this same group of revelers – "How awful is this silence!" she complains – (p. 200) illustrates the vacuity of this milieu, in which empty talk continually propels itself on, but nothing substantial is ever really said.

The fact that the masquerade is both showcased at the center of *Walsingham*, but at the same time is not completely distinct, or distinguishable from the goings-on of society in general, reflects Robinson's use of the convention as a critique of the contemporary social world, one which, moreover, represents an interesting departure from what Castle identifies as a prominent function of masquerade episodes in eighteenth-century fiction. Castle argues that:

> the masquerade episode precipitates plot ... a comic plot in particular. It engenders a rewarding or euphoric pattern of narrative transformation, even for characters ... whom one would not expect to benefit from its disarming travesties. [...] [T]he masquerade stands out in eighteenth-century

narrative as an indispensable event … without which the comic destiny of characters could not be realized.[40]

The masquerades in *Walsingham* deviate from this pattern, leading to neither reward nor euphoria. Rather, the first masked ball sets up a plot situation that will result in tragedy following the second, and cannot really be seen, even within the overall conceptualization of the narrative, as generating its eventual comic resolution – the union of Walsingham and Sidney. Walsingham, despite the seriousness with which he perceives himself, is drawn into the destructive energy of the masquerade and succumbs with little resistance to the force of its promiscuous potential. His initial reluctance to attend the first ball is replaced by an immediate determination to attend the second one as he *"flew* to the scene of folly and intrigue" (p. 284). Although his determination is motivated by the desire to confront his beloved Isabella once more – and indeed, he perceives himself surrounded by "at least, a dozen Isabellas" (p. 285) – Walsingham eventually makes Amelia the victim of his negative impulses. Mistaking her in her disguise for the woman he loves, he leads her first into a carriage and then into his bed. The moment of seduction is characterized by an overall sense of the mistaken perception that constitutes the most prominent feature of the masquerade itself:

> The inordinate quantity of wine which in my rage and vexation I had swallowed, soon took possession of my brain. I knew not where I was; the image of Isabella still predominated, while indignation and revenge occupied the throne of reason! I fetched the light which my servant had left upon the table to see whether her features began to reanimate; my limbs were unsteady – I reeled – the candlestick fell from my hand; while the faintest dawn of day entered between the shutters. I fell at the feet of my beautiful *incognita*. – She wept, and sighed; she hid her face upon my shoulder…all the laws of honour were violated – and – I was a villain! (p. 290)

The seduction does indeed have a tragic outcome. Amelia is unable to overcome the remorse which follows her willingness to have sex with Walsingham, and wastes away in grief until her eventual death. Likewise, the incident does not – to understate the issue – bring out the best in Walsingham: his repeated refusal to accept responsibility for his actions, which, as convention dictated, would include marriage to Amelia, posits him at best as a libertine, and qualifies his insistent self-portrayal as the perpetual victim of unscrupulous society.[41] Walsingham's equivocal and evasive behavior towards Amelia, and the eventual tragedy of her death locate the masked ball as an "exemplary locus" of a "World Turned Upside Down",[42] which, rather than enabling a recuperative movement in the text, serves to characterize and foreground the negative energy of the society that Robinson portrays, and which is especially pernicious in regard to economically or socially vulnerable women.

Yet despite his troubling complicity with the norms of the masquerade, and thus with the decadent social order in general (behavior which recalls Hubert de Sevrac's use of the *lettre de cachet*) it is clear that Walsingham can both victimize and be victimized at the same time. The various ways in which he is pursued by society include three cases of false arrest as well as ongoing humiliation and ridicule at the hands of the nobility. The accumulative effect of Walsingham's series of misfortunes serves to emphasize the vulnerability – indeed the utter helplessness – of the disempowered subject when confronted with institutional systems of power. Bisset, in *The Anti-Jacobin*, was quick to recognize the political element of such a representation, writing in his review of *Walsingham* that:

> [Robinson's] peers and peeresses are all either weak or wicked. The miseries and the vices of the *low* are uniformly deduced from the oppressions and the vices of the *high*; ... [t]his representation is hurtful, because it tends to encourage the dislike for nobility, which, from the spirit of insubordination, and the fanciful notions of equality, is already too prevalent.[43]

As Bisset correctly notes, Robinson concentrates primarily on the manners and intrigue of the upper classes to delineate a staunchly political worldview. At the same time, an anti-nobility bias is also expressed by the working-class characters in the novel and contributes to the overall sense of insubordination which causes the periodical's reviewer so much unease. Thus, the turnkey who ostensibly guards Walsingham during one of his sojourns in prison says:

> vy ve have a bit of a club here in the wicinity of the prison, and it vou'd make your hair stand on end, vas you but to hear how ve talks politics! [. . .] ve begins to know a thing or two, and to walue our rights and our priwleges, as vell as our betters. (pp. 249–50)

Likewise, a conversation among a group of undertakers whom Walsingham meets on one of his adventures provides another representation of working-class political awareness: "There's more fuss about one titled carcase [*sic*] than about twenty wholesome bodies [one coffin-bearer says.] But all trades must thrive; and half the great folks we convey home are better dead than living," (p. 330).

The *Anti-Jacobin's* review also refers to the one scene in *Walsingham* in which Robinson enables her protagonist to engage in an outright political confrontation with his noble opponents, and in which the novel's ideological agenda is explicitly aligned to the French Revolution. Soon after his abandonment of Amelia, Walsingham arrives at Bath, where, upon entering the library, he encounters some of his fashionable acquaintances. Their attitude towards him, that of "insolent contempt" (p. 334) receives a parallel in their disregard to literary texts themselves: "[p]lays, pamphlets, novels, magazines and reviews were handed round, and as quickly, with their leaves unopened, returned to the librarian" (p. 334). The literary chatter of the nobles is intermixed with repeated attempts to incite and humiliate Walsingham, and the discussion soon becomes marked along political, class-based lines. Thus, in response to a comment that "some law should be made to rescue people of rank from the animadversions of impertinent scribblers" (p. 343), he replies that "the most powerful of the human race, in these momentous times, are *men of letters*, not men of *titles*: – those who can guide the *pen*, and influence the country by the genuine language of truth and philanthropy" (p. 345).

This representation of the tension between a redemptive, meritocratic and morally-engaged literary labor and the political reality that surrounds it reiterates a popular Robinson theme. Significantly here, the oppositional and marginalized status of the artist is directly linked to an identification with the values of the French Revolution, as Robinson's protagonist extends his argument:

> the convulsions of France are like the contending symptoms of vitality where the object has been benumbed by suspended circulation. The ears of princes in the atmosphere of Versailles were deaf to supplicating merit: their hearts were closed against suffering talents, by a petrifying torpidity, and their minds contaminated by false and vicious counselors, – till nature shuddered at their injustice, and reason nerved her arm to scourge them. Every neglected man of genius became the enemy of despotism; every exalted son of illustrious intellect flew to the standard of tremendous retribution. (p. 346)

In considering this social commentary – the ongoing, strident critique of nobility and the vindication of the original revolutionary effort – we must remember that while Walsingham is speaking in late 1791, when such views were part of prevailing liberal thought,[44] Robinson is writing in 1797, when those same views were conspicuously outside of the consensus. This is another illustration of the distancing strategy that we viewed in *Hubert de Sevrac* where, it will be recalled, the characters of the novel were able to articulate a pro-Revolution stand that preceded, and thus was able to circumvent, the atrocities of the Terror.

Accordingly, although Walsingham/Robinson specifically links revolutionary energy to the triumph of "supplicating merit" and "suffering talents", this vision is contradicted by the bleakness of the social arena in which it is enacted. Literary merit, as we see in the scene in the Bath library, is marginalized by the power of those who reign in society by virtue of inherited privilege. Clearly reflecting the climate in which her novel was written rather than that in which it takes place, Robinson's depiction of the cultural landscape illustrates her understanding that the Revolution was ultimately unable to revitalize literature as a site of political influence or to resolve issues of tyranny and social inequality. As she repeatedly shows us, the "petrifying torpidity" which had characterized *ancien régime* France is a prominent feature of contemporary British society. Just as her novel satirizes this society, it recognizes (and mourns) past aspirations and a failed reformist vision.

It is not surprising then that the scene in the Bath library also includes a reference to free speech and censorship. In praising the liberal daily newspapers, Walsingham warns against a time "when that source of public information, which has so long been the pride of Englishmen, shall be closed and annihilated" (p. 343). This warning is scorned by his noble auditors, and the conversation almost immediately ends, but the seriousness of the subject – and the fact that the curtailing of free speech is an issue that deeply concerns Robinson – is evinced when Walsingham addresses the matter once again following his return to Glenowen. In arriving at a neighboring public house, he thinks: "it is there that the wants of the little, and the follies of the great, are investigated with that freedom of speech which is the birthright of mankind, and which was once the pride of a degenerated people" (p. 480). As Julie Shaffer notes, Robinson is alluding here to the Treasonable Practices Act and the Seditious Meetings Act that had been passed late in 1795,[45] and which granted the authorities strict control over public meetings and gatherings convened for the purposes of political debate. This reference once again calls attention to the 1797 (rather than 1791) awareness that permeates the novel and to its study of political defeat.

Nowhere in *Walsingham* is this general sense of defeat more conspicuous than in the character of Sidney Aubrey. Cross-dressed since birth, Sidney exemplifies both a critique of "the passage of property from male to male that left women by and large economically handicapped"[46] as well as functioning as a signifier of the overall destabilization of society itself that Robinson presents. Thus, while recent criticism of the novel contextualizes Sidney's transvestism within a tradition of crossdressing in the eighteenth century,[47] I believe that her particular case does not signal the continuity of, or identification with, an implied exuberance of blurring, or of upsetting gender boundaries, but rather, foregrounds the victimization inherent in the masquerade which she is forced to perform. The fact that Sidney herself unwillingly complies with this masquerade is evinced in the following cry of despair, one which occurs early in the novel: "Oh Walsingham! [she says] ... what a devoted wretch am I! What a despicable, monstrous hypocrite! Could you behold my palpitating heart; could you but read the dark and cureless sorrows of my destiny,"(p. 151).

Sidney's sense of herself as a "devoted wretch" attests to the fact that her disguise is sustained only through obedience to her mother's demands, which originate in the material goals of inheritance and property. And yet, Lady Aubrey's insistence on passing her daughter off as male derives not only from the fact that she is attempting to manipulate a reality defined by male privilege and power. Notwithstanding either her original motives, or her daughter's evident distress, she appears intent upon perpetuating the masquerade only because she is vulnerable to the blackmail of the housekeeper Mrs Blagden, whose own actions are motivated by both greed and revenge. Yet, as events tumultuously unfold in *Walsingham's* denouement, and secret after secret is revealed, we learn that even Mrs Blagden, the "tyrant of Glenowen" (p. 450), is responding to her own, personal experience of loss, as the abandoned lover of Walsingham's father, and in the words of Walsingham's half-brother, "the early victim of our fickle parent's violated promises" (p. 485). As Setzer notes, "the story might have been different had it been told from her point of view ... [that of] the displaced object of Mr Ainsforth's attentions and the bearer of his child."[48] Thus, while Mrs Blagden is the source of the misguided scheme that generates the novel's narrative action, Robinson also reminds us that she, too, has been subjected to injustice. Mrs Blagden is yet another victim among the many who populate *Walsingham*: Sidney, Lady Aubrey, Amelia Woodford and Colonel Aubrey (who not only loses his fiancée, Amelia, to Walsingham's seduction and its tragic consequences, but also, through Lady Aubrey's deception, his right to inherit his brother's property) and, of course, Walsingham himself. Marginalized by either status or gender or both, *Walsingham's* various victims signify in their aggregate the delineation of oppression as Robinson's central thematic concern.

Despite this focus, Robinson concedes to convention by allowing a fortuitous conclusion to her protagonist's story – he marries the woman he loves and is awarded the financial security that has always been legally his due. Before that can occur, however, there is one more obstacle to overcome: Walsingham, soon after learning Sidney's true gender, inadvertently gives her a dose of laudanum and leaves her in a near-death state, escaping to the Continent to await the outcome of the event (and to write the long letter to Rosanna which comprises the novel). While calling attention to the somewhat immature and irresponsible behavior that has characterized Walsingham throughout the narrative, this sequence of events – Sidney's near-fatal illness and his abrupt retreat from her bedside – also has a necessary thematic function. As Chris Cullens explains:

> the text of the novel, which is also the story of the narrator's life, is fashioned during precisely that interval in which Sidney's refashioning as female occurs offstage – and whether Sidney is actually alive during this interval seems oddly irrelevant to the narrator and author ... [For] the transvestite Sidney must "die" as a male, or at least be confined to the passivity of unconscious immobility, in order to be reborn female.[49]

Yet, in spite of the ease and expediency with the novel concludes, in which Walsingham and a "completely... changed... purely gentle... feminine" (p. 495) Sidney are united, *Walsingham*, to cite Cullens again, "taken in total, also consists of an articulate sigh, as well as an at times numbingly monotonous howl of rage."[50] The scars that remain from the struggle for survival in an unjust world, which, as Robinson knows well, cannot simply be erased, are fittingly displayed in Walsingham's concluding letter to Rosanna:

> retired from the busy varying scenes of noise and folly, I leave those trifling vicious reptiles whom you have met with during the progress of my disastrous story, to the infamy that will mark their names... If they continue to triumph over the children of worth and genius, it will only prove that, in this indefinable sphere, where the best and wisest cannot hope for happiness, the *demons of art* are permitted to oppress with wrongs, while they lift the empty brow of arrogance above the illustrious pupils of GENIUS, TRUTH, and NATURE! (p. 496)

Calling attention to alienation and oppression rather than to conjugal felicity, these concluding comments ultimately testify to the bleakness of Robinson's vision.

Robinson's understanding that "the best and wisest cannot hope for happiness" indirectly points us once more to her engagement with the place of the artist in society, the consciousness of which continues to inform her literary project. One of her final works, the *Sylphid*, which appeared regularly in the *Morning Post* in a series of installments in 1799–1800, and which was later included in Volume III of her *Memoirs*, includes numerous and varied references to "neglected genius" and to an artistic struggle for survival. As Robinson's airy, bodiless sylph traverses Britain and beyond, it repeatedly juxtaposes this struggle to the same "brilliant scenes of dissipated folly"[51] that she addresses so frequently. Thus, the sylph observes:

> the genuine sons and daughters of the Muses, pining in obscure poverty, and labouring incessantly for a scanty pittance. No splendours decorated their neglected habitation; no luxuries were seen on the board of weary toil. Ah! Race neglected by the proud, unhonoured by the ignorant! TIME will record your names and consecrate your labours! (p. 19)

This is familiar rhetoric from Robinson in its depiction of ostracized intellectual endeavor and which, as we have seen, is repeatedly intertwined within her representations of social and political upheaval during those same years when she herself "labour[ed] incessantly" at writing. Thus, in 1790, the "best and the wisest", personified in Robert Merry, were envisioned as holding a privileged role in shaping a new and vibrant society that lay just within reach, just as the failure of the Revolution later inscribed their marginality. As her portrayal of the literary landscape signals this movement, it also stresses the ideological provenance of her work. In doing so, it insistently reminds us of the brief moment of hope enabled by the unique historical period in which she wrote, but even more so, expresses an articulate sigh that acknowledges what might have been.

IV

I want to conclude my discussion of Mary Robinson by briefly discussing her friendship with William Godwin in the final years of her life, a friendship that acknowledges the kind of literary, intellectual, politically progressive community that she repeatedly privileges in her writing.[52] Robinson was first introduced to Godwin by Robert Merry in February 1796, and Godwin's diary for that year and for early 1797 provides evidence of their frequent contact: he would meet her, often with mutual friends such as Mary Wollstonecraft, Mary Hays, Amelia Opie, Thomas Holcroft and Samuel Jackson Pratt, for dinner, supper or tea. Godwin stopped seeing Robinson after his marriage to Wollstonecraft in April 1797, but their meetings resumed in 1799, with Godwin now a widower, at times on an almost daily basis. For instance, during the first two weeks of June 1800, Godwin and Robinson met eight times. Again, they were often joined by other writers and artists, including, in this period, Samuel Taylor Coleridge, John and Eliza Fenwick, the painter James Northcote, John Wolcot (Peter Pindar) and the novelist Jane Porter.

While Robinson's letters clearly indicate the social and intellectual benefits she derived from her friendship with Godwin, we may also note in passing that the connection was advantageous for him as well. Judith Pascoe, in her discussion of Robinson's role as poetry editor of the *Morning Post*, has shown that "the paper's allusions to those she knew fluctuated according to their place in her affections", hence, as her friendship with Godwin grew stronger, he "became the recipient of a number of compliments" in the newspaper. For example, on 13 August 1800, the *Post* wrote that "Mr. Godwin is so popular in Ireland, that he is courted and caressed in all the most distinguished societies, both of *genius* and of *political* importance".[53]

In the late summer of 1800, in fact, just around the time the *Morning Post* bestowed this praise on Godwin, his friendship with Robinson was being severely tested. Paula Byrne suggests that the two had quarreled over money matters: in the spring of that year Robinson had been arrested for debt and it is likely that Godwin had paid the £63 necessary to secure her release but had asked for some form of security in return for the loan.[54] It is also possible that Robinson was more immediately upset by Godwin's suggestion that she receive a visit from his friend, the Irish barrister John Philpot Curran; the subject of his proposed visit repeatedly appears in their correspondence as a matter of contention. The intensity of the feelings that the row exposed on both sides is striking, as Godwin and Robinson address the tensions that had emerged in the course of their friendship. In the letters exchanged between the two in late August and early September there is a sense of deep personal hurt. Godwin accuses Robinson of "inconstancy in friendship", of "alternate kindness and indifference" and of having a "cold heart."[55] She, in turn, claims that he had, in "mixed societies ... appeared to feel pleasure, in humbling [her] vanity", and felt little esteem for her "humble Talents" in general.[56] Notwithstanding her literary achievements, Robinson was oppressed with feelings of failure, which were surely exacerbated by the bluntness of Godwin's remarks and by her sense of the vulnerability of her present situation – ill, poor and away from the metropolis.[57] "You tell me that I have 'literary Fame'," she writes to him, "How comes it then that I am abused, neglected, – unhonoured, – unrewarded [?]"[58] On 1 September, Godwin visited Robinson at her home in Englefield Green, seventeen miles outside London, and her letter to him written the next day suggests that amends were eventually made during his stay. She died on 26 December; Godwin noted her death in his diary. On 30 December he would return to Englefield Green for her funeral.

I find this exchange compelling for the way it illuminates various aspects of community and isolation in the radical literary milieu of the late 1790s, and provides access, however brief, to ideological and philosophical concepts such as truth and sincerity as they come under the pressures of lived experience. Godwin's gradual acknowledgement of the place of the feelings, and his own greater acquiescence to sensibility has been amply discussed, in particular in the context of his relations with Mary Wollstonecraft, but also with his wider social circle. Most recently, Pamela Clemit has shown how Godwin's letters reveal "the dictates of pure theory [that have] been modified in the crucible of experience", and how in the aftermath of Wollstonecraft's death, his "vulnerable interior voice register[s] the moment when his theories had come smack against the rock of experience."[59] Mark Philp mentions Robinson as among those besides Wollstonecraft to whom Godwin is indebted for the revision of his philosophical worldview, as moral obligations become grounded "more consistently in the emotions and feelings of the individual – in the natural sympathies rather than in reason."[60] Godwin's "natural sympathies" were also noted by Robinson herself in her letter of 24 August, written in the midst of their dispute:

> I ventured to know you, rather to wonder at your wisdom, than to idolize your heart. I met you as a tutor of the <u>mind</u>, and I never expected to find you, as associate of the <u>soul</u> ... I have, from time to time, seen you in new points of view. I have <u>wondered</u>, – pardon the expression, at your sensibility!^[61]

It seems likely that Robinson's and Godwin's final meeting was motivated by a flexible application of philosophical principles and "sensibility" – of reason, emotion and sincerity – which ensured that, although they might not have resolved all their differences, they did at least part friends.[62]

Around the same time as her quarrel with Godwin, Robinson wrote to her friend, the novelist Jane Porter, of her vision of a "select society…a little colony of mental powers, a world of talents, drawn into a small but brilliant circle." This letter at first displays a more optimistic tone than the letters to Godwin, in projecting Robinson's view of a privileged artistic community. As the letter continues, however, we also see the signs of the disappointment she had so lately and deeply felt, and the feelings of neglect such as she had conveyed to Godwin: "Visionary idea! [she writes to Porter] It can never be!"[63] Similarly to what had appeared in her published writings, Robinson can still identify with, and cling to, a vision of shared intellectual endeavor, with its comforts of friendship and mutual esteem. Yet at the close of her life, and for life itself, she cannot provide a felicitous conclusion, as she also acknowledges the reality of her isolation.

5

"Newgate Before My Eyes": Elizabeth Inchbald I

Of the three authors whom I discuss in this study, Elizabeth Inchbald (1753–1821) is the one most prominently identified as a radical. Gary Kelly famously inscribed her (together with William Godwin, Thomas Holcroft and Robert Bage) as one of the "English Jacobins" whose work helped shape political thinking during the Revolutionary decade, and who formed a "community of reaction towards the events and issues of the time, which in turn shaped their community of ideas in common ways."[1] Kelly's observation reflects the perception of Inchbald's contemporaries as well: both the *Anti-Jacobin Review* and *The True Briton* singled her out for particular censure, calling attention to her "democratic" principles.[2]

Alongside this recognition of her political affiliations, Inchbald's career was also informed by caution. Widowed at a young age, she valued above all her financial stability and independence, having struggled in her early life, working first as an actress before eventually publishing twenty plays, two novels and a substantial body of theatre criticism. And as a successful yet politically-engaged author, Inchbald was cognizant of the need to accommodate her published writings within the realms of institutional approval, although not necessarily of popular consensus, ever aware of the censorial forces at work during the times in which she wrote. In a letter written to William Godwin while she was completing her novel *Nature and Art* (1796) she states that she has "Newgate before [her] eyes"[3] a comment that exemplifies her consciousness of the oppressive climate that characterized England during the 1790s and of the limitations that restrained her presentation of a political agenda. This understanding was most certainly (and ominously) reinforced by personal experience: as her biographer James Boaden writes, "she used to receive anonymous letters occasionally, of *caution*, as to [her] publications."[4]

Yet in spite of these pressures, Inchbald was unable, or unwilling to distance herself from an association with the turbulent issues that were unfolding during the 1790s. Her recognition of the fine line that she had to negotiate in publishing politically contentious material manifests itself in various thematic strategies present in her work, as well as in the compromises she ultimately had to make. These compromises are particularly evident in her work for the stage, where, as we will see in the following chapter, political matters are presented only to be ambivalently resolved in conclusions that belie the ideological force with which they were introduced.

Inchbald herself addressed the issue of political awareness as it traverses both novels and drama in an essay written in 1807 for Prince Hoare's periodical *The Artist*:

> The Novelist is a free agent. He lives in a land of liberty, whilst The Dramatic Writer exists but under a despotic government. – Passing over the subjection in which an author of plays is held by the Lord Chamberlain's office, and the degree of dependence which he has on his actors – he is the very slave of the audience. He must have their tastes and prejudices in view, not to correct, but to humour them.[5]

Inchbald emphasizes here the limitations of genre, acknowledging the institutionalized censorship of the theatre which legally forbade during the 1790s the production of plays supporting the French Revolution or criticizing the British government, or addressing oppositional issues at all.[6] However, her use of metaphors of liberty and tyranny also suggests the ubiquity of the political awareness that pervades her writings regardless of genre and whose tensions and manifestations she openly avows.

At the same time, Inchbald's political engagement is treated ambivalently by her biographers. Boaden conceives of her politics as of a "temporary nature"[7] and mainly as an extension of her personal friendship with Godwin and Thomas Holcroft, and thus as those of someone who had simply fallen "into the wrong hands."[8] Likewise, Annibel Jenkins concludes her recent biography of Inchbald by writing:

> Mrs. Inchbald had a wide knowledge of the political scene from 1780–1810, but she is never outspoken about the government ... [S]he must have heard over and over the views of both Holcroft and Godwin, and for that matter she must have heard both Kemble and Sheridan make comments ... As we look back on Inchbald's life and work, it is not possible to speak definitely about her political views, especially since those were the years when England became embroiled in the war with France.[9]

Note how this argument stresses Inchbald's passivity: she has heard the men speak, and it is this act of listening which, for Jenkins, defines Inchbald's own political presence. Although she concedes that Inchbald had "strong opinions"[10] those opinions are rarely given center stage in her study, but rather linked, as in Boaden, to personal friendships and social interaction.

Despite this marginalization of Inchbald's politics, Jenkins's grouping of Holcroft and Godwin, on the one hand, and of John Phillip Kemble and Richard Sheridan on the other, is instructive, as it connects Inchbald's politics to her movement within different literary circles, and thus reflects her own parallel literary work – in novel writing and in the theatre. The fact that Inchbald *was* more circumspect as a playwright may partially explain the perception of her biographers, who view the accumulative effect of her writing as a whole, and thus, under the impression of the prudence of her staged work are able to relegate her radicalism (when they are forced to admit of its existence) merely to social connections or to a passing fashion. Conversely, Gary Kelly, interested primarily in Inchbald's novels, can unequivocally acknowledge her "Jacobinism" by virtue of a more exclusionary generic focus.[11]

In this chapter, I will present a discussion of Inchbald's novels – *A Simple Story* (1791) and *Nature and Art* (1796) that shows how they repeatedly articulate those concerns which were thrust into the forefront of public consciousness by the French Revolution and the struggle for domestic reform: hierarchal social structures, tyrannical patriarchy and institutional injustice. And yet it is important to note that Inchbald's work during this period, excepting the suppressed play *The Massacre* (1792, which will be discussed in the following chapter) is devoid of outright references to specific contemporary events, a fact that may appear curious in light of the conspicuousness of her political identification, but which actually attests to the complexity of its expression. Thus, among the questions that I will be asking in my discussion of Inchbald are: How can we attribute a certain, at times diffuse, ideological awareness to a pro-Revolution stand? In what forms of indirection is it articulated? How does Inchbald navigate the politically-charged issues which attracted her, and from which, despite her caution, she could not dissociate herself? In attempting to answer these questions, I will be attentive to instances of silencing and censorship, extra-literary ones, to be sure, but also representations within the texts themselves that reflect the external pressures that accompanied their publication. What emerges, I will argue, is the recognition that Inchbald's work is indeed characterized by an "outspokenness", as she presents a consistent critique of institutional systems of power and the domestic rebellion that is always ultimately subdued.

I

In 1791, after years of writing, revising, combining and setting aside, Inchbald published *A Simple Story*, her two-generational story of rebellion and submission.[12] Notwithstanding its name, the novel is, in Boaden's words, "anything but simple", an assessment with which present-day critics, despite their varied readings of the text, unanimously agree.[13] The novel tells the story of Miss Milner, a rich, high-spirited and independent-minded young woman and her love for her guardian, Dorriforth, a Catholic priest. After inheriting the title of Lord Elmwood and being released from his vows, and after a stormy courtship period, the two marry. Moving seventeen years ahead in time, it transpires that, after a blissful beginning, the marriage had ended in disaster following Miss Milner's affair with a suitor from her past while her husband had been abroad. Overcome with guilt and remorse upon his return, she accepts a life of banishment and exile, one that is imposed upon their daughter, Matilda, as well, by her unforgiving father. The second part of the novel relates Lord Elmwood's vengeful behavior towards, and later reconciliation with Matilda, who, unlike her mother, is attracted rather than repelled by the exertion of patriarchal authority.

The radicalism of *A Simple Story* appears in its delineation of character and theme, with Inchbald's progressive views appearing most prominently in the portrayal of Miss Milner as the embodiment of an exuberant, libertarian impulse towards female freedom and independence. Her presence controlling the entire first half of the narrative, Miss Milner is, in Terry Castle's words, a heroine whose "desires repeatedly triumph over masculine prerogative; familial, religious and psychic patterns of male domination collapse in the face of her persistent will to liberty."[14] The energy and vitality of this character have led many critics, beginning with Boaden, to note the autobiographical parallels which underline Inchbald's portrayal of her central heroine, not least the possibility that Dorriforth was modeled after the actor and theatre manager John Phillip Kemble, a close friend of Inchbald's and a man with whom, perhaps, she had been in love.[15]

While an autobiographical parallel may in fact resonate throughout the novel, I believe there is another, more pertinent form of self-reflexivity present in *A Simple Story*, one which manifests itself in the ways the two halves of the narrative inform one another to exhibit a broader, more nuanced political consciousness. For Inchbald's worldview is implicated not only in her portrayal of Miss Milner, but also, to a certain degree, in that of Matilda, that is to say, both in the desired resistance to hierarchal systems of power, but also in the realization of the limitations, indeed, of the futility of that resistance. After briefly rehearsing the radical implications of the character of Miss Milner, I want, in the discussion that follows, to focus on this movement between idealism and reality, between radicalism and caution, for the ways that it exposes the self-conscious political tensions underlying *A Simple Story*. This is a positioning that will, in various ways, persist as a prominent feature of Inchbald's presentation of a progressive political agenda throughout her literary career.

Inchbald's ideological concerns are immediately evident with the introduction of Miss Milner into the narrative. If, as Claudia Johnson writes, "innovative social conduct ... feminine desire and illicit sex" are the major themes appropriated by women writers in shaping their response to Burke's *Reflections on the Revolution in France*, and thus to the revolutionary discourse that dominated the 1790s,[16] then Miss Milner may serve as an exemplary representation of this response. Not only does she desire – "I love [Dorriforth] with all the passion of a mistress and all the tenderness of a wife," she exclaims to her companion Miss Woodley – but her desire is, furthermore, directed towards an object doubly forbidden; Dorriforth is not only her guardian, but also a Catholic priest.[17] The centrality of the guardian/ward, or tutor/pupil love plot within the novel, radical in itself in English fiction of the period,[18] at once points to Inchbald's aim of collapsing socially-imposed barriers of hierarchy, propriety and convention. The significance that Inchbald assigns to this theme (as well as to female desire itself) is underscored in its appearance elsewhere in her writings. Note, for example, the similarity between Miss Milner's impassioned confession and one that occurs in Inchbald's play *The Child of Nature* (1788). There, Amanthis, a young woman raised in seclusion by her father's friend, Almanza, cries out, at the moment when she recognizes her love for her guardian, "Ah! can I behold you at my feet? You to whom I ought to kneel as my father; but whom I would rather thus tenderly embrace as a lover."[19]

Alongside desire, Miss Milner's conception of love also implies power, freedom and independence. The fact that it is during the period following her engagement to Dorriforth that she appears most unsettled and restless – she spends money recklessly, stays out till late hours and behaves insolently, purposely disobeying her guardian's orders – points to her attempt to grasp whatever power she can, in the brief moment *when* she can. As she says to Miss Woodley, "As my guardian, I certainly did obey him; and I could obey him as a husband; but as a lover, I will not" (p. 154). Miss Milner's recognition of the male privilege that proscribes and limits female behavior acknowledges then, in spite of her valiant attempt to oppose them, her own consciousness of her "lack of power within the fictional world."[20] And Inchbald, notwithstanding the bold presentation of this struggle, can portray it only as one which is doomed to failure; knowing as she does the ways of the world, it can hardly be otherwise. In doing so, she replaces acts of rebellion with those of submission: Miss Milner's and Elmwood's marriage suddenly and immediately reverses the cancellation of their engagement (that had resulted from her ultimate act of disobedience, attendance at a masquerade) and is precipitated by Sandford, Elmwood's friend and spiritual guide, who, in urging them along, presents the event as a disciplinary act: "Now then, Lord Elmwood, this moment give her up for ever; or this moment constrain her by such ties from offending you, she shall not *dare* to violate" (p. 191). Although ostensibly fulfilling Miss Milner's aspirations, this moment in effect signals the success of her subjugation. Marriage, in Patricia Spacks's words, "provides the definitive means to quell female insubordination."[21]

Thus, although the marriage is described as an event of "happiness most supreme" (p. 193), it is also portrayed in terms of loss. As George Haggerty argues, the "wedding itself is a time of mourning: in finally gaining Lord

Elmwood, Miss Milner loses herself."[22] This movement is epitomized in the appearance of the mourning ring which Elmwood in his haste inadvertently gives to his bride, and whose presence gives her "excruciating shock" (p. 193) at the conclusion of Volume II of the novel. J.M.S. Tompkins claims that the ring was added at a later stage of the composition of *A Simple Story*, and views its presence as an example of the uneven connection between the two halves of the novel, as an "omen" for future unhappiness that Inchbald belatedly added when she decided to expand her original two-volume work. (A striking example of this "unevenness" and the perceived disparity between the two halves of the novel appears in the French translation of *A Simple Story*. The translator, Jean-Marie Deschamps, published the novel as two separate texts.)[23] However, I prefer to see the ring not just as a signifier of future foreboding, and the eventual collapse of the union so intensely desired. Rather, it also serves as a marker of her heroine's *present* loss – and the mourning – entailed in the moment when she willingly succumbs to the limitation of her own independence.[24]

With that in mind, the mourning ring should be seen as a sign of cohesiveness rather than disunity, as it signals the loss of self that defines the stories of both Inchbald's female protagonists: Miss Milner's rebellion and eventual failure, and her daughter Matilda's submission and ultimate "victory." To cite Spacks again, a "profound unity" in *A Simple Story* is in fact evident by virtue of this two-generation narrative, and the way it tells two different versions of the same story. Taken together, she writes:

> it becomes clear that the "daughter" can't win: either she destroys her marriage (as Lady Elmwood does) or she submits, in her own view, to becoming a cipher. The second-generation daughter, the *real* daughter, has learned the lessons of cipherhood.[25]

The second half of *A Simple Story* is concerned with what seems to be solely the desire to submit to patriarchal authority. Matilda's attraction to the exertion of her father's power is evident in her response upon hearing that he has agreed to let her live in Elmwood Castle:

> She listened sometimes with tears, sometimes with hope, but always with awe, and terror, to every sentence wherein her father was concerned. Once she called him cruel – then exclaimed "he was kind;" but at the end of Sandford's intelligence, concluded she was happy and grateful for the boon bestowed. – Even her mother had not a more exalted and transcendent idea of Lord Elmwood's worth, than his daughter had formed. (p. 218)

By appropriating the vocabulary of Gothic sublimity to introduce the second father/ daughter relationship, Inchbald calls attention once more to the preeminent theme of her novel – the exploration of power and desire and the ways that they reinforce patriarchal control. The Gothic genre is conducive for this portrayal, with its amplification of the terms in which female subjugation is enacted: Elmwood's "implacable rigour and injustice" (p. 195) together with the "forlorn . . . sedateness" (p. 216) of his daughter display the far less subtle demarcation of the lines of power that Inchbald draws in the second half of her narrative.

While I do not mean to claim that *A Simple Story* should be perceived as a Gothic novel, elements of that genre are central to Matilda's story and its ongoing portrayal of the distribution of power and helplessness. This Gothic consciousness is evident most prominently in her relegation to a secluded set of apartments for the duration of her father's visits to Elmwood Castle. And yet, although the very fact of her confinement is the most prominent indicator of her helplessness, it (also typically for the Gothic) suggests the possibility of some degree of self-empowerment. Thus, while Matilda retains an attraction to anything even remotely connected with her father – she stares for hours at his portrait (p. 220) takes "delight" in hearing of his every action (p. 241) and fetishizes his pen and hat (pp. 245–6) – she exhibits, at the same time, her own desire for power, and at times an imperiousness of spirit that defines her relations with the other members of the little community to which she has access at the Castle. For example, upon hearing that Miss Woodley has agreed to dine with Sandford and Harry Rushbrook (her cousin, and Lord Elmwood's heir) she, "for the first time in her life, darted upon her kind companion, a look of the most cutting reproach and haughty resentment" (p. 258). Another time, in her dismay at being denied her father's presence, she "called upon her mother and reproached her memory" (p. 244).

However, Matilda's resentment is most apparent in her attitude to Rushbrook, who had himself as a young boy been victim to Lord Elmwood's intransigence (he had been disowned along with his mother, Elmwood's sister, who had married against her brother's wishes) and was only restored to his favor through the intervention of Miss Milner. Matilda repeatedly rejects Rushbrook's professions of friendship, once going so far as to say, upon hearing that he had gone out shooting with Lord Elmwood, "All the pleasure is now eclipsed which I used to take in listening to the report of my father's gun, for I cannot now distinguish his from his parasite's"(p. 232).

Significant issues are exposed in Matilda's comment. First, notice the way that, in making Rushbrook the target of her resentment, she is replicating that same practice of assigning "guilt by proxy" that characterizes her father's actions. The absence of Miss Milner's generous "good nature" (p. 105) and the aiming of displaced anger at one who has not personally wronged her mark Matilda more as her father's daughter than her mother's. More importantly, Matilda's use of the term "parasite" acknowledges the material basis of her hostility. Rushbrook is, after all, not only her father's favorite, but the acknowledged heir of his immense fortune as well. Although initially it is solely filial "tenderness" (p. 225) that she craves, her cousin's arrival at her father's estate at once reminds Matilda (and us) of her economic as well as emotional disenfranchisement, and her utter financial helplessness.

Thus, while critics of *A Simple Story* have discussed extensively the oedipal elements of Matilda's attraction to Elmwood, we should not underestimate the material concerns that underlie her actions. This economic anxiety is initially brought to the forefront in the story of Edwards, a long-time gardener for the family, who is dismissed upon breaking the rule of the house when he inadvertently mentions the name of Lady Elmwood. In informing us that Edwards has a "large indigent family of aged parents, children, and other relatives, who subsisted wholly on the income arising from his place" and who, the following day, are evicted from their home (pp. 270–1) Inchbald registers her awareness of the financial implications of disobedience, no matter how unintentional, to the tyrannical patriarch. Hearing Edwards's story, Matilda cannot but recognize the precariousness of her own situation; the "melancholy incident perhaps affected [her] ... beyond any other that had occurred since [her mother's] death" (p. 272).

Matilda's desire for paternal recognition, then, is not limited exclusively to the realm of emotional needs. Compliance with patriarchal fiat is necessary for survival itself. The fact that a short while later she, too, unintentionally trespasses her father's restrictive orders, is subsequently banished from the estate, and then abducted by a dissolute nobleman, Lord Margrave, exposes her vulnerability at its most literal level; it is what Margrave himself calls her "indigence" (p. 301) that makes her such an easy victim.

The sequence of Matilda's abduction and her eventual rescue by her father enables the resolution of the domestic plot, yet at the same time displays Inchbald's cognizance of the implacable power that continues to motivate it. That is to say, there is no movement in which Elmwood becomes less authoritarian, and Matilda anything other than abject. Haggerty describes the initial moment of reconciliation between father and daughter as one that reinforces rather than disrupts the existing configuration of power:

> The Lord ... asserts his heroic posture and her abjection without even thinking. The act of "folding" his brutally rejected daughter seems to assume that no explanation of his past behavior is necessary – she becomes in any case a mute object.[26]

Accordingly, then, the father–daughter rapprochement does not signal a concurrent restoration of Matilda's material rights. Although she is now safely ensconced in her father's residence, Rushbrook remains his heir: "never did [Elmwood] indulge ... the idea of replacing her exactly in that situation to which she was born, to the disappointment of all his nephew's expectations" (p. 334). That is, not until Rushbrook acknowledges his love for Matilda. Elmwood's immediate response upon hearing of his nephew's desire to marry her – he orders him to "quit [the] house, and never dare to return" (p. 335) – exhibits yet again his sheer imperiousness. Thus, while Elmwood ultimately allows Matilda herself to accept or reject Rushbrook's proposal, her actions are subordinated to and enacted within the framework of patriarchal edict. Amidst the domestic harmony exhibited at the conclusion of *A Simple Story*, Inchbald once more reminds us of the linkage between authority, disobedience and its material as well as emotional manifestations.

And, if the conclusion of her plot is not reminder enough, Inchbald articulates this awareness in the authorial rejoinder that appears at the very end of the text:

> what may not be hoped from that school of prudence – though of adversity – in which Matilda was bred? And Mr. Milner, Matilda's grandfather, had better have given his fortune to a distant branch of his family – as Matilda's father once meant to do – so had he bestowed upon his daughter A PROPER EDUCATION. (p. 338)

The force of Inchbald's final pronouncement overshadows the fact that the material concerns of the text – specifically, the connection between obedience and financial security – are foregrounded yet again. The linking of "fortune" to a "proper education" is, it seems to me, more than merely a syntactical construction. Rather, Matilda's education in the school of adversity enables not only the fortuitous resolution of her story but also, in this summation, her retroactive reinstatement as heiress to the family fortune. Inchbald writes here that "Matilda's father *once* meant" to give his fortune to a "distant branch of the family" but recall that only a few pages earlier we were told that notwithstanding his reconciliation with his daughter, Elmwood still recognized Rushbrook as his intended heir. Although, obviously, the marriage of daughter and heir implies a shared enjoyment of the financial boon, the allusion to Matilda's re-enfranchisement, linked as it is to Miss Milner's reappearance in the narrative, once more reminds us of the stakes involved in submission and rebellion.

Indeed, Matilda *has* received a proper education, one that has directed her towards a realistic perception of the existing institutions of power and the possibilities for action within them. As Spacks puts it, "she knows enough not to want too much."[27] This conclusion, in which the felicitous resolution of Matilda's story is juxtaposed to the tragic outcome of Miss Milner's own faulty education, is, however, complicated by Inchbald herself who, years after the publication of *A Simple Story*, returns to present this issue in a somewhat different light. In the preface to her play *Wives As They Were and Maids As They Are* (one of the 125 critical prefaces that she wrote by commission for

Longman's *The British Theatre* (1806–9)) she asserts, regarding the heroine of that play:

> Miss Dorrillon is by far the most prominent and interesting [character] in the piece; and appears to have been formed of the same matter and spirit as compose the body and mind of the heroine of the "Simple Story" – A woman of fashion with a heart – A lively comprehension, and no reflection: – an understanding, but no thought. – Virtues abounding from disposition, education, feeling: – Vices obtruding from habit and example.[28]

Inchbald's later assessment acknowledges both the vitality that later readers have continued to identify in the presentation of Miss Milner, as well as the ideological awareness that informs it. In presenting her as *the* (only) heroine, she retrospectively valorizes the radical consciousness of the first half of her novel rather than the portrayal of compromise and submission – the lesson in survival – that follows it. It is significant then that education, one presumably common to both Miss Milner and Miss Dorrillon, is associated here with "virtue" rather than "vice." (I read Inchbald's use of the term "virtue" here according to the OED definition as "superiority or excellence ... merit or distinction.") On one level, this alignment calls into question those readings which take the novel's final proclamation – "A PROPER EDUCATION" – at face value, as a proscriptive decree for female behavior, such as Mary Wollstonecraft's contemporary assessment, in which she writes, "Mrs. I. had evidently a very useful moral in view, namely to show the advantage of a good education" or that of Gary Kelly, who asserts that "[Matilda's] education, directed by Sandford, has given her the intellectual resources that Miss Milner ... fatally lacked."[29] Conversely, the recognition of Miss Milner's education as a positive element seems to indicate Inchbald's retrospective acknowledgement of the value inherent in the attempt to re-negotiate the boundaries of power, desire, authority and obedience. While this is, admittedly, a later assessment, it is suggestive of the intentions that most probably motivated Inchbald's original portrayal of her heroine in 1791, as well as of the ambivalence that marks the progression of her story.

Inchbald's self-reflexivity in delineating these issues is evident not only in a retrospective context. In the closing lines of her preface to *A Simple Story* she alludes to the financial needs that motivated the writing of the novel:

> Welcome, then, thou all-powerful principle, NECESSITY! – THOU, who art the instigator of so many bad authors and actors – but, to their shame, not of all: – THOU, who from my infancy seldom hast forsaken me, still abide with me. – I will not complain of any hardship thy commands require, so thou doest not urge my pen to prostitution. – In all thy rigour, oh! do not

force my toil to libels – or, what is equally pernicious – panegyric on the unworthy! (p. 2)

In prefacing her text with an emphasis on "necessity" as well as on authorial integrity, Inchbald calls attention to the way in which her novel, and her authorship, are informed by the tension inherent in the intersection of ideological and material concerns, one which manifests itself in a radical vision, but also in the awareness of the pressures which continually limit its presentation. While she is never forced to the extremes of either libel or panegyric, the compromise is, nonetheless, inevitably exacted.[30]

II

The tension that results from the entwining of political and economic consciousness remains, in varying degrees, as a pervasive feature of Inchbald's writing, appearing most prominently in her staged and published plays. (Miss Dorrillon and *Wives As They Were* mentioned above, is, as I will argue later in this book, a prominent example.) However, there is one work that notably deviates from this pattern – Inchbald's second and final novel *Nature and Art* (1796), where her social criticism receives what is perhaps its clearest and most forthright expression.

Nature and Art tells the story of two brothers, William and Henry Norwynne, who come, penniless, to London to make their fortunes. Henry achieves fame and financial stability as a violin player, his success enabling him to provide his brother with a formal education and later, through his connections, to obtain for him a position in the Church. As he rises in public prominence, William marries the proud and class-conscious Lady Clementina and, partly at her urging, renounces his brother, who, after the death of his own wife, takes his infant son, also named Henry, and joins a party of Englishmen going to the African island, Zocotora. There the colonizers are all killed in a local uprising except the two Henrys, who are taken prisoner on the island. Years pass, and Henry manages to have his son smuggled out of Africa, and turned over to the care of his brother. William, overcome with guilt, takes him into his household to be raised alongside his own son, also named William. The narrative traces the fortunes of the two young men, contrasting the "natural" upbringing of young Henry with the elite but artificial education of his cousin.

The result of their different educations becomes apparent as the two boys reach adulthood. William has become proud, selfish and class-conscious, willing to manipulate those beneath him in rank for his own personal benefit. Henry retains the innocence of his early, "natural" boyhood, and never really internalizes the values of the society into which he has been adopted, functioning as an observer who exposes the inequality and injustice that he constantly meets as a member of his uncle's household. The crisis appears at the family's summer home in Anfield; William meets a young cottager, Hannah Primrose, whom he seduces and then abandons. Hannah's story – her pregnancy, the abandonment and later reunion with her child, and her descent into poverty and crime, followed by her inevitable death – becomes the main focus of the remainder of the novel. Alongside Hannah's decline, we see William attain professional success, accompanied by guilt and remorse (in a scene of compelling irony, he is the judge who, without recognizing her, sentences Hannah to death) and Henry return to rescue his long-lost father from captivity. *Nature and Art* concludes with Henry reunited with his father and with Rebecca, the woman who has loyally waited for him, living in a cottage at the edge of the sea, in a voluntary exile from the cruel and hypocritical society whose pernicious effects have been exposed throughout the novel.

The critical reception of *Nature and Art* unanimously acknowledges the foregrounded political agenda in the novel. The reviewer for the conservative *British Critic*, although admitting that "the book throughout is remarkably well written", observes that he has:

> [a]very serious quarrel with many of the principles which are here inculcated; many misrepresentations of characters and situations; many inaccuracies, which a candid enquiry, or a little careful deliberation, would have prevented. We lament that it should be thought necessary, by some of the most accomplished persons in this branch of writing, to exhibit the errors or weaknesses of those in exalted rank, in the most odious and exaggerated representations.[31]

In 1796, *The Anti-Jacobin Review* had not yet appeared, but a later comment in the periodical, in a 1800 footnote to a review of Godwin's *St. Leon*, much more bluntly conveys the contemporary conservative response, calling the novel "the most impudent, malignant, and audacious heap of absurdity" and Inchbald herself a "scavenger of democracy."[32]

Mary Wollstonecraft, writing in *The Analytical Review* from a different political perspective, acknowledges the ideological provenance of *Nature and Art*, but also qualifies her overall aesthetic assessment of the work: "The present novel, though written with a more philosophical spirit than the simple story, has not, on that very account, perhaps, an equally lively interest to keep the attention awake."[33] This observation underscores the way that *Nature and Art* participates in a late eighteenth-century novelistic tradition – what Gary Kelly would call a "Jacobin" tradition – that privileged the promotion of a political worldview over a more nuanced development of character and theme, and in which, in Patricia Spacks's words, "political and moral agendas often supersede psychological ones."[34]

Yet although Wollstonecraft's review calls our attention to the polemical nature of *Nature and Art* (and contrasts it to the psychological subtlety and complexity of *A Simple Story*) the very force of the social critique invested in Inchbald's plot is precisely where other readers find the strength of her narrative. William Hazlitt, for example, writes that:

> *Nature and Art* is one of the most pathetic and interesting stories in the world ... The effect of this novel upon the feelings, is not only of the most distressing, but withering kind ... The conclusion ... is a scene of heartless desolation, which must effectually deter any one from ever reading the book twice.[35]

As opposed to the disparaging comments of the *Analytical Review*, Hazlitt's response suggests Inchbald's success in emotionally engaging her readers through the presentation of a profoundly political message. And yet, as we will see, this is a message that has in itself undergone substantial revision, a fact that implies both an even more radical awareness that had been envisioned for *Nature and Art*, as well as Inchbald's understandable anxiety in publishing it. Together, they exhibit the customary caution that is so pervasive in her work, but also, in this particular novel, the strength of her political commitment and the direction in which she was willing to take it.

The two working titles of *Nature and Art* prior to its publication, "The Prejudice of Education" and "A Satire Upon the Times"[36] reflect Inchbald's aim of consciously addressing relevant contemporary concerns. Her hesitation over the name of her book suggests the desire to retain an allusion to its polemical nature, yet through a more abstract display of the issues involved, and thus also calls attention to the anxiety surrounding the composition and revision of the novel as a whole. Boaden informs us that Inchbald began preparing *Nature and Art* for publication in January 1794, during which time she showed her manuscript to her friends Godwin, Holcroft and George Hardinge.[37] As Kelly relates it, Hardinge:

> as one of the Queen's attorneys-general ... was perhaps so situated as to be able to warn his friend that it was a most inauspicious time to publish a novel expressing liberal views. [He] himself liked the novel at first, but soon turned violently against it.[38]

Kelly's reference to an "inauspicious time" acknowledges in particular a culture that in the second half of the year 1794 would be gripped by the Treason Trials, in which Inchbald's close friend, Holcroft, was one of the accused. The fact that she apparently followed the advice of her friends and withheld *Nature and Art* from publication while at the same time, in spite of her prudence, remained loyal to Holcroft, visiting him in prison while he awaited trial,[39] is yet another example of the combination of caution and integrity that accompanies the appearance of the novel.

Although originally withheld, *Nature and Art* was finally published in 1796, and in a cultural climate no less inhospitable to a progressive political agenda, nor less affected by the same sense of oppression. The suspension of *habeas corpus*, decreed concurrent to the Treason Trials, was still in effect, and the "Two Acts", which extended treason to include writing and speaking against the government, were passed by Parliament in the winter of 1795–6.[40] In this context, Inchbald's critique of British society and its pervasive but empty institutions of power, appears all the more compelling.

The political self-consciousness that accompanies the publication of *Nature and Art* repeatedly appears within the novel itself. Inchbald acknowledges the contemporaneousness of her narrative in various ways, including references to censorship, the power of the law (including two crucial trial scenes), and the ambiguous representation of colonial space. These issues, which later become integral elements of the plot as they shape the fortunes of her central characters, are initially introduced through the perspective of the young Henry, whose British education seems to lie solely in questioning the premises of the society into which he has been adopted.

One of the most powerful examples of Henry's interrogation of British society occurs in a family discussion of the word "massacre." The scene begins as the family hears the firing of cannons and the ringing of bells.

> "Then I dare say" cried Henry, "there has been another massacre." The dean [as the elder William is frequently called] called to him in anger "Will you never learn the right use of words? You mean to say a battle." "Then what is a massacre?" cried the frightened, but still curious Henry. "A massacre" replied his uncle, "is when a number of people are slain –" "I thought," returned Henry, "soldiers had been people!"[41]

The conversation continues, until Henry is eventually silenced by his uncle's authority, although, the narrator adds:

> he had an answer at the veriest [*sic*] tip of his tongue, which it was torture to him not to utter. What he wished to say must ever remain a secret. – The church has its terrors as well as the law, and Henry was awed by the dean's tremendous wig, as much as Pater-noster Row is awed by the attorney-general. (Vol. i., p. 84)

Inchbald's choice of words here is telling. The references to "torture", "secret", the "terror" of Church and State, as well as the publishing community's "awe" of the attorney-general, all linked to a discussion of war and its casualties, prominently display the intensity of her political engagement as well as her anxiety in presenting it, and which, just as significantly, she openly shares with her readers.

As with the discussion on massacre, Henry's naïve, humane reflection on the world is associated throughout *Nature and Art* with his outsider status, his natural upbringing outside "civilization" enabling him to expose the injustices of his adopted society. His cousin William, alternately, is defined by his elite English education, which has made him devoid of imagination, curiosity and the ability to think for himself. As Inchbald describes him, "[William] could talk on history, on politics, and on religion; surprisingly to all who had never listened to a parrot or a magpie – for he merely repeated what he had heard" (Vol. i., p. 46). In this condemnation of a system of education that discourages independent thinking, Inchbald also seems to be alluding to, and reversing Hume's infamous remark in his "Essay: Of National Characters." "In Jamaica", Hume writes, "they talk of one negroe as a man of parts and learning; but 'tis likely he is admired for very slender accomplishments, like a parrot who speaks a few words plainly."[42] On the one hand, through her allusion to Hume, Inchbald ostensibly collapses the Enlightenment dialectic in which, as Emmanuel Chukwudi Eze writes, " 'civilization' became almost synonymous with 'white' people and northern Europe, while unreason and savagery were conveniently located among the non-whites, the 'black', the 'red', the 'yellow' outside Europe."[43] This reversal, and the implication that it is William who is uncivilized, introduces a paradigm that repeatedly appears in the novel to register Inchbald's dismay with British society. For example, Hannah Primrose, after being abandoned, tells Henry: "I always heard that you were brought up in a savage country; but I suppose it was a mistake; it was your cousin William" (Vol. ii., p. 56).

At the same time, Inchbald's equation works only to a limited degree, serving primarily to emphasize the brutality of English society, while Africa, rather than functioning as a benevolent and humane alternative, is ambivalently presented. For example, we recall that the party of colonizers was massacred on the island of Zocotora, and although the natives are seemingly released from guilt – the elder Henry writes to his brother in the letter smuggled out with his son, "we had no business to invade their territories" (Vol. i., p. 51) – this remark only reflects the humanity of the enlightened colonizer rather than that of the inhabitants of the island, who are never given a voice in the narrative. Moreover, after his rescue, the elder Henry realizes that he "had [on the island] no friend with whom he wished to shake hands at his departure" (Vol. ii., p. 125), and England, although portrayed throughout the text as savage, now provides a degree of relief, as "he slept on board an English vessel, with Englishmen his companions" (Vol. ii., p. 126). It appears that the Africa Inchbald valorizes through her portrayal of Henry refers to an abstract signification of "nature", one that serves as a locus for a natural, Rousseauvian education. In contrast, Africa as a *geographical* territory, as Zocotora, cannot function as an idyllic alternative to corrupt England, but rather, is portrayed as inhospitable – a place of danger, massacre and isolation.[44] The overall feeling of distress that Hazlitt describes in reference to *Nature and Art* comes from this recognition: there *is* no alternative, no place where one can escape to unscathed by the relentless brutality of social experience.

This sense of unremitting persecution receives its most prominent expression in the character of Hannah Primrose, the country girl who falls victim to William's selfish passion, and whose story controls the second half of the narrative. Susan Staves has argued that the figure of the seduced maiden appears in eighteenth-century texts in a fairly standard form, with attributes – youth, beauty, sensibility – that render these women "especially pathetic . . . because their seducers seemed to have unfair advantage over them."[45] The relationship of William and Hannah is typical of this paradigm, as evident in Hannah's reflection on their relationship prior to her seduction:

> [H]ad she [Hannah thinks] been accustomed to the conversation of men in William's rank of life, she had, perhaps, treated William's addresses with indifference; but in comparing him with her familiar acquaintance, he was a miracle! His unremitted [*sic*] attention seemed the condescension of a superior being, to whom she looked up with reverence, with admiration, with awe, with pride, with sense of obligation. (Vol. i., p. 143)

Hannah's musings reinforce a binary of power and abjection, the recognition of which informs Inchbald's worldview and epitomizes her social criticism. And, as Inchbald reminds us, a poor woman is not only especially susceptible to social persecution, but also denied the means with which to articulate the full awareness of her own vulnerability. The written communication between Hannah and William following her seduction is characterized by this very lack. It takes her a "fortnight" (Vol. i., p. 160) to read the letter that he eventually writes to her from London, and although she writes him back, it is an arduous task: it takes her "generally a week to write a letter of ten lines" (Vol. i., p. 160). At the same time, as this rudimentary communication indicates, a critical insistence on the *complete* silencing of the lower-class woman in this novel, such as Shawn Maurer's claim that "Hannah, deprived of education by her poverty and of authority by her sex, has no voice with which to speak"[46] is not entirely accurate. Not only does she write William two letters of her own (the second one before her execution (Vol. ii., pp. 154–6)) but, moreover, reads the prison calendar and so learns that he will be the judge at her trial. In the early stages of their relationship at least, she responds to him verbally, as well: "Enchant[ed]" by William's eloquence as he courts her, she "gave to him, her most undisguised thoughts" (Vol. i., p. 140). Hannah's unchecked verbosity contributes, of course, to her fall, exhibiting how, not exactly voicelessness, but rather the inability to manipulate, control and efficiently use language repeatedly signals her marginality and enforces her victimization.[47]

Yet, while Hannah is doubly victimized because of gender and class, the "unfair advantage" (to use Staves's term again) that her story displays is also a ubiquitous feature of society as a whole.[48] Consider, for example, the "first family" of Anfield, the "Lord of the Bedchamber" and his wife, Lord and

Lady Bendham. Imperious, hypocritical, wasteful in their personal economy but penurious to the poor, the portrayal of the Bendhams enables Inchbald to articulate a direct critique of the nobility itself, one which is even further enabled by her own emphasis on their function as "type" rather than as character. Thus, her initial presentation of the Lord almost immediately dissolves into a generalized political statement:

> Lord Bendham, besides a good estate, possessed the office of a lord of the bed-chamber to his majesty. Historians do not ascribe much importance to the situation, or to the talents of nobles in this department, nor shall this little history. A lord of the bed-chamber is a personage well known in courts, and in all capitals where courts reside ... in becoming acquainted with one of those noble characters, you become acquainted with all the remainder ... a lord of the bed-chamber must necessarily be the self-same creature: one, wholly made up of observance, of obedience, of dependence, and of imitation – a borrowed character – a character formed by reflection. (Vol. i., pp. 119–20)

I quote this passage at length not only for its blunt depiction of the vacuity of noble hierarchy and rank. For Inchbald's portrayal receives additional significance when considered in light of the circumstances surrounding her composition of *Nature and Art*, and the attention that she herself gave to the presentation of her "lord of the bedchamber." As we learn from an undated letter to Godwin, she had intended this character to represent the King himself:

> And now I will discover to you a total want of *aim*, of *execution*, and every particle of genius belonging to a writer, in a character in this work, which from the extreme want of resemblance to the original, you have not even reproached me with the fault of drawing accurately. I really and soberly meant (and was in hopes every reader would be struck with the portrait) Lord Rinforth to represent his Most Gracious Majesty, George the 3rd. I said at the commencement all Lords of Bedchambers were mirrors of the Grand Personage on whom they attended, but having Newgate before my eyes, I dressed him in some virtues, and (notwithstanding his avarice) you did not know him.[49]

Godwin had not recognized the King in Inchbald's Lord of the Bedchamber in the draft version of *Nature and Art*, nor does the present-day reader, reading the final revised edition of the text. Not only has the name of this character been changed from Rinforth to Bendham; the comment "at the commencement" that "Lords of the Bedchamber were mirrors of the Grand Personage" is also, tellingly, absent. Furthermore, later in her letter to Godwin Inchbald states that she had thought:

how pleased Mr. Godwin will be at my making the King so avaricious, and there, (said I to myself) how pleased the King will be at my making him so very good at the conclusion, and when he finds that by throwing away his money he can save his drowning people he will instantly *throw it all away* for flannel shirts for his soldiers, and generously pardon me all I have said on *equality* in the book, merely for giving him a good character.[50]

These remarks reveal further evidence of Inchbald's revisions. In the published novel Bendham does not "throw away his money" to save his tenants, and at no point assumes a positive, or even a major role in the narrative. Rather, he dies of "the effects of intemperance" (Vol. ii., p. 193) and Henry, upon seeing his monument, thinks of him only as "a man, whose best advantage is to be forgotten" (Vol. ii., p. 186).

While no extant copy exists of the original draft of *Nature and Art*, and we can only conjecture as to the depth and breadth of the radical message that Inchbald had initially wished to convey in her novel in general, and in her portrait of the lord of the bedchamber in particular, her comments to Godwin suggest, at the very least, the boldness of her intention. And although the consciousness of "Newgate before [her] eyes" renders the final result suitably muted as opposed to her original plan, it still remains compelling to a certain degree. Let us look, for example, at the conversation between Henry and Bendham as they discuss the latter's treatment of his tenants. After learning that the Lord had given those tenants one hundred pounds as a Christmas gift, Henry exclaims, "How prudent!" (Vol. i., p. 126). The Dean attempts to silence him, but Lord Bendham wishes to have an explanation. The discussion continues as Henry elaborates:

I thought it was prudent in you to give a little; lest the poor, driven to despair, should take all. [Bendham responds that] "And if they had they would have been hanged." "Hanging, my lord [Henry replies] our history, or some tradition says, was formerly adopted as a mild punishment, in place of starving." (Vol. i., p. 127)

The fact that the Dean attempts to end this conversation – "[D]o not ask for an explanation" (Vol. i., p. 126) he anxiously intervenes – points, together with the earlier instance when Henry refrains from speaking his mind, to an ongoing awareness of the need to silence politically imprudent speech. This awareness is further reinforced at the very end of this scene. Bendham does not reply to Henry's suggestion to extend financial relief to his impoverished tenants, but whispers to himself, "I had rather keep my ——." The narrator, as if to make sure that we are aware of the omission, then adds, "His last word was lost in the whisper" (Vol. i., p. 129). While perhaps mainly pointing to the greed of Bendham, this dialogue provides additional evidence of deliberately concealed speech and of the pervasiveness of censorship as a recurrent concern in the novel. Nonetheless, Henry, in this instance, still manages to conclude his thoughts with a practical suggestion for Bendham: "For if my lord would only be so good as to speak a few words for the poor as a senator, he might possibly for the future keep his hundred pounds, and yet they may never want it" (Vol. i, p. 129).

Various issues appear in this dialogue that call our attention once more to the anxious contemporary referentiality of *Nature and Art*, in which the allusions to starvation, punishment and hanging collectively acknowledge not only the famine of 1795 (the year before *Nature and Art* was published) but also the overall fear of the insurrection of the working class that accompanied it.[51] As Kelly notes, Inchbald is responding here, and throughout the novel, to both Evangelical and government attitudes towards the poor as they appeared in the speeches of Bishop Samuel Horsley and the 1795 debate on the "Poor Law", and in fictional texts such as Hannah More's *Cheap Repository Tracts*, specifically "Village Politics."[52] Kelly's claim that *Nature and Art* responds to a certain contemporary discourse on the subject can be further illustrated by comparing the novel to More's text "The Riot", which was "written during the Scarcity of 1795."[53] There, More presents a dialogue in which the prudent Jack Anvil dissuades his friend, the impetuous Tom Hod, from instigating a riot and tearing down the local mill. While More, like Inchbald, also acknowledges the pervasiveness of hunger, want and starvation and, similarly to Inchbald's Henry, hints at the responsibility of "King and Parliament" (p. 444) for alleviating the situation, her argument focuses, typically, on the practical advantages of hard work and the stoic acceptance of things as they are. As the sober-minded Jack says:

> And though I've no money, and though I've no lands,
> I've a head on my shoulders and a pair of good hands;
> So, I'll work the whole day, and on Sundays I'll seek
> At church how to bear all the wants of the week.
>
> (p. 444)

The churchmen in *Nature and Art* offer no such spiritual sustenance for their "Jack Anvils": "[R]igid attention to the morals of people in poverty, and total neglect of their bodily wants, was the dean's practice" (Vol. i., p. 153), just as hard work in itself cannot stave off the effects of indigence –"every cottage [in Anfield] was crammed with half-starved children, whose father from week to week, from year to year, exerted his manly youth and wasted his strength in vain to protect them from hunger" (Vol. i., p. 124). However, common to both Inchbald and More is the recognition that the threat of hanging is always in the background. Bendham refers to that method of punishment in response to Henry's warning on the despair of the poor, and it is also the means by which Jack eventually quells the rebellious impulses of his friend:

"And when of two evils I'm asked which is best, / I'd rather be hungry than hang'd, I protest" (p. 445).[54]

Whereas in "The Riot" the threat of the ultimate punishment enables an immediate, renewed acceptance of the political and social status quo, in *Nature and Art* it is the critique of a ubiquitous apparatus of government oppression that is reinforced and sustained in the novel's two trial scenes. This is a society in which individuals struggle for justice in the face of ecclesiastical and legal, as well as political, authority. Inchbald's worldview is further apparent in the way that, as Vivien Jones suggests, her courtroom scenes draw upon the precedent established by Godwin in *Caleb Williams* by exhibiting a plea for justice within the context of a radical novel,[55] but also the inefficacy of the attempt to obtain it.

The two trial scenes in *Nature and Art* center around Hannah Primrose; the first one, an informal hearing led by the Dean, in which the matter of the parentage of her abandoned baby is investigated, and the second, after her descent into crime, when she appears on trial for forgery in front of a court over which his son William (now a judge) presides. Hannah is conspicuously absent from the Dean's "courtroom"; it is Henry who is interrogated regarding the infant whom he had found and then turned over to the care of his beloved Rebecca. The questioning revolves around the assumption that Henry and Rebecca are the child's parents, and the proceedings attempt both to verify this fact under oath, as well as to take punitive measures against this breach of morality, for, as Staves reminds us, "seduced maidens were guilty of fornication, a crime punishable in the ecclesiastical courts."[56] Staves singles out *Nature and Art* as perhaps the only fictional text of the period that acknowledges the actual function of the law, and specifically, the ecclesiastical system of discipline in the treatment of seduced women, which "had become a class-based system, exacting compliance only from the lower classes, and the rural lower classes at that."[57]

Inchbald stresses both the class bias that motivates the proceedings and the hypocrisy that surrounds them. William, who is present as an observer, remarks that no "punishment could be too great for the seducer of innocence" (Vol. ii., pp. 23–4) although, he, obviously, is that very seducer, and Lady Bendham, upon hearing of the events, was "most of all shocked and offended" (Vol. ii., p. 35) although in town she herself "visited and received into her house the acknowledged mistresses of a man in elevated life" (Vol. i., p. 123). The narrator's comments in this context sum up the prevailing attitude: "it was not ... the crime, but the rank which the criminal held in society" (Vol. i., p. 123) that determines an ethical stance among Inchbald's upper-class characters. Moreover, Henry's and Rebecca's trial underscores a legal as well as a moral relativity in the pursuit of justice, for not only does the law exert itself forcibly only towards the disempowered; in this instance, the combined forces of rank, religion and law pervert rather than serve the cause of truth. (Later, it should be noted, the truth *does* emerge, but only when Hannah reveals the child's parentage to the Dean who insists that the matter be silenced from then on.)

The second trial in which Hannah is implicated ostensibly dispenses justice, for, as a result of her poverty and distress, she had "become an accomplice in negotiating bills forged on a country banker" (Vol. ii., p. 133) a crime punishable by death according to the law of the land. However, the efficient workings of the courtroom over which William presides only serve to expose, in the emotional climax of the novel, the larger injustice that motivates Hannah's story. The irony of the situation is made apparent in the following courtroom dialogue:

> "Have you no one to speak for your character?" [William asks] The prisoner answered, "No." A second gush of tears followed this reply, for she called to mind by *whom*, her character had first been blasted. (Vol. ii., p. 142)

William indeed sentences Hannah to death, and her impassioned response – "Not from *you*" (Vol. ii., p. 143) – resonates throughout the courtroom, reiterating in its unintelligibility to her auditors the abjectness of her situation (she is presumed mad) and to Inchbald's readers, the ultimate display of unfair advantage.

If Hannah's story illustrates social and economic vulnerability in its most heightened expression, then the conclusion of *Nature and Art* resituates Inchbald's bleak vision in a more ambivalent social space, and in more muted terms. The end of the novel finds Henry and Rebecca, along with the elder Henry, in a cottage by the side of the sea, living by "cheerful labour of fishing, or the tending of a garden" (Vol. ii., p. 197), in a tranquil existence where they constantly reflect upon their own happiness as opposed to the cruel and empty social world to which their lives have been contingent in varying degrees. Yet, the repeated remarking upon the vices of the rich, as it registers the memory and the scars of their own experience, leaves us with an ongoing awareness of injustice and inequality rather than a sense of "cheerfulness" or reconciliation as the final word of the text. Henry's concluding comments further disrupt the seeming tranquility at the seaside, as he reiterates the need for social change:

> and yet those in poverty, ungrateful as they are, murmur against that government from which they receive the blessing; and, unlearned as they are, would attempt to alter it. – We leave to the physician the care of restoring our health, we employ the soldier in fighting our battles, and the lawyer in defence of our fortunes, without presuming to interrupt them in their vocations – then why not leave, and without molestation, those to govern a kingdom who have studied the science of politics? (Vol. ii., p. 202)

Notice the progression of this argument – the mention of the "ungrateful poor" and the "government . . . blessing" illustrating in ironic reversal the caution through which Inchbald conveys her political message, while the claim against monarchy immediately restates her agenda in clear and direct terms. Henry's argument, in its subject as well as its structure encapsulates the movement that we have seen throughout the novel in a final acknowledgement of the tense times in which the book was written.

And, staying for another moment with this conclusion, it is clear that insofar as the monarchy in particular is concerned, the anxious contemporary awareness in Inchbald's novel is in fact quite profound. *Nature and Art* was first published on 11 January 1796, closely following events in which the King's well-being had been at the center of public, political and legal attention. On 29 October 1795, his carriage had been attacked on its way to the opening of Parliament. As John Barrell describes it:

> As the procession left the palace and turned into the Mall, it ran immediately into a hostile crowd chanting "Down with George!", "No King!", "No George!", along with some less treasonable prayers and imprecations, "Peace, peace!", "Bread, bread", "No famine!", "No War"!, "No Pitt!" . . . According to one anti-royalist report, some of the crowd succeeded in climbing the gate; eventually they forced the locks and burst into Whitehall . . . [and] in Parliament Street the procession continued to be hooted, hissed, groaned at, and pelted with mud; stones were thrown at the state coach and one or two of its windows were broken or cracked.[58]

Following these disturbances, the government carried through with plans for new legislation, the Treasonable Practices Bill and Seditious Meetings Bill, which would further clamp down on freedom of assembly and speech, justified by what was clearly perceived as the threat to the personal safety of the monarch. Inchbald's reference to a government led by those who have studied the "science of politics", with the echoes of "No King! No George!" resonating insidiously underneath the surface, marks the conclusion of *Nature and Art* as a conscious stand on the premier radical issue of its time.

Kelly identifies in the denouement of *Nature and Art* "a kind of Pantisocracy which is the logical ending for a book which certain events had inspired, and then passed by."[59] In light of the social brutality that Inchbald portrays, a quiet, self-imposed exilic existence, with, perhaps, a nod to an ideological conception of a better, more just world was all she could offer. At the same time, Kelly's claim that *Nature and Art* is somewhat anachronistic, along with his observation that "[p]erhaps prudence induced Mrs. Inchbald to soften the ending of [the book] to accord more with the political atmosphere of 1796 than of early 1794"[60] arouses our curiosity as to what we could learn about Inchbald's politics from a hypothetical reading of the original draft of the novel. Would we find revolutionary energy instead of resignation and retreat, a vibrant rather than a quietist ending, a detailed program for radical action? Although the evidence from her letters to Godwin hints at her intentions, it is unlikely that we will ever know the specificities of the political ideas that she had originally wished to convey.

The aftermath of this "Jacobin" cultural moment is conveyed even more precisely in the 1797 edition of *Nature and Art*, in which the ending of the novel is revised and the emphasis altered. Henry's final speech, with its disparaging remarks on the monarchical system of government, is entirely omitted, exhibiting the fact that, in terms of an outright political agenda at least, Inchbald's conclusion is even more subdued and cautious in the second edition of the text than in the first one.[61] Keeping in mind the intensity of the backlash and the new government legislation, it could hardly be otherwise. What emerges is an intensification of her characters' anger at the prevailing systems of power, with much of their fury directed towards the poorer classes' own acceptance of the status quo. The emphasis is now on the inability to effect social change, which results from an "education" that is nothing more than a learned helplessness. As the elder Henry asserts:

> Our children observe us pay respect, even reverence, to the wealthy, while we slight or despise the poor. The impression thus made on their minds in youth is indelible during the more advanced periods of life; and they continue to pine after riches, and lament under poverty.[62]

His son responds in a rejoinder that concludes the text:

> Let the poor, then … no more be their own persecutors – no longer pay homage to wealth – instantaneously the whole idolatrous worship will cease – the idol will be broken. (pp. 201–2)

The naïve and gentle humanity that had characterized the young Henry throughout *Nature and Art* is replaced here with prophetic anger. And yet, in light of the consciousness of the abjection of the lower classes, of the incapacity of the present state of education to improve society and of the marginality of Henry's own subject position as he speaks, the realization of his future vision is negated even as he articulates it, leaving a grim yet ineffectual aggressiveness as the final word of the text.

These alterations further widen the gap between Inchbald's first draft of *Nature and Art* and what appears in 1797 as a depiction of frustrated powerlessness and defeated expectations unmediated by the presentation of an alternative agenda; the different revisions of the novel are thus an important indication of the deepening entrenchment of the reactionary backlash and of Inchbald's own response to it. At the same time, however, other overt political statements that we viewed, such as the discussion on massacre, the reference to censorship and Paternoster Row, and the introduction of the lord of the bedchamber, remain intact in the 1797 and 1810 editions of *Nature and Art*, indicating that although Inchbald's expression of a progressive worldview (especially regarding the monarchy) had been modified, her social and political critique had not really been abandoned. Ultimately, both versions of the novel that she eventually wrote rather than the one she wanted to write exhibit, as her original title indicates, a satire, even a mourning, but above all a reflection upon her times, one that may perhaps miss its moment for promoting social change, but accurately captures in its critiques and in its silencing, but also in the presentation of the vestiges of a radical vision, the cultural climate in which it was written.

The publication and later re-publication of *Nature and Art* is significant not only for its expression of, and contextualization within, a particular cultural moment, but also as it reflects the intersection of the various motivations that accompanied Inchbald's authorship as a whole. Novel writing came neither easily nor quickly to her, as evinced in the two-to-three year germination period of *Nature and Art*, and what some scholars see as a period of twelve years for *A Simple Story*.[63] Her own thoughts on the difficulty of writing fiction as opposed to drama are evident in a letter to Godwin, regarding the earlier novel:

> My health suffered much during this confinement, my spirits suffered more on publication; for though many gentlemen of the first abilities have said to me things high in its favour, it never was liked by those people who are the readers and consumers of novels; and I have frequently obtained more pecuniary advantage by ten days' labour in the dramatic way than by the labour of this ten months.[64]

Inchbald's comments reinforce how sensitivity to audience approbation and the financial reward that results in its stead are issues that repeatedly surround her authorship. Her allusion to "pecuniary advantage" reminds us that *A Simple Story*, like *Nature and Art* a novel of radical aspirations and defeated possibilities, was accompanied by a preface that emphasized economic necessity as a factor that both dictates and restrains the presentation of the narrative. *Nature and Art* appears without prefatory remarks, but it is safe to assume that had a preface been included, it would not have called attention to Inchbald's economic situation: by 1796 she was living in comfortable lodgings in Leicester Square, investing in the stock market as well as having the means to assist her needy brothers and sisters.

Is it likely then that financial gain was a factor in Inchbald's decision to publish another novel, and a polemical one at that? Judging by the £150 that she received for *Nature and Art*, compared to the far more substantial sums that she had been earning for her plays (£900 and £700 respectively for *Such Things Are* and *Every One Has His Fault*, to cite just two examples)[65] the answer is probably no. Rather, a clue to her motivations can be found by returning to her essay in *The Artist*, which I quoted at the beginning of this chapter, where she asserts that "[t]he Novelist is a free agent. He lives in a land of liberty, whilst The Dramatic Writer exists but under a despotic government." That Inchbald positions herself within this metaphorical "land of liberty" at the very moment when government repression took on its most bleak literality represents possibly a unique moment in her literary career – the offering of a political intervention "for itself", unfettered by material concerns. (As we will see, her play *The Massacre* was written with a similar intention but never reached either the stage or the press during her lifetime.) That is to say, despite the element of caution in her negotiation of her subject matter, the decision to print such a politically-volatile literary work – even in its revised version – exposes above all an underlying ideological commitment, the strength of which emerges in *Nature and Art* to transcend the other, more quotidian pressures that informed her career.

6
"Under a Despotic Government": Elizabeth Inchbald II

"The Novelist is a free agent. He lives in a land of liberty, whilst The Dramatic Writer exists but under a despotic government."[1] I begin my discussion of Elizabeth Inchbald's plays by once more calling attention to her reflection on the difference between writing novels and drama. For although it was more time consuming, stress-inducing and less financially profitable for her than writing for the stage, Inchbald knew that prose fiction was still the literary form most conducive for articulating a political position. Having spent all her adult life in theatre circles, she was well aware of the multiple levels of restraint imposed on the dramatic writer – the theatre managers who were to accept, revise and modify the manuscript play, the all-powerful audience, whose approbation was continually a source of anxiety for her and the Chief Examiner of Plays, who was to scrutinize its political and otherwise objectionable references.

These sites of authority were particularly evident throughout the Revolutionary decade; through the policy of John Larpent, the Chief Examiner between the years 1778–1824, urgent contemporary issues raised by the French Revolution and by the concern with social reform were virtually nonexistent on the stage. As L.W. Conolly writes, "in 1789 the stages of the patent theatres were the only places in Britain where discussion and comment on the French Revolution were legally prohibited" and although in later years allusions to the events in France were allowed to appear, all plays on the subject were "very carefully scrutinized by the Examiner of Plays." Larpent succeeded, thus, throughout the 1790s, in "isolating the theatre from the vigorous debates about reform, republicanism, and revolution which were being conducted in just about every other place and medium in Great Britain."[2]

And yet, politics were not entirely absent from the theatre during the Revolutionary decade. Through a discussion of two of Inchbald's most successful plays, *Every One Has His Fault* (1793) and *Wives as They Were and Maids as They Are* (1797), this chapter will show how a progressive political engagement did in fact appear on the London stage during the 1790s. As will become clear, Inchbald's distinction between the writing of fiction and drama belies the fact that she *was* able to negotiate quite successfully the limits and strictures that she herself acknowledges and present plays that exhibited her social critique while calling attention to the repressive institutional systems in which it is enacted. Similarly to what we have seen in *A Simple Story* and *Nature and Art*, Inchbald's presentation of her politics once more illustrates that combination of pragmatism and integrity that characterizes her work in general; the boundary between the "land of liberty" and the "despotic government" was at times quite permeable. Furthermore, my reading of her unpublished and unstaged play, *The Massacre* (1792) presents a view of her writing as it existed before reaching the public domain in its final form. Positioned on the borders between public intervention and private sentiment, the play uniquely exhibits an engagement with contemporary political developments that has not been subjected to managerial revisions and Larpent's judgment and is dissociated to a certain extent from the anticipation of audience approbation.

I

As Ellen Donkin has shown, the already formidable obstacles facing any writer of drama were even more difficult to overcome for the woman playwright attempting to have her work accepted for production.[3] Donkin singles out Inchbald as one of the few "survivors" of this system, and notes that her success was achieved due to the fact that she was one of the few women playwrights who crossed over to writing from a career as an actress, and, as a result of her years of work on the stage and familiarity with its procedures, had an insider's knowledge that facilitated access to the theatre managers, who would then more readily read her manuscript plays.[4] As Annibel Jenkins notes, Inchbald's presence in green-room circles meant "being in the center of the London world."[5] Inchbald's prominence and success as a playwright is evinced in the repeated and consecutive staging of her plays and in her earnings. Judith Stanton has provided statistical evidence that places Inchbald as the third most successful woman dramatist between the years 1660–1800.[6]

Initially made possible by her relatively easy access to theatre managers, Inchbald's success as a writer of dramatic texts was sustained by her ability to maneuver herself within the overt as well as the more discrete systems of power surrounding the theatrical world. For example, her recognition of the all-important issue of audience approval repeatedly appears in her prefaces to the *British Theatre* to exhibit this subject as one that is particularly important for her. Consider, for example, this passage in her remarks on Addison's *Cato*:

> The joy or sorrow which an author is certain to experience upon every new production, is far more powerful in the heart of a dramatist, than in that of any other writer. The sound of clamorous plaudits raises his spirits to a kind of ecstacy; whilst hisses and groans, from a dissatisfied audience,

strike on the ear like a personal insult, avowing loud and public contempt for that, in which he has been labouring to show his skill.[7]

Significantly, this comment is immediately preceded by one acknowledging the political resonances of Addison's play: "It was indebted", Inchbald writes, "to the political circumstances of the times, for that enthusiastic applause with which it was received by the town."[8]

The discussion of Addison exemplifies how the interlocking issues of audience, politics and censorship inform Inchbald's criticism as well as her imaginative writing. In the preface to *Cato* the political reference alludes to a more distant past (*Cato* was first performed in 1713) but elsewhere in the *Remarks* she addresses the intersection of theatre and politics in her own time and exhibits her understanding of the Examiner's authority, especially as it was exerted in contemporary political matters. Thus, in her preface to *Julius Caesar* she writes that, "it has been thought advisable, for some years past, that this tragedy should not appear on the stage ... [for] when the circumstances of certain periods make certain incidents of history most interesting, those are the very seasons to interdict their exhibition."[9] Likewise, regarding Otway's *Venice Preserved*, she asserts:

[This play] is the favourite work of Otway. It is played repeatedly every year; except when an order from the Lord Chamberlain forbids its representation, lest some of the speeches ... should be applied, by the ignorant part of the audience, to certain men or assemblies in the English state.[10]

Inchbald would certainly have been thinking here of the uproar surrounding the October 1795 production of *Venice Preserved* at Drury Lane. It was the play's theme of rebellion, but also, as contemporary accounts indicate, the audience's heightened response to its politically inflected speeches, that caused the government's anxious response to the production and the cancellation of its run.[11]

In the preface to Frederick Reynolds's *The Dramatist*, Inchbald addresses the matter succinctly: in the past, authors could write "without political or moral restraint. Uncurbed by law or delicacy, they wrote at random."[12] This assessment, written with a retrospective view of the events, illuminates Inchbald's understanding of the limitations and restrictions, "moral restraint" and "delicacy", to be sure, but also her consciousness of "political restraint" and "law", as it accompanied her own authorship of drama during the revolutionary years. Her negotiation of the system was indeed very successful: while Conolly provides numerous examples of plays written during the 1790s in which Larpent forbade the presentation of speeches that criticize the aristocracy or acknowledge social difficulties in general, Inchbald's manuscript plays submitted during that period, in which she variously addresses these same issues, were left virtually untouched by the Censor. For instance, while

Larpent refused to license Thomas Dibdin's musical entertainment *The Two Farmers* on the grounds that it dealt with "the scarcity and high price of corn in the country", repeated comments in *Every One Has His Fault* on the scarcity of food in London escape the verdict of his pen.[13]

I have called attention to the seeming tolerance that characterizes Larpent's reception of Inchbald's plays, but was it really leniency and if so, why, we may ask, does it matter? Submission of manuscript plays was anonymous and I have found no evidence to show that Larpent was aware of Inchbald's authorship, and if he were, whether it would have affected the process of approval.[14] Thus, we can safely discard the possibility that it was personal identification of Inchbald with the manuscript plays that dictated Larpent's reading of her work. At the same time, however, this positive reception points to the subtlety of her social critique and the progressive agenda that accompanies it. Because it is embedded within domestic plots and conciliatory closures – in the discrete representation, or cautious resolution of political issues – her social criticism was less likely to arouse the uneasiness of the Chief Examiner of Plays or perhaps even to catch his attention, suggesting the success of her negotiation of the institutional strictures of the system.

Inchbald's political critique may have escaped the attention of the Censor, but in fact received anxious notice elsewhere. Nowhere was the public response to Inchbald's dramatic writing more conspicuous than in the reception of *Every One Has His Fault*. First performed on 29 January 1793 at Covent Garden,[15] the play critiques contemporary British society through the contemplation of marriage and patriarchy and how they compel obedience and submission. Specifically, the play tells the story of a group of friends and relations who all experience domestic unhappiness – the elderly bachelor Mr Solus, who seeks marriage as an escape from loneliness; the unhappily married Mr Placid, who dreams of a separation from his domineering wife; Sir Robert Ramble, a professed libertine in the first stages of regret following his recent divorce, and his ex-wife (now called Miss Wooburn) who has ambivalent feelings following the event; and Captain and Lady Eleanor Irwin, who have recently returned, penniless, from America, where they had gone after being disowned by Lady Eleanor's father, Lord Norland, because she had married an army officer of a lower social class against his wishes. In what functions as a sentimental counterpoint to the social comedy of the different marriage plots, we see the Irwins abandoned by all their friends, as their increasing sense of despair culminates in Irwin's thoughts of suicide, and his robbery of his father-in-law at gunpoint.

Connecting these characters is Mr Harmony, a self-acknowledged philanthropist whose main aim is to promote peace and happiness among friends and strangers alike. Harmony, sensitive and benevolent, is not involved in an emotional engagement of his own, but rather, exerts himself in order to ease the distress of his acquaintances, and does so through the telling of white lies which, in causing the other characters to believe that good rather than bad is thought of them, precipitates reconciliation, goodwill and appeasement. Harmony's efforts are successful: the end of the play finds the various marriages renewed or happily re-intact, and the Irwins recognized by the formerly imperious Lord Norland, as well as reunited with their eldest son, Edward, who had been left behind when they went to America, and unbeknownst to them, raised by Norland himself.

Every One Has His Fault was an immediate success, having an initial run that extended to thirty-one nights.[16] Among the attention it received on the morning after its premiere was a notice in the government-supported newspaper *The True Briton*. There, the reviewer acknowledges Inchbald's success in emotionally engaging her audience, but at the same time raises objections to the play's content, mentioning the incident in which Irwin robs his father-in-law, and also making the following observations:

> It has another tendency, and that highly objectionable. Allusions are made to the dearness of provisions in this Metropolis; and in several sentences the *Democrat* displays a cloven foot ... We are at a loss what to term this new species of composition; 'tis neither Comedy, nor Tragi-Comedy, but something anomalous in which the two are jumbled together.[17]

The True Briton, established, in James Boaden's words, "for the avowed object of supporting Mr. Pitt in his endeavours to suppress the revolutionary spirit",[18] was, a week after the execution of Louis XVI and shortly before France's declaration of war on Britain, eager to identify and root out "Jacobinism" anywhere it could be found. The newspaper's anxiety is underscored in its physical layout, as the review of Inchbald's play appears alongside articles calling readers' attention to the whereabouts of Jean-Paul Marat, the actions of Marie Antoinette, reported sightings of French privateers, as well as an ongoing commentary on the death of the French king. Surrounded by this tense perception of a pervasive French threat, Inchbald's theatrical production, with its allusions to a kind of contemporary social decay, points not only to government nervousness in general, but also to the recognition that the theatre, and, moreover, a production that "kept [the audience] alive throughout the whole of the performance" was, notwithstanding the strict system of censorship, a potent site for disseminating radical and contentious ideas.

Yet, *The True Briton's* attention to Inchbald and *Every One Has His Fault* did not end with the 30 January edition of the newspaper. On 1 February, it published further comments, claiming that Inchbald had deleted certain provocative elements from her play following its original performance. Under the title "EVERY ONE HAS HIS FAULT", the writer immediately proceeds with his accusations, which are worth quoting in their entirety:

> Mrs. Inchbald, too, has her's [*sic*]; for she has acknowledged as much. The exceptional parts of her Play, which we, *only*, pointed out to her, have

been expunged, at least nearly so – and we can now, without a violation of justice and propriety, bestow upon it some portion of praise.

In the criticism which we made upon this Piece, we did not mean to attribute to MRS. INCHBALD any improper motives in the sentiments which seemed to predominate in her Piece; but, as TRUE BRITONS, we confess ourselves awake to every insinuation that affects the character, the peace, or the interests of our Country – There were expressions which we could not but be alarmed at, and which we felt it our duty to condemn: these expressions are omitted; and independent of any moral or political considerations, we think the Piece seriously the better for it.

Last night there was a very crowded house – we hope the third will prove equally so, and that MRS. INCHBALD will in consequence no longer have reason to cry out against the *dearness of provisions*, when she counts her gains from the generosity of a British Public.[19]

The True Briton, while exculpating Inchbald from its original claim for "improper motives" (and at the same time congratulating itself both on its coercive power and its journalistic scoop) is actually restating its accusations in different yet more ominous terms. This reconfiguration is apparent both on the level of ideology – the political "insinuations" in her play are now expanded, and viewed as such that could potentially influence "the character, the peace, or the interests of [the] Country" – and also insofar as they implicate her personal life and career. For despite the newspaper's ostensible applauding of Inchbald's "revisions", the charge that she had altered her work and thus compromised her authorial integrity appears (invidiously) *before* the crucial third-night benefit that would entitle her to most of the proceeds earned from the performance.[20]

At once acknowledging the possible backlash that could be caused by these assertions, Inchbald responded that same day in a letter to the newspaper *The Diary*:

After the most laborious efforts to produce a dramatic work deserving the approbation of the town; after experiencing the most painful anxiety till that approbation was secured; a malicious falsehood, aimed to destroy every advantage arising from my industry, has been circulated in a print called "The True Briton;" in which I am accused of conveying seditious sentiments to the public. This charge I considered of little importance, while an impartial audience were, every evening, to judge of its truth: – but my accuser having, in this day's paper, taken a different mode of persecution, saying I have expunged those sentences which were of dangerous tendency, the play can, now, no longer be its own evidence: I am, therefore, compelled to declare, in contradiction to this assertion, that not one line, or one *word*, has been altered or omitted since the first night of representation. As a further proof of the injustice with which I have been treated, had I been so unfortunate in my principles, as to have written anything of the nature of which I am accused, I most certainly should not have presented it for reception to the manager of Covent-garden theatre.[21]

The same pragmatic awareness that characterizes Inchbald's presentation of her politics in her imaginative writing appears in this rebuttal to *The True Briton*. Rejecting, of course, the possibility that she had conveyed "seditious sentiments" in the first place, she does not, however, disclaim the political elements in her play, but rather the polarized formation in which the newspaper's attack is articulated.[22] In doing so, she calls the reviewer's very interpretation of her work into question: if there *had* been a "dangerous tendency" there, the "impartial audience" surely would have noticed it. Furthermore, in explaining at the conclusion of this letter that "had [she] written anything of the nature of which [she was] accused", she would certainly have not submitted it to the Covent Garden Theatre, she calls attention to her self-reflexivity as a writer – her own consciousness of what limits she must not trespass – just as she foregrounds her knowledge of the systems of power that motivate the theatrical world.

While Inchbald obligatorily denies being "unfortunate in her principles", what particularly worries her here is not the actual defense of her politics – for she did *not* respond to *The True Briton's* original piece – but rather the attack on the integrity of her authorship and the concomitant financial loss that could result from the public's response to the newspaper's accusations. And Inchbald's shrewd survival instincts are evident in the fact that by immediately publishing *Every One Has His Fault* that same month, she was able to provide textual evidence against the charges of the newspaper, performing, as Thomas C. Crochunis writes, "a kind of forthright openness to public judgment that contributed to her reputation as an author."[23]

There is one further element of the Inchbald/*True Briton* incident that merits notice here. It concerns John Taylor, the newspaper's theatre critic in 1793, and on the basis of that role the person whom we can assume to have been responsible for the repeated attacks on Inchbald and her play. John Taylor was an eye doctor as well as at different periods editor of *The Morning Post* and *The Morning Herald*, a man enamored with the theatrical world and with its actors and actresses and well connected with other prominent cultural figures of the period. Taylor was a personal friend of Inchbald, even devoting an entire chapter of his memoirs, *Records of My Life* (1832), to her life and to her connections with him. (Taylor had also been a close friend of Mary Robinson, although, perhaps not unexpectedly, given her notoriety, he does not mention her in even one word in his memoirs.) Although John Barrell has recently shown that this was not, as previously assumed, the same John Taylor who had spied on meetings of the London Corresponding Society and had testified at the 1794 Treason Trials against John Thelwall, he was nonetheless "a known and convinced Tory and a devotee of ... William

Pitt."[24] The intensity of Taylor's political loyalties is evident in his apparent willingness – in spite of his friendship with Inchbald – to use his post as theatre critic to repeatedly and publicly attack her politics, to insinuate against her integrity and to potentially damage her career. It is puzzling that, following the review of *Every One Has His Fault,* the two remained friends.[25]

The contemporary reception of *Every One Has His Fault* was otherwise generally favorable. None of the other reviews acknowledge the "seditious" and "democratic" politics that had so vexed *The True Briton,* yet like that newspaper, they attend to its generic novelty, and how, in the words of the *Critical Review,* Inchbald combines "comic humour and the pathetic"[26] in a way that was considered innovative at the time. Thus, when *The Star* asserts that "[t]his piece may more properly be called a dramatized novel than a Comedy" and the *Thespian Magazine* states that "we should have thought ourselves at a tragedy,"[27] we can see the play's position as, in Frank Ellis's words, the "sentimental comedy in the process of becoming melodrama"[28] and with it the recognition of the energy of Inchbald's social critique and her success in imparting it. And while *The True Briton's* repeated attacks on the play derive more from the government anxiety which was so profound in early 1793 rather than from the radicalism of the work itself, it is this understanding that it is indeed a careful and intensely realized response to social concerns of the time on which I want to base my reading of the play. Indeed, it is the availability of Inchbald's political message, together with the repeated attacks of *The True Briton* which most probably led to the sometimes hostile reception of *Every One Has His Fault* in the provincial theatres.[29]

Anne Mellor's observation that "implicit in Inchbald's plays is the argument that Britain is not the land of liberty it claims to be, that its wives are prisoners, its subjects the victims of an oppressive class system [and] ... [o]nly through the agency of benevolent sensibility can social improvement come" succinctly describes the political basis of Inchbald's dramatic writing.[30] Although Mellor does not refer to *Every One Has His Fault* in particular, her understanding of the means through which Inchbald delineates a political worldview is especially relevant for this play, in its representation of the power of patriarchal institutions as well as in the vision of a possible mode of individual action based on sympathy and goodwill, which is presented not to inculcate a general reform of the prevailing cultural order (which, as Inchbald knows well, it cannot do) but only to suggest a way of ameliorating the oppressiveness of social experience.[31]

The initial introduction of Mr Harmony emphasizes a disinterested model of philanthropy as a central issue in the play. As he informs his cousin, Miss Spinster,

> since I can remember, I have felt the most unbounded affection for all my fellow creatures. I even protest to you, dear madam, that, as I walk along the streets of this large metropolis, so warm is my heart towards every

person who passes me, that I long to say, "How do you do?" and "I am glad to see you" to them all.[32]

Miss Spinster's reply infuses this discourse with that particular social relevance that had been identified by *The True Briton*:

> Let me tell you, kinsman, all this pretended philanthropy renders you ridiculous. There is not a fraud, a theft, or hardly any vice committed, that you do not take the criminal's part, shake your head, and cry, "Provisions are so scarce!" And no longer ago than Last Mayor's Day, when you were told that Mr. Alderman Ravenous was ill with an indigestion, you endeavoured to soften the matter, by exclaiming, "Provisions are so scarce!" (I, ii, p. 13)

The repeated acknowledgement of a relevant contemporary issue and the laughter it most probably elicited from the audience justifies, to a certain degree, the anxiety of *The True Briton*. For although the subject of food shortages is articulated by Miss Spinster, a minor figure who will reappear only at the very end of the play, it is associated with Mr Harmony, a central, positive character whose actions ultimately restore order to the discordant social milieu upon which Inchbald focuses her attention.

This interchange serves as a preamble to the presentation of Harmony's main "fault": he tells lies in order to promote social tranquility and goodwill, an action he represents as "saying a few harmless sentences . . . being soothing and acceptable to the person offended" and as a result seeing "hearts cold and closed to each other, warmed and expanded, as every human creature's ought to be" (I, ii, p. 14). It is significant that, besides Miss Spinster, none of Harmony's acquaintances seem to be aware of this tendency on his part: they believe his falsehoods, and thus willingly opt into the scenarios he sets up. For example, following the conversation between Harmony and Miss Spinster Mr Solus arrives at his house; Harmony persuades him to stay for supper with Miss Spinster and himself by telling him that "one of [Miss Spinster's] greatest joys is to be in [his] company" (I, ii, p. 15) when in fact the opposite is the case. In doing so, he initiates a rapprochement which results in the marriage of the two at the end of the play. (Miss Spinster, too, joins the dinner party after hearing that Solus, in turn, thinks well of her but her credulity is curious in light of the way that it was she who had called attention to Harmony's propensity for lying in the first place.)

This is only the first of Harmony's efforts to reconcile hostile parties. Later he will soften, by the same means, the mutual resentment of Lord Norland and Sir Robert Ramble (the latter has forced a divorce upon his wife, who is Norland's ward) as well as that of Norland towards his daughter and son-in-law, the Irwins. Yet, beyond the comic effect of these developments – they precipitate laughter through the audience's ironic knowledge of the true state of the characters' feelings – Harmony's falsehoods take on a deeper serious-ness and a moral urgency in the final dramatic action to reiterate, even as they resolve, the issues at the heart of the play.

Let us briefly look at this concluding scene, which commences with Miss Wooburn and Mrs Placid arriving at the house of Robert Ramble on the pre-tense (contrived by Harmony) that Ramble and Mr Placid have been seriously wounded in a duel. The expectation of imminent death exposes the true feelings of the women and motivates the reconciliation with their respective partners. Although in the case of Miss Wooburn this reunion is problematic (after learning of the ploy she changes her mind, and only agrees to a remar-riage after repeated coercion and the approval of Lord Norland) these issues are immediately set aside, as Harmony startles the company with yet another lie: Irwin has died. This announcement elicits the following response from his shocked companions:

> *Lord Norland*: Do you mean the husband of my daughter?
> *Solus*: Do you mean my nephew?
> *Placid*: Is it my friend?
> *Sir Robert*: And my old acquaintance?
> *Harmony*: Did Mr. Irwin possess all those titles you have given him, gen-tlemen? Was he your son? . . . Your nephew? . . . Your friend? . . . And your old acquaintance? How strange, he did not know it!
> *Placid*: He did know it.
> *Harmony*: Still more strange, that he should die for want, and not apply to any of you?
> *Solus*: What! Die for want in London! Starve in the midst of plenty!
>
> (V, iii, p. 85)

While Harmony's story at first motivates the characters' retrenchment into their own falsehoods ("he did know it", Placid insists) it also enables a pro-cess of recognition in which they will be confronted with the larger truth of the injustice of their own behavior accompanied by the requisite emer-gence of a greater sense of social responsibility. The fact that this awareness is achieved against, and enmeshed within a contemporary topicality renders it culturally pertinent as well as sentimentally affective – the earlier references to the "scarcity of provisions" remind us that one *can* starve in London. (As if to make sure we have remembered, Inchbald inserts a brief comic inter-lude amidst these dramatic events. Solus and Miss Spinster arrive on the scene to inform the company of their marriage, Miss Spinster justifying the surprising event by reminding her cousin, Harmony, that "you can never want an excuse for me, when you call to mind the scarcity of provisions" (V, iii, p. 84).)[33]

The subsequent appearance of the Irwin family, alive and well, reiterates this lesson in social awareness as the final word of the play. At the same time, the effects of Irwin's inhospitable reception in society cannot really be erased, and thus he tells Lord Norland at the moment of reconciliation: "I come to offer my returning reason; to offer my vows that, while that reason continues, so long will I be penitent for the phrensy which put your life in danger" (V, iii, p. 87). In the recollection of his earlier robbery of his father-in-law and the way that social brutality destabilizes rational behavior, we are reminded of the savagery that defines the experience of the dispossessed, and which Irwin himself had expressed earlier in the play: "Is this my native country? Is this the hospitable land which we describe to strangers? No – we are savages to each other; nay, worse" (II, i, p. 27). In *Nature in Art*, the tension between civilization and savagery was only resolved by having the virtuous characters reside at the borders of society. (Similarly, we recall, Charlotte Smith's novels of social defeat conclude at a distance from upper-class London, replaced with the exile of Verona, Switzerland, or the New World.) In contrast, *Every One Has His Fault* ends with the Irwins welcomed back into their social milieu and domestic peace generally restored. The different ways in which the "savage-civilized" opposition is treated in the novel and in the play underline how genre dictates Inchbald's management of her ideological concerns, as Irwin's acknowledgement of the scars of his experience is subsumed into the comic structure of the play, and played out in the heart of the metropolis. At the same time, this conformity to the requirements of genre cannot erase the effect (and affect) of the Irwin subplot: when the *Analytical Review* writes that Irwin's story "is the best part of the play", when Inchbald herself recalls that during the performance "some were heard to laugh, and some were seen to weep"[34] it is clear that the melodramatic urgency of the play's social message was a key force in its success and was what made it memorable for its original audiences.

The play's cultural awareness is also linked, to be sure, to its engagement with the concept of truth – Harmony's prevarications are what lead to the felicitous conclusion of events not only insofar as the Irwins are concerned but regarding the other characters as well. Through this movement of cause and effect, whereby deliberate lying enables reconciliation and "harmony", Inchbald implies that there is a value to falsehood. In doing so, she presents a view opposed to the one held by her friends William Godwin and Thomas Holcroft, who believed in the idea of "truth" as a central tenet of their ideological project.[35] So strong was Holcroft's conviction regarding the efficacy of truth that even in 1798, when other aspects of his political worldview had undergone revision, he could still assert that:

> wherever I perceive any glimmering of truth before me, I readily pursue and endeavour to trace it to its source, without any reserve or caution of pushing the discovery too far, or opening too great a glare of it to the public. I look upon the discovery of any thing which is true, as a valuable acquisition to society; which cannot possibly hurt or obstruct the good

effect of any other truth whatsoever; for they all partake of one common essence, and necessarily coincide with each other.[36]

It is not surprising then that in his review of *Every One Has His Fault*, Holcroft pays particular attention to this subject:

> Of Mr Harmony, we cannot help saying that we are out of patience with his benevolent lies; that is, we feel a very sincere concern that the deeply-rooted prejudice of mankind "that falsehood may be beneficial" is thus so forcibly inculcated. The very merit of the writing increases the sin; and the auditors will go home well satisfied that the lies, which they may have ever told, were all for some good purpose or other, and therefore that they, like Mr. Harmony, are all very good people.[37]

Shortly afterwards, Inchbald would herself explore the possibility of the benevolent truth teller through the character of the young Henry in *Nature and Art*, who is subjected to ridicule, exile and defeat. For her, unlike for Holcroft, it is this naïve sincerity that is inefficacious in the effort to reform society, thus the very act of lying becomes a subversive critique of institutional repression by exposing the hypocrisy that motivates its all-encompassing systems of power.

In its apparent tidiness, then, the conclusion of *Every One Has His Fault* exhibits, as Misty Anderson argues, "the more cynical implication ... that social harmony, if not social justice cannot be achieved naturally. Harmony's lying and the rapid succession of marriages and reconciliations foreground the artificiality of the ending."[38] Anderson ascribes this artificiality, this sense of a contrived closure, both to the demands of Inchbald's chosen genre, which necessitate the culmination of the plot in marriage and to her conceptual concerns – the representation of the abuse of patriarchal authority, but also the fear of "social dissolution ... in a society that rejects marriage." Anderson suggests that what underpins the play is an increasing cultural anxiety surrounding divorce, together with the recognition that "ties of marriage and family must be ... maintained with love and commitment."[39] Yet, although the movement towards reconciliation in *Every One Has His Fault* implies a retreat from divorce as a desirable solution, the alternative is shown to be not much more agreeable, and one which, as opposed to Anderson, I would contend is descriptive rather than prescriptive. That is to say, what emerges in the play is not so much a depiction of "love and commitment" but rather (as elsewhere in Inchbald's writings) the delineation of power and repression and the immoveable patriarchal presence that informs them.

These issues are prominently displayed not only in the Irwins' story of social banishment, but also in the play's central marriage plot – Sir Robert Ramble's desire to re-marry Miss Wooburn, his divorced wife. Lord Norland plays a crucial role in both plots, a double father figure (Lady Irwin is his daughter and Miss Wooburn, his ward) whose imperatives disrupt and then restore domestic order. It is telling that while the Rambles' separation had originally resulted from the profligacy of Sir Robert, the guardian's edicts are what reinforce the powerlessness of the rejected wife. Thus, even as Norland witnesses Miss Wooburn's grief over the divorce, he immediately proposes to marry her off again (obviously, to a man of his own choice) and in response to her increasing unease makes the following assertion:

> And where is the woman who marries the man she would chuse? You are reversing the order of society; men only have the right of choice in marriage. Were women permitted theirs, we should have handsome beggars allied to our noblest families, and no such object in our whole island as an old maid. (III, i, p. 46)

Inchbald, through the words of the imperious aristocrat, acknowledges a present reality of class and gender hierarchies but also a contrasted ideal – an alternative, egalitarian society that could be shaped by women. Although the vision is brief and elusive, Norland's anxious reaction to this possibility – "were women permitted" – is further exemplified in the dialogue that immediately follows the above speech:

> *Miss Wooburn*: But being denied that choice, why am I forbid to remain as I am?
> *Lord Norland*: What are you now? Neither a widow, a maid, nor a wife. If I could fix a term to your present state, I should not be thus anxious to place you in another. (III, i, p. 46)

"Neither a widow, a maid, nor a wife." Lord Norland's words succinctly encapsulate the disruptive potential inherent in the lack of marital status for women.[40] And although his choice of a second husband for Miss Wooburn – the worthy Mr Harmony himself – may perhaps make the end result, and her renewed place within the social order, appear more tolerable, it does not mitigate the force of the patriarchal command, one that, in Anderson's words, "acknowledges Norland's real social power while it exposes its abuse."[41] The extent of Norland's power, and the way that it encompasses class as well as gender prerogatives, is further evident in Harmony's own unwilling compliance with this plan – he, too, must succumb to the aristocratic decree.

Miss Wooburn's reunion with Sir Robert enables structural as well as thematic closure yet, while the rapprochement releases her and Harmony from an unwanted marriage, it at the same time calls attention to the abjection of her position. The meeting between the estranged couple is based, as we recall, on the false premise that Sir Robert had been wounded in a duel, and her response to the supposed crisis causes public acknowledgement of her love towards her former husband, but also, when the true state of events is revealed, public humiliation at the exposure of her vulnerability. It is this sense of vulnerability that prevails at the conclusion of Miss Wooburn's story, as, significantly, it is Lord Norland himself who decides upon the remarriage: "I do at last say to that lady, she has my consent to trust you again" (V, iii, p. 85). Sir Robert's reply – And she will trust me: I see it in her smiles" (V, iii, p. 85) – recognizes *his* perception of her happiness, but also reinforces her own voicelessness, as the two men speak about her, but not to her. Miss Wooburn herself not only remains silent as her fate is decided; the gesture of her ostensible consent – her smile – is not given a presence even in the stage directions, but rather is acknowledged solely by her former and future husband.[42]

The couple's reconciliation signals the final convergence of the philosophical and social issues that shape the course of the dramatic narrative – benevolence and the inefficacy of truth on the one hand, and the power of marriage and patriarchy, on the other. And because truth is ineffectual in promoting public good and in collapsing the existing apparatus of power, all Inchbald can offer is the benevolent lie and the elusive presence of Miss Wooburn's smile: an acquiescence to the belief that the affective domestic experience within the confining limits of a class and gender-based society can be tolerable, even desirable to a certain extent.

II

Inchbald's conception of the oppressiveness of marriage and patriarchy receives further and even starker expression in her 1797 play, *Wives as They Were and Maids as They Are*. Originally submitted to the Chief Examiner of Plays on 10 February 1797 as *The Primitive Wife and the Modern Maid*, the final title aptly conveys her cultural critique in this work, as it echoes the radical preoccupation with "things as they are" – a key phrase for signaling, in Patricia Spacks's words, the treatment of "social actualities in relation to imagined options."[43] Yet, the futility of any agenda of social reform in 1797 is evident in the play's conceptual concerns and thematic closure, as Inchbald focuses on gender relations in order to delineate an oppressive present reality and a grim future vision.

Wives as They Were and Maids as They Are presents the story of Maria Dorrillon, an energetic, high- spirited young woman who strives to assert her independence amidst the dissipated world of fashionable London society. Miss Dorrillon lives with her guardian, Mr Norberry, unaware of the fact that his houseguest, the irascible Mr Mandred, is actually her father, Sir William Dorrillon, who has returned from a stay of many years in India in order to secretly observe her behavior. Father and daughter engage in often acrimonious discussions that focus on female independence and patriarchal command: Sir William, despite his disguised identity, expects (and demands) filial discipline and submission from Miss Dorrillon, while she treats him as just another one of the many men that surround her, and as such, as yet another male figure whose authority must be questioned.

Miss Dorrillon typically lives the life of a fashionable woman. She is courted by many suitors, most prominently the sincere and sober-minded Sir George Evelyn and his dissolute rival, the libertine Mr Bronzely, and is also deeply in debt as a result of losses at gambling. However, she valiantly attempts to live her life according to an idealized view of female subjectivity; as a result, she is unwilling to accept Sir George's offer of financial aid because of her perception that it compromises her integrity, and is unable to receive money from her father because of his objection to her strong-willed behavior. Miss Dorrillon becomes increasingly vulnerable financially and is eventually sent to debtors' prison, where she learns the true identity of her father, and (somewhat surprisingly, in light of what has passed) willingly submits to his authority, including his command that she marry Sir George.

While Miss Dorrillon exhibits the conception of "maids as they are", the second plot of the play focuses on "wives as they were" through the story of Lord and Lady Priory, who also arrive as guests at Norberry's house. Lord Priory is tyrannical to the extreme, imposing a strict disciplinary regimen on his wife in which she must exclude herself from society and basically function as a servant who caters to all his demands, embodying as such a perception of (as the other characters view it) *past* marital rigor. Lady Priory's submission to this mode of existence is challenged when she is first sexually assaulted by Mr Bronzely and later compelled by her husband to meet her assailant in private to hear his further offers of seduction, as a test of her fidelity and as a justification to the other male observers for his strict mode of behavior. The plan "succeeds", and Lady Priory returns willingly to her imperious spouse, yet in doing so articulates an awareness of her subordinate position, which questions even as it upholds a resolution in which female subjugation and silence predominate.

Notwithstanding this discrete moment of resistance, the troubling conclusion of *Wives as They Were and Maids as They Are* in which silent, compliant women voluntarily submit to all-encompassing male authority, exhibits a view of women's position within society that is all the more bleak because it is unaccompanied by mitigating factors such as the subversive presence of the benevolent lie in *Every One Has His Fault*, or the more fully expressed (although similarly futile) vision of rebellion that appears in *A Simple Story*. Years later, however, in her preface to *Wives as They Were* in the *Remarks for the British Theatre*, Inchbald, tellingly, qualifies this portrayal of willing female submission by presenting an openly critical discussion of her work. Beginning with the comment that "[she] has failed in the execution of a proper design", she then elaborates:

> The first act promises a genuine comedy; and the authoress appears to have yielded up her own hopes with reluctance. In the dearth of true

comic invention, she has had recourse at the end of her second act, to farce; [...] she essays successively, the serious, the pathetic, and the refined comic; failing in turns by them all, although by turns producing chance effect; but without accomplishing evident intentions, or gratifying certain expectations indiscreetly raised.[44]

Indicating her dissatisfaction with the play in regard both to style and to the unfulfilled expectations of the plot, Inchbald's remarks succinctly exhibit the limitations of her chosen genre. Thus, the comedy fails *as comedy* because her subject matter – the depiction of the binary of power and subordination that underpins gender relations – is not at all amusing: in Misty Anderson's words, "there is no joke that can moderate the power of husbands and fathers."[45] Moreover, since comic closure insists upon restored domestic tranquility and social order, Inchbald is compelled to present a resolution that reverses rather than sustains the critiques that appear throughout the play.

Taking my cue from Inchbald's disparaging comments in the *Remarks* and the regret expressed there over her unachieved aspirations in the play, I want to present a reading of *Wives as They Were and Maids as They Are* that focuses once more on that tension (so prevalent in her writings) between radical consciousness and practical enactment, and thus which also speculates upon what her "evident intentions" might have been. In doing so, my argument differs from recent critical discussions of the play that view Inchbald's seemingly complacent closure as an affirmation of bourgeois values and of a more conservative political worldview.[46] I want to propose instead a reading in which the reconciliation exhibited at the conclusion of the play takes on a more nuanced perspective – that is to say, one that does not necessarily signal an acceptance of the values it ostensibly endorses. Rather, the retreat to conformity and with it, the dissonance between desired rebellion and ultimate submission, serve to illustrate and amplify the very invincibility of the forces under consideration.

Before turning to the play itself, I would like to remain another moment with Inchbald's prefatory comments in the *Remarks* and the possible insights they provide to the motivations underlining the dramatic narrative. There, Inchbald writes that Miss Dorrillon and Miss Milner in *A Simple Story* have been formed of the "the same manner and spirit", and thus suggests a conscious appropriation of this character type to demonstrate the possibilities of female rebellion but also the price that is paid in attempting it.[47] Yet she also undermines that alignment to a certain extent when she states that the "part [of Miss Dorrillon] was written purposely for Miss Farren; but the very season she should have performed it, she quitted the stage, to appear in a more elevated character."[48] In referring to the life story of the actress Elizabeth Farren, who had left the stage in 1797 after a successful career to marry her long-time lover, the Count of Derby, Inchbald suggests an alternative to the female plot that she herself presents – not in the end result of marriage itself, but rather by calling her readers' attention to a conspicuous unconventionality that is rewarded, in its very unconventionality, with an "elevated character" and (as her readers would certainly have known) a noble title.[49] By stressing the fact that she had written the part of Miss Dorrillon with Farren in mind, Inchbald reinforces her approval of her friend and colleague through the linkage to her own authorial work.

The mention of Miss Milner (but *not* of the other heroine of *A Simple Story*, the conventional Matilda) and the reference to Elizabeth Farren exhibit at the outset the prominence Inchbald assigns to an energetic and unorthodox female presence in *Wives as They Were and Maids as They Are*. And although Inchbald's original audiences and early readers were viewing (and reading) the play without the benefit of this retrospective assessment, they, too, were introduced to the dramatic narrative through prefatory material – the prologue to the play – which foregrounds the tension between energy and acquiescence. Thus, we almost immediately learn from the speaker in the prologue that:

> My client is a more experience'd dame
> Tho' not a Veteran, not unknown to Fame,
> Who thinks your favours are an honest boast,
> Yet fears to forfeit what she values most.[50]

Presented in terms of gain and loss, this frank reference to Inchbald's cautious approach to her subject matter and the compromise that it entails is underscored in the final section of the prologue:

> Our author would your loudest praise forego
> Content to feel within "what passes show"
> "But since" (she says) "such hopes cannot be mine,
> Such bold pretensions I must needs resign" [.]

Through an enmeshment with the authorial voice, the anonymous writer of the prologue calls attention to the specific position of the woman writer and the anxiety that accompanies and limits her presentation of a social critique. The phrase "what passes show", an allusion to *Hamlet*, "But I have that within which passeth show" (I. ii, 266) suggests here a recognition of the possibilities of authentic expression that must be yielded up through conscious submission to the exigencies of genre, gender, censorship and public approbation.

It is significant then that among the mixed reviews that *Wives as They Were and Maids as They Are* received in the periodicals the prologue was singled out for particular attention, its deliberate, self-conscious awareness of ideological compromise accurately perceived by contemporary critics.[51] Thus, the liberal *Monthly Review* publishes a substantial extract from the Prologue, including the passage expressing the "fears to forfeit" that I quoted above.[52] Likewise, the conservative *British Critic,* while admiring the play itself, notes its displeasure with the prologue and the epilogue, citing "evident marks of haste and incorrectness,"[53] a comment that may reflect the reviewer's concern over the woman writer who openly acknowledges the power of the cultural forces that surround her. Equally significant is the fact that, unlike the case of *Every One Has His Fault*, the status of *Wives as They Were* as *comedy* is not a point of discussion in the contemporary reception of the play. Inchbald's comments in her preface regarding "the dearth of true comic invention", her dissatisfaction in the movement between "farce", "the serious", "the pathetic" and the "refined comic", and her sense of "failing in turns by them all" are not similarly acknowledged by the original reviewers. For them, but not for her, the failure of female rebellion and the willing submission to patriarchal authority seem to be accepted as a matter of course, complacently acknowledged in a "successful" comic closure.

Inchbald's concern with women's place within society is most prominently evident in the character of Miss Dorrillon and her active expressions of the desire for female independence and in the ambivalent way in which her story is resolved. Yet Miss Dorrillon's vitality receives even further force when viewed in contrast to the submissiveness of Lady Priory, the second heroine of the play. Ostensibly embodying Inchbald's conception of "wives as they were," Lady Priory is initially introduced through her husband's boast of "always having treated [her] according to the ancient mode",[54] a remark that is elucidated when we learn that she does not go to public places, never entertains at home, is forced to rise every morning at five o'clock and basically performs the functions of a servant, in short, "practis[ing] the same humble docile obedience" (I, i, p. 12) as did women of former times. And yet, despite the apparent archaism of Lady Priory's situation and the binary suggested in the play's title, "past" and "present" are fluid constructions throughout *Wives as They Were and Maids as They Are*, exhibiting in light of what eventually transpires an ironic awareness not of a bifurcation but rather of a continuum of women's experience. As we will see, Lady Priory's function within the dramatic narrative is not exactly to expose the rigors of a "primitive" (to use Inchbald's original title) age, but to convey an understanding of *present* times: the implied modernity that informs Miss Dorrillon's actions is in fact quite tenuous.[55]

That Inchbald in effect destabilizes the temporal equation that she herself presents is apparent when Lady Priory is assaulted by Bronzely, the dissipated libertine and erstwhile suitor of Miss Dorrillon. Lady Priory's unwitting entry into "modern" life finds her actually quite resourceful, as amidst her cries for help she also succeeds in cutting off a piece of her attacker's jacket as evidence of the crime. (Later Bronzely will give the torn jacket to Sir William Dorrillon, who then haplessly attempts to hide himself along with the incriminating evidence.) While in her preface Inchbald alludes to this sequence and its aftermath when she cites her "recourse ... to farce", the assault on Lady Priory actually represents in very serious ways, in fact encapsulates, the continuities of women's oppression which are at the center of her play.

Underpinning this depiction of sexual violence against women is, as Daniel O'Quinn has shown, Inchbald's personal experience as a victim of sexual aggression. He cites an incident, originally related by Inchbald's friend John Taylor, involving the theatre manager Thomas Harris, in which, when assaulted by Harris, Inchbald "found no recourse but in seizing him by the hair, which she pulled with such violence that she forced him to desist."[56] The manager / actress relationship parallels to a certain extent that of the "husband's governance of the marriage state," suggesting Inchbald's awareness of the ubiquity of male power as it is exhibited in sexual predation, but also manifested within a wider alliance of patriarchal control. As O'Quinn explains:

> when the [torn] coat passes from Bronzely to Sir William the exposure encompasses a wider field of signification. The coat now exposes linked patterns of gendered power: a relationship is drawn between socially unacceptable acts of sexual violence and socially condoned acts of parental control. Inchbald literally clothes the tyrannical father and the rapist with the same skirtless coat.[57]

The strength of the patriarchal imperative is most prominently exhibited in *Wives as They Were and Maids as They Are* through the successive adventures of Lady Priory, not only as a potential rape victim, but also in her seemingly unquestioned acceptance of her husband's strict domestic control. The extent of Lady Priory's submissiveness is apparent when Bronzely persists in his attempts to seduce her, and then learns that she had told her husband of his intended visit:

> *Mr. Bronzely*: I charged you to keep what I had to tell you a profound secret.
> *Lady Priory*: Yes; but I thought you understood I could have no secrets from my husband.
> *Mr. Bronzely*: You promised no one should know it but yourself.
> *Lady Priory*: He is myself.
>
> (IV, ii., pp. 50–1)

Lady Priory's rejoinder acknowledges the legal reality that frames the dramatic narrative, at once calling to mind Sir William Blackstone's *Commentaries on the Laws of England* (1765) and the famous description there of women's status within the married state:

> By marriage the husband and wife are one person in law; that is, the very being or legal existence of the woman is suspended during the marriage, or

at least is incorporated and consolidated into that of the husband; under whose wing, protection, and cover she performs every thing ... For this reason, a man cannot grant any thing to his wife, or enter into covenant with her: for the grant would be to suppose her separate existence.[58]

Lady Priory's behavior throughout the play functions, in its very extremeness, as a literalization of this legal reality –"he is myself" – but inherent in her comment is also, crucially, a critical, self-reflexive consciousness of its power. Thus, when she next addresses Bronzely, it is to articulate this awareness: "your sex, in respect to us, are all tyrants. I was born to be the slave of some of you – I make the choice to obey my husband" (IV, ii, p. 51).

The reference to slavery implies the totality of female oppression in general – one is reminded of Mary Wollstonecraft's similar phrasing of the issue in her novel *Maria, or the Wrongs of Woman*, written in the same year as *Wives as They Were* and published posthumously in 1798, in which the eponymous heroine thinks, "Was not the world a vast prison, and women born slaves?"[59] However, the condition of slavery, as Wollstonecraft and Inchbald know well, is also specifically one of economic powerlessness. Thus, when Lady Priory is finally brought to Bronzely's isolated estate, her insistence on an immediate return home acknowledges more than just an emotional context. In spite of her insular existence, Lady Priory was probably well aware of the fact that divorce laws at this time substantially favored the husband, and, as Eve Tavor Bannet has shown, "women's sexual freedom was linked to their economic independence ... 'free love' came with a cruel and devastating price tag for women."[60] Lady Priory's recognition of Bronzely's offer as "so bad a bargain" (V., i., p. 64) suggests the pragmatic realization that life with him would afford no real improvement of her situation.

Inchbald's economic concerns are evident in her depiction of rebellion as well as submission, and Miss Dorrillon's struggle for independence is shown, similarly, as contingent to her financial vulnerability. It is important to note here that although Miss Dorrillon's financial troubles were brought about by her propensity to gamble, gambling itself does not appear as a focus of Inchbald's condemnation in this play. Rather, an early mention of the subject, "I love to part with my money ... I like to see the joy sparkle in another's eye" (I, i, p. 15) exhibits, uniquely, I believe, in Inchbald's works, a positive dimension, stressing the generosity that marks Miss Dorrillon as an approved character worthy of our interest and identification.[61] In this brief glimpse of active female agency Miss Dorrillon, in O'Quinn's words, "indulges in the fantasy economy in which women are independent, yet prudently protects herself from non-legally binding offers of support from the men around her."[62]

That it is indeed a fantasy to which she clings, Miss Dorrillon, in spite of herself, seems to know as well. Thus, when her father (disguised as Mr Mandred) attempts to promote Sir George's suit, she represents her position as that of a defendant in an imagined courtroom scene, and after acknowledging "great lawyers study[ing] Blackstone", asserts:

> You mean to say, "That if A is beloved by B, why should not A be constrained to return B's love?" Counsellor for defendant – "Because, moreover, and besides B ... there are also C, D, E, F, and G; all of whom put in their separate claims – and what, in this case, can poor A do? She is willing to part and divide her love, share and share alike; but B will have all, or none: so poor A must remain A, by herself, A." (II, i, pp. 27–8)

The fact that Miss Dorrillon's "playful legalese"[63] is preceded by the mention of Blackstone qualifies this lyric vision of selfhood, his *Commentary* once more alluded to in the text, as it frames the witty legal fantasy with a very real legal reality. The reference to Blackstone renders the fleeting ideal exhibited in Miss Dorrillon's "courtroom" particularly tenuous and her presentation of the alternative to marriage – "poor A must remain A, by herself, A" – wistfully ironic, as it registers the consciousness of a powerful legal truth that is always in the background and the "suspension of existence" which is continuously at stake.

It is the eventuality of marriage which, of course, prevails: "B will (and does) have all." That Miss Dorrillon's independence is only temporary, and her subordination imminent is apparent when she is arrested for debt.[64] Her imprisonment suggests the "female gothic" inflection of this play, not only through its exhibition of forced confinement but also in how the cell functions concurrently as a refuge which energizes rather than subdues her in her struggle against institutional exertions of power. In refusing to comply with Sir William's conditions for paying the money to release her from prison – the regulation of her behavior – Miss Dorrillon once more displays her independent spirit as well as her generosity. And when he finally agrees to give her the money without condition, she immediately offers to send it to her father instead, who is represented as living in poverty and sickness (although it is he, still disguised as Mr Mandred, whom she is in fact addressing). Her plea, "I shall be happy in this prison, indeed I shall, so I can but give a momentary relief to my dear, dear father" (V, ii, p. 71) renders the physicality of the prison superfluous through the projection of an active philanthropy and a foregrounded, transcendent sense of self.

The filial devotion that motivates Miss Dorrillon's behavior enables a final moment of idealized energy, one that is especially telling in light of what immediately follows. Upon learning from Mr Norberry of Mandred's true identity, she collapses into a faint, a literal moment of non-being from which she is reborn to silence, submission and conformity, as she emerges from her cell only to enter into the larger prison of women's experience. Significantly, then, just like Miss Wooburn in *Every One Has His Fault*, the "new"

Miss Dorrillon is marginalized at the very moment when her future – the choice of her husband – is decided:

> *Sir William*: ... you [Mr. Bronzely] will not be surprised, if the first command I lay upon my daughter is – to take refuge from your pursuits, in the protection of Sir George Evelyn.
> *Sir George*: And may I hope, Maria –
> *Miss Dorrillon*: No – I will instantly put an end to all your hopes.
> *Sir George*: How?
> *Sir William*: By raising you to the summit of your wishes.
> Alarmed at my severity, she has owned her readiness to become the subject of a milder government.
>
> (V, iv, pp. 77–8)

Unlike Miss Wooburn, however, Miss Dorrillon attempts to speak at the crucial moment when her fate is decreed. What she says – "I will instantly put an end to all your hopes" – suggests that she just may rebel against her father's plans, allowing us for a brief moment to once more anticipate the "old" Miss Dorrillon articulating an ideal of independent selfhood. Yet we never learn what she had intended to say. The fact that she is silenced by her father's anxious interjection, only to be readdressed indirectly, and through metaphors of government, ultimately signals the triumph of patriarchal power. The ease and efficiency with which Miss Dorrillon submits to Sir William's control, curious in light of her earlier actions, lead to an even greater dissonance when she finally speaks again in the closing lines of the play. Speaking only because invited to do so by her husband-to-be, she asserts, "A maid of the present day shall become a wife like those – of former times" (V, iv, p. 78).[65] Her subordination, it seems, is complete.

O'Quinn contends that this conclusion, and Miss Dorrillon's willingness to become "the subject of a milder government" reflects Inchbald's endorsement of "reasonable patriarchal government in the private sphere" which seeks, ultimately, to "restrain masculine fantasies of domination in favor of socio-economic stability."[66] "Socio-economic stability" was also, to be sure, a key issue for Inchbald herself, and the fashioning of her dramatic text in such a way so as not to contemplate the outcome of a sustained rebellion would be in line with, if not a conscious ideological positioning, then at least a cautious authorial stance – doubly cautious in her writing for the theatre and always aware of its "despotic government." This was especially true in 1797, a period when John Larpent was particularly vigilant in denying the stage to any work that so much as hinted at the promotion of a subversive social agenda[67] and a time when the world had seen all too clearly the price exacted by the toppling of tyrannical institutions. Perhaps then, acquiescence to a milder form of patriarchy could be a reasonable and pragmatic goal towards which she could lead her fictive characters and espouse on the public stage.

And yet, that having been said, I am still compelled by Inchbald's prefatory remarks to this play and the disappointment expressed there over her lack of success in "accomplishing evident intentions." Could those "intentions" have included a less forceful and troubling erasure of female subjectivity? Could she be alluding to a more qualified acceptance of "reasonable patriarchal government"? If we return to the final scene of *Wives as They Were and Maids as They Are*, we can find various moments that undermine the conclusion that Inchbald presents, suggesting that the dissatisfaction she *later* felt might have also manifested itself in a subtle subversion of her apparent message at the moment of its presentation. For example, when Miss Dorrillon asserts that "a maid of the present day shall become a wife like those – of former times" the word "shall" is itself ambiguous, not necessarily signaling a prescriptive decree for female behavior, but perhaps simply recognition of the authority to which she has succumbed. As the OED informs us, "shall" can be expressive of varying degrees of willingness, representing mere futurity as well as voluntary action; expectation accompanied by hope but also by fear; duty and obligation alongside propriety. It is important, furthermore, to remember that these lines immediately follow Sir William's earlier remark that Miss Dorrillon had consented to marry because she was "alarmed at [his] severity." What had he told his daughter that enabled such immediate submission – how was that severity expressed? Because that conversation occurs off stage, we are left to imagine, or Inchbald assumes that we already know, the invincibility of patriarchal tyranny.

"A maid of the present day shall become a wife like those – of former times." Were these lines spoken on stage, we may also wonder, with spirit or irony; with conviction or resignation? And, we may further ask, did Inchbald have Elizabeth Farren herself in mind when writing them? It would be tempting to consider the subversive possibilities inherent in the performance of this scene as Inchbald had originally conceived it at her writing table. Farren, in her unconventional personal life, was certainly no model of a woman "of former times" and a vision of her delivering this final speech infuses it with an ironic awareness that would qualify the unequivocal submission it promotes, inviting us to imagine, if even for a fleeting moment, a different outcome to the daughter's rebellion, as well as an alternative to what emerges as an elusive, ultimately fictive temporal dichotomy of female experience.

III

Inchbald's commentary in her *Remarks* on the writing of *Wives as They Were and Maids as They Are* provides a suggestive glimpse of her approach to her work, affording us brief access to the authorial motivations that accompany the process of composition in its early stages as well as to a later, self-reflexive assessment of the eventual result. A reading of her suppressed play *The Massacre* offers additional insights into a kind of "original intention." The story of a family destroyed by violent events in a time of political turmoil, ostensibly during the St Bartholomew's Day massacres, the play is also a quite personal reflection on the possibilities of representation – in *Britain* – regarding the French Revolution itself.

Although *The Massacre* was completed in early 1792 and later typeset for publication, it was neither performed nor published, appearing in print only in 1833 when included by James Boaden as an appendix to his biography of Inchbald. Boaden alludes to the tense political climate that character-ized the year of the play's composition in comments immediately prefacing the work – "The play was suppressed, though printed, before publication, in deference to public opinions" – and in the biography itself, stating that Inchbald had shown her manuscript to Thomas Harris at Covent Garden and George Colman at the Haymarket, but "the stage declined so disagree-able a subject."[68] Boaden notes that Inchbald had circulated *The Massacre* among others as well: Godwin, Holcroft and George Hardinge all agreed that "[her] fame would not have been advanced by either the performance, or the publication of [the play.]"[69]

Among the recipients of the manuscript not mentioned by Boaden is John Taylor, who thus remembered the events years later:

> Besides her well-known plays and farces, Mrs. Inchbald wrote a tragedy in prose on the French revolution, and the fate of the unfortunate Louis XVI. It was printed, but never published. She sent a copy of it to me, with the following note, which I insert, because I cannot but be proud that such a woman should have paid such a compliment to my opinion: – "I am undetermined whether to publish this play or not – do, dear creature, give me your opinion. I will send for an answer to-morrow, or if you call here, leave a note if I am from home." As far as I can recollect, I advised her to suppress it.[70]

Taylor's recollection of *The Massacre* is important, as it exhibits Inchbald's manner of inviting comments and criticism on her work from friends on both sides of the political spectrum. (And just how much Taylor's politics were opposed to Inchbald's would become evident the following year in his scathing attack on *Every One Has His Fault* in *The True Briton*.) At the same time, Taylor himself seems preoccupied in this anecdote with emphasizing his close personal relationship with Inchbald rather than with the play itself, his status as "dear creature" more worthy of attention than the controversial political text for which his opinion was requested. This emphasis is in accor-dance with the way Taylor downplays his politics in general in his memoirs and is indicative of the change in the political climate in the intervening years: in 1832, the year of the passing of the Reform Bill, the political divi-siveness of the 1790s was viewed in quite a different light.[71] As Taylor wants to show here, it is indeed barely remembered.

What do we find in *The Massacre* that, in 1792, had disturbed Godwin and Holcroft on the one hand, and Taylor on the other? Boaden surmises that Inchbald's radical friends "dreaded the exposure of republican horrors"[72] implicated in the play's portrayal of party uprising; Taylor, conversely, was probably taken aback by the speeches of the benevolent, articulate judge, Glandeve, who promotes a vision of "liberty ... peace and charity"[73] dissociated from the violent excesses accompanying the promotion of the cause. Although it seems that Inchbald had that view of representing a tolerant "liberty, peace and charity" in mind when writing *The Massacre*, the portrayal of these issues within a more nuanced and complex context might explain why the play was received with unease by her friends on both sides of the political divide.

Inchbald revealingly tells of her intentions in writing the play in a letter to Godwin, which, although undated, was probably written in early 1792:

> There appears an inconsistency in my having said to you, "I have no view to any public good in this piece," and afterwards alluding to its preventing future massacres: to this I reply that it was your hinting to me that it might do harm which gave me the first idea that it might do good.[74]

This letter sheds light on the tension between "public" and "private" authorship that informs the composition of *The Massacre*. Thus, while on the one hand Inchbald asserts that she had "no view to any *public* good" when writing the play, the fact that the manuscript was offered to the theatre managers implies that she had entertained at least a faint hope of having her work staged. Knowing that *The Massacre* actually lay on the desk of George Colman, awaiting his verdict –"I will, now, attend to [the Tragedy] very speedily", he had informed Inchbald in a letter dated 7 February 1792[75] – challenges the view that the play was written "expressly to intervene in the private political discussions of the Jacobin circle."[76] Given the date of Colman's letter, it is also clear that the play was not written, as is sometimes assumed, as a direct response to the massacres which occurred in Paris in September 1792.[77] Even before the massacres, events such as the "Great Fear" of 1789, the attacks on refractory priests, the killings on the Champ de Mars in the summer of 1791 and the food riots in Paris at the beginning of 1792, provided Inchbald with ample evidence of the Revolution's potential for generating scenes of random violence.

The tentative status of *The Massacre* as an attempt to "do good" beyond a small circle of friends is further evinced in Inchbald's introductory advertisement to the printed text. Explaining why this work had never been produced, she quotes Horace Walpole's postscript to his own unacted play, *The Mysterious Mother*:

> From the time that I first undertook the foregoing scenes, I never flattered myself that they would be proper to appear on the stage. The subject is

so horrid, that I thought it would shock, rather than give satisfaction, to an audience. Still, I found it so truly tragic in the essential springs of *terror* and *pity,* that I could not resist the impulse of adapting it to the scene, though it could never be practicable to produce it there.

Inchbald aptly applies Walpole's recognition of different authorial motivations, yet in doing so she is also somewhat disingenuous, for she *had* submitted *The Massacre* to at least one theatre manager. Furthermore, although she had informed Taylor that she was "undetermined whether to publish this play or not" the very presence of an advertisement reflects the moment, disclaimer aside, when she assumes a wider audience than the few friends to whom she had shown her manuscript, if not in performance, than at least as text. Why, after all, write an advertisement in the first place? Why have the play typeset for publication?

Staying for a moment with the advertisement, we see additional evidence of this move towards public presentation. Inchbald states there that the play was "founded upon circumstances that have been related as facts," and on the title page adds that it was "taken from the French." She thus simultaneously grounds the dramatic narrative within a specific historical reality but also purposely distances it, both as an adapted text, and as one that is supposedly set during the time of the St Bartholomew's Day massacres – although that setting and historical context receive no explicit substantiation in the play itself.[78] The act of historically displacing politically relevant plays was itself a common strategy during the revolutionary years and may further hint at an original intent of performance on the part of Inchbald through a self-conscious allegorizing of earlier yet parallel, recognizable, events.[79] This introductory material, along with the various letters to and from Inchbald, signal together an ongoing uncertainty as to the play's final status, exhibiting for future readers the vacillation between private and public desires, illustrating the attempt to intervene in political discourse as well as the various factors that combine to restrain it.

Despite the ambivalence inherent in this positioning, *The Massacre* at the same time offers a revealing view of Inchbald deviating from her customary pragmatism. While not exactly a unique instance of ideological conspicuousness (recall, in particular, *Nature and Art*) nor an endeavor entirely dissociated from the pressures of stage politics (for she *had* tried to have the play produced) it nonetheless reflects a singular moment in Inchbald's career in which she abandons social comedy and a critique of domestic institutions in order to engage directly with political events. And because *The Massacre* is an overt political critique, tragedy rather than comedy, and is unfettered by necessary accommodations (had it been produced) to censorial restrictions, I will be especially attentive in my discussion of the play to how Inchbald explicitly represents those themes which in her other works are embedded in a repertoire of symbolic replacements, particularly as they pertain to gender and silencing.

The Massacre tells the story of the Tricastin family, whose tranquil domestic existence is disrupted and then destroyed by violent political upheaval. Eusèbe Tricastin returns to his family after witnessing and escaping the brutal slaughter taking place on the streets of Paris, only to hear that a mob is approaching their estate and demanding his arrest. The family makes hurried plans to flee but is overcome by enemy forces. Through a ploy, Mme Tricastin is removed from the scene, while Eusèbe and his father are brought to a hastily organized trial, where they face the benevolent judge Glandeve. Condemning random acts of violence, Glandeve releases them, only for the group to learn that, in their attempted flight, Mme Tricastin and her children have been killed by the riotous mob. The play concludes as a tolerant, non-violent worldview is espoused alongside the removal of the bodies of the slain family. As this brief summary makes clear, repeated references to mob violence, party and class struggle and political trials, as well as its French setting, underscore the play's topicality and it is this link with current (1792) rather than sixteenth-century events that Inchbald's original readers, such as Godwin and Taylor, immediately identified.

Although introduced through prefatory material that acknowledges its political relevance, the play itself initially focuses on what appears to be solely a scene of conjugal distress. Mme Tricastin complains about her husband's prolonged stay in Paris in an opening sequence that conceals, however briefly, the political upheavals that are so central to the dramatic action. Mme Tricastin is apparently unaware of any sort of external exigency that would account for her husband's absence, and of the political unrest that is at that very moment occurring. This initial allusion to Mme Tricastin's insularity from the outside world and the brief aspersion regarding her husband's behavior – "it is cruel of him to find delight in the society of his friends" – she complains (I, p. 360) suggests a familiar context of domestic instability that is introduced, only to be discarded.

Even as the impending danger becomes clear to those who surround her, Mme Tricastin is repeatedly denied information (by her friends Conrad and Amédée as well as by the elder Tricastin, her father-in-law) about what is happening:

> *Mme. Tricastin*: [*Going to Amédée*] Amédée, whatever makes you look thus pale, do not be afraid to tell it to me.
> *Conrad*: [*In a low voice to Tricastin*] Permit me to speak a word to you alone.
> *Tricastin*: Alone? – Why? Wherefore? [*Trembling*] I protest you alarm me almost as much as my daughter is alarmed!
> *Conrad*: Follow me into another room. [*Still in a low voice*]
> *Tricastin*: But, if I do, her friend will tell her the secret.
> *Conrad*: She has promised me she will not.

Tricastin: Don't mind her promise; she can't help it. However, I'll go with you. [*Going*]
Mme. Tricastin: Sir! Conrad! Whither are you both going? Oh! whatever has befallen my husband, do not conceal it from me.
Conrad: I do not know that anything has befallen him – upon my word of honour, I speak the truth.
Mme. Tricastin: Then why these terrifying looks?

(I, pp. 361–2)

This conversation introduces an emphasis on female powerlessness as a prominent concern in the play. Yet the attempt to insulate Mme Tricastin from impending danger generates, not fortitude, but only fear, as her companions ineffectually strive to uphold a public / private – gendered – sense of decorum that is collapsing even as they speak. In its emphasis on female vulnerability, this sequence exemplifies a political critique in which, as Daniel O'Quinn argues, the "sequestration of women and children in ostensibly 'safe spaces' ... allows the family and the political to become realms of exclusively male homosocial transactions" which are eventually unable to protect them.[80]

At the same time, Inchbald's critique throughout the play is also aimed at the indiscriminateness of the violence itself. Thus, she depicts a landscape of terror in which both women *and* men are among the victims: the actions of the mob are, as she clearly shows, impervious to gender difference. Conrad's disclosure of a report that "speaks of children torn from the breast of their mothers, husbands from the arms of their wives, and aged parents from their agonizing families" (I, p. 362) serves only as a preamble to Eusèbe's eventual arrival and his account of the scenes he has witnessed, including the murder of his wife's family: "these stains came from the veins – of thy mother – thy uncles – thy sisters – and all of those, who clung fast around me, and I tried in vain to defend" (I, p. 364). He then further specifies:

I found I clasped nothing but dead bodies. – I rose from the horrid pile, and by a lamp discerned (all gashed with wounds) faces, that but a few hours before I had seen shine with health and benevolence ... I saw poor females, youths, and helpless infants try to ward off the last fatal blow ... aged men dragged by their white hairs ... infants ... stab other infants sleeping in their cradles. (I, pp. 364–5)

The accounts of Eusèbe and Conrad, remarkable in their graphic explicitness, would seem to indicate a universal rejection of "party" violence; it is telling then that both men express a desire for vengeance in a way that does not preclude their own employment of brutal means in attaining it. It is not through the site of "male homosocial transactions," to use O'Quinn's term again, that, Inchbald implies, future massacres will be prevented.

This propensity to violence is challenged, however, even if unsuccessfully, by the elder Tricastin, who repeatedly calls for restraint, most notably when he states that "by pursuing retaliation, we shall assume the power of God, and forfeit the rights of man" (Act I, p. 365). This terminology acknowledges the contemporaneousness of the dramatic narrative for Inchbald's implied audience; the phrase "the rights of man", anachronistic in relation to the period of the St Bartholomew's Day massacres, shows the slippage of her allegorical framework and the explicit emergence of the actual political context in which she is interested. At the same time, the "rights of man" is also incongruous here because it is associated with an obsolete worldview rather than with an emerging political modernity. The clash between the old and new orders is evinced in the elder Tricastin's failed attempt at assuming his son's identity as the mob reaches his house, as well as in the reasons he employs to forestall the attack. His futile attempt to placate his adversaries and their leader, Dugas – "Many little acts of friendship have passed between us … little kindnesses … do not imbrue your hand in your neighbour's blood" (Act II, p. 373) – exhibits the voice of moderation, but one that is based on "little", individual acts of neighborly relations and solely on an out-dated *personal* civility whose time has irretrievably passed.

In contrast, Glandeve, the judge before whom the elder Tricastin and his son Eusèbe are brought to trial is a figure firmly located within the present political moment. Immediately identified (by two villagers sympathetic to the Tricastins) as "strong in the opposite party" (III, p. 374), his presence within the narrative implies that a compassionate revolutionary activism in which "'tis liberty to do good, not ill – liberty joined with peace and charity" (III, p. 375) could, perhaps, still exist. Glandeve's enlightened vision is further evident as the court proceedings continue:

> *Dugas*: … Every one present knows the crimes of Eusèbe.
> *Glandeve*: What are they?
> *Dugas*: All know – he does not think with us.
> *Glandeve*: And how long (answer me, some of my friends) has it been a capital offense – *to think as you please?* If I am a friend to freedom, my first object is, freedom of *thought*.
>
> (III, pp. 375–6)

It is telling that Inchbald's representation of an idealized revolutionary viewpoint – the one that opposes its violent excesses – includes a particular emphasis on those abstract universal values whose relevance extends beyond revolutionary France. In foregrounding the defense of "freedom of thought" she expresses both an ideological positioning and a plea for open-mindedness that together, it seems to me, also accommodate a self-referential awareness of the circumstances that accompanied the writing of *The Massacre* and the thoughts that she must have had as to whether it would ever be published or performed. Appearing *before* the punitive legislation of the mid-1790s, in which the right to *"think as you please"* came under constant attack, Inchbald's play is a reflection on cultural discourse that foresees the censorial forces that will ultimately prevail.

Accordingly, *The Massacre*, as a conscious intervention on behalf of a progressive political agenda which is also as a self-reflexive commentary upon the attempt to do so, concludes with an act of silencing. Just at the moment when the Tricastin men are saved, the news arrives that Mme Tricastin and her children have been killed by the riotous mob. Replicating the death of her mother that had occurred under the same circumstances the day before, Mme Tricastin's murder illustrates in the extreme the continuity of female silencing that accompanies and indeed characterizes male governance; Glandeve's courtroom, as all of Inchbald's "courtrooms", is exposed as embodying exclusively a male prerogative.

The body of the dead woman on stage at the end of the play may also symbolically represent Inchbald's own recognition of the limitations of speech and of action – especially for women, always the most vulnerable of subjects – at the particular moment when, in concluding her play, she also contemplates its future status. And yet, as I hope to have demonstrated, Inchbald herself was neither silenced nor excluded from contemporary political debate. Although *The Massacre* did not appear before the public, ideological concerns exhibited in the play appear in other, albeit more nuanced, ways throughout her literary oeuvre: the right to "freedom of thought" along with the pervasiveness of silencing and censorship; the critique of intolerance and the wish to "prevent future massacres", but also the representation of an idealistic effort that has somehow gone wrong; the recognition of the forces that continually impinge upon a woman's attempt to assert an independent selfhood, and indeed the depiction of female vulnerability itself. Two comments that appear in Inchbald's letters to Godwin during the writing of her most overtly political texts (*The Massacre* and *Nature and Art*) summarize together the awareness that accompanied her anxious but ultimately successful navigation of the pressures of politics and publishing – the attempt to "do good" alongside the consciousness of "Newgate before [her] eyes" – exemplifying a cautious pragmatism but also an idealized, consciously radical vision.

IV

In concluding this chapter with these references, it is important to note that, unlike Charlotte Smith and Mary Robinson, Inchbald was not in contact with Godwin at the end of the revolutionary decade. In their friendship, which was more intense and sustained on personal as well as professional levels (Godwin and Inchbald had been friends since 1791, had read and commented on drafts of each other's works and had often gone to the theatre together) the break was also more profound. A brief mention of the collapse of the Godwin/Inchbald relationship may serve as a coda to my discussion of Inchbald through its encapsulation of those tensions that accompanied her both in her private life and in the presentation of her politically-inflected writing. Inchbald's friendship with Godwin effectively ended on 19 April 1797 at Drury Lane theatre, following an incident in which she behaved unkindly towards Mary Wollstonecraft, whom Godwin had married a few weeks earlier. Inchbald does not emerge well from the events surrounding Godwin's marriage. Her sharp note upon hearing of the news, "If I have done wrong, when you next marry, I will act differently",[81] and her public snubbing of Wollstonecraft a few days later at Drury Lane display a degree of insensitivity and a lack of generosity that is so unlike what we would want, or expect, to see from Inchbald, who was otherwise generally regarded as a loyal and liberal-minded friend. At the same time, Godwin's own insensitivity is also revealed in the events surrounding the altercation at the theatre. He had been Inchbald's regular companion in the period immediately preceding and following his marriage (his diary notes seven different meetings between them in the days leading up to and following the event) and the revelation of the secret he had been keeping during that time would have been insulting not only on a personal level but, in light of Wollstonecraft's visible pregnancy and the assumption that the she and Godwin had been married much earlier, socially compromising for Inchbald as well.[82] The anger felt by both parties following the clash was profound. Even some months later, upon hearing from Godwin of Wollstonecraft's death, Inchbald wrote to him that she was shocked "beyond expression [but did not feel] the smallest portion of remorse [for her earlier behavior]." In his reply, Godwin wrote with bitterness of her "base, cruel and insulting" behavior towards his late wife.[83] Nonetheless, he did try to resume the connection in later years. Inchbald may have been cordial towards him, but the friendship never retrieved its earlier intensity.[84]

Opposing, clearly insurmountable, gender-driven expectations in regard to reputation, propriety and integrity dictate Inchbald's and Godwin's behavior. For Inchbald, the desirability of Godwin's friendship was outweighed by what she perceived as a threat to her reputation and thus to social and financial survival. Conversely, Godwin's claim, in the course of their correspondence following the altercation, that Inchbald kept "no circles to debase & enslave" her[85] may have been intended as a compliment, but more pertinently reflects his failure to appreciate her sense of the precariousness of her social position. As he should have known, "circles" of public approbation do, in fact, enslave. It was Inchbald's acquiescence to the demands of those circles, and her cautious negotiations with all the despotic governments in which she was, variously, a subject, that insured her literary success and financial independence, and in doing so acknowledge her understanding of rebellion and submission but also the price they exact.

Conclusion

Anne Janowitz concludes her study of Mary Robinson and Anna Barbauld by calling attention to a collection of *Odes* published in Ludlow in 1800 by George Nicholson and distributed in London by radical bookseller Henry Symonds. Janowitz cites the collection as reflective of the final defeat of the radical moment, writing that "it is a sad booklet, suffused with the voices of resignation and retreat of radicals and reformers and bluestockings and sold by a bookseller recently associated with Paine's red-hot republicanism."[1] Among the contributors whose works Nicholson gathered for the volume and who would have known in their own lives the energy but also the defeat of the radical moment were Anna Barbauld, the satirist Peter Pindar (John Wolcot), Robert Burns and, as I have tried to show in this book, Mary Robinson. The poems themselves foreground various modes of introspection – in their titles, with odes to melancholy, reflection, sympathy, and despondency (to name a few) and in their subject matter, which for the most part displays a kind of quietist pastoral retirement, frequently adorned with classical images but with little, if any, contemporary referentiality.[2]

"To Meditation", the Robinson poem that appears in the *Odes*, is a shorter version of a piece originally published in the newspaper *The Oracle* on 26 December 1789. It had been reprinted in Robinson's *Poems* (1791) and would later be included in the 1806 *Poetical Works* edited by her daughter, Maria Elizabeth.[3] Thus, although the poem complements the other works in the Nicholson collection by exhibiting the similar theme of a country retirement infused with melancholy memory, it is not in a historical sense indicative of the cultural moment in which the volume was compiled. The world had profoundly changed between 1789 and 1800 and Robinson's poetical reflections in that earlier period, although informed by the personal experience of ostracism, had yet to be mediated by the climate of political repression.

Janowitz's reference to the *Odes* is illuminating as an indication of the radical literary endeavor at the close of the revolutionary decade. Yet I want to conclude my discussion of Mary Robinson, Charlotte Smith and Elizabeth

Inchbald by pointing to a different direction, to those later works of the three writers which exhibit, even if obliquely, timely political resonances all but absent from the Nicholson volume. Just as in the other representations of resignation and defeat that we viewed throughout this book, such as the conclusions to *Walsingham*, *The Young Philosopher*, and *Nature and Art*, in which the memory and aftereffects of social oppression cannot be erased even amidst conjugal harmony and financial sufficiency, the final works of Robinson, Smith and Inchbald do not retreat from an acknowledgement of contemporary issues nor indulge in the comforts of a fictive, pastoral abode.

A few representative but necessarily very brief examples evince this topical, contemporary engagement. Mary Robinson, for one, continued to call attention to the pressures that limit free speech. In her novel *The False Friend* (1799) there are repeated allusions to the issue, including a sequence in which the protagonist, Gertrude St Leger, defends the "liberty of . . . conscience" not long before she is threatened by her perfidious landlady, who openly announces herself as a government spy and paid informer, and who insinuates that "it is the duty of every loyal subject to be careful."[4] In "The Progress of Liberty" (1801), her two-book poem that revisits both the aspirations and the excesses of the French Revolution, Robinson would yet again link the prisoner who "[d]ared talk of Freedom" to the "liberty" that is "reason's birthright, and the gift of God!"[5]

Charlotte Smith, as we saw earlier, continued in the *Letters of a Solitary Wanderer* to express a critical social worldview, prefacing her comments with anxious references to the criticism incurred by those who articulated what was seen as a "Jacobin" positioning.[6] Her final work, the posthumously published blank-verse poem *Beachy Head* (1807) further exhibits Smith's political awareness as it appears at the end of her life. The poem presents a vast panorama viewed from the Sussex seashore. The poet-narrator gradually moves down from the summit, depicting a landscape inflected with inverted pastoral underpinnings – this is a world of poverty, wet and shivering sheep, smugglers, alienated recluses and insane vagrants. Smith's expressive and meticulously detailed landscape is, moreover, informed by her conception of the grand scale of history itself. In viewing the English history that resonates in Beachy Head, the poem suggests a "subversive historiography"[7] which privileges common English-French origins and in doing so works against the prejudicial divisions which had reached a peak during the Napoleonic wars.

In her prefaces to Longman's *The British Theatre* (1806–9) Elizabeth Inchbald repeatedly called attention to the political conditions under which British drama was written and performed. Her final play, *To Marry or Not to Marry* (1805), exhibits another dimension of her later political awareness. In the play Inchbald returns to address those themes that had featured in her earlier works – authenticity as opposed to artifice, truth versus falsehood and marriage as a signifier of institutional power. Despite the genuine love felt by the individualistic, idealistic, Sir Oswin Mortland and Hester Lavensforth, there is repeated emphasis on the coercive forces that discipline them into marriage, and with it, into an approved social conformity. *To Marry or Not to Marry* exhibits, furthermore, a specific contemporary awareness as well. The reference to Sir Oswin's involvement in a case of political impeachment led to speculation by the *Anti-Jacobin Review* that Inchbald's play was a commentary upon the real-life impeachment, over corruption charges, of Henry Dundas (Lord Melville), the First Lord of the Admiralty. The impeachment effort was led by Samuel Whitbread, a Whig MP who was known for his progressive, if not radical opinions. In her preface to the play for the *British Theatre*, Inchbald neither refutes nor admits the *Anti-Jacobin's* charge, but acknowledges it as a "remarkable observation . . . worthy of insertion."[8] And yet, in the play itself Sir Oswin learns to regret his earlier political interventions; his lesson in conformity on the domestic front carries with it a parallel rejection of his earlier involvement in the public sphere of politics, replaced by compassion for his rival's banishment and suffering.

Inchbald's critique of a heightened, energetic, political involvement in *To Marry or Not to Marry* is counterbalanced by the attention she gives to the *Anti-Jacobin's* aspersions over the political provenance of her play, as she persists in reminding her readers of her *own* political awareness. This positioning similarly reflects the ideological reminders that we have seen in the final works of Charlotte Smith and Mary Robinson as well. After the revolutionary decade and the energy, fervor, hopes, aspirations and, ultimately disappointment of the 1790s, there still remained the possibility of expression, muted, perhaps, but far from abandoned; of what was lost but also of what has been retained – those "revolutionary imaginings" that still and yet are presented in print publications.

Notes

Introduction

1. William Godwin, "Essay against re-opening the war with France" (1793), quoted in Mark Philp, "Thompson, Godwin and the French Revolution", *History Workshop Journal* 39 (1995), p. 95.
2. Jürgen Habermas, *The Structural Transformation of the Public Sphere*, trans. Thomas Burger (Cambridge, MA: MIT Press, 1989), p. 51.
3. Habermas, p. 56. For examples of feminist responses to Habermas see Nancy Frazer, "Rethinking the Public Sphere: A Contribution to the Critique of Actually Existing Democracy", in *Habermas and the Public Sphere*, ed. Craig Calhoun (Cambridge, MA: MIT Press, 1992), 109–42 and Joan B. Landes, "The Public and the Private Sphere: A Feminist Reconsideration", in *Feminists Read Habermas: Gendering the Subject of Discourse*, ed. Johanna Meehan (New York and London: Routledge, 1995), 91–116. Frazer argues that Habermas's conception of a single public sphere consisting of bourgeois men ignores other, competing public spheres. Landes focuses on the way women's participation in politics in pre-revolutionary and revolutionary France contests Habermas's claim for the marginalization of women in the public sphere of discourse.
4. Anne Mellor, *Mothers of the Nation: Women's Political Writing in England, 1780–1830* (Bloomington and Indianapolis: Indiana University Press, 2000), p. 3.
5. Ibid.
6. Thompson briefly acknowledges the political importance of both Wollstonecraft and More. He mentions "the intellectual tradition of Godwin and Mary Wollstonecraft", p. 179, as well as her writings on behalf of women's rights (p. 94) but does not expand his discussion of her work beyond a few passing comments. Regarding More, he writes, "The sensibility of the Victorian middle class was nurtured in the 1790s by frightened gentry who had seen miners, potters and cutlers reading [Paine's] *Rights of Man*, and its foster-parents were William Wilberforce and Hannah More", p. 57. Nonetheless, in spite of the prominence he assigns her, More and her writings are mentioned later only briefly, anecdotally, in passing. (Wilberforce is discussed more.) Goodwin's references to Wollstonecraft and More are even briefer. He mentions Wollstonecraft only through her relationship to Godwin, and although he notes the importance of More's *Cheap Repository Tracts* – they "outsold even Paine and long outlasted the Loyalist associations which had sponsored them" (p. 265) – that remark is the sole acknowledgement of her, or her work, in his book. Goodwin relates, in passing, to Anna Barbauld and Amelia Opie as members of the Norwich Dissenting circles, but does not discuss their writings. See E.P. Thompson, *The Making of the English Working Class* (New York: Vintage Books, 1966) and Albert Goodwin, *The Friends of Liberty: The English Democratic Movement in the Age of the French Revolution* (Cambridge, MA: Harvard University Press, 1979).
7. Philp, "Thompson, Godwin and the French Revolution", p. 90. See also Marilyn Butler, *Burke, Paine, Godwin and the Revolution Controversy* (Cambridge: Cambridge University Press, 1984). As Butler writes, Thompson's view "tends to obscure the

role of the middle class writer, who ... often remained attached to radicalism until the end of 1796, or later", p. 233, n.

8. It is significant that other historians, in their work to recover women's past political presence, note the need to examine a variety of discursive genres but at the same time continue to overlook, or marginalize the radical group of women writers in the 1790s. For example, Kathryn Gleadle and Sarah Richardson, in the introduction to their collection of essays, *Women in British Politics, 1760–1860: The Power of the Petticoat* (Basingstoke: Macmillan – now Palgrave Macmillan, 2000) write that "the broadening of the concept of the political also calls for a reappraisal of the genres which might serve to constitute women's political engagement", p. 13. However, while their collection includes an essay on Hannah More, it does not include similar contributions on the women writing from the opposite side of the political spectrum.

9. Smith's lifelong financial struggle is a major theme in her work, appearing in her literary texts themselves and in the prefaces that accompany them. Smith's struggle to raise her large family and to receive her rightful share of her father-in-law's inheritance has been well-documented. See Judith Phillips Stanton "Charlotte Smith's 'Literary Business': Income, Patronage and Indigence", *The Age of Johnson: A Scholarly Annual* 1(1987) 375–400, and Loraine Fletcher, *Charlotte Smith, A Critical Biography* (New York: St. Martin's Press – now Palgrave Macmillan, 1997). Smith's letters relate her financial situation in meticulous detail, *The Collected Letters of Charlotte Smith*, ed. Judith Phillips Stanton (Bloomington and Indianapolis: Indiana University Press, 2003). Robinson's financial distress, resulting, in part, from the Prince of Wales's delinquency in paying the annuity which he had promised her, is documented by Robinson herself in *The Memoirs of the Late Mrs. Robinson, Written By Herself* (London: R. Phillips, 1801). See also Judith Pascoe, Introduction, Mary Robinson, *Selected Poems*, ed. Pascoe (Peterborough, Ontario: Broadview Press, 2000), pp. 33–4, and Jan Fergus and Janice Farrar Thaddeus, "Women, Publishers and Money, 1790–1820", *Studies in Eighteenth-Century Culture* 17 (1987), pp. 196–7. For accounts of Inchbald's early poverty, see James Boaden, *Memoirs of Mrs. Inchbald: Including her Familiar Correspondence with the most distinguished persons of her time* (London: Richard Bentley, 1833) and Annibel Jenkins, *I'll Tell You What: The Life of Elizabeth Inchbald* (Lexington: University Press of Kentucky, 2003).

10. Barbara Taylor, *Mary Wollstonecraft and the Feminist Imagination* (Cambridge: Cambridge University Press, 2003), p. 178.

11. Ibid., p. 180.

12. Ibid., pp. 182–92.

13. Influential works on this subject are Marilyn Butler, *Jane Austen and the War of Ideas* (London: Oxford University Press, 1975), and Claudia Johnson's response to Butler, *Jane Austen: Women, Politics and the Novel* (Chicago and London: University of Chicago Press, 1988). Other important studies of women's writing in the 1790s include Mellor, *Mothers of the Nation*, Claudia Johnson, *Equivocal Beings: Politics, Gender, and Sentimentality in the 1790s* (Chicago and London: University of Chicago Press, 1995), Gary Kelly, *Women, Writing, and Revolution 1790–1827* (Oxford: Clarendon Press, 1993) and "Women Writers and the French Revolution Debate: Novelizing the Revolution/Revolutionizing the Novel", *Eighteenth-Century Fiction* 6:4 (1994) 369–88, and Harriet Guest, *Small Change: Women, Learning and Patriotism 1750–1810* (Chicago: University of Chicago Press, 2000) for an important discussion which suggests the broader scope of women's writing throughout

the long eighteenth century. Two collections of essays likewise include important interventions: *Rebellious Hearts: British Women Writers and the French Revolution*, eds. Adriana Craciun and Kari Lokke (Albany: State University of New York Press, 2001), and *Women, Revolution and the Novels of the 1790s*, ed. Linda Lang-Peralta (East Lansing: Michigan State University Press, 1999).

14. Margaret Ezell, *Writing Women's Literary History* (Baltimore and London: Johns Hopkins University Press, 1993), p. 2. Although Ezell is primarily concerned with pre-1700 women's writing, she reminds us of the importance of the self-reflexivity that must accompany the presentation of women's literary history in any historical period in light of an emerging canon, and of the critical pressures that motivate, but also limit that presentation.

15. Claudia Johnson, *Equivocal Beings*, p. 2.

16. For a comprehensive survey of anti-Jacobin literary works, including many by women, see M.O. Grenby, *The Anti-Jacobin Novel: British Conservatism and the French Revolution* (Cambridge: Cambridge University Press, 2001). The case for More as arguably "the most influential woman living in England during the Romantic period" is persuasively made by Mellor, *Mothers of the Nation*. See especially Chapter One, "Hannah More, Revolutionary Reformer." For a discussion that links the radical Helen Maria Williams and Mary Hays together with the loyalist Elizabeth Hamilton as participants in the cultural revolution that detached the middle classes from the cultural and ideological domination of the aristocracy, see Gary Kelly, *Women, Writing and Revolution 1790–1827*.

17. Butler, ed., *Burke, Paine, Godwin*, p. 150.

18. See, for example, West's *A Tale of the Times* (London: Longman and Rees, 1799) and Hamilton's *Memoirs of Modern Philosophers* (1800) ed. Claire Grogan (Peterborough, Ontario: Broadview Press, 2000). *A Tale of the Times* tells the story of Geraldine Powerscourt, a young heiress who marries the selfish and spoiled Lord Monteith. After four years of relative tranquility, Geraldine meets the devious Fitzosborne, who has returned from France professing revolutionary ideals and a deist philosophy, and from the outset plots Geraldine's seduction. Geraldine, who is also implicitly critiqued for succumbing, because of her own vanity, to Fitzosborne's flattering advances, is eventually tricked into eloping with him. Soon abandoned, she realizes her errors, and dies of sorrow and remorse. Although West's novel also puts some of the blame, as it were, on Geraldine, as well as on her ineffectual father and husband, the negative energy is firmly located in Fitzosborne and in his identification with reformist theories and ideals. A far less nuanced position appears in *Memoirs of Modern Philosophers*, in which one of the central figures of the novel, Brigetina Botherim, is an outright caricature of Mary Hays. While Brigetina's misadventures seem to provide, for Hamilton, some element of comedy (but also exhibit, in the repeated references to her awkward physical appearance and her various humiliations, a strong degree of cruelty) the main threat to social harmony appears in Vallaton, a man of obscure origin who has returned from France promoting republican ideals (as well as explicitly Godwinian beliefs) and plans the seduction of a naïve young woman, Julia Delmond. Like Geraldine in *A Tale of the Times*, Julia is seduced and abandoned, and likewise dies of grief.

19. Thomas J. Mathias, *The Pursuits of Literature: A Satiric Poem in Dialogue with Notes* (1794) 4th edition (London: T. Becket, 1797), p. 14.

20. A possible exception, the lack of political resonance of Robinson's poem *Ainsi Va Le Monde*, will be discussed in Chapter 3.

21. Mathias, *The Pursuits of Literature*, 4th edn., 1797, p. ii.

22. Interestingly, in the 1812 edition of *The Pursuits of Literature*, which was published in a large, ornate format, with over one hundred portraits of the authors mentioned in the poem, Smith is one of only four women whose pictures appear in the volume. And, in 1812, Mathias was able to add, "Mrs. Charlotte Smith has great poetical powers, and a pathos which commands attention," Mathias, *Pursuits*, 16th edn., (1812), p. 74.

23. Heath is identified as the author of this review by Emily de Montluzin, *The Anti-Jacobins 1798–1800: The Early Contributors to the Anti-Jacobin Review* (Basingstoke: Macmillan – now Palgrave Macmillan, 1988), p. 185.

24. *The Anti-Jacobin Review* 6 (1800), p. 152. The review of *St. Leon* appears in Vol. 5 (pp. 23–9) and Vol. 6 (pp. 145–53).

25. De Montluzin, p. 106. As she elaborates, " 'The 'Wollstonecraft school', [Heath] was convinced, was aiming at nothing less than to turn English women into 'revolutionary agents', not 'dutiful daughters, affectionate wives, tender mothers, and good Christians.' To a loyal anti-Jacobin like Heath, convinced as he was that the morality of English womanhood was the nation's first defense against Radicalism and irreligion, the implications of such activities were terrifying."

26. *The Anti-Jacobin Review* 6 (1800), p. 152.

27. The fact that I cite two anti-Jacobin critics in order to posit the identification of Smith, Robinson and Inchbald as radicals, reinforces Grenby's claim that "the most obvious testimony of [the] existence of [Jacobin productions] is provided by its opponents rather than exponents", p. 19.

28. In representing the centrality of Burke I am also aware of the need to recognize the more nuanced nature of the debate as a whole. See, for example, Kevin Gilmartin, *Writing Against Revolution: Literary Conservatism in Britain 1790–1832* (Cambridge: Cambridge University Press, 2007), for a discussion of the Revolution debate that warns against the tendency of presenting an overly reductive identification of Burke as "conservative," pp. 7–9.

29. Iain Hampsher-Monk, ed., *The Impact of the French Revolution* (Cambridge: Cambridge University Press, 2005), p. 57.

30. Edmund Burke, *Reflections on the Revolution in France* (1790), ed. J.C.D. Clark (Stanford: Stanford University Press 2001), p. 183.

31. Butler, ed., *Burke, Paine, Godwin*, p. 35.

32. John Barrell and Jon Mee, "Introduction", *Trials for Treason and Sedition*, 8 vols. eds. Barrell and Mee (London: Pickering and Chatto, 2006–2007), i., p. xiii. My discussion here follows this introduction as well as John Barrell, *Imagining the King's Death* (Oxford: Oxford University Press, 2000).

33. Barrell and Mee, eds., *Trials for Treason and Sedition*, vol. viii, "The Trial of Mr. John Thelwall", p. 16, p. 84. Mr Serjeant Adair, the representative for the prosecution, stated, in his closing remarks, that the works of Paine and Barlow contained "the most wild, wicked and cruel doctrines ... subversive not only of this government but of all governments and of all order, " p. 84.

34. William Godwin, *Things as They Are, or the Adventures of Caleb Williams* (1794), ed. Maurice Hindle (London: Penguin, 1988), pp. 3–4. This comment, along with the original preface, appeared in the second edition of *Caleb Williams*, and is dated 29 October 1795.

35. Goodwin, *The Friends of Liberty*, pp. 387–8.

36. John Barrell, *Imagining the King's Death*, p. 568. The performance described here was the third night of the play's run. As Barrell notes, the speeches of the republican protagonists in the play were also later published separately in newspapers and handbills, thus keeping the controversy alive.

37. Jenkins, *I'll Tell You What*, p. 272, p. 364.
38. Mark Philp, *Godwin's Political Justice* (London: Duckworth, 1986), pp. 171–2.
39. Ibid., pp. 31–2.
40. Raymond Williams, *Keywords, A Vocabulary of Culture and society* (London: Fontana, 1976), p. 15. Williams gives his own example of a word – "sentimental" – that had cultural relevance in the eighteenth century, but which has lost its significance today.
41. The volumes of William Godwin's diary are catalogued as [Abinger] Dep. e.196–227 in the Bodleian Library. I am grateful to the Bodleian Library, University of Oxford for permission to cite from the Diary.
42. Smith to William Davies, 21 May 1797; Smith to Cadell and Davies, 24 June 1797, in Judith Stanton, ed. *The Collected Letters of Charlotte Smith*, p. 276, pp. 279–80. Smith informs her publishers that Inchbald was receiving higher payment for her novels than she was.
43. Inchbald to Godwin, 10 September 1797, in C. Kegan Paul, *William Godwin: His Friends and Contemporaries* (London: Henry S. King and Co., 1876), p. 277. I will discuss the altercation between Inchbald and Wollstonecraft in Chapter 6.
44. Smith to William Davies, 25 April 1797, in Stanton, ed. *Letters*, p. 268. As Smith writes, "I hope You will take such precautions as are in your power to prevent [her portrait from] being exhibited in Magazines 'with anecdotes of <u>this</u> admir'd <u>Authoress</u>' like Mrs. Mary Robinson & other Mistresses whom I have no passion for being confounded with."
45. Mary Robinson, "Sonnet to Mrs. Charlotte Smith, on Hearing that Her Son was Wounded at the Siege of Dunkirk", in Pascoe, ed., *Selected Poems*, p. 290, line 12. Smith's son, Charles Dyer Smith, was indeed wounded at Dunkirk in September 1793 and had a leg amputated as a result.
46. In *The Poems of Charlotte Smith*, Stuart Curran has included seventy-nine shorter poems, in addition to the Sonnets, *The Emigrants* and *Beachy Head*. *The Poems of Charlotte Smith*, ed. Curran (New York: Oxford University Press, 1993).
47. Pascoe, Introduction, Mary Robinson, *Selected Poems*, p. 19. As Pascoe writes, the number is uncertain because Robinson's poetry was "so widely disseminated under multiple pseudonyms", p. 19.
48. For an excellent recent survey of women's writing during the revolutionary decade, see William Stafford, *English Feminists and their Opponents in the 1790s* (Manchester: Manchester University Press, 2002). Stafford provides a wealth of information and a meticulously detailed account of this body of writing. In tracing various themes as they appear in texts across this period, he, obviously, is unable to provide extended readings of the works that he discusses.
49. Charlotte Smith, *Desmond* (1792) eds. Antje Blank and Janet Todd (London: Pickering and Chatto, 1997), p. 6.

1   Precarious Bread: Charlotte Smith I

1. *European Magazine* 22 (1792), p. 380. Stuart Curran entitles this poem, "Written for the benefit of a distressed player, detained at Brighthelmstone for debt, November, 1792", as it was subtitled in the *European Magazine*. Curran, ed. *The Poems of Charlotte Smith* (New York: Oxford University Press, 1993), p. 99.
2. This note is included in the version of the poem that appeared in the *Elegiac Sonnets*, Curran, ed., *Poems*, p. 100. For the emergence of the *sans culottes* in the

second half of 1792, see David Andress, *The Terror: The Merciless War for Freedom in Revolutionary France* (New York: Farrar, Straus and Giroux, 2005), Chapter Three.

3. Judith Phillips Stanton, ed. *The Collected Letters of Charlotte Smith,* (Bloomington: Indiana University Press, 2003), p. 629. The comment appears in a letter from Smith to her former patron, Lord Egremont dated 27 June 1804.

4. *The Anti-Jacobin Review* 1 (1798), p. 188. The reviewer has been identified as Bisset by Emily de Montluzin, *The Anti-Jacobins 1798–1800: The Early Contributors to the Anti Jacobin Review* (Basingstoke: Macmillan now Palgrave Macmillon, 1988), p. 166. As de Montluzin writes, "Bisset was [a] ... fanatical Jacobin-hater ... [who] sought to alert his readers against the foes he saw on all sides ... A hallmark of [his] literary style was the extreme intensity and personal hatred with which he approached his opponents in the press," p. 58. At the same time, Bisset elsewhere expressed a grudging admiration for Smith. For example, in his novel *Douglas, or the Highlander* (1800), he writes that Smith, along with Ann Radcliffe and Frances Burney, writes "performances of the epic kind", Robert Bisset, *Douglas, or the Highlander,* 4 vols. (London: C. Chappel, 1800), p. xx.

5. For modern-day discussions of Smith that argue for her disavowal of a pro-Revolution viewpoint, see M.O. Grenby, *The Anti-Jacobin Novel: British Conservatism and the French Revolution* (Cambridge: Cambridge University Press, 2001) and Gary Kelly, *The English Jacobin Novel* (Oxford: Clarendon Press, 1976).

6. Charlotte Smith, *Desmond* (1792), ed. Antje Blank and Janet Todd (London: Pickering and Chatto, 1997), pp. 36–7. All further references will be from this edition and cited parenthetically in the text.

7. The precise dating of the letters in *Desmond* has been noted by Margaret Doody, who writes, "The characters' letters are dated, and the author is evidently careful to ensure that people mention events at the time they would first have heard of them", Margaret Doody, "English Women Novelists and the French Revolution", *Le Femme en Angleterre et Dans Les Colonies Americaines aux XVIIe et XVIIIe Siecles* (Lille: Publications de l'université de Lille III, 1975), p. 182. Angela Keane likewise notes the immediacy of the novels' relation to political events, *Women Writers and the English Nation in the 1790s* (Cambridge: Cambridge University Press, 2000), p. 82.

8. Marilyn Butler, ed. *Burke, Paine, Godwin and the Revolution Controversy* (Cambridge: Cambridge University Press, 1984), p. 108.

9. Iain Hampsher-Monk writes that "[Paine's] demonstrative ability to write clearly and accessibly about politics to the disenfranchised populace was part of the process of creating a public political world in which they could claim a space," "Introduction", *The Impact of the French Revolution: Texts from Britain in the 1790s*, ed., Iain Hampsher-Monk (Cambridge: Cambridge University Press (2005), p. 21.

10. For a comprehensive discussion that examines the 1688 Revolution as a crucial context of the 1790s Revolution debate, and as central to the formation and development of Romantic literature itself, see Anthony Jarrells, *Britain's Bloodless Revolutions: 1688 and the Romantic Reform of Literature* (Basingstoke: Palgrave Macmillan, 2005).

11. For *Desmond's* rejection of the compact of 1688 as binding, see p. 157; for an attack on the peerage system and its corruption, see p. 350, and for the mention of the subject of game rights, see pp. 118–19. This, however, is Smith's own parallel, rather than Desmond's – the story of the Breton appears in a letter dated 2 October 1790, before Paine's text was published. Desmond writes his response to *The Rights of Man* in a letter dated 10 April 1791.

12. Diana Bowstead, "Charlotte Smith's *Desmond*: The Epistolary Novel as Ideological Argument", in *Fetter'd or Free?* eds. Mary Anne Schofield and Cynthia Macheski (Athens, Ohio: Ohio University Press, 1986), p. 237.

13. In addition to Bowstead, see also Alison Conway, "Nationalism, Revolution, and the Female Body", *Women's Studies* 24:5 (1995), p. 399, Katherine Binhammer, "Revolutionary Domesticity in Charlotte Smith's Desmond", in *Women, Revolution and the Novels of the 1790s*, ed. Linda Lang-Peralta (East Lansing: Michigan State University Press, 1999), p. 32 and Nicola Watson, *Revolution and the Form of the British Novel 1790–1825* (Oxford: Clarendon Press, 1994), pp. 38–9.

14. Chris Jones, *Radical Sensibility: Literature and Ideas in the 1790s* (New York and London: Routledge, 1993), p. 163. See also Blank's and Todd's introduction to *Desmond* for a reading which extends Jones's observations by viewing Geraldine's willingness to expose herself to life-threatening situations as a suicide wish, pp. xxxiii–xxxiv.

15. In her discussion of this tension, Anne Mellor persuasively argues that Geraldine's actions throughout the novel reflect Smith's articulation of "an early version of ... standpoint theory [in which] no single 'objective' understanding of social or political institutions is possible because the position that any one observer inhabits in relation to those institutions always already determines one's (necessarily limited) cognition of them." Thus, her behavior is not really idiosyncratic, but rather determined by the fact that her "reality" is that of "one completely without power, without choice, one whose mind and body are at the service of others, of men", Anne Mellor, *Mothers of the Nation: Women's Political Writing in England 1780–1830* (Bloomington and Indianapolis: Indiana University Press, 2000), p. 113, p. 117.

16. Edward Copeland, *Women Writing About Money* (Cambridge: Cambridge University Press, 1995), p. 37. Copeland writes that "what informs Charlotte Smith's novels with genuine power is her anger, her blazing fury at women's 'exile', as she repeatedly calls it, from social and economic power, the two conditions of women's existence that are hardly separable in her mind", p. 51.

17. For example, it is Geraldine's "generous tenderness" (p. 404) that had persuaded Josephine to entrust her with her daughter.

18. Mellor, *Mothers of the Nation*, p. 117. See also Keane, p. 88. Both Mellor and Keane call attention to Desmond's repeated use of possessive pronouns as he describes his domestic bliss: "My Geraldine, You my dear Bethel and your sweet Louisa – my friend Montfleuri and his Fanny", p. 408.

19. Janet Gurkin Altman, *Epistolarity: Approaches to a Form* (Columbus: Ohio State University Press, 1982), p. 150.

20. See especially the Introduction and Chapter 1.

21. Watson, p. 17.

22. Ibid., p. 39.

23. Susan Lanser, *Fictions of Authority: Women Writers and Narrative Voice* (Ithaca and London: Cornell University Press, 1992), p. 46.

24. Ibid, p. 64.

25. Holcroft and Smith are associated with the same cultural milieu, and there is evidence from William Godwin's diary that they met at least once, although long after *Desmond* and *Anna St. Ives* were published. On 10 January 1798 Godwin records having tea at Smith's with HT (Holcroft) and Thomas Newhouse, Smith's son-in-law, the husband of her daughter Lucy. Godwin's diary, Bodleian Library, Dep. e.196–227. For Godwin's use of the abbreviation HT for Holcroft, see Philp,

Godwin's Political Justice (London: Duckworth, 1986) p. 129. However, there is no mention of Smith in Holcroft's autobiography, and, likewise, no references to him in Smith's letters. *Anna St. Ives* was published in February 1792, four months before *Desmond*.

26. Reviews of *Desmond* appeared in the *European Magazine*, the *Analytical Review*, the *Critical Review* and the *Monthly Review* in July, August, September and December 1792, respectively. Common to these reviews is the emphasis on the political content of the novel.

27. The *European Magazine* 22 (1792), p. 22. This was the same issue which published Smith's "Occasional Address" cited at the beginning of this chapter.

28. William Cowper to William Hayley, 21 May 1793. In his letter, Cowper related to Hayley a rumor that he had heard earlier that month from his cousin, Lady Hesketh. He was quick to reject it, responding to her, "I cannot believe that Mrs. Smith has ever been paid by a party." A short while later he wrote to Hayley of the exchange. Cowper's letters appear in *The Letters and Prose Writings of William Cowper*, 5 vols., *Vol. IV: Letters 1792–1799* eds. James King and Charles Ryskamp (Oxford: Clarendon Press, 1984), p. 341, p. 336.

29. Quoted in both David V. Erdman, *Commerce des Lumieres: John Oswald and the British in Paris 1790–1793* (Columbia: University of Missouri Press, 1986), p. 230, and in Adriana Craciun and Kari Lokke, "British Women Writers and the French Revolution", *Rebellious Hearts: British Women Writers and the French Revolution*, eds. Craciun and Lokke (Albany: State University of New York Press, 2001), p. 3.

30. Erdman, p. 229.

31. Erdman describes the circumstances surrounding the publication of the British Club manifesto and the publicity generated by the 18 November celebration in *Commerce des Lumieres*, noting also the presence of the British government spy, Captain George Monro. He also includes a reproduction of the signed document. See especially pp. 229–31 and Appendix E.

32. Erdman identifies the toasts at the British Club as follows: "to the French Republic, the French armies, and the destruction of tyrants and tyranny, the National Convention, the coming convention of England and Ireland, the union of France, Great Britain and Belgium . . . the Republic of Men . . . the destruction of the Germanic Circle . . . [the] abolition of hereditary titles . . . Lord E. Fitzgerald and Sir R. Smyth, Tomas Paine . . . Mrs. (Charlotte) Smith and Miss H.M. Williams . . . the women of France, especially those who have had the courage to take up arms to defend the cause of liberty . . . and Universal Peace, based on universal liberty", p. 230. Smith's fellow toastee, Helen Maria Williams, was recognized not for fiction but for her *Letters Written in France*, first published in 1790 and continuing in additional installments through 1796, a work whose veracity as factual reportage was, as Neil Fraistat and Susan Lanser write, accepted "by most reviewers and readers . . . even when they did not share her enthusiasm or her point of view", Fraistat and Lanser, Introduction to *Letters Written in France* (Peterborough, Ontario: Broadview Press, 2001), p. 39.

33. Charlotte Smith to Joel Barlow, 3 November 1792, Stanton, ed., *Letters*, p. 49.

34. Loraine Fletcher, *Charlotte Smith: A Critical Biography* (New York: St. Martin's Press – now Palgrave Macmillan, 1998), p. 192.

35. Stanton, *Letters*, p. 49. Fletcher merely paraphrases Smith's opening comments, summarizing them as a reaffirmation of "her loyalty to the ideals of the Revolution," p. 192.

36. Joel Barlow, *Advice to the Privileged orders in the Several States of Europe, Resulting From the Necessity and Propriety of a General Revolution in the Principle of Government* (London: J. Johnson, 1792), and *Letter to the National Convention, on the Defects in the National Constitution of 1791*, (London: J. Johnson, 1792).

37. John Barrell and Jon Mee, eds. *Trials for Treason and Sedition 1792–1794*. 8 vols (London: Pickering and Chatto, 2006–2007, Vol. 8, "The Trial of Mr. John Thelwall", p. 15.

38. Fletcher, p. 193.

39. Barlow, *Advice to the Privileged orders*, p. 24, pp. 133–4.

40. Stanton, ed., *Letters*, p. 49.

41. Paula Backscheider, *Eighteenth-Century Women Poets and their Poetry: Inventing Agency, Inventing Genre* (Baltimore: Johns Hopkins University Press, 2005), p. 362.

42. For a very good discussion of the shift in public opinion in Britain following the September massacres, see Deborah Kennedy, *Helen Maria Williams and the Age of Revolution* (Lewisburg: Bucknell University Press, 2002), especially Chapter 3. Kennedy calls attention to the way that the support of British liberals for the Revolution was specifically directed to the Girondin political faction, and opposed to what was perceived as the "unruly, Jacobin-duped mob", p. 112. This is a stance that reflects Smith's position as well.

43. Quoted in Sarah M. Zimmerman, *Romanticism, Lyricism and History* (Albany: State University of New York Press, 1999), p. 66.

44. At the same time, the response to the situation of the emigrants also cut across political lines. For example, Thomas J. Mathias, who was a leading figure in the Anti-Jacobin circle, was also a fierce foe of the emigrants themselves. For a detailed discussion of the reception of the French emigrants in Britain, see Kirsty Carpenter, *Refugees of the French Revolution: Émigrés in London, 1789–1802*, (Basingstoke: Macmillan – now Palgrave Macmillan, Press, 1999).

45. Claudia Johnson, Introduction to Hannah More, *Considerations on Religion and Public Education* and Frances Burney, *Brief Reflections Relative to the Emigrant French Clergy*. The Augustan Reprint Society Publication Number 262 (William Andrews Clark Memorial Library, University of California, Los Angeles, 1990), p. 4. Hereafter cited parenthetically in the text.

46. Johnson, Introduction, *Considerations*, p. viii.

47. Stuart Curran, "The 'I' Altered", *Romanticism and Feminism*, ed. Anne K. Mellor (Bloomington and Indianapolis: Indiana University Press, 1988), p. 201.

48. Linda Colley, *Britons: Forging the Nation 1707–1837* (New Haven and London: Yale University Press, 1992), p. 53.

49. Charlotte Smith, *The Emigrants*, in Stuart Curran, ed. *The Poems of Charlotte Smith*, p. 133. Hereafter cited parenthetically in the text. Cowper responded in a letter to Smith dated 25 July 1793 which he had written upon receiving his copy of *The Emigrants* and expressed his pleasure in reading her dedication, *The Letters and Prose Writings of William Cowper*, eds. King and Ryskamp, Vol. iv., p. 373. Cowper's own view of the events in France during the time immediately preceding the publication of *The Emigrants* is exhibited in a letter written to William Hayley on 1 April 1793: "In short I think that the Exiles themselves cannot be treated with too much tenderness . . . nor the tyrants in Paris with too much severity. But whether my views of this matter coincide with yours and Mrs. Smith's, I doubt, and in this uncertainty I find a check that hinders me when I would suggest any thing on the subject", *Letters*, eds. King and Ryskamp, Vol. iv., p. 319.

50. Stanton, ed., *Letters*, p. 64. Smith's letter to Walker is dated 20 February 1793, when the poem was still in the planning stages.
51. For a thorough, well-documented account of Smith's financial struggles, see Judith Phillips Stanton, "Charlotte Smith's 'Literary Business': Income, Patronage and Indigence", *The Age of Johnson* 1 (1987), pp. 375–400. These struggles are also, of course, very forcefully conveyed in Smith's own words in very many of her letters.
52. As Chris Jones writes, "[Smith's] powers of natural description are impressive, but after each evocation of the beauty of nature and the beneficence of God she interposes the barrier of human suffering", *Radical Sensibility*, p. 201. See also Mellor, *Mothers of the Nation*, pp. 73–4.
53. Curran identifies the reference for the modern reader in *Poems*, p. 148n.
54. Ibid., p. 149n.
55. Robert J. Griffin, *Wordsworth's Pope* (Cambridge: Cambridge University Press, 1995), p. 60.
56. Charlotte Smith, *The Letters of a Solitary Wanderer* (1800) (New York: Woodstock Books, 1995), Vol. iii, p. 252, and *Marchmont* (1796) (Delmar, New York: Scholars' Facsimiles and Reprints, 1989), Vol. iv, pp. 211–12.
57. Mellor, *Mothers of the Nation*, p. 74.
58. Kevis Goodman has brief references to *The Emigrants* and Smith's other extended blank-verse poem, *Beachy Head* (1806) in her *Georgic Modernity and British Romanticism* (Cambridge: Cambridge University Press, 2004). Annabel Patterson's comprehensive study, *Pastoral and Ideology*, provides a detailed account of the political motivations that underlie the use of the pastoral in its various appropriations throughout literary history. Patterson identifies the Georgic as a signifier of seventeenth and eighteenth-century concerns regarding "political representation and franchise and the class implications of enclosures versus common land, and hence, ultimately, the class system itself", Annabel Patterson, *Pastoral and Ideology* (Berkeley and Los Angeles: University of California Press, 1987), p. 135. Kurt Heinzelmann extends this argument by locating the issues which the particularized use of the Georgic both reflects and addresses in the late eighteenth and early nineteenth centuries. Kurt Heinzelmann, "Roman Georgic in the Georgian Age: A Theory of Romantic Genre", *Texas Studies in Language and Literature* 33:2 (1991), pp. 182–214. For other studies that deal with the Georgic in this period, see also John Murdoch, "The Landscape of Labor: Transformations of the Georgic", *Romantic Revolutions: Criticism and Theory*, eds. Kenneth Johnston, Gilbert Chaitin, Karen Hanson and Herbert Marks (Bloomington and Indianapolis: Indiana University Press, 1990), pp.176–193, and Bruce Graver, "Wordsworth's Georgic Beginnings", *Texas Studies in Language and Literature* 33:2 (1991), pp. 137–59.
59. Heinzelmann, p. 188.
60. Patterson, p. 278.
61. See, for example, the critique in *Desmond* of the ways in which the natural landscape is abused by the excesses of the newly-rich Sir Robert Stamford, p. 167.
62. The quotation, and description of the political climate in England during and after the Treason Trials are taken from E.P. Thompson, *The Making of the English Working Class* (New York: Vintage Books, 1966), p. 132. For a description of the anti-radical violence during the trials, see especially chapters 1 and 5. For a detailed account of the Trials and the anti-radical persecution that preceded and followed them, see John Barrell, *Imagining the King's Death* (Oxford: Oxford University Press, 2000). For a discussion of the development of fiction during this time see Patricia Meyer Spacks, "Novels of the 1790s: Action and Impasse", *The Columbia History of*

the British Novel, ed. John Richetti (New York: Columbia University Press, 1994), pp. 247–74. *The Banished Man* was published in July 1794 (Smith's preface is dated 30 July), after the arrest of the men but before they were brought to trial.
63. *Letters*, ed. Stanton, p. 175.
64. Philp, p. 58. As Philp explains, even before the Treason Trials, "the remaining sympathizers [to the cause of the Revolution] ... suffered at the hands of the government: printers, publishers, writers and booksellers were prosecuted for their production and circulation of radical works – particularly Paine's *Rights of Man, Part Two*."
65. Charlotte Smith, *The Banished Man* 4 vols. (London: Cadell and Davies, 1794), p. viii. Further references will be from this edition and cited parenthetically in the text.
66. *The Analytical Review* 20 (1794), p. 254.
67. *The British Critic* 4 (1794), p. 623.
68. *The Analytical Review* 20 (1794), p. 255, *The British Critic* 4 (1794), p. 623, respectively.
69. See Gary Kelly, *The English Jacobin Novel* and M.O. Grenby, *The Anti-Jacobin Novel*. In the introduction to his edition of *The Banished Man* (part of Pickering & Chatto's *The Works of Charlotte Smith*), Grenby revises his position to some degree, and ultimately concludes that what motivated Smith in her writing of *The Banished Man* was the saleability of the novel, the "desire to please the widest possible constituency" (*The Works of Charlotte Smith, Volume 7, The Banished Man*, London: Pickering & Chatto, 2005), p. xxxii. Critics who stress the ongoing radical engagement of *The Banished Man* include Judith Davis Miller, "The Politics of Truth and Deception: Charlotte Smith and the French Revolution", in *Rebellious Hearts*, eds. Craciun and Lokke, pp. 337–63. For other discussions of *The Banished Man*, see Doody, "English Women Novelists and the French Revolution", Katharine Rogers, "Inhibitions on Eighteenth-Century Women Novelists: Elizabeth Inchbald and Charlotte Smith", *Eighteenth-Century Studies* 11 (1977), 63–78, and Rogers's "Romantic Aspirations, Restricted Possibilities: The Novels of Charlotte Smith", in *Re-Visioning Romanticism: British Women Writers, 1776–1837*, eds. Carol Shiner and Joel Haefner (Philadelphia: University of Pennsylvania Press, 1994), pp. 193–209, and Harriet Guest, "Suspicious Minds: Spies and Surveillance in Charlotte Smith's Novels of the 1790s", in *Land, Nation and Culture, 1740–1840: Thinking the Republic of Taste*, eds. David Simpson, Nigel Leask and Peter de Bolla (Basingstoke: Palgrave Macmillan, 2005), pp. 169–87.
70. The "Avis au Lecteur" has generated very little critical attention. Rictor Norton has, however, included it in his collection, *Gothic Readings: The First Wave, 1764–1840* (London and New York: Leicester University Press, 2000) in the section on contemporary critical debate of the Gothic, a move which acknowledges the inherently critical nature of the passage, and its distinction from the rest of the novel.
71. Smith slightly misquotes the text here. In Corporal Trim's efforts to begin his story he is repeatedly interrupted by Uncle Toby, and never manages to complete the sentence as Smith represents it. Laurence Sterne, *The Life and Opinions of Tristram Shandy* (1760–1767) ed. Ian Campbell Ross (Oxford and London: Oxford University Press, 1983), pp. 450–5.
72. Sterne, p. 450. Corporal Trim makes it clear that his story is a fiction. Smith was an admirer of Sterne's writings: later in the "Avis" she praises his "light and forcible pencil", p. i.

73. The charge of plagiarism was one that haunted Smith from early on in her literary career. In 1785 after she had translated the Abbé Prevost's *Manon L'Escaut*, a letter appeared in the *Public Advertiser* suggesting that Smith's translation had been a "literary fraud." As Catherine Anne Dorset, Smith's sister, writes in her memoir: "Thus were Mrs. Smith's laudable exertions embittered by the attacks, either of wanton and unprovoked malice, or the artifice of a concealed enemy; and in aggravation of her private misfortunes, she was taught to feel all the penalties and discouragement attached to the profession of an author," Catherine Anne Dorset, "Charlotte Smith", *The Miscellaneous Prose Works of Sir Walter Scott, vol. iv; Biographical Memoirs of Eminent Novelists and Other Distinguished Persons, Vol. ii* (Edinburgh: Robert Cadell; London: Whittaker and Co, 1834), p. 45. For another account of this event, see Fletcher, pp. 82–3. Undoubtedly, this early incident had a profound effect on the experience of authorship for Smith.

74. Smith's insistence on the "fictionality" of her text is also contradicted by a comment in her letter to her publisher Thomas Cadell on 16 December 1793. There, she writes of beginning her work on *The Banished Man* and notes that the novel is "partly founded in Truth", *Letters*, p. 88.

75. Ronald Paulson, *Representations of Revolution (1789–1820)* (New Haven and London: Yale University Press, 1983), p. 217. See also Fred Botting, *Gothic* (London and New York: Routledge, 1996) and David Punter, *The Literature of Terror* (London: Longman, 1980) for discussions that contextualize the Gothic as a response to the political upheavals of the revolutionary decade.

76. Margaret Doody, "Deserts, Ruins and Troubled Waters: Female Dreams in Fiction and the Development of the Gothic Novel" *Genre* 10 (1977), pp. 562–3. Doody's recognition of Smith's imaginative limitations underscores Smith's own awareness of this lack.

77. Smith anticipated the criticism that she would receive for this autobiographical portrayal. In the opening preface, she writes: "The insults I have endured, the inconveniences I have been exposed to, are not to be described – but let it not be a matter of surprise or blame, if the impression made by them on my mind affects my writings…a Novelist, from the same causes, makes his drawing to resemble the characters he has had occasion to meet with…", p. ii. Later, after initially introducing Mrs Denzil to the reader, she adds in a note the following wry observation: "Lest any part of the sketches given of Mrs. Denzil's history should be supposed too strongly to resemble my own, I beg this circumstance, so totally different, may be adverted to: not one of my children's relations ever lent them a house, though some of them have contributed all in their power to take from them the house we possess of our own," Vol. ii., p. 215.

78. Guest, p. 175.

79. Margaret Doody, "English Women Novelists and the French Revolution", pp. 182–3.

80. Colley, pp. 254–5.

81. Mary Wollstonecraft, *An Historical and Moral View of the French Revolution*, quoted in Colley, p. 255.

82. For a discussion of this issue, see Lynn Hunt, "The Many Bodies of Marie Antoinette: Political Pornography and the Problem of the Feminine in the French Revolution", in Hunt, ed. *Eroticism and the Body Politic* (Baltimore and London: Johns Hopkins University Press, 1991), especially pp. 124–6.

83. Jones, p. 176.

84. Stanton, *Letters*, p. 50. This representation of the King as "the Grandson of Louis the 15th" accords with the way that his tragedy was perceived in England above all as a domestic one. As John Barrell has shown, the representation (and sentimentalizing) of the King's execution derived from how he was repeatedly portrayed in terms of his domestic relations. As Barrell explains, this representation "provides multiple opportunities for sympathetic identification with the characters in the narrative, multiple points of entry into the scene, and thereby into the sufferings of a family", John Barrell, *Imagining the King's Death*, p. 72. Although Smith had written her letter to Barlow a little over two months *before* Louis's guillotining, it anticipates the very way in which he would later be eulogized by the British public.
85. Jones, p. 176.
86. Albert Goodwin, *The Friends of Liberty: The English Democratic Movement in the Age of the French Revolution* (Cambridge: Harvard University Press, 1979), pp. 177–8.
87. *The Anti-Jacobin Review* 1 (1798), p. 188.
88. Jones, p. 175.
89. Keane, p. 94.
90. The identification with exile underscores another autobiographical parallel in *The Banished Man* – Smith's desire, like that of Mrs Denzil, to leave England. In a letter written to Joseph Cooper Walker on 25 March 1794, when the novel was nearing completion, she wrote: "I assure you that I have neither naturally nor artificially the least partiality for my native Country, which has not protected my property by its boasted Laws, & where, if the Laws are not good, I know nothing that is, for the climate does not agree with me, who am another creature in France ... Therefore, if Death or Justice or any other <u>decisive</u> personification, should happen to interfere on my poor childrens [sic] behalf ... I wd not hesitate a moment (that is if I am able to move) to bid to 'the Isle Land that pushes from her all the rest' a long & last Adieu", Stanton, ed., *Letters*, p. 105. Interestingly, this same quote – "this Land, that pushes from her all the rest" appears, as we have seen, in the novel itself, preceding Mrs Denzil's comment that in England "she has lost everything but [her] head" (Vol.i., p. 259). Smith, of course, remained in England – working until the end of her life to settle her father-in-law's will.
91. Adriana Craciun, *British Women Writers and the French Revolution: Citizens of the World* (Basingstoke: Palgrave Macmillan, 2005), p. 157. See also Keane, p. 94.
92. Guest, pp. 178–9, p. 185.
93. The references are to the dissenting minister Richard Price (1723–1791) whose sermon, "A Discourse on the Love of our Country" at the Old Jewry on 4 November 1789 was a focal point for Burke's arguments in the *Reflections on the Revolution in France* (1790) and Joseph Priestley (1733–1804), a prominent scientist and dissenter, whose radical religious and political views led to the burning of his house during the 1791 "Church and King" Birmingham riots.

2 "A Disciple of a Better System": Charlotte Smith II

1. Mark Philp, *Godwin's Political Justice* (London: Duckworth, 1986), p. 227. For Philp's discussion of the idea of community, and his view of the Godwin circle as such, see Chapters 6, 8 and the appendices.
2. For Smith's own desire to leave England, see Chapter 1, note 89.

3. See Anne Mellor, "Embodied Cosmopolitanism and the British Romantic Writer", *European Romantic Review* 17:3 (2006), pp. 290–300, Angela Keane, *Women Writers and the English Nation in the 1790s* (Cambridge: Cambridge University Press, 2000), William Brewer, "Charlotte Smith and the American Agrarian Ideal", *Modern Language Notes* 40:4 (2003), pp. 51–63, Leanne Maunu, "Home is Where the Heart Is: National Identity and Expatriation in Charlotte Smith's *The Young Philosopher*" *European Romantic Review* 15:1 (2004), pp. 51–71, and Adriana Craciun, *British Women Writers and the French Revolution: Citizens of the World* (Basingstoke: Palgrave Macmillan, 2005).

4. The volumes of William Godwin's diary that cover 1796–1800 are catalogued as [Abinger] Dep. e.196–227 in the Bodleian Library.

5. Pamela Clemit, ed. and Intro., "Charlotte Smith to William and Mary Jane Godwin: Five Holograph Letters", *Keats-Shelley Journal* 55 (2006), pp. 29–40, p. 31. In a letter dated 27 February 1800, Smith writes of her approval of Coleridge and in doing so, alludes to her desire for this type of literary society in general. Thus she remarks to Godwin, "If you can make me acquainted with any other literary Man as pleasant as Mr. Coleridge, pray do", p. 38. I wish to thank Arnold Markley for first calling my attention to these letters.

6. Clemit, ed., *Letters*, p. 38. The friend to whom Smith is referring remains unidentified. The volume in question contains reviews of Richard Phillips's *Annual Necrology for 1797–8*, and in which Mary Wollstonecraft, Mary Hays and "the philosopher Godwin and his worthy disciples" are attacked, *Anti-Jacobin Review* Vol. 5 (January 1800), p. 39. In addition, the first part of Godwin's *St. Leon* is reviewed and criticized. Smith and Godwin were linked together in the subsequent issue of the *Anti-Jacobin Review* in February 1800, when (as we saw in the Introduction) Smith had been criticized in a footnote to the second part of the review of *St. Leon*.

7. Smith was unaware, of course, of the unfortunate timing of this letter, written two days after the birth of Godwin's and Wollstonecraft's daughter, and mailed on 4 September, after Wollstonecraft had developed the symptoms of the infection from which she would later die. See Clemit, p. 32, n. 12.

8. Clemit, ed., *Letters*, p. 34. p. 33. Charles Dyer Smith had been wounded at the siege of Dunkirk, where he had lost a leg. Nonetheless, he returned to active duty and at the time of the writing of this letter was home on leave. As Clemit notes, Charles was the "'victim of our accursed systems' twice over": as a soldier, he received little financial compensation from the government for his injury and as a heir to his grandfather's will, he was denied his part of the inheritance (along with his siblings) because of the interminable legal proceedings surrounding the settlement of the will, Clemit, p. 33, n. 21.

9. *Elegiac Sonnets* was first published in 1784 and went through six editions until this expanded two-volume edition appeared in 1797.

10. Stanton, ed., *Letters*, p. 267. In another letter Smith writes to her publishers Cadell and Davies that it is her "wish and purpose to make the volume as large and good as I can", *Letters*, p. 257. Smith's correspondence with her publishers reveals fascinating details of her involvement with the publication of the second volume of the *Elegiac Sonnets*, and exhibit not only her awareness of the publication process but also many examples of her sharp wit, especially in her criticism of the engravings that accompany the volume. See for example the letter from Smith to William Davies of 25 April 1797 in Stanton's edition, pp. 266–9.

11. Ibid., p. 268, n. 1.

12. Ibid., p. 268 n. 2. On 3 June 1787 Smith had written to her publisher, Thomas Cadell Sr. of how her "friends and several persons of high fashion [had] express'd a wish that the Edition of Sonnets ... may be publish'd with plates by subscription," Stanton, ed., *Letters*, p. 11.

13. Jacqueline M. Labbe, *Charlotte Smith: Romanticism, Poetry and the Culture of Gender* (Manchester and New York: Manchester University Press, 2003), p. 11.

14. Paula Backscheider, *Eighteenth-Century Women Poets and their Poetry: Inventing Agency, Inventing Genre* (Baltimore: Johns Hopkins University Press, 2005), p. 337.

15. Stuart Curran, ed., *The Poems of Charlotte Smith* (New York and Oxford: Oxford University Press, 1993), p. 71, line 13. Further references to Smith's poems will be from this edition and cited by page and line numbers in the text.

16. Ibid., p. 71, Smith's note.

17. Charlotte Smith, *Rural Walks: in Dialogues intended for the use of young persons*, 2 vols. (London: Cadell and Davies, 1795), Vol. ii., pp. 22–3, pp. 28–9. Robert Burns, "Man was Made to Mourn", in *Poems, chiefly in the Scottish dialect*, third edn., (London: 1787), p. 231, lines 55–6. Smith includes "To a Mountain Daisy" in its entirety, except, as her note tells us, for the omission of one stanza, the one in which Burns compares "the artless Maid ... By Love's simplicity betrayed" to the mountain daisy, a subject which she must have deemed inappropriate for a children's book.

18. Burns, "To a Mountain Daisy", *Poems*, p. 251, line 43.

19. Ibid., lines 37–42.

20. Smith's note continued to appear in subsequent editions of the *Elegiac Sonnets* published in 1811 and 1827 and her use of the phrase "the rights of man" continued even later to generate anxious attention. In 1903, in a biographical sketch of Smith written for the *Cornhill Magazine*, the Viscount St Cyres mentions "The Dead Beggar", stating that "[i]It is a wonder Mrs. Smith was not prosecuted for sedition, after explaining how 'In Earth's cold bosom [lie the] Rights of Man' within a short time of the execution of Louis XVI." "The Sorrows of Mrs. Smith", *The Cornhill Magazine* XV (1903), pp. 683–96, p. 691.

21. Quoted in Edward Copeland, *Women Writing about Money* (Cambridge: Cambridge University Press, 1995), p. 48.

22. Loraine Fletcher, *Charlotte Smith: A Critical Biography* (New York: St. Martin's Press – now Palgrave Macmillan, 1998), p. 278. *The Young Philosopher* has been receiving increased critical attention. In addition to Fletcher's discussion of the novel, see Chris Jones, *Radical Sensibility: Literature and Ideas in the 1790s* (New York and London: Routledge, 1993), Keane, *Women Writers and the English Nation*, Eleanor Ty, *Unsex'd Revolutionaries: Five Women Novelists of the 1790s* (Toronto and London: University of Toronto Press, 1993), Maunu, "Home is Where the Heart Is", pp. 51–71 and Brewer, "Charlotte Smith and the American Agrarian Ideal", pp. 51–61. Brief discussions of the novel also appear in Nicola Watson, *Revolution and the Form of the British Novel* (Oxford: Clarendon Press, 1994) and Ann B. Shteir, *Cultivating Women, Cultivating Science* (Baltimore and London: Johns Hopkins University Press, 1996).

23. Stanton, ed. *Letters*, pp. 233–4.

24. Ibid., p. 284.

25. Philp, p. 133. The second edition of *Political Justice* was published at the end of November 1795. The third and even more heavily revised edition appeared only in December 1797.

26. Charlotte Smith, *The Young Philosopher* (1798), ed. Elizabeth Kraft (Lexington: University Press of Kentucky, 1999), p. 247. Further references will be from this edition and cited in the text.

27. Philp, p. 138. Judith Davis Miller notes the way *The Young Philosopher* is in dialogue with Godwin's writings, arguing that the novel also critiques *Political Justice* when Smith has her characters conceal the truth from each other in order to protect them, instead of adhering to the sometimes "painful" insistence on truth that Godwin had advocated. Judith Davis Miller, "The Politics of Truth and Deception: Charlotte Smith and the French Revolution", in *Rebellious Hearts: British Women Writers and the French Revolution*, eds. Adriana Craciun and Kari Lokke (Albany: State University of New York Press, 2001), pp. 337–63, p. 357. In June 1798 Godwin recorded in his diary his own reading of *The Young Philosopher*.

28. *The Young Philosopher* was also reviewed in *The Monthly Review* 28 (1799), the *Critical Review* 24 (1798) and the *Analytical Review* 28 (1798), in reviews which likewise note the novel's engagement with contemporary political concerns. For example, the *Analytical*, writing from a different political viewpoint from that of the *Anti-Jacobin*, remarks that "the story...possesses considerable merit and interest; the characters are drawn with spirit, and well sustained; the incidents contrived and managed with ingenuity and effect; the whole is pervaded by a vein of good sense, liberal sentiment, and just observation", p. 73.

29. De Montluzin identifies Bisset as the reviewer of *Walsingham*, p. 166.

30. *The Anti-Jacobin Review* 1 (1798), p. 190.

31. As Chris Jones writes, "*The Young Philosopher* [as] a...committed radical work, amply justifies its inclusion in "The New Morality", *Radical Sensibility: Literature and Ideas in the 1790s* (New York and London: Routledge, 1993), p. 177. Among the other works that appear in the plate are Mary Wollstonecraft's *Maria, or the Wrongs of Woman*, John Horne Tooke's *Speeches*, the *Monthly Magazine*, Priestley's *Political Sermons* and John Thelwall's *Lectures*. This is auspicious company indeed for Smith's novel, and is additional evidence for its reception as a radical text.

32. Markman Ellis, in *The Politics of Sensibility* (Cambridge: Cambridge University Press, 1996) discusses Gillray's plate and stresses the ambiguous way in which sensibility was constructed in the 1790s. He argues that the picture is a marker of how sensibility was eclipsed following the violence of the French Revolution and thus denied any redemptive power. However, he also notices that "whereas in content the caricature is censorious of sensibility, in form it is less so." See especially pp. 194–7. For a brief overview of Gillray's life and work, including his adoption of anti-Jacobin views, see Marilyn Butler, *Romantics, Rebels and Reactionaries* (Oxford and New York: Oxford University Press, 1981), especially chapter 1.

33. *The Anti-Jacobin Review* 1 (1798), p. 188.

34. Ibid.

35. Ibid., p. 190.

36. Charlotte Smith, *The Banished Man* (London: Cadell and Davies, 1794), Vol.i., p. 259.

37. Keane, p. 102, Maunu, p. 58.

38. Medora's engagement with botany is described as follows: "The perfection she attained, in delineating some of the earliest plants which the fields, as well as the garden and the conservatory produced, was a source of the most delightful amusement to her," pp. 154–5.

39. Smith herself, it appears, would have endorsed that view of her political positioning in 1798. In a letter to Joseph Cooper Walker dated 9 January 1799, she writes

that she was "very glad" that Walker liked *The Young Philosopher*, "notwithstand-ing *the politics* which I thought by no means thickly sewn or offensive", *Letters,* ed. Stanton, p. 321.

40. Jones, p. 177. Brewer, similarly, argues for a correspondence between Glenmorris's opinions and those of Thomas Paine, p. 54.
41. The first edition of Godwin's *Memoirs of the Author of a Vindication of the Rights of Woman* appeared in January 1798. That same month Godwin also published the *Posthumous Works of the Author of a Vindication of the Rights of Woman,* which included the unfinished novel, *Maria.* Smith dates her preface to *The Young Philoso-pher* 6 June 1798. For an account of the public response to Godwin's memoir, see Pamela Clemit's and Gina Luria's introduction to *Memoirs of the Author of a Vin-dication of the Rights of Woman* (Peterborough, Ontario: Broadview Press, 2001), pp. 32–6.
42. Kraft, ed. *The Young Philosopher,* p. 355, n. 59.
43. Ibid., pp. 357–8, n. 27.
44. Leonore Davidoff and Catherine Hall, *Family Fortunes: Men and Women of the English Middle Class 1780–1850* (London: Hutchinson, 1987), p. 82. E.P. Thomp-son also discusses the religious revival of the late 1790s, although his focus is specifically on how the radical enthusiasm generated by the French Revolution on the working classes became channeled into a religious fervor "upon the ruins of the political messianism which had been overthrown", p. 388. *The Young Philoso-pher,* conversely, portrays its religious zealots as part of the dominant system of power.
45. Davidoff and Hill, especially chapter 1, and Mary Poovey, *The Proper Lady and the Woman Writer* (Chicago and London: University of Chicago Press, 1984), p. 9.
46. Edmund Burke, *Reflections on the Revolution in France* (1790), ed. J.C.D. Clark (Stanford: Stanford University Press, 2001), pp. 183–4.
47. Mary Wollstonecraft, *A Vindication of the Rights of Men* (1790) in *Political Writings,* ed. Janet Todd (Buffalo and Toronto: University of Toronto Press, 1993), p. 23.
48. Burke had written the remark in the context of his discussion of the nobility and the clergy as the purveyors of manners and civilization in traditional society. As the result of the current upheavals, he warns, "learning will be cast into the mire, and trodden down under the hoofs of a swinish multitude", *Reflections,* p. 242.
49. Thompson, p. 90.
50. Ibid., p. 177.
51. Maunu, p. 56.
52. *The Anti-Jacobin; or Weekly Examiner,* 14 May 1798, p. 211. This weekly magazine was the predecessor of the *Anti-Jacobin Review and Monthly.*
53. Charlotte Smith, *The Emigrants,* in *The Poems of Charlotte Smith,* ed. Curran, pp. 133–4.
54. William Godwin, *Enquiry concerning political justice, and its influence on morals and happiness,* 2nd ed., (London: G.G. and J. Robinson, 1796), p. xii.
55. Fletcher, p. 272.
56. As we recall, the criticism of *The Banished Man* censured Smith's portrayal of Mrs Denzil on these very grounds. In his review of *The Young Philosopher,* Bisset writes that, "with considerable talents for fictitious biography, Charlotte Smith mingles a degree of egotism, which renders many parts of her work tired to any reader acquainted with her former publications", *Anti-Jacobin Review* 1 (1798), p. 187. Smith would continue to rebut these charges, as she had done in *The Banished Man* (see note 80), denying that her portrayals of financially and legally vulnerable

women are of an autobiographical nature. Her comments in the preface to Vols. IV and V of *The Letters of a Solitary Wanderer* are especially trenchant, although perhaps disingenuous: "it is observed, by one of these critics, that 'MRS. SMITH is too fond of representing the distresses of *middle-aged ladies*; and has given the same character, under different names, in all her novels [...] Surely no impartial reader will judge in this manner; or imagine I could be guilty of such foolish egotism as to represent myself under these different characters, and under circumstances which, in no single instance, bear any relation to my private life", *Letters of a Solitary Wanderer* Vols. IV–V (London: Longman and Rees, 1802), pp. vi–vii. Indeed, present-day criticism concurs with this perception, continuing to mark these portrayals as "autobiographical" or "semi-autobiographical."

57. Mary Wollstonecraft, *Maria, or the Wrongs of Woman* (1798), (New York and London: W.W. Norton, 1994), p. 11. Keane briefly discusses the ways in which Smith's and Wollstonecraft's novels "ironically comment upon one another", p. 107.

58. Thus, Leanne Maunu claims that the American identity chosen by Smith's characters represents a status of particular merit, and Angela Keane argues that *The Young Philosopher* offers "the most complete fantasy of spatial and historical relocation, of a new and equal community, of republican romance," Maunu, p. 65, Keane, p. 106.

59. It is interesting that modern scholarship and publication practices have reproduced the very fragmentation which accompanied the original appearance of *The Letters of a Solitary Wanderer*. In 1995 Woodstock Books published an edition of the novel as part of its series *Revolution and Romanticism 1789–1834*. However, the edition includes only the first three volumes of Smith's text, and Jonathan Wordsworth, in his introduction to the work, makes no mention of the existence of the remaining two volumes. Throughout my discussion of the *Solitary Wanderer*, I will be referring to the 1995 Woodstock edition for Volumes I–III and to the 1802 Longman edition for Volumes IV–V, and hereafter cited by volume and page numbers parenthetically in the text.

60. Altman, p. 37.

61. Ibid., p. 150.

62. See Watson's introduction and chapter 1. Watson does not mention *The Letters of a Solitary Wanderer* in her study although the novel seems to affirm her claim for the connection between the collapse of the radical narrative and the way in which the letter itself becomes a marker of instability. Furthermore, in a manner conducive to Watson's argument for *La Nouvelle Heloise* as the recurring subtext in the epistolary novels of the 1790s (in this case, the way that the acknowledgement of Rousseau's text extends into the early years of the nineteenth century), Guilelmine, a character in Vol. V., specifically refers to herself as Rousseau's Julie: "Situated in many respects like Julie, I fancied that I should emulate her character in all but its fatal errors...Can you wonder that my heart sought a St. Preux and a Claire?" Vol. v., pp. 180–1.

63. Adriana Craciun and Kari Lokke, "Introduction", "British Women Writers and the French Revolution", *Rebellious Hearts*, eds. Craciun and Lokke, p. 14.

64. Rousseau, conversely, writes that when he was distressed, he would "wander at random through the woods and mountains, not daring to think for fear of stirring up my sufferings. My imagination...let my senses give themselves up to the light but sweet impressions of surrounding objects . . . I delighted in this ocular recreation which in misfortune relaxes, amuses, distracts the mind, and suspends the troubled feeling", Jean-Jacques Rousseau, *The Reveries of the Solitary Walker*,

trans. Charles E. Butterworth, in Roger D. Masters and Christopher Kelly, eds., *The Collected Writings of Rousseau*, 12 vols. (Hanover and London: University Press of New England, 2000), Vol. 8, p. 59.

65. Rictor Norton notes the mutual influence that Smith and Ann Radcliffe had on each other's work: "Smith may be entitled to rank as co-creator of the School of Radcliffe. [Smith's early novels] *Emmeline* and *Ethelinde* ... influenced Radcliffe, though in turn Radcliffe influenced Smith's *The Old Manor House*, which in turn influenced Radcliffe's *Udolpho*, which in turn influenced Smith's later novels, which became more decidedly Gothic", *Gothic Readings: The First Wave 1764–1840* (London and New York: Leicester University Press, 2000), p. 286.

66. George Cheyne, *The English Malady* (1733) in *Patterns of Madness in the Eighteenth Century, A Reader* ed. Allan Ingram (Liverpool: Liverpool University Press, 1998), p. 84. In 1810 the London physician William Black tabulated the causes of insanity among the admissions to Bethlem Hospital; under "family and heredity" he listed 115 cases. Roy Porter, *Mind-Forg'd Manacles: A History of Madness in England from the Restoration to the Regency* (London: Athlone Press, 1987), pp. 33–4.

67. This is the case with Medora in *The Young Philosopher*, Emmeline, in the novel of that name and Henrietta in Volume II of *The Letters of a Solitary Wanderer*.

68. Johnson arrives at this subject after informing Warton of the death of the wife of the publisher Dodsley: "You know poor Mr. Dodsley has lost his wife: I believe he is much affected. I hope he will not suffer so much as I yet suffer from the loss of mine ... I have ever since seemed to myself broken off from mankind; a kind of solitary wanderer in the wild of life, without any direction, or fixed point of view: a gloomy gazer on a world to which I have little relation", James Boswell, *Boswell's Life of Johnson* (1791) (London: Oxford University Press, 1953), p. 196.

69. Charlotte Smith to Sarah Farr Rose, 14 February 1804, Huntington Library HM 18034. This letter is not included in Stanton's edition of the *Letters*.

3 "Poetry [and] Politics": Mary Robinson I

1. I state the generally accepted date of Robinson's birth, although lately that has come under question. See Paula Byrne, *Perdita: The Life of Mary Robinson* (New York: HarperCollins, 2004), Appendix: "The Mystery of Mrs. Robinson's Age", pp. 429–30, for a discussion of this issue.

2. Jan Fergus and Janice Farrar Thaddeus trace the lifelong financial struggle that accompanied Robinson's literary career, "Women, Publishers and Money, 1790–1820", *Studies in Eighteenth-Century Culture*, Vol. 17, eds. John Yolton and Leslie Eileen Brown (East Lansing, Michigan: Colleagues Press, 1987), pp. 192–7.

3. Stuart Curran, "Mary Robinson's *Lyrical Tales* in Context", in *Re-Visioning Romanticism: British Women Writers 1776–1837*, eds. Carol Shiner Wilson and Joel Haefner (Philadelphia: University of Pennsylvania Press), p. 31.

4. Mary Robinson, *Walsingham* (1797), ed. Julie A. Shaffer (Peterborough, Ontario: Broadview Press, 2003), p. 170.

5. *The General Magazine* 4 (1790), p. 548.

6. See, among others, Robert Bass, *The Green Dragoon* (New York: Henry Holt, 1957.) While Bass provides a detailed chronological survey of the publication of Robinson's works, his discussion of the political events of the late eighteenth century – both in Britain and in France – is solely in relation to Tarleton. Thus, for example, his account of the publication of the highly political *Ainsi Va Le Monde* neglects

to mention its subject matter – the French Revolution, pp. 300–1. For another account of Robinson's life which ignores her political interventions, see Stanley Makower, *Perdita, A Romance in Biography* (London: Hutchinson and Co., 1908).

7. Thomas J. Mathias, *The Pursuits of Literature*, 4th edn., (London: T. Becket, 1797), p. 14.

8. William Gifford, *The Baviad and The Maeviad*, 8th edition (London: Becket and Porter, 1811), pp. 55–6. This comment appeared only in the 1811 edition of the work. Gifford's willingness to incorporate cruel personal attacks against the writers whom he is criticizing exhibits itself repeatedly throughout all the editions of the poem, as evinced in his comment on Robinson's physical disability: "See Robinson forget her state, and move / On crutches tow'rds the grave," (lines 26–7). It is perhaps in this context that William Hazlitt writes, "[Gifford's] attacks on Mrs. Robinson were unmanly," *The Spirit of the Age* (1825), (London: Oxford University Press, 1954), p. 206.

9. Richard Polwhele, *The Unsex'd Females* (London: Cadell and Davies, 1798), p. 17.

10. Anne K. Mellor, "Mary Robinson and the Scripts of Female Sexuality", *Representations of the Self from the Renaissance to Romanticism*, eds. Patrick Coleman, Jayne Lewis and Jill Kowalik, (Cambridge: Cambridge University Press, 2000), p. 256.

11. *Ibid.*, p. 256.

12. *Ainsi Va Le Monde* was originally published under the name of Laura Maria by John Bell in 1790, and republished a year later under Robinson's own name in her *Poems* (1791). Robinson's movement back and forth between anonymity, pseudonymity and the use of her own name throughout her work illustrates Robert Griffin's understanding of the dialectic of anonymity and identity, and the possibility that one is not necessarily replaced by the other in a historical sequence, "Anonymity and Authorship", *New Literary History* 30 (1999), p. 890. Griffin's insights into the various factors that inform the presence, absence or replacement of the authorial name are, likewise, useful for the particularized case of Robinson's writing. For example, he suggests that the various pseudonyms under which Robinson published her poetry in *The Morning Post* were an attempt to conceal the fact that so many of the poems appearing in the newspaper were written by the same author, p. 886. See also Paula Feldman, "Women Poets and Anonymity in the Romantic Era", *New Literary History* 33 (2002), pp. 279–89, and Judith Pascoe, "Mary Robinson and the Literary Marketplace", *Romantic Women Writers: Voices and Countervoices* (Hanover and London: University Press of New England, 1995), pp. 252–68, for additional examples of Robinson's use of pseudonyms in her writing.

13. Robert Merry, *The Laurel of Liberty* (London: John Bell, 1790), line 51. Further references will be cited in the text.

14. Jerome McGann, *The Poetics of Sensibility* (Oxford: Clarendon Press, 1996), p. 81.

15. Mary Robinson, *The Memoirs of the Late Mrs. Robinson, Written By Herself* 4 vols. (London: R. Phillips, 1801), Vol. ii, p. 127. Although the writer here cites the date of the poem's publication as 1791, it originally appeared in 1790, and the emphasis on the immediacy of Robinson's response would certainly refer to that earlier moment of publication. This remark is quoted in the introductory note to the poem in Mary Robinson, *Selected Poems*, ed. Judith Pascoe, (Peterborough, Ontario: Broadview Press, 2000), p. 103. All references to Robinson's poems, unless otherwise noted, will be from this edition, and hereafter cited parenthetically in the text.

16. *Memoirs*, Vol. ii, p. 179. Judith Pascoe notes a similar sense of reciprocal energy in the poetic correspondence between Robert Merry and Hannah Cowley, in the

exchange which served as the defining moment of the Della Cruscan movement. As Pascoe writes, "each poet is in love with the other's power to thrill him or her into writing," *Romantic Theatricality* (Ithaca and London: Cornell University Press, 1997), pp. 75–6.

17. Coleridge, in the "Monody on the Death of Chatterton" links "Otway's famish'd form" (line 32) to Chatterton and to Britain's neglect of poetic genius. The poem appears in Thomas Chatterton, *The Rowley Poems* (1777) (Oxford and New York: Woodstock Books, 1990), pp. xxv–xxviii. William Hayley posits the connection between "A future Chatterton by poison dead, / An Otway fainting for a little bread," in his *Essay on Epic Poetry* (1782) cited in David Fairer, "Chatterton's Poetic Afterlife, 1770–1794: A Context for Coleridge's *Monody*", in *Thomas Chatterton and Romantic Culture*, ed. Nick Groom (Basingstoke Macmillan – now Palgrave Macmillan 1999), p. 235. Thomas Holcroft decries "ill-treated " genius: "Oh Otway, Oh Chatterton!", in *The Adventures of Hugh Trevor* (1794–1797) ed. Seamus Deane (Oxford: Oxford University Press, 1978), p. 232. Bridget Keegan notes the ways in which "the very act of mourning [Chatterton's] loss" enabled his attainment of a privileged status as a "prototype for concepts of Romantic genius," "Nostalgic Chatterton: Fictions of Poetic Identity and the Forging of a Self-Taught Tradition", in Groom, ed. *Thomas Chatterton and Romantic Culture*, p. 212. David Fairer briefly mentions Robinson's "Monody", in his study of many of the poetic tributes to Chatterton that appeared in the decades following his death, p. 237. For Robinson's allusions, see *Walsingham*, pp. 170–1, *The Natural Daughter* (Peterborough, Ontario: Broadview Press, 2003), p. 227, *Angelina* (London: 1796), Vol.i. p. 72, and *The Sylphid* (included in the *Memoirs*), Vol. iii., p. 10.

18. McGann has recognized that "[t]he basic structure of the verse is exactly erotic because it proceeds by acts of intercourse that are at once perfectly immediate and purely imaginative", p. 82.

19. E.P. Thompson, *The Making of the English Working Class* (New York: Vintage Books, 1966), p. 105. For a good general overview of the British reaction to, and approval of the Revolution in its early stages, in which the events in France were viewed as basically the extending of the British system of constitutional monarchy, see Fraistat and Lanser, Introduction to Helen Maria Williams, *Letters Written in France* (1790) eds. Fraistat and Lanser (Peterborough, Ontario: 20001), pp. 9–50.

20. *The Critical Review* 1 (1791), p. 75.

21. Quoted in Stuart Semmel, *Napoleon and the British* (New Haven and London: Yale University Press, 2004), p. 116.

22. Anne Janowitz, *Women Romantic Poets: Anna Barbauld and Mary Robinson* (London: Northcote House, 2004). As Janowitz explains, Robinson is "the newcomer to the poetic tradition she has earlier outlined", p. 74.

23. *The Analytical Review* 8 (1790), pp. 550–1. Janet Todd and Marilyn Butler attribute this review to Wollstonecraft, based on the use here of her characteristic signatory initial "M". Todd and Butler, *The Works of Mary Wollstonecraft, Vol. 7*, "On Poetry, Contributions to the *Analytical Review*, 1788–1797", (New York: New York University Press, 1989), p. 331.

24. These comments appear in the hypertext edition of *Ainsi Va Le Monde* for "Romantic Circles." Adriana Craciun, ed. http://www.rc.umd.edu/editions/contemps/robinson/mrainsi06frst.htm.

25. *The Poetical Works of the late Mrs. Robinson, written by Herself* (London: 1806), p. 19.

26. Ibid., p. 21. The discrepancy in the line numbers in the two versions of the poem results from the insertion, in 1806, of an additional four lines to the poem. In the

section of the poem which relates to the current cultural climate, Maria Elizabeth, in referring to the "empty witlings" (131) who dominate society, adds the following lines, in what appears to be a specific reference to her mother's own personal experiences:

> Who with obsequious smiles mislead the mind,
> And prove most mischievous, by seeming kind;
> Pour on the Ear soft adulation's sound,
> And give to infamy the fame they wound.
> (141–4)

27. If, as many critics have argued, the continuation of Robinson's *Memoirs* was indeed written by Maria Elizabeth Robinson, this editorial work would complicate the assertion, stated in the *Memoirs* soon after the text assumes a third-person narration (and which I quoted at the outset of my discussion), that "in the poem entitled '*Ainsi Va le Monde*' Mrs. Robinson is at once the animated eulogist of Mr. Merry's talents, the dignified assertor of her own, and the graceful and intrepid champion of Freedom." Linda Peterson identifies Maria Elizabeth Robinson as the author of the completion of the *Memoirs*, whereas Judith Pascoe argues that although Maria Elizabeth, as well as the publisher of the *Memoirs*, Richard Phillips are possible candidates for author of the "Continuation", it is also possible that Robinson herself completed the text, using the third-person narrative as a distancing strategy. Linda Peterson, "Becoming an Author: Mary Robinson's *Memoirs* and the Origins of the Woman Artist's Autobiography", in *Re-Visioning Romanticism*, eds. Wilson and Haefner, p. 44, and Pascoe, *Romantic Theatricality*, p. 117n. M. Ray Adams, conversely, asserts that the "Continuation" was written by Peter Pindar (John Wolcot) although he does not provide any evidence to support this claim, *Studies in the Literary Backgrounds of English Radicalism* (Lancaster, Pennsylvania: Franklin and Marshall College Studies, 1947), p. 105. The discontinuity as it relates to Merry and his (non)presence in the poem evinced in these two assessments of *Ainsi* would seem, to my mind, to work against the claim for Maria Elizabeth's authorship of the "Continuation."

28. See David Erdman *Commerce des Lumieres: John Oswald and the British in Paris 1790–1793*, (Columbia: University of Missouri Press, 1986), pp. 305–6 and Jon Mee, " 'Reciprocal expressions of kindness': Robert Merry, Della Cruscanism and the limits of sociability", in *Romantic Sociability: Social Networks and Literary Culture in Britain 1770–1840*, eds. Gillian Russell and Clara Tuite (Cambridge: Cambridge University Press, 2002), pp. 104–22.

29. Mee's essay gives a detailed account of Merry's literary and political career that charts his move from the sociability of the Della Cruscan effusion to that of more radical, working class circles, culminating in his eventual exile from England.

30. Mathias, *Pursuits* (1797) Advertisement to Part IV, p. ii.

31. Ibid., p. 4. In perusing this list, one wonders if Mathias was aware of the fact that "Laura Maria" and "Mary Robinson" are indeed one and the same author, or if this is merely an oversight on his part.

32. McGann, p. 81. Gifford's attacks on Della Cruscan poetry have traditionally been recognized as a central factor in the demise of the convention.

33. William Gifford, *The Baviad* (London: Beckett and Porter, 1791), note to line 40. Gifford repeatedly and mistakenly calls the poem *The Wreath of Liberty*.

34. Ibid., In the 1800 and 1811 editions of the text, the epithet "Mrs. R——" is replaced by "Mrs. Robinson."
35. Gifford, *The Baviad and The Maeviad* (London: Becket and Porter, 1797), pp. 60–1.
36. Gifford (1811), pp. 55–6.
37. Mathias, p. 14.
38. Richard Polwhele, *The Unsex'd Females*, p. 17.
39. As far as this awareness relates to the writing of the 1790s, two major critics who reinforce the prominence of the novel in conveying a political viewpoint are Gary Kelly, in *The English Jacobin Novel* (Oxford: Clarendon Press, 1976) and "Women Novelists and the French Revolution Debate: Novelizing the Revolution/Revolutionizing the Novel", *Eighteenth-Century Fiction* 6:4 (1994), pp. 369–88, and Marilyn Butler, *Jane Austen and the War of Ideas* (Oxford: Clarendon Press, 1975). Both Butler and Kelly downplay Robinson's contribution to the political engagement with the French Revolution. Butler writes that Robinson was "not such [a] conscientious polemicist but intermittently would reveal liberal sympathies" (p. 31), while Kelly contends that she "could display some talent and . . . partook of that 'brisk traffic in opinions' around William Godwin," *English Jacobin Novel*, p. 12.
40. Kelly, "Women Novelists and the French Revolution Debate: Novelizing the Revolution/Revolutionizing the Novel", p. 374.
41. Recent studies of women's writing of this period point to the generic diversity of women's political engagement. See Craciun and Lokke, Introduction, *Rebellious Hearts: British Women Writers and the French Revolution, 1789–1815* (Albany NY: State University of New York Press, 2001), pp. 3–30 and Anne K. Mellor, *Mothers of the Nation: Women's Political Writing in England, 1780–1830* (Bloomington and Indianapolis: Indiana University Press), 2000.
42. See Janowitz, *Women Romantic Poets*, pp. 72–4, for the only sustained recent discussion of the poem.
43. For discussions of the highly sexualized representations of Marie Antoinette in pamphlets and the popular press, see Lynn Hunt, "The Many Bodies of Marie Antoinette", in *Eroticism and the Body Politic*, ed. Hunt (Baltimore and London: Johns Hopkins University Press, 1991), pp. 108–30, Terry Castle, "Marie Antoinette Obsession", *Representations* 38 (1992), pp. 1–38, and Pierre Saint-Amand, "Adorning Marie Antoinette", *Eighteenth-Century Life* 15:3 (1991), pp. 19–34. These studies stress the ways in which these portrayals included implications of lesbianism, and later accusations of incest and child abuse.
44. Robinson, *Memoirs*, Vol. ii, p. 177.
45. Fergus and Thaddeus, "Women, Publishers and Money, 1790–1820", p. 194.
46. Robinson, *Memoirs*, Vol. ii, p. 190. This description occurs soon after the narrative is broken off, and after the editorial rejoinder "Continuation. By a Friend", following which the text resumes with a third-person narrator.
47. Ibid., p. 193.
48. Pascoe, *Romantic Theatricality*, p. 121. Pascoe describes the meeting between Robinson and Marie Antoinette in detail, in a reading of the event that emphasizes a "reciprocal fetishization" (p. 119) as the women admire each other's bodies, clothes and ornaments. Later, Robinson loans the queen the miniature of the Prince of Wales that she had been wearing, and the queen responds by giving her the gift of a hand-netted little purse. Pascoe uses this exchange to illustrate Robinson's deployment of a "theatrical femininity" and thus a sense of "her own spectacular power" (p. 119).

49. Robinson's reference to the King's "late flight" points to the fact that this tract was published following the ill-fated escape to Varennes, *Impartial Reflections on the Present Situation of the Queen of France* (London: John Bell, 1791), p. 25. This text was originally published anonymously, under the title "A Friend to Humanity," hereafter cited parenthetically in the text.
50. Saint-Armand, p. 28.
51. Hunt, p. 123. As Hunt notes, this anxiety was not limited to the treatment of the monarchy, but was exhibited in various ways throughout the political spectrum. Thus, two weeks before Marie Antoinette's execution, all women's political clubs, including the radical "Société des républicaines Révolutionnaires" were shut down by order of the Convention, p. 124.
52. Ibid., p. 126.
53. Simon Schama, *Citizens, A Chronicle of the French Revolution* (New York: Vintage Books, 1989), pp. 550–51, David Andress, *The Terror: The Merciless War for Freedom in Revolutionary France* (New York: Farrar, Straus and Giroux, 2005), p. 54. Despite the different historiographical positions of Schama and Andress, they agree on the active, central role Marie Antoinette played during the early stages of the Revolution.
54. Robinson is slightly misquoting here. Burke had written that "the age of chivalry is gone," Edmund Burke, *Reflections on the Revolution in France*, ed. J.C.D. Clark, (Stanford: Stanford University Press, 2001), p. 238.
55. Burke's description of the invasion of the Queen's bedroom, on 6 October, 1789, is as follows:

> From this sleep the queen was first startled by the voice of the sentinel at her door, who cried out to her, to save herself by flight – that this was the last proof of fidelity he could give – that they were upon him, and he was dead. Instantly he was cut down. A band of cruel ruffians and assassins, reeking with his blood, rushed into the chamber of the queen, and pierced with an hundred strokes of bayonets and poniards the bed, from whence this persecuted woman had but just time to fly almost naked, and through ways unknown to the murderers had escaped to seek refuge at the feet of a king and husband, not secure of his own life for a moment.

Burke, *Reflections*, ed. J.C.D. Clark, p. 232.
56. Claudia Johnson, *Equivocal Beings* (Chicago and London: University of Chicago Press, 1995), pp. 2–3.
57. Johnson notes that such was the power of Burke's rhetoric that it "hardly matters that the Queen may not deserve to be adored", p. 6. Indeed, as J.C.D. Clark writes, "Burke's famous apostrophe of the Queen was a piece of carefully-judged public rhetoric. In private, he was often highly critical", J.C.D. Clark, Introduction, *Reflections on the Revolution on France* (Stanford: Stanford University Press, 2001), p. 37.
58. Clark, p. 38.
59. Curran, "Mary Robinson's *Lyrical Tales* in Context", p. 31. Curran singles out Robinson's poems "Edmund's Wedding", "The Deserted Cottage", "The Widow's Home", "The Hermit of Mont-Blanc", "The Fugitive", "Poor Marguerite", "The Alien Boy", "The Negro Girl", "Lascar", "All Alone", "The Shepherd's Dog" and "The Poor Singing Dame" as particularly representative of this awareness.

60. Mary Robinson, "Marie Antoinette's Lamentation", in Pascoe, ed., *Selected Poems*, pp. 135–7. Further references will be cited by line numbers parenthetically in the text.
61. Pascoe, Introduction, *Selected Poems*, p. 53.
62. Hunt, p. 122. Hunt quotes from the bill of indictment at the Queen's trial proceedings regarding this charge:

> the widow Capet, immoral in every way, new Agrippina, is so perverse and so familiar with all crimes that, forgetting her quality of mother and the demarcation prescribed by the laws of nature, she has not stopped short of indulging herself with Louis-Charles Capet, her son, and on the confession of this last, in indecencies whose idea and name make us shudder with horror. (p. 108).

Saint-Amand provides a similar account of these allegations, p. 27.
63. Mary Robinson, "Monody to the Memory of the Late Queen of France" (London: 1793). Hereafter cited by line number parenthetically in the text.
64. *The Monthly Review* 13 (1794), p. 117.
65. Saint-Amand, p. 29. Robinson's particular attention to the Queen's hair likewise acknowledges the widely disseminated account of how her hair had instantly lost its color. As Saint-Amand writes, "Back from Varennes, in a moment of fright, her hair lost its beautiful sheen and turned instantly white." He also acknowledges how this change in the Queen's appearance was perceived by the opposite side of the political spectrum: "The revolutionaries took care not to show this violent metamorphosis: the queen went to the guillotine wearing a simple bonnet," p. 29.
66. This is not the only allusion to Burke's *Reflections* present in this poem. For example, in a passage describing the ruin of the royal court, Robinson writes: "Where the rich banquet met the dazzling eye,/A thousand sheathless poniards glitt'ring lie;" (lines 241–2).
67. See Chapter 1, pp. 38–9.
68. Castle, p. 14.
69. The "Monody to the Memory of the Late Queen of France" was reviewed by the *Monthly Review* 13 (1794), the *Critical Review* 10 (1794), the *Analytical Review* 18 (1794), the *British Critic* 3 (1794) and the *European Magazine* 25 (1794). The *Monthly* writes, in a review that is indicative of the general tenor of the reception of the poem that "the public has often been addressed both in verse and in prose: but we have seen nothing on this subject that, in our apprehension, can more deeply excite the reader's tenderest feelings, than the verses of Mrs. Robinson", p. 116.
70. *The European Magazine* 25 (1794), p. 31.
71. *The Analytical Review* 18 (1794), p. 200.
72. Unlike the review of *Ainsi Va Le Monde*, the *Analytical's* review of the "Monody" was *not*, according to Todd and Butler, written by Wollstonecraft, *The Complete Works of Mary Wollstonecraft*, eds. Todd and Butler, Vol. 7.

4   "The Best and the Wisest": Mary Robinson II'

1. Mary Robinson, *Walsingham* (1797), ed. Julie Shaffer (Peterborough, Ontario: Broadview Press, 2003), p. 496. All references will be to this edition and hereafter cited parenthetically in the text.

2. Adriana Craciun has called attention to this letter in "The New Cordays: Helen Craik and British Representations of Charlotte Corday, 1793–1800", in *Rebellious Hearts: British Women Writers and the French Revolution*, eds. Adriana Craciun and Karri Lokke (Albany: State University of New York Press, 2001), p. 204. The letter itself, from which I quote directly, is located in the National Archives, London, and is catalogued as HO 102/10.

3. Although Robinson links Skirving, Margarot and Muir together, Muir was tried in August 1793, before the Edinburgh convention, and Skirving and Margarot in its aftermath, in January 1794. For accounts of what would become known as the "Scottish treason trials", see John Barrell, *Imagining the King's Death* (Oxford: Oxford University Press, 2000), pp. 142–69 and Albert Goodwin, *The Friends of Liberty* (Cambridge, MA: Harvard University Press, 1979), pp. 268–306.

4. John Barrell and Jon Mee, "Introduction", *Trials for Treason and Sedition*, eds. John Barrell and Jon Mee, 8 vols. (London: Pickering and Chatto, 2007), Vol. i., p. xxiv.

5. See Judith Pascoe, "Mary Robinson and the Literary Marketplace", in *Romantic Women Writers: Voices and Countervoices*, eds. Paula R. Feldman and Theresa M. Kelley (Hanover and London: University Press of New England, 1995), pp. 260–1, for a discussion of Robinson's use of the pseudonym of Tabitha Bramble and its indication of a political stance. Robinson herself addresses the use of this pseudonym in a letter to Samuel Jackson Pratt dated 31 August 1800. In mentioning her poetic contributions to the *Morning Post*, she writes: "all the Oberons [,] Tabithas [,] M.R.'s and most of the Poetry, you see there is mine", in *Shelley and his Circle 1773–1822*, 2 vols. ed. Kenneth Neill Cameron (Cambridge, MA: Harvard University Press, 1961), Vol. i., p. 232.

6. Paula Byrne, *Perdita: The Life of Mary Robinson* (London: HarperCollins, 2004), p. 350, cites March–April 1797 as the period in which Robinson's relationship with Tarleton effectively ended.

7. Jerome McGann, *The Poetics of Sensibility* (Oxford: Clarendon Press, 1996), p. 95.

8. Conversely, McGann views the Della Cruscan convention as laying the groundwork for the kind of sensibility that Robinson displays in the sonnet sequence. In placing an emphasis on the aesthetic aspects of her poetry, he recognizes a continuity, rather than a rupture between Robinson's earlier poetry and *Sappho and Phaon*. McGann argues that the "ultimate issues [at stake] here [are] aesthetic ones – and socio-political to the extent that we can appreciate the socio-political dimensions of aesthetic ones," p. 97. McGann views the radicalism of the poem (and its prefatory material) in its theorizing of the deployment of sensibility.

9. Preface to *Sappho and Phaon*, in Mary Robinson, *Selected Poems*, ed. Judith Pascoe, (Peterborough, Ontario: Broadview Press, 2000), p. 148. All references will be to this edition and hereafter cited parenthetically in the text.

10. McGann, pp. 100–2.

11. Ibid., p. 102.

12. Joan DeJean, *Fictions of Sappho* (Chicago and London: University of Chicago Press, 1989), p. 160. In using Barthélemy as her authority on Sappho, Robinson is also following the "standard [eighteenth-century] heterosexual scenario" of Sappho's life (p. 140), a point which is conspicuously evident in the sonnets themselves.

13. Ibid., p. 157.

14. For a reading that stresses the overt political nature of Barthélemy, see McGann, especially p. 115. For an opposing view, see Anne Janowitz, *Women Romantic Poets: Anna Barbauld and Mary Robinson* (London: Northcote House, 2004), p. 75.

15. Yopie Prins, *Victorian Sappho* (Princeton: Princeton University Press, 1999), pp. 183–4. Prins's reference to the "I" alludes to her engagement with Stuart Curran's groundbreaking essay on late eighteenth-century and early nineteenth-century women writers, "The 'I' Altered." Her argument for the disappearance of the woman poet opposes Curran's claim for the dispossessed, alienated subjectivity which characterizes this writing. As should be clear by now, my study of Mary Robinson and Charlotte Smith is much indebted to Curran's work, and to his conceptualization of the sense of tenuous existentiality that informs their literary projects.
16. Prins, p. 183.
17. DeJean, p. 157.
18. Richard Polwhele, *The Unsex'd Females* (London: Cadell and Davies, 1798), p. 17. See Chapter 3 of this study for a survey of the "Anti-Jacobin" response to Robinson's politics.
19. Robert Bass, *The Green Dragoon* (New York: Henry Holt, 1957) gives the date of the publication of *Sappho and Phaon* as 22 October 1796, and of *Hubert de Sevrac* as 26 November that same year, pp. 369–71.
20. Robinson locates the beginning of her novel in "the summer of 1792" (Vol. i., p. 7). If we take into consideration the time of the de Sevracs' stay at the castle of Montnoir, Hubert's long incarceration, the time spent in the cottage in the mountains, as well as the family's later adventures, a time frame extending until 1794 would seem a likely approximation of the period covered in the narrative.
21. Mary Robinson, *Hubert de Sevrac*, 3 vols. (London: Hookham and Carpenter, 1796), Vol. iii, p. 316. Further references will be cited parenthetically in the text.
22. See for example, the *Monthly Review*, whose reviewer writes: "We could point out many parts of these volumes that are delineated with strength and spirit: but, as a whole, the composition rather fails in effect, owing to the multiplicity of characters & incidents and to the frequent change of scene," quoted in Bass, p. 371. Mary Wollstonecraft concurs, in her discussion of the novel in the *Analytical Review*: "Mrs. Robinson writes so rapidly, that she scarcely gives herself time to digest her story into a plot, or to allow those incidents gradually to grow out of it, which are the fruit matured invention", *The Analytical Review* 25 (1797), p. 523. For the attribution of this review to Wollstonecraft see Janet Todd and Marilyn Butler, *The Complete Works of Mary Wollstonecraft*, Volume VII, *Contributions to the Analytical Review* (New York: New York University Press, 1989), p. 486.
23. Bass notes the popularity of *Hubert de Sevrac*, and adds that within a year it had been translated into French and German, pp. 371–2.
24. E.P. Thompson, *The Making of the English Working Class* (New York: Vintage Books, 1966), p. 147.
25. William Brewer, "The French Revolution as a Romance: Mary Robinson's *Hubert de Sevrac*", *Papers on Language and Literature* 42:2 (2006), pp. 115–49, presents a reading of the novel that foregrounds its political awareness and locates censorship specifically as a prominent theme.
26. Ibid., p. 119.
27. *The Analytical Review*, 25 (1797), p. 523.
28. See, for example, Claudia Johnson, *Jane Austen: Women, Politics and the Novel* (Chicago and London: University of Chicago Press, 1988) for an excellent discussion of the way the private, domestic sphere is political in both radical and anti-Jacobin novels during the 1790s.

29. Mary Favret, *Romantic Correspondence* (Cambridge: Cambridge University Press, 1993), p. 60.

30. See Chapter 2, pp. 61–8 for the discussion of Charlotte Smith's *Letters of a Solitary Wanderer*. Robinson certainly embraced the epistolary form. In addition to *The False Friend*, her novels *The Widow* (1794) and *Angelina* (1796) are also novels of letters.

31. At the same time, this narrative "preparation", as it were, is really only apparent upon a second reading of the novel. As Julie Shaffer writes, Robinson's readers "are fooled" by Sidney's appearance and behavior. Likewise, "[n]o one in the novel guesses that Sidney is not the man she appears to be unless her secret has been told or overheard," "*Walsingham*: gender, pain, knowledge", *Women's Writing* 9:1 (2002), p. 71.

32. These reviews appear in Appendix A of the Broadview edition of *Walsingham*, ed. Julie Shaffer: *The Analytical Review* 27 (1798), p. 500 and *The Monthly Review* 26 (1798), p. 497. In my references to the contemporary reviews of the novel I will cite the page numbers as they appear in the Broadview edition.

33. *The Anti-Jacobin Review* 1 (1798), pp. 502–3. Robert Bisset has been identified as the author of this review by Emily De Montluzin, *The Anti-Jacobins 1798–1800: The Early Contributors to the Anti Jacobin Review* (Basingstoke: Macmillan – now Palgrave Macmillan, 1988), p. 166. *The British Critic* 12 (1798), likewise foregrounds Robinson's politics in the novel: "The services of Rousseau and Voltaire, in delivering the earth from the shackles of tyranny and superstition, are *not* much acknowledged 'in this little island,' which is *exempt* (as the author words it) from the rest of the inhabitable globe; [...] When will authors, possessing any shadow of credit, cease to surfeit us with such disgusting and depraved absurdities?" p. 509.

34. See Chapter 2, p. 52.

35. Sharon Setzer, "The Dying Game: Crossdressing in Mary Robinson's *Walsingham*", *Nineteenth-Century Contexts* 22 (2000), p. 321. Setzer connects Robinson's support of the Revolution in *Walsingham* to the ways that the text itself responds to, and aligns itself with France, and particularly with the Chevalier d'Eon affair, a story which Robinson had engaged with in her *Letter to the Women of England, on the Injustice of Mental Subordination* (1799). There, Robinson had cited d'Eon as an example of the double standard, in which, as Setzer puts it, "what is 'laudable' in man [is]reprehensible, if not preposterous in woman," p. 305.

36. Chris Cullens, "Mrs. Robinson and the Masquerade of Womanliness", *Body and Text in the Eighteenth Century*, ed. Veronica Kelly and Dorothea von Mucke (Stanford: Stanford University Press, 1994), p. 275.

37. Terry Castle, *Masquerade and Civilization: The Carnivalesque in Eighteenth-Century Culture and Fiction* (Stanford: Stanford University Press,1986), p. 98.

38. Cullens points to Robinson's repeated focus on costume and on the awareness of her own dress as a marker of this consciousness of fashion, pp. 281–2. Shaffer connects Robinson's consciousness of fashion to the decline of crossdressing itself towards the end of the eighteenth century, "*Walsingham*: gender, pain, knowledge", p. 71.

39. Castle, p. 59.

40. Ibid., p. 122. Castle does not include *Walsingham* in her discussion of the representations of masquerade in eighteenth-century fiction.

41. As Setzer writes, "Of all the episodes that threaten to undermine the reader's sympathy for Walsingham, this is certainly the most disturbing," p. 318.

42. Cullens, p. 278.

43. *The Anti-Jacobin Review* 1 (1798), pp. 503–4.
44. I date this conversation according to the temporal markers that appear throughout the novel. The long letter to Rosanna that constitutes most of the text is dated "February 1792", and Walsingham's flight from England, upon learning both of Sidney's true gender and of her poisoning, occurs two months earlier, in December 1791. As this conversation in Bath occurs not long before Walsingham's return to Glenowen, and the denouement, we can safely assume that it takes place in the latter part of 1791.
45. Shaffer, ed., *Walsingham*, p. 480, n. 1.
46. Ibid., p. 71.
47. See, for example, Setzer, "The Dying Game", and Shaffer, "Walsingham: gender, pain, knowledge." Setzer, in linking Sidney's transvestism to the affair of the Chevalier d'Eon argues that in stressing the improbability of *Walsingham's* plot, the contemporary reviews of the novel overlook the story of d'Eon. The cultural work performed by these reviews is thus "symptomatic of a lingering tendency to forget that plausibility is not an objective, universal standard but a normative, regulatory construct, serving to discredit fictions that violate the conventions of gender and genre," pp. 306–7. Shaffer, while noting the decline in crossdressing at the end of the eighteenth century, both in the lives of real women, and in breeches parts performed on the stage, nevertheless views Sidney's actions within the continuum of a voluntary cultural act, pp. 70–1.
48. Setzer, "The Dying Game", p. 313.
49. Cullens, p. 272.
50. Ibid., p. 289.
51. *The Memoirs of the Late Mrs. Robinson, Written By Herself.* 4 vols. (London: R. Phillips, 1801), Vol. iii., p. 21. Further references will be cited parenthetically in the text.
52. The course of this friendship – along with Robinson's place more generally within the radical literary and intellectual circles of the late 1790s – has been most recently discussed in Paula Byrne's biography of Robinson. See also Mark Philp, *Godwin's Political Justice* (London: Duckworth, 1986) for a discussion of these intellectual circles in general.
53. Judith Pascoe, "Mary Robinson and the Literary Marketplace", p. 259, p. 314, n. Godwin had been on a visit of a few weeks to Ireland at this time.
54. Byrne, pp. 389–90, p. 405.
55. Mary Robinson to William Godwin, 28 August 1800. We do not have Godwin's earlier letter, and his comments mentioned above are available to us from being re-quoted by Robinson [Abinger] Dep. b.215/2.
56. Ibid.
57. To be sure, Godwin had quarreled with others as well because of the directness of his criticisms. See Pamela Clemit, "Holding Proteus: William Godwin in his letters", in *Repossessing the Romantic Past*, eds. Heather Glen and Paul Hamilton (Cambridge: Cambridge University Press: 2006) pp. 109–11 and Barbara Taylor, *Mary Wollstonecraft and the Feminist Imagination* (Cambridge: Cambridge University Press, 2003), p. 187 for Godwin's experience with Mary Hays.
58. Mary Robinson to William Godwin, 28 August 1800. [Abinger] Dep. b. 215/2.
59. Clemit, "Holding Proteus", p. 102, p. 104. See also Taylor, especially chapter 5. For a discussion of how Godwin's beliefs and the move towards sympathy is represented in his philosophical writings, especially in *An Enquiry Concerning Political Justice* and its different revisions, see Philp, *Godwin's Political Justice*.

60. Philp, p. 217.
61. Mary Robinson to William Godwin, 24 August 1800. [Abinger] Dep. b. 215/2.
62. The differences seem to have revolved around John Philpot Curran. Robinson explains to Godwin in her letter of 2 September the various reasons why she will not receive Curran, whom she feels is an improper associate for her, who had been used to the company of "the first talents in the world, in the society of the most enlightened men," Mary Robinson to William Godwin, 2 September 1800, [Abinger] Dep. c. 507/7. Godwin, in his reply, rose to Curran's defense, but also wrote, "There is nothing to which I should be more averse than putting the smallest force on your inclination." Godwin's letter appears in Pamela Clemit, "William Godwin and James Watt's Copying Machine: Wet-transfer Copies in the Abinger Papers", *Bodleian Library Record*, 18:5 (2005), pp. 532–60, p. 553. Robinson wrote Godwin one more letter, on 10 October, in which she thanks him for his "very kind attention" (but with no details as to what that attention could have been). Mary Robinson to William Godwin, 10 October 1800, [Abinger] Dep. b. 215/2.
63. Quoted in Byrne, p. 403. This letter is undated in Byrne, but she places it in September 1800.

5   "Newgate Before My Eyes": Elizabeth Inchbald I

1. Gary Kelly, *The English Jacobin Novel* (Oxford: Clarendon Press, 1976), p. 8. At the same time, Kelly admits that the term "Jacobin" is itself misleading: "[M]ost of those in Britain who bore that label were in fact Girondins in their principles and beliefs, and took their political thought from native rather than French precedents", p. 7. E. Tangye Lean devotes a chapter to Inchbald in *The Napoleonists: A Study in Political Disaffection 1760–1960* (London: Oxford University Press, 1970) but he focuses more on Inchbald's later years and her various responses to the Napoleonic Wars than to her political involvement during the 1790s. Lean relies exclusively on Inchbald's biographer James Boaden for the account of her life, while noting at the same time that Boaden's work is "exasperating in its omissions", p. 372.
2. *The Anti-Jacobin Review* 6 (1800), p. 152, *The True Briton*, 30 January 1793, 1 February 1793.
3. Inchbald's letter to Godwin, undated, appears in C. Kegan Paul, *William Godwin: His Friends and Contemporaries* (London: Henry S. King and Co., 1876), p. 140.
4. James Boaden, *Memoirs of Mrs. Inchbald: Including her Familiar Correspondence with the most distinguished persons of her time*. 2 vols. (London: Richard Bentley, 1833), Vol. i., p. 330.
5. Elizabeth Inchbald, "To the Artist", *The Artist: A Collection of Essays Relative to Painting, Poetry, Sculpture, Architecture, the Drama, Discoveries of Science, and Various Other Subjects*, Vol. i., 14 (1807), p. 16.
6. L.W. Conolly, *The Censorship of English Drama 1737–1824* (San Marino: The Huntington Library Press, 1976), p. 83.
7. Boaden, Vol. i., p. 330.
8. Boaden's approach is thus described by Kelly, p. 69. Kelly adds that "the whole tendency of [Boaden's] *Memoirs* ... is to underplay any seriousness on [Inchbald's] part, whether it is her early passion for self-improvement, her English Jacobinism or her later religiosity," p. 72.
9. Annibel Jenkins, *I'll Tell You What: The Life of Elizabeth Inchbald* (Lexington: University Press of Kentucky, 2003), pp. 518–19. Jenkins's view of the political and

intellectual culture of the 1790s in general is evident in the following comment: "Godwin actually was never an important political figure...and neither [he nor Holcroft] had an important role in the actual political events of the 1790s; only Holcroft's unfortunate experience in the Treason Trials and Godwin's letter of defense made a political footnote," p. 518.

10. Ibid., p. 324.

11. Although Kelly focuses almost exclusively on Inchbald's two novels, he does briefly discuss her play *Such Things Are* (1787) as a text that exhibits both "her own peculiar brand of satire and sentiment" (p. 94), as well as an early engagement with political issues and topical themes.

12. Inchbald wrote the first draft of *A Simple Story* in 1777 and continued to revise it, after soliciting comments from friends. However, in 1780, after failing to find a publisher, she put it aside. She came back to the novel only in 1789, and after more revisions, it was finally accepted by George Robinson, who published it in early 1791, Jenkins, pp. 274–5.

13. Boaden, Vol. i., p. 274. For discussions of the novel see for example, Kelly, *The English Jacobin Novel*, Terry Castle, *Masquerade and Civilization* (Stanford: Stanford University Press, 1986), Katharine M. Rogers, "Inhibitions on Eighteenth-Century Women Novelists: Elizabeth Inchbald and Charlotte Smith" *Eighteenth-Century Studies* 11 (1977), pp. 63–78, Patricia Meyer Spacks, *Desire and Truth: Functions of Plot in Eighteenth-Century Novels* (Chicago and London: University of Chicago Press, 1990) and "Novels of the 1790s: Action and Impasse", *The Columbia History of the British Novel*, (New York: Columbia University Press, 1994), pp. 247–74, Catherine Craft-Fairchild, *Masquerade and Gender* (University Park: Pennsylvania State University Press, 1993), Jane Spencer, *The Rise of the Woman Novelist: From Aphra Behn to Jane Austen* (Oxford: Basil Blackwell, 1986), Eleanor Ty, *Unsex'd Revolutionaries: Five Women Novelists of the 1790s* (Toronto and Buffalo: University of Toronto Press, 1993), Nora Nachumi, " 'Those Simple Signs' The Performance of Emotion in Elizabeth Inchbald's *A Simple Story*" *Eighteenth-Century Fiction* 11:3 (1999), pp. 317–38, Jo Alyson Parker, "Complicating *A Simple Story*: Inchbald's Two Versions of Female Power", *Eighteenth-Century Studies* 30:3 (1997), pp. 255–70, Paula Byrne, "*A Simple Story*: From Inchbald to Austen", *Romanticism* 5:2 (1999) pp. 161–71, and George Haggerty, "Female Abjection in Inchbald's *A Simple Story*", *Studies in English Literature* 36:3 (1996), pp. 655–72.

14. Castle, p. 292.

15. See, for example, J.M.S. Tompkins's note to the Oxford edition of the novel, p. 342n. Whether or not they had been in love during the early period of their lives, Inchbald and Kemble remained lifelong friends. A particularly moving expression of Kemble's admiration for Inchbald appears in a letter that he wrote to her upon hearing of the successful premiere of her first play, *The Mogul's Tale* (1784). Thus Kemble writes, "If I cou'd write [poetry] I wou'd – I cannot – so you must receive Esteem instead of Flattery, and Sincerity for wit, when I swear there is no woman I more truly admire, nor any man, whose abilities I more highly value," Kemble to Inchbald (17 July 1784), Victoria and Albert Museum, Forster Collection MS 322.

16. Claudia Johnson, *Jane Austen: Women, Politics and the Novel* (Chicago and London: University of Chicago Press, 1988), p. 6.

17. Elizabeth Inchbald, *A Simple Story* (1791), ed. J.M.S. Tompkins (Oxford: Oxford University Press, 1986), p. 72. Hereafter cited parenthetically in the text. Tompkins views the issue of Dorriforth's priesthood as a biographical referent to Kemble, who, like Dorriforth had studied for the priesthood in France, p. 339, n.

18. As Castle explains, "[t]he guardian / ward relationship is typically a sacrosanct one in English fiction of the period – sentimental in form and nonsexual in nature", p. 299. Inchbald is appropriating the French tradition here, as it features most prominently in Rousseau's *La Nouvelle Heloise.*

19. Elizabeth Inchbald, *The Child of Nature* (1788) in *Cumberland's British Theatre* (London: 1829), Vol. 11, p. 30. This play was an adaptation of Mme de Genlis's *Zélie*, which Inchbald had translated and adapted from the French. The issue of tutor / pupil love also appears in *Lovers' Vows*, a play that Inchbald had translated and adapted from Kotzebue's *Child of Love*. The contemporary perception of *Lovers' Vows*, as famously seen in Jane Austen's *Mansfield Park*, suggests that, even as an adaptation, her rendition of the Amelia / Anhalt relationship retained much notoriety. See Byrne for a discussion which emphasizes the interconnectedness of *A Simple Story*, *Lovers' Vows* and *Mansfield Park* as it is exhibited through the presentation of a pupil / tutor relationship.

20. Castle, p. 307.

21. Spacks, *Desire and Truth*, p. 198.

22. Haggerty, p. 661.

23. Tompkins, ed. *A Simple Story*, p. 344n. Deschamps wrote to Inchbald in January 1792, acknowledging his edition of *A Simple Story*, while admitting that he had only translated the first two volumes of the novel. Asking her "forgiveness", he writes that "it has cost me much in taking upon myself to separate what you believed must be united. But this union of two different stories in the same framework would have passed with us for such boldness that even success would not have justified." Deschamps's letter appears in Boaden, Vol. ii, p. 373 (my translation.)

24. It is instructive to view, in this context, Inchbald's own attitude to marriage as it is reflected in her personal life. Although widowed at the age of 26, she never remarried, despite the fact that she had had many offers. Her friend John Taylor writes that when he asked her why she had not married again, her answer was, "That for wedlock, friendship was too familiar, and love too precarious," John Taylor, *Records of My Life*, 2 vols., (London: Edward Bull, 1832), Vol. i., p. 409.

25. Spacks. "Novels of the 1790s: Action and Impasse", p. 273, p. 267.

26. Haggerty, p. 669.

27. Spacks, *Desire and Truth*, p. 200.

28. Elizabeth Inchbald, *Remarks for The British Theatre* (1806–1809) (Delmar, NY: Scholars Facsimiles and Reprints, 1990), "Wives As They Were and Maids As They Are", p. 5. The *Remarks* themselves are a series of biographical and critical prefaces that accompanied the 25-volume collection of plays, *The British Theatre*. In addition to *Wives As They Were*, four of Inchbald's other plays were also anthologized in *The British Theatre*: *Such Things Are*, *Every One Has His Fault*, *Lovers' Vows*, and *To Marry or Not to Marry*.

29. *The Analytical Review* 10 (1791), pp. 101–3. This review is attributed to Wollstonecraft by Marilyn Butler and Janet Todd eds., *The Complete Works of Mary Wollstonecraft*, Vol. 7, *Contributions to the Analytical Review* (New York: New York University Press, 1989). See also Kelly, pp. 90–1. Kelly asserts that "the first two volumes of *A Simple Story* dwell on the errors of an 'ill-educated woman', but the second part of the novel restores the balance, as Mrs. Inchbald clearly intended, by showing the positive results of an academic and stoical training in Miss Milner's daughter Matilda", p. 72.

30. This preface is omitted from later editions of the novel.
31. *The British Critic* 7 (1796), p. 263, p. 261. *Nature and Art* was also reviewed in *The Analytical Review* 23 (1796), *The Monthly Review* 19 (1796) and *The Critical Review* 16 (1796). For recent discussions of the novel, see Kelly, *The English Jacobin Novel*, as well as Shawn L. Maurer, both in her introduction to the Pickering and Chatto edition of the book (1997) and in her essay, "Masculinity and Morality in Elizabeth Inchbald's Nature and Art", *Women, Revolution, and the Novels of the 1790s*, ed. Linda Lang-Peralta (East Lansing: Michigan State University Press, 1999), pp. 155–76, and Eleanor Ty, *Unsex'd Revolutionaries: Five Women Novelists of the 1790s*. Brief discussions of various aspects of the novel also appear in Mona Scheuermann, *Her Bread to Earn: Women, Society and Money from Defoe to Austen* (Lexington: University Press of Kentucky, 1993), Vivien Jones, "Placing Jemima: Women Writers of the 1790s and the Eighteenth-Century Prostitution Narrative", *Women's Writing* 4:2 (1997), pp. 201–20 and Susan Staves, "British Seduced Maidens", *Eighteenth-Century Studies* 14:2 (1980), pp. 109–34.
32. *The Anti-Jacobin Review* 6 (1800), p. 152. See Introduction, pp. 8–9.
33. *The Analytical Review* 23 (1796), p. 511. Todd and Butler attribute this review to Wollstonecraft, p. 462.
34. Spacks, "Novels of the 1790s: Action and Impasse", p. 260. Much of Spacks's essay is devoted to the ways in which Inchbald's other novel, *A Simple Story*, diverges from this tradition.
35. William Hazlitt, "Lectures on the Comic Writers" (1819), in *The Collected Works of William Hazlitt* (12 vols.) eds. A.R. Waller and Arnold Glover (London: J.M. Dent, 1902–1904), Vol. 8, pp. 127–8.
36. Boaden, Vol. i., p. 346.
37. For Boaden's account of the events surrounding the composition of *Nature and Art*, see Vol. i., pp. 315–30.
38. Kelly, p. 98. See also Jenkins, p. 372.
39. As Boaden relates it, "when Holcroft was committed to prison on a charge of high treason, [Inchbald] neither felt alarm about *herself*, nor would desert her *friend*; but went immediately with Robinson the publisher in a coach to Newgate to visit him", Vol. i., p. 330.
40. E.P. Thompson, *The Making of the English Working Class* (New York: Vintage Books, 1966), p. 145, and Philip A. Brown, *The French Revolution in English History* (London: Frank Cass, 1965), p. 152.
41. Elizabeth Inchbald, *Nature and Art*, 2 vols. (1796) (Oxford and New York: Woodstock Books, 1994), Vol. i., p. 81. All references will be to this edition and hereafter cited parenthetically in the text. Shawn Maurer has edited two editions of *Nature and Art*, for the "Pickering Women's Classics" series (1997) and for Broadview Press (2005). She has chosen the 1797 edition as the source text for these editions, citing the more "readable" nature of this text for her decision to use it, "Note on the Text", (1997), p. liv. Maurer includes the original ending of the novel in her appendices, calling it "strangely ironic" and acknowledging that Inchbald had probably revised it because of the radical implications of the 1796 conclusion, p. 152, n. 55. This later ending remains intact in subsequent editions of *Nature and Art*. The final edition of the text that Inchbald herself corrected appeared in 1810 in Anna Barbauld's *British Novelists* series, where a conspicuous (though thematically unimportant) alteration occurs in the changing of Hannah Primrose's name to Agnes. I have chosen to work with the original 1796 edition precisely for its more energetic radical stance.

42. David Hume, "Essay: Of National Characters", in *The Philosophical Works / David Hume*, 4 vols., eds., Thomas Hill Green and Thomas Hodge Grose (London: 1882), Vol. i., *Essays Moral, Political and Literary* (1748) p. 252.

43. Emmanuel Chukwudi Eze, *Race and the Enlightenment* (Cambridge, MA. and Oxford: Blackwell, 1997), p. 5.

44. For discussions on the representation of the East in Inchbald's plays, see Betsy Bolton, "Farce, Romance, Empire: Elizabeth Inchbald and Colonial Discourse", *The Eighteenth Century: Theory and Interpretation*, 39:1 (1998), pp. 3–24, and Daniel O'Quinn, "Inchbald's Indies: Domestic and Dramatic Re-Orientations", *European Romantic Review* 9:2 (1998), pp. 217–31. Neither Bolton nor O'Quinn mentions the colonial element of *Nature and Art*. Although Zocotora is not exactly "East" Inchbald presents it as an exotic locale and as a foil for viewing cultural issues central to British society.

45. Staves, p. 120.

46. Maurer, Introduction, *Nature and Art*, p. xix.

47. For a discussion of Hannah's marginalized position as seen through her access to language see also Ty, p. 108.

48. Scheuermann argues that it is Hannah's lower-class status only, and not her gender, that dooms her. As she writes, "Inchbald sees class rather than gender as the determinant of victimization: rich women are as obnoxious as rich men," *Her Bread to Earn*, p. 169. While she is correct in stating that women in *Nature and Art* appear as oppressors as well as the oppressed, she ignores the fact that it is the convergence of class *and* gender that makes Hannah so very vulnerable. In viewing the way that her gender contributes to her downfall it is sufficient to compare her arrival, destitute, to London with that of the Norwynne brothers, who eventually attain social mobility.

49. Inchbald's letter to Godwin appears in C. Kegan Paul, pp. 140–1.

50. C. Kegan Paul, p. 141. Jenkins includes this letter in her biography of Inchbald, yet, and, typically of her focus, writes merely, "We evidently cannot know exactly the details of [Inchbald's] composition, but her letter does show her awareness of the current criticism [of the King] as he was said to be", p. 347.

51. For the connection between the food shortages and the fear of a popular insurrection see John Barrell, *Imagining the King's Death* (Oxford: Oxford University Press, 2000), pp. 551–6.

52. Kelly, pp. 105–7. Kelly makes the connection between the pro-government pamphlets written by Inchbald's Dean William and "the sermon which Horsley had preached in January 1793, 'before the House of Lords at Westminster Abbey, depicting the dangers of the revolutionary spirit,' " p. 105.

53. Hannah More, "The Riot; or Half a Loaf is Better than No Bread", *Cheap Repository Shorter Tracts* (London: 1800), p. 442. Further references will be cited parenthetically in the text.

54. As Anne Mellor notes, Hannah More and her *Cheap Repository Tracts* were crucial in stemming the tide of a working-class insurrection in England. Mellor singles out "The Riot" (which is written in the form of a ballad) as a particularly influential text, and notes that it was sung in 1795 in Bath and Hull in order to calm down rioting colliers. Mellor, *Mothers of the Nation: Women's Political Writing in England, 1780–1830* (Bloomington and Indianapolis: Indiana University Press, 2000), p. 15.

55. Jones, p. 210.

56. Staves, p. 122.

57. Ibid., p. 123.

58. Barrell, p. 556.
59. Kelly, p. 111.
60. Ibid., p. 104.
61. Kelly makes no mention of the revised 1797 edition of *Nature and Art*, although the elements present in its conclusion strengthen his analysis of the novel.
62. Inchbald, *Nature and Art* (2nd edn.) (London: G.G. and J. Robinson, 1797), Vol. ii., p. 201.
63. See note 12.
64. Inchbald's letter to Godwin appears in C. Kegan Paul, pp. 74–5, and in Jenkins, pp. 316–17.
65. For Inchbald's earnings for *Nature and Art*, see Jenkins, p. 372. For a full list of Inchbald's earnings for her plays, see Misty Anderson, *Female Playwrights and Eighteenth-Century Comedy* (New York and Basingstoke: Palgrave – now Palgrave Macmillan, 2002), p. 26.

6 "Under a Despotic Government": Elizabeth Inchbald II

1. Elizabeth Inchbald, "To The Artist," *The Artist: A Collection of Essays Relative to Painting, Poetry, Sculpture, Architecture, the Drama, Discoveries of Science, and Various Other Subjects* 1: 14 (1807), pp. 9–19, p. 16.
2. L.W. Conolly, *The Censorship of English Drama 1737–1824* (San Marino: The Huntington Library Press, 1976), pp. 92–3, p. 106. Conolly meticulously documents the censorship of drama during the revolutionary years, providing examples of plays that were submitted to the censor and then either simply rejected, or caused to be substantially revised.
3. Ellen Donkin, *Getting Into the Act: Women Playwrights in London 1776–1829* (London and New York: Routledge, 1994) p. 3. Donkin details the hurdles that a playwright of either gender would have to overcome in order to have his or her work seen, read, approved and eventually staged. She cites two areas – education and conduct – which made the process doubly difficult for women, who were constrained by lack of formal education, by lack of access to systems of networking that facilitated contact between male playwrights and theater managers, and by conduct literature, which circumscribed the theatre as a dangerous and inhospitable environment for women: "Playwriting, as a profession, violated all rules of conduct," p. 18. Jeffrey Cox cites Joanna Baillie, Sarah Siddons and Anna Larpent as examples of women who prominently held "social and cultural power" in the late eighteenth and early nineteenth-century theater world, "Baillie, Siddons, Larpent: gender, power and politics in the theatre of Romanticism", *Women in British Romantic Theatre: Drama, Performance and Society, 1790–1840*, ed. Catherine Burroughs (Cambridge: Cambridge University Press, 2000), p. 42.
4. Donkin, pp. 110–14.
5. Annibel Jenkins, *I'll Tell You What: The Life of Elizabeth Inchbald* (Lexington: University Press of Kentucky, 2003), p. 149.
6. Judith Phillips Stanton, " 'This New-Found Path Attempting': Women Dramatists in England 1660–1800", *Curtain Calls: British and American Women and the Theatre 1660–1820*, eds. Mary Anne Schofield and Cecilia Macheski (Athens, Ohio: Ohio University Press, 1991), pp. 325–54. See especially Table 6, p. 36.
7. Elizabeth Inchbald, *Remarks for The British Theatre* (1806–1809) (Delmar, NY: Scholars Facsimiles and Reprints, 1990), "Cato", p. 5. Since each preface is paginated

separately in this edition, I will, in referring to the *Remarks*, cite the titles of the plays referred to, followed by the relevant page number of that preface. See also, for example, the prefaces to George Farquhar's "The Inconstant", p. 1, and to Charles Macklin's "The Man of the World", p. 4.

8. Inchbald, *Remarks*, "Cato", p. 5.
9. Ibid., "Julius Caesar", p. 1.
10. Ibid., "Venice Preserved", p. 1. Although I have been referring to the Chief Examiner of Plays for his role in censoring or forbidding the production of manuscript plays submitted to him, it was the Lord Chamberlain in whom the authority for the task was ultimately invested, although the actual work was delegated to the Examiner. See Conolly, pp. 15–16.
11. See John Barrell, *Imagining the King's Death* (Oxford: Oxford University Press, 2000), pp. 567–9, for an account of the events surrounding the 1795 production of *Venice Preserved* and how they reflected in a wider sense the political tensions and divisions of the period. As Barrell has shown, these events also played a role in motivating the government's legislation of the Two Acts.
12. Inchbald, *Remarks*, "The Dramatist", p. 1.
13. For the Dibdin text and other examples, see Conolly, pp. 104–6. I have checked the following Inchbald plays that were written during the 1790s in the Larpent Collection of Manuscript Plays in the Huntington Library: *The Hue and Cry* (1791) (LA 900), *Next Door Neighbours* (1791) (LA 912), *Every One Has His Fault* (1793) (LA 967), *The Wedding Day* (1794) (LA 1044), *Wives As They Were and Maids as They Are* (1797) (LA 1155), and *The Wise Man of the East* (1799) (LA 1271). The one instance in which a phrase is crossed out in an Inchbald play in the Larpent copy, appears in *Such Things Are* (1786) (LA 761).
14. As Dougald Macmillan explains, "Most copies [of plays sent to the Examiner] are accompanied by a formal application for license to perform, signed by the manager of the theatre; and the name of the author only rarely appears upon the play, except on title-pages of printed copies, submitted instead of manuscripts", *Catalogue of the Larpent plays in the Huntington Library* (San Marino: Huntington Library Press, 1939), p. vii. Inchbald's plays in the Larpent collection do not have her name appearing anywhere in the manuscript.
15. James Boaden, *Memoirs of Mrs. Inchbald: Including her Familiar Correspondence with the most distinguished persons of her time*, 2 vols. (London: Richard Bentley, 1833), Vol. i., p. 309.
16. Misty Anderson, *Female Playwrights and Eighteenth-Century Comedy* (New York and Basingstoke: Palgrave – now Palgrave Macmillan, 2002), p. 183. Anderson also notes that the play was popular in the United States, and was performed in Philadelphia in 1794, p. 232, n.
17. *The True Briton*, 30 January 1793.
18. Boaden, Vol. i., p. 310.
19. *The True Briton*, 1 February 1793.
20. As Donkin explains, "As a general rule, playwrights received a benefit on the third, sixth and ninth evening, if they were lucky enough to have a play last that long. A benefit meant that once a certain specified amount of overhead had been cleared at the box office, the remaining box office take went to the playwright", p. 7.
21. Inchbald's letter appears in Boaden, Vol. i., p. 311. It is dated 1 February 1793 (the same day that *The True Briton's* second response had appeared) a fact that calls attention to the immediacy of Inchbald's reply.

22. For this insight, I am indebted to Angela Smallwood's conference paper, "Women Playwrights, Politics and Convention: The Case of Elizabeth Inchbald's 'seditious' comedy *Every One Has His Fault* (1793)", presented at the conference *Women's Writing in Britain 1660–1830*, University of Southampton, July 2003.

23. Crochunis, "Authorial performances in the criticism and theory of Romantic women Playwrights", in *Women in British Romantic Theatre*, ed. Burroughs, p. 233. Betsy Bolton mentions the Inchbald/*True Briton* incident as an example of how the need to insure professional and economic survival forced women to adapt a politically- neutral stand. She thus views Inchbald's letter to *The Diary* as a retraction, rather than as a more politically ambiguous and subtle response to the charges against her, Bolton, *Women, Nationalism and the Romantic Stage: Theatre and Politics in Britain 1780–1800* (Cambridge: Cambridge University Press, 2001), p. 39.

24. John Barrell, "The Reptile Oculist", *London Review of Books* 26:7 (1 April 2004), p. 19.

25. It was Taylor who wrote the lines of the rhyming butler for Inchbald's play *Lovers' Vows* in 1799. John Taylor, *Records of My Life*, 2 vols. (London: Edward Bull, 1832), Vol. i., p. 402.

26. *The Critical Review* 7 (1793), p. 224.

27. *The Star* (30 January 1793) and *The Thespian Magazine* (March 1793), both included in the appendix of *The Broadview Anthology of Romantic Drama*, eds. Jeffrey N. Cox and Michael Gamer (Peterborough, Ontario: Broadview Press, 2003), p. 318, p. 322.

28. Frank H. Ellis, *Sentimental Comedy: Theory & Practice* (Cambridge: Cambridge University Press, 1991), p. 112. The original reviews of the play also note Inchbald's originality in the construction of her various characters. The *Critical Review* cites Sir Robert Ramble as a figure who is "new on the stage", p. 224 and *The Analytical Review* cites Mr. Harmony as a character who is "founded on an idea which was perhaps never realized in the extent here represented," *The Analytical Review* 15 (1793), p. 458. Two lengthy reviews of the play were written by Inchbald's close friends – William Godwin in *The European Magazine 23* (1793) and Thomas Holcroft in *The Monthly Review 10* (1793). Godwin, after claiming that *Every One Has His Fault* "rises above any of her former theatrical essays" (p. 105) nonetheless qualifies his praise by stating that the play is "too rich in ideas", p. 106, that is, Inchbald should have concentrated more fully on only one of her plots, rather than diffusing many themes through the multiple stories and characters that appear in the work. As he writes, "He who would contemplate the genius of Mrs. Inchbald in its full lustre, must read the Simple Story", p. 106. Holcroft's review in the *Monthly*, while admitting of the "well imagined variety of character" (p. 302), is also more critical of the piece as a whole, especially as it pertains to Mr. Harmony, a character whose actions imply that "falsehood may be beneficial", p. 304, a point I will discuss more fully above.

29. As Gillian Russell has shown, the first performance of *Every One Has His Fault* in Brighton, in August 1793, was disrupted by army officers, although their ire was, it seems, not directed specifically at the play, but towards the radical Rev. Vicesimus Knox, who was present in the audience. Another incident occurred in 1795, during the performance of the play in Portsmouth. As Russell relates it, the riot was "caused by a group of young officers who rushed into the playhouse with a 'hideous yell' and 'terminated the performance'", Gillian Russell, *The Theatres of*

War: Performance, Politics and Society, 1793–1815 (Oxford: Clarendon Press, 1995), pp. 111–12.

30. Anne K. Mellor, *Mothers of the Nation: Women's Political Writing in England, 1780–1830* (Bloomington and Indianapolis: Indiana University Press, 2000), p. 68.

31. Katherine S. Green's essay, "Mr. Harmony and the Events of January 1793: Elizabeth Inchbald's *Every One Has His Fault*," *Theatre Journal* 56:1 (March 2004), pp. 47–62, presents a reading of *Every One Has His Fault* that, like my own discussion, focuses on the political awareness that infuses the play and, similarly, contextualizes it within the particular cultural moment in which it was written. While my argument generally concurs with Green's, particularly in the recognition of the cautious strategies that Inchbald employed to articulate her political message, and in her rejection of the Godwin–Holcroft notion of "truth", it differs regarding Inchbald's presentation of the aristocracy. As will become clear, I cannot agree in particular with Green's claim that Inchbald "never overtly questions patriarchal privilege", p. 58.

32. Elizabeth Inchbald, *Every One Has His Fault*, in Roger Manvell, ed. *Elizabeth Inchbald, Selected Comedies* (Lanham, New York, London: University Press of America, 1987), I,. ii, p. 13. All further references will be from this edition and cited parenthetically in the text.

33. Besides this reference to the "scarcity of provisions" and the two times the phrase appears in Miss Spinster's speech in Act I, it appears yet again in Act III, scene i. Lord Norland has just informed Mr. Harmony of the attempt to rob him the previous night, saying "It is amazing we cannot put a stop to such depradations." Harmony replies, "Provisions are so scarce!" (p. 39). Unlike the other three times when the phrase is spoken, here it does not appear in a comic context, but rather as a direct reference to the connection between a rising crime rate and the current economic situation.

34. *The Analytical Review* 15 (1793), p. 458, Inchbald, *Remarks for the British Theatre*, "Every One Has His Fault", p. 4.

35. For Godwin and Holcroft, as Gary Kelly writes, "[t]ruth, once known, must prove invincible, and it was every man's social duty to make the truth known as widely as possible," *The English Jacobin Novel* (Oxford: Clarendon Press, 1976), p. 135.

36. This comment appears in Holcroft's diary entry for 22 June 1798. It is included in *The Life of Thomas Holcroft, Written By Himself, Continued to the Time of his Death from his Diary Notes and Other Papers by William Hazlitt* (1816) 2 vols., ed. Elbridge Colby (London: Constable and Co., 1925), Vol. ii., pp. 123–4. Holcroft's treatment of the issue of "truth" appears in his fictional works as well. For example, in his 1792 novel *Anna St. Ives* the approved characters repeatedly and forcefully articulate its defense. To cite just one example, Anna, the eponymous heroine, writes to her friend: "The diffusion of knowledge, or more properly of truth, is the one great good to which wealth, genius, and existence ought all to be applied. This noble purpose gives birth to felicity, which is in itself grand, inexhaustible, and eternal", Thomas Holcroft, *Anna St. Ives*, 7 vols. (London: 1792), Vol. vi, pp. 150–1.

37. *The Monthly Review* 10 (1793), pp. 303–4.

38. Anderson, p. 190.

39. Ibid., pp. 184–5. Anderson's larger argument is concerned with the way in which Inchbald and other women playwrights addressed, through the genre of comedy, the historical changes that were occurring in the eighteenth century. Regarding

Inchbald specifically, she claims that her plays exhibit "marriage law and divorce as both a cultural crisis and a generic dilemma", p. 172.

40. The lines also clearly echo Shakespeare's *Measure for Measure* and the Duke's inter-rogation of Mariana's similarly vague marital status: "Neither maid, widow, nor wife?" (V.i. 2584).

41. Anderson, p. 187.

42. The omission of a stage direction at this moment is a reversal of Inchbald's usual procedures. As Nora Nachumi has shown, physical gestures played a crucial role in Inchbald's plays, and especially at moments of heightened emotion: "Although her twenty-one plays rarely *describe* individual gestures, Inchbald's stage directions insist that actors physically illustrate their characters' emotional states." In this final scene of *Every One Has His Fault*, this practice is reversed. Miss Wooburn's smile is described, but absent from the stage directions. Nora Nachumi, " 'Those Simple Signs': The Performance of Emotion in Elizabeth Inchbald's *A Simple Story*", *Eighteenth-Century Fiction* 11:3 (1999), p. 323.

43. Patricia Meyer Spacks, "Novels of the 1790s: Action and Impasse", *The Columbia History of the British Novel*, ed. John Richetti (New York: Columbia University Press, 1994), p. 255. Spacks cites several titles and subtitles that reflect this concern: *Ellinor, or The World As It Is*; *Man As He Is*; *Hermsprong, or Man As He Is Not*; *Caleb Williams, or Things As They Are*. The Larpent copy of the play (LA 1155), besides exhibiting Inchbald's original title, reveals that she had changed the names of some of the main characters. The Dorrillons were originally called Sir William and Maria Merrideth and Mr Norberry was first named Mr Auberry. The choice of the name Dorrillon for her central characters, and its resemblance to the name Dorriforth, may be yet another example of the echoes of *A Simple Story* that figure so prominently in the play.

44. Inchbald, *Remarks*, "Wives As They Were and Maids As They Are", p. 1.

45. Anderson, p. 192.

46. For example, Anderson claims that Inchbald's politics reflect an "affective individ-ualism" as the only possible solution to constricting gender relations, and that in presenting this solution, her politics are "hardly feminist", p. 199. See also Daniel O'Quinn "Scissors and Needles: Inchbald's *Wives As They Were, Maids As They Are* and the Governance of Sexual Exchange", *Theatre Journal* 51:2 (1999), in which O'Quinn asserts that *Wives as They Were* advocates "reasonable government" and can be read as a "political allegory that argues for the value of hegemony for the emergent bourgeoisie,", p. 124.

47. *Remarks*, "Wives as They Were and Maids as They Are", p. 5.

48. Ibid.

49. Suzanne Bloxam, in her biography of Elizabeth Farren, makes repeated efforts to show that the relationship between Farren and Derby was a platonic one, in which they were in effect "engaged" until the time when Derby's estranged wife would die and they would be able to marry. Bloxam bases her claim on the fact that Farren's mother was a constant companion – "Mrs. Farren, who always resided with her daughter, was present in every step of their advancement", Suzanne Bloxam, *Walpole's Queen of Comedy: Elizabeth Farren, Countess of Derby* (Ashford, Kent: 1988), p. 112. In keeping with this focus, Bloxam necessarily downplays the fact that Farren and Derby were indeed a subject for gossip and conjecture, citing these sources only indirectly and then in order to contradict them. The following comment is indicative of her approach: "Elizabeth's success and her acceptance in High Society engendered some envy but according to all contemporary sources,

any satire steered clear of imputations on her virtue," p. 112. However, the fact that they *were* the subject of satire in itself points to the conspicuous unconventionality of their relationship. James Gillray, for example, drew two caricatures of the couple, "A Peep at Christies" (September 1796) and "The Marriage of Cupid and Psyche" (May 1797) a piece whose title may suggest a view of the relationship opposed to that presented by Bloxam. It is interesting to note that Derby's wife eventually died on 14 March 1797, ten days after *Wives as They Were* was first performed, and Farren continued to act on the stage until 8 April. Thus, in spite of Inchbald's comments on writing the part of Miss Dorrillon with Farren in mind, but with the implication that Farren *was unable* to perform it, she was not cast in the role, even though her upcoming marriage was not an issue when the play was in rehearsal and production.

50. Elizabeth Inchbald, *Wives As They Were and Maids As They Are* (London: G.G. and J. Robinson, 1797), p. iii. This prologue was written "By a Friend" and does not appear in the Manvell edition of the play. It was spoken by the actor Mr Waddy, who played Mr Norberry, the guardian of Miss Dorrillon, a more moderate and less conspicuous patriarchal figure than Sir William Dorrillon.

51. *Wives As They Were and Maids As They Are* received mixed reviews from contemporary critics. *The Monthly Review*, while commending the "spirit, ease, and sprightliness of the dialogue" in the play, at the same time criticizes the improbability of its plot, and what the reviewer sees as "the writer's disregard of the laws of the drama", *Monthly Review* 23 (1797), p. 463. *The Analytical Review* is even less generous, noting the play's popularity, but also that "a crowded house ... is but a very equivocal test of merit", also stating that "we do not find any character to be particularized for it's [sic] energy or eccentricity", *Analytical Review* 25 (1797), p. 602. The more conservative *British Critic*, not surprisingly, applauds the character of Lady Priory while being less at ease with that of Miss Dorrillon: "The wife of the former days is here happily delineated; the maid of the present time, we trust, is somewhat overcharged", in general commenting that "the whole is so well written, that it could not fail to produce a strong effect upon an audience", *British Critic* 10 (1797), pp. 133–6.

52. *The Monthly Review* 23 (1797), p. 462.

53. *The British Critic* 10 (1797), p. 136.

54. Elizabeth Inchbald, *Wives As They Were and Maids As They Are*, in Roger Manvell, ed. *Elizabeth Inchbald, Selected Comedies* (Lanham, New York, London: University Press of America, 1987), I, i., p. 10. All further references will be from this edition and cited parenthetically in the text.

55. As Anderson writes, "The historical gesture of the title [of this play] tends to collapse temporal distance even as it hints at historical change; marriage preserves the past as the living legacy of women", p. 196.

56. Taylor, *Records of My Life*, Vol. i., p. 399. Taylor himself presents this incident in a comical, even farcical manner. As he continues the story, "[Inchbald] then rushed out of the house, and proceeded in haste to the green-room of the theatre, where the company were then rehearsing. She entered the room with so wild an air, and with such evident emotion, that all present were alarmed. She hastily related what had happened as far as her impediment [a recurrent stutter] would permit her, and concluded with the following exclamation: 'Oh! If he had wo-wo-worn a wig, I had been ru-ruined'", Taylor, Vol. i., p. 399.

57. O'Quinn, "Scissors and Needles", p. 111, p. 109.

58. Sir William Blackstone, *Commentaries on the Laws of England*, 4 vols. (1765) (Chicago and London: University of Chicago Press, 1979), Vol. i, p. 430.

59. Mary Wollstonecraft, *Maria, or the Wrongs of Woman* (1798), (New York and London: W.W. Norton, 1994), p. 11.

60. Eve Tavor Bannet, "The Marriage Act of 1753: 'A Most Cruel Law for the Fair Sex' ", *Eighteenth-Century Studies* 30:3 (1997), pp. 243–4.

61. Negative portrayals of gambling in Inchbald's work appear through the characters of Lady Clementina and Lady Bendham in *Nature and Art*, Sir George Splendorville and Lady Caroline in *Next-Door Neighbours* (1791) and Claransforth and Lady Mary Diamond in *The Wise Man of the East* (1799). These portrayals focus on the more conventional depiction of gambling in order to present a social critique of dissipated aristocratic society.

62. O'Quinn, "Scissors and Needles", p. 122.

63. Bolton, *Women, Nationalism and the Romantic Stage*, p. 223.

64. It may be significant that at this very moment, as legal and patriarchal power combine to imprison her, Maria Dorrillon is mistakenly referred to with Inchbald's own name – "Elizabeth" (IV, iii, p. 56). This original error appears in the Larpent copy of the play, and was never corrected, continuing in the first and then in all successive editions of the printed text.

65. In the Larpent manuscript of the play, these lines read: "A modern maid shall become a primitive wife."

66. O'Quinn" Scissors and Needles", p. 124.

67. See Conolly, especially pp. 100–6, for examples of Larpent's treatment of social issues which did not directly refer to the French Revolution, but nonetheless reflected its concerns.

68. Boaden, Vol. i., appendix and p. 303.

69. Ibid., pp. 303–4.

70. Taylor, *Records of My Life*, Vol. i., p. 407.

71. Barrell, "The Reptile Oculist", p. 23.

72. Boaden, Vol. i., p. 304.

73. Elizabeth Inchbald, *The Massacre*, in Boaden, *Memoirs of Mrs. Inchbald*, Act III, p. 375. Further references will be from this edition and cited parenthetically in the text by act and page numbers as they appear in Boaden. The prefatory material appears on unnumbered pages and will be hereafter simply cited in the text under the headings in which they appear.

74. This letter appears in C. Kegan Paul, *William Godwin: His Friends and Contemporaries*, 2 vols. (London: Henry S. King and Co, 1876), Vol. i., p. 74. Inchbald begins the letter by responding to Godwin's apparent criticism of the lack of factual accuracy in the play, writing that, "like half [of] England", she relies on the newspapers for accounts of the events in France.

75. Although, to the best of my knowledge, there is no evidence of the actual responses of the theatre managers to the manuscript of *The Massacre*, this letter from George Colman to Inchbald tellingly locates the play as it awaited his reading and subsequent decision whether to produce it. As he writes, "I confess myself a woeful delinquent, as far as relates to the Tragedy: – but I will, now, attend to it very speedily," (Colman to Inchbald, 7 February 1792. Forster Collection, Victoria and Albert Museum. MS 116).

76. Daniel O'Quinn, "Elizabeth Inchbald's The Massacre: Tragedy, Violence and the Network of Political Fantasy" British Women Playwrights Around 1800. June 1999.

8 pars. http://www.etang. umontreal.ca/ bwp1800/essays/oquinn_massacre.html par.1.

77. Terence Hoagwood, for example, states that "Inchbald's play represents directly the September massacres of 1792," "Elizabeth Inchbald, Joanna Baillie, and Revolutionary Representation in the 'Romantic' Period", in Adriana Craciun and Kari Lokke, eds., *Rebellious Hearts: British Women Writers and the French Revolution* (Albany: State University of New York Press, 2001), p. 303.

78. Hoagwood, citing Jeffrey Cox, suggests that the source text for *The Massacre* could be Marie-Joseph Chenier's 1788 play *Charles IX*, which "also includes a massacre in Paris followed by counsel against massacre." He also acknowledges the importance of Inchbald's notes to the play, and the way they impose a factual reality on to the "imaginary space of the dramatic illusion", p. 305.

79. For a brief yet informative discussion of this issue, see Ronald Paulson, *Representations of Revolution (1789–1820)*, (New Haven and London: Yale University Press, 1983), p. 145. Conolly also discusses many specific examples of plays that employed this kind of historical displacement.

80. O'Quinn, "Elizabeth Inchbald's *The Massacre*", par. 6.

81. Inchbald to Godwin, 11 April 1797, quoted in C. Kegan Paul, Vol. i., p. 240.

82. See Judith Barbour, " 'Obliged to make this sort of deposit of our minds': William Godwin and the sociable contract of writing", in *Romantic Sociability: Social networks and Literary Culture in Britain 1770–1840*, eds. Clara Tuite and Gillian Russell (Cambridge: Cambridge University Press, 2002), pp. 166–85, for a discussion of Godwin's less than exemplary behavior following his marriage, not only in regard to Inchbald, but towards Wollstonecraft as well. See also Jenkins, pp. 401–5 for a discussion of these events that takes a benign view of Inchbald's role in her quarrel with Godwin.

83. C. Kegan Paul, Vol. i., p. 276, p. 278.

84. Godwin and Inchbald were in intermittent contact until the end of her life. In 1820, a year before her death, it appears that she had refused to see him, following which he wrote to her, "I have had the happiness to know you five & twenty years; & in all that time I can fully acquit you of any capricious actions towards me" (Godwin to Inchbald, 11 February 1820, Forster Collection, Victoria and Albert Museum, MS 226). He had actually known her for twenty-nine years.

85. C. Kegan Paul, p. 278.

Conclusion

1. Anne Janowitz, *Women Romantic Poets: Anna Barbauld and Mary Robinson*, (London: Northcote House, 2004), p. 105. Symonds had spent two years in jail, from 1793, for selling Paine's *The Rights of Man, Part II*.

2. *Odes*, by George Dyer, M. Robinson, AL. Barbauld, J. Ogilvie, &c. &c. ([Ludlow]: George Nicholson, 1800).

3. Judith Pascoe notes the original publication date in the *Oracle* in Mary Robinson, *Selected Poems*, ed. Judith Pascoe (Peterborough: Broadview Press, 2000), p. 410.

4. Mary Robinson, *The False Friend*, 4 vols., (London: Longman & Rees, 1799), Vol. iii, p. 242, p. 297.

5. "The Dungeon", from "The Progress of Liberty", in Pascoe, ed. *Selected Poems*, p. 311, lines 62, 70. The poems that make up "The Progress of Liberty" were originally published separately in the *Morning Post* between 1798–1800 (as well as one poem published in the *Monthly Magazine*.) They were published together as "The

Progress of Liberty" in Volume iv of Robinson's Memoirs in 1801. Pascoe details this publication history in *Selected Poems*, p. 298.

6. See Chapter 2, p. 67.

7. Matthew Bray, "Removing the Anglo-Saxon Yoke: The Francocentric Vision of Charlotte Smith's Later Works", *The Wordsworth Circle* 24:3 (1993), p. 156.

8. The original commentary appears in *The Anti-Jacobin Review and Magazine*, 24 (1806), p. 98. Inchbald's remarks appear in *Remarks on the British Theatre* (1806–1809), (Delmar, NY: Scholars Facsimiles and Reprints, 1990), "To Marry or Not to Marry", pp. 4–5. For a discussion of what became known as the Melville–Whitbread affair, see Roger Fulford, *Samuel Whitbread 1764–1815: A Study in Opposition* (London: Macmillan, 1967), chapter 11, "The Impeachment of Melville".

Works Cited

Manuscripts and manuscript letters

Uncollected manuscript letters

Tabitha Bramble [Mary Robinson] to Robert Dundas. 23 January 1794 National Archives, London HO 102/10

Mary Robinson to William Godwin.
24 August 1800. Bodleian Library. [Abinger] Dep. b. 215/2
28 August 1800. Bodleian Library. [Abinger] Dep. b. 215/2
2 September 1800. Bodleian Library. [Abinger] Dep. c. 507/7.
10 October 1800. Bodleian Library [Abinger] Dep. b. 215/2

Charlotte Smith to Sarah Farr Rose. 14 February 1804. Huntington Library. HM 18034.

William Godwin to Elizabeth Inchbald. 11 February 1820. Forster Collection. National Art Library. Victoria and Albert Museum, MS 226.

George Colman to Elizabeth Inchbald. 7 February 1792. Forster Collection. National Art Library. Victoria and Albert Museum. MS 116

John Philip Kemble to Elizabeth Inchbald. 17 July 1784. Forster Collection. National Art Library. Victoria and Albert Museum. MS 322.

Larpent collection of manuscript plays. Huntington Library, San Marino, California

Such Things Are (1786) LA 761
The Hue and Cry (1791) LA 900
Next-Door Neighbours (1791) LA 912
Every One Has His Fault (1793) LA 967
The Wedding Day (1794) LA 1044
Wives As They Were and Maids As They Are (1797) LA 1155
The Wise Man of the East (1799) LA 1271

Eighteenth-century newspapers and periodicals

The Analytical Review:
8 (1790)
10 (1791)
15 (1793)
18 (1794)
20 (1794)
23 (1796)
25 (1797)

27 (1798)
28 (1798)

The Anti-Jacobin; or Weekly Examiner. 14 May 1798.

The Anti-Jacobin Review:

1 (1798)
5–6 (1800)
24 (1806)

The British Critic:
3 (1794)
4 (1794)
7 (1796)
10 (1797)
12 (1798)

The Critical Review:
1 (1791)
7 (1793)
10 (1794)
16 (1796)

The European Magazine:
22 (1792)
25 (1794)

The General Magazine:
4 (1790)

The Monthly Review:
10 (1793)
13 (1794)
19 (1796)
23 (1797)

The True Briton
30 January 1793
1 February 1793

Pre-twentieth-century works

Barlow, Joel. *Advice to the Privileged Orders in the Several States of Europe, Resulting from the Necessity and Propriety of a General Revolution in the Principle of Government,* London: J. Johnson. 1792.
—— *Letter to the National Convention, on the Defects in the National Constitution of 1791,* London: J. Johnson. 1792.
Bisset, Robert. *Douglas, or the Highlander.* 4 vols. London: C. Chappel. 1800.
Blackstone, Sir William. *Commentaries on the Laws of England.* 4 vols. (1765) Chicago and London: University of Chicago Press. 1979.

Boaden, James. *Memoirs of Mrs. Inchbald: Including her Familiar Correspondence with the most distinguished persons of her time.* 2 vols. London: Richard Bentley. 1833.

Boswell, James. *Boswell's Life of Johnson* (1791). London: Oxford University Press. 1953.

Burke, Edmund. *Reflections on the Revolution in France* (1790). Ed. J.C.D. Clark. Stanford: Stanford University Press. 2001.

Burney, Frances. *Brief Reflections Relative to the Emigrant French Clergy* (1793). The Augustan Reprint Society Publication Number 262. William Andrews Clark Memorial Library. University of California, Los Angeles. 1990.

Burns, Robert. *Poems, chiefly in the Scottish dialect,* 3rd edn. London: A. Strahan, T. Cadell. 1787.

Chatterton, Thomas. *The Rowley Poems* (1777). Oxford and New York: Woodstock Books. 1990.

Cheyne, George. *The English Malady* (1733) in *Patterns of Madness in the Eighteenth Century, A Reader.* Ed. Allan Ingram. Liverpool: Liverpool University Press. 1998.

Dorset, Catherine Anne. "Charlotte Smith." *The Miscellaneous Prose Works of Sir Walter Scott,* Vol. iv; *Biographical Memoirs of Eminent Novelists and Other Distinguished Persons,* Vol. ii. Edinburgh: Robert Cadell; London: Whittaker and Co. 1834. 20–70.

Gifford, William, *The Baviad.* London: Becket and Porter. 1791.

—— *The Baviad and the Maeviad.* London: Becket and Porter. 1797. Sixth Edition. 1800. Eighth Edition. 1811.

Godwin, William. *An Enquiry concerning political justice, and its influence on morals and happiness,* 2nd edn. London: G.G. and J. Robinson. 1796.

—— *Things as They Are, or the Adventures of Caleb Williams* (1794). Ed. Maurice Hindle. London: Penguin. 1988.

—— *Memoirs of the Author of the Vindication of the Rights of Woman* (1798). Eds. Pamela Clemit and Gina Luria Walker. Peterborough, Ontario: Broadview Press. 2001.

Hamilton, Elizabeth. *Memoirs of Modern Philosophers* (1800). Ed. Claire Grogan, Peterborough, Ontario: Broadview Press, 2000.

Hazlitt, William. *The Life of Thomas Holcroft Written By Himself, Continued to the Time of his Death from his Diary Notes and Other Papers by William Hazlitt,* (1816) 2 vols. Ed. Elbridge Colby. London: Constable and Co. 1925.

—— "Lectures on the Comic Writers" (1819) in *The Collected Works of William Hazlitt* 12 vols. Eds. A.R. Waller and Arnold Glover. Vol. 8. London: J.M. Dent. 1902–1904.

—— *The Spirit of the Age* (1825). London: Oxford University Press. 1954.

Holcroft, Thomas. *Anna St. Ives.* 7 vols. London: Shepperson and Reynolds. 1792.

—— *The Adventures of Hugh Trevor* (1794–1797). Ed. Seamus Deane. Oxford: Oxford University Press. 1978.

Hume, David. "Essay: Of National Characters" (1748) in *The Philosophical Works / David Hume.* 4 vols. Eds. Thomas Hill Green and Thomas Hodge Grose. London: 1882. Vol. 1. *Essays Moral, Political and Literary.* 244–58.

Inchbald, Elizabeth. *The Child of Nature* (1786). *Cumberland's British Theatre.* London: 1829. Vol. 11.

—— *Such Things Are.* London: G.G. and J. Robinson. 1788.

—— *A Simple Story* (1791). Ed. J.M.S. Tompkins. Introduction. Jane Spencer. Oxford: Oxford University Press. 1986.

—— *The Massacre* (1792). In Boaden.

—— *Every One Has His Fault* (1793), *Elizabeth Inchbald: Selected Comedies.* Ed. Roger Manvell. Lanham, NY and London: University Press of America. 1987.

—— *Wives As They Were and Maids As They Are* (1793) in Manvell, ed. *Selected Comedies.*

—— *Nature and Art* (1796). Oxford and New York: Woodstock Books. 1994.

—— *Nature and Art.* 2nd. edn London: G.G. and J. Robinson: 1797.

—— *To Marry or Not to Marry.* London: Longman, Hurst, Rees and Orme. 1805.

—— "To the Artist." *The Artist: A Collection of Essays Relative to Painting, Poetry, Sculpture, Architecture, the Drama, Discoveries of Science, and Various Other Subjects* 1:14. (1807) 9–19.

—— *Remarks for the British Theatre* (1806–1809). Delmar, NY: Scholars Facsimiles and Reprints. 1990.

Mathias, Thomas J. *The Pursuits of Literature: A Satirical Poem in Dialogue with Notes.* London: T. Becket. 1794. Third Edition: 1796. Fourth Edition: 1797. Sixteenth Edition: 1812.

Merry, Robert. *The Laurel of Liberty.* London: John Bell. 1790.

More, Hannah. *Considerations on Religion and Public Education with Prefatory Address to the Ladies &c of great Britain and Ireland in Behalf of the French Emigrant Clergy.* The Augustan Reprint Society Publication Number 262. William Andrews Clark Memorial Library. University of California, Los Angeles. 1990.

—— "The Riot; or Half a Loaf is Better than No Bread." *Cheap Repository Shorter Tracts.* London: 1800.

Nicholson, George. *Odes,* by George Dyer, M. Robinson, A.L. Barbauld, J. Ogilvie, &c. &c. [Ludlow]: 1800.

Paul, C. Kegan. *William Godwin: His Friends and Contemporaries.* London: Henry S. King and Co. 1876.

Polwhele, Richard. *The Unsex'd Females.* London: Cadell and Davies. 1798.

Robinson, Mary. *Selected Poems.* Ed. Judith Pascoe. Peterborough, Ontario: Broadview Press. 2000.

—— *Impartial Reflections on the Present Situation of the Queen of France.* London: John Bell, 1791.

—— *Monody to the Memory of the Late Queen of France.* London: 1793.

—— *Angelina.* 3 vols. London: Hookham and Carpenter. 1796.

—— *Hubert de Sevrac.* 3 vols. London: 1796.

—— *The False Friend.* 4 vols. London: Longman & Rees. 1799.

—— *The Memoirs of the Late Mrs. Robinson, Written By Herself.* 4 vols. London: R. Phillips. 1801.

—— *The Poetical Works of the Late Mrs. Robinson, Written By Herself.* 1806.

—— *Walsingham* (1797). Ed. Julie A. Shaffer. Peterborough, Ontario: Broadview Press. 2003.

—— *The Natural Daughter* (1799). Ed. Sharon Setzer. Peterborough, Ontario: Broadview Press. 2003.

Rousseau, Jean-Jacques. *The Reveries of a Solitary Walker* (1778). Trans. Charles E. Butterworth. *The Collected Writings of Rousseau,* 12 vols. Vol. 8, ed. Christopher Kelly. Hanover and London: University Press of New England. 2000.

Smith, Charlotte. *Desmond* (1792). Ed. Antje Blank and Janet Todd. London: Pickering and Chatto. 1997.

—— *The Banished Man.* 4 vols. London: Cadell and Davies. 1794.

—— *Rural Walks: in Dialogues intended for the use of young persons.* 2 vols. London: Cadell and Davies. 1795.

—— *Marchmont* (1796). Delmar, NY: Scholars' Facsimiles and Reprints. 1989.

—— *The Young Philosopher* (1798). Ed. Elizabeth Kraft. Lexington, Kentucky: University Press of Kentucky. 1999.

—— *The Letters of a Solitary Wanderer (Vols. I–III).* (1800). New York: Woodstock Books. 1995.

Smith, Charlotte. *The Letters of a Solitary Wanderer (Vols. IV–V)*. London: Longman and Rees. 1802.
—— *Elegiac Sonnets*. London: 1811; London: 1827.
—— *The Poems of Charlotte Smith*. Ed. Stuart Curran. New York: Oxford University Press. 1993.
Sterne, Laurence. *The Life and Opinions of Tristram Shandy* (1760–1767). Ed. Ian Campbell Ross. Oxford and New York: Oxford University Press. 1983.
Taylor, John. *Records of My Life*. 2 vols. London: Edward Bull. 1832.
West, Jane. *A Tale of the Times*. 3 vols. London: Longman and Rees. 1799.
Williams, Helen Maria. *Letters Written in France* (1790). Eds. Neil Fraistat and Susan S. Lanser. Peterborough, Ontario: Broadview Press, 2001.
Wollstonecraft, Mary. *Political Writings*. Ed. Janet Todd. Buffalo and Toronto: University of Toronto Press. 1993.
—— *Maria, or the Wrongs of Woman* (1798). New York and London: W.W. Norton. 1994.

Twentieth- and twenty-first-century works

Adams, M. Ray. *Studies in the Literary Backgrounds of English Radicalism*. Lancaster, Pennsylvania: Franklin and Marshall College Studies. 1947.
Altman, Janet Gurkin. *Epistolarity: Approaches to a Form*. Columbus: Ohio State University Press. 1982.
Anderson, Misty. *Female Playwrights and Eighteenth-Century Comedy*. New York and Basingstoke: Palgrave – now Palgrave Macmillan. 2002.
Andress, David. *The Terror: The Merciless War for Freedom in Revolutionary France*. New York: Farrar, Straus and Giroux. 2005.
Backscheider, Paula. *Eighteenth-Century Women Poets and their Poetry*. Baltimore: Johns Hopkins University Press. 2005.
Bannet, Eve Tavor. "The Marriage Act of 1753: 'A Most Cruel Law for the Fair Sex'." *Eighteenth-Century Studies* 30:3 (1997). 233–54.
Barbour, Judith. " 'Obliged to make this sort of deposit of our minds': William Godwin and the sociable contract of writing." *Romantic Sociability: Social Networks and Literary Culture in Britain 1770–1840*, eds. Clara Tuite and Gillian Russell. Cambridge: Cambridge University Press. 2002. 166–85.
Barrell, John. *Imagining the King's Death: Figurative Treason, Fantasies of Regicide 1793–1796*. Oxford: Oxford University Press. 2000.
—— "The Reptile Oculist", *London Review of Books* 26:7, 1 April 2004.
Barrell, John and Jon Mee, eds. *Trials for Treason and Sedition*. 8 vols. London: Pickering and Chatto. 2006–7.
Bass, Robert. *The Green Dragoon: The Lives of Banastre Tarleton and Mary Robinson*. New York: Henry Holt. 1957.
Binhammer, Katherine. "Revolutionary Domesticity in Charlotte Smith's *Desmond*." *Women, Revolution and the Novels of the 1790s*. Ed. Linda Lang-Peralta. East Lansing: Michigan State University Press. 1999. 25–46.
Blank, Antje and Janet Todd. Introduction. *Desmond*. London: Pickering and Chatto. 1997. xi–xxxix.
Bloxam, Suzanne. *Walpole's Queen of Comedy: Elizabeth Farren, Countess of Derby*. Ashford, Kent: 1988.
Bolton, Betsy. "Farce, Romance, Empire: Elizabeth Inchbald and Colonial Discourse." *The Eighteenth Century: Theory and Interpretation* 39:1 (1998). 3–24.
—— *Women, Nationalism and the Romantic Stage: Theatre and Politics in Britain 1780–1800*. Cambridge: Cambridge University Press. 2001.

Botting, Fred. *Gothic*. London and New York: Routledge. 1996.

Bowstead, Diana. "Charlotte Smith's *Desmond*: The Epistolary Novel as Ideological Argument." *Fetter'd or Free?* Ed. Mary Anne Schofield and Cynthia Macheski. Athens: Ohio University Press. 1986. 237–63.

Bray, Matthew. "Removing the Anglo-Saxon Yoke: The Francocentric Vision of Charlotte Smith's Later Works." *The Wordsworth Circle* 24:3 (1993). 155–8.

Brewer, William D. "Charlotte Smith and the American Agrarian Ideal." *English Language Notes* 40:4. (2003). 51–61.

—— "The French Revolution as a Romance: Mary Robinson's *Hubert de Sevrac*." *Papers on Language and Literature* 42:2 (2006). 115–49.

Brown, Philip A. *The French Revolution in English History*. London: Frank Cass. 1965.

Butler, Marilyn. *Jane Austen and the War of Ideas*. London: Oxford University Press. 1975.

—— *Romantics, Rebels and Reactionaries*. Oxford and New York: Oxford University Press. 1981.

—— Ed., *Burke, Paine, Godwin and the Revolution Controversy*. Cambridge: Cambridge University Press. 1984.

Byrne, Paula. "*A Simple Story*: From Inchbald to Austen. *Romanticism* 5:2 (1999). 161–71.

—— *Perdita: The Life of Mary Robinson*. New York: HarperCollins. 2004.

Cameron, Kenneth Neill, ed. *Shelley and His Circle 1773–1822*. 2 vols. Cambridge: Harvard University Press. 1962.

Carpenter, Kirsty. *Refugees of the French Revolution: Émigrés in London, 1789–1802*. Basingstoke: Macmillan – now Palgrave Macmillan. 1999.

Castle, Terry. *Masquerade and Civilization*. Stanford: Stanford University Press. 1986.

—— "Marie Antoinette Obsession." *Representations* 38 (1992). 1–38.

Clark, J.C.D. Introduction. Edmund Burke, *Reflections on the Revolution in France*. Stanford: Stanford University Press. 2001. 23–111.

—— "William Godwin and James Watt's Copying Machine: Wet-transfer Copies in the Abinger Papers." *Bodleian Library Record*, 18:5 (2005). 532–60.

Clemit, Pamela. "Holding Proteus: William Godwin in his letters." *Repossessing the Romantic Past*. Eds. Heather Glen and Paul Hamilton. Cambridge: Cambridge University Press. 2006. 98–115.

—— Ed. and Intro. "Charlotte Smith to William and Mary Jane Godwin: Five Holograph Letters", *Keats-Shelley Journal* 55 (2006). 29–40.

—— and Gina Luria. Introduction. Godwin, William. *Memoirs of the Author of a Vindication of the Rights of Woman*. Peterborough, Ontario: Broadview Press. 2001. 11–36.

Colley, Linda. *Britons*. New Haven and London: Yale University Press. 1992.

Conolly, L.W. *The Censorship of English Drama 1737–1824*. San Marino, CA: The Huntington Library Press, 1976.

Conway, Alison. "Nationalism, Revolution, and the Female Body." *Women's Studies* 24:5: (1995). 395–409.

Copeland, Edward. *Women Writing About Money*. Cambridge: Cambridge University Press. 1995.

Cox, Jeffrey. "Baillie, Siddons, Larpent: gender, power and politics in the theatre of Romanticism." *Women in British Romantic Theatre*. Ed. Catherine Burroughs. Cambridge: Cambridge University Press. 2000. 23–47.

—— and Michael Gamer, eds. *The Broadview Anthology of Romantic Drama*. Peterborough, Ontario: Broadview Press. 2003.

Craciun, Adriana. "The New Cordays: Helen Craik and British Representations of Charlotte Corday, 1793–1800." *Rebellious Hearts: British Women Writers and the French Revolution.* Eds. Adriana Craciun and Kari Lokke. Albany: State University of New York Press, 2001. 193–232.

—— Ed. Hypertext edition, *Ainsi Va Le Monde.* http://www.rc.umd.edu/editions/contemps/robinson/mrainsi06frst.htm

—— *Fatal Women of Romanticism.* Cambridge: Cambridge University Press. 2003.

—— *British Women Writers and the French Revolution: Citizens of the World.* Basingstoke: Palgrave Macmillan. 2005.

—— and Karri Lokke. "Introduction: British Women Writers and the French Revolution, 1789–1815." *Rebellious Hearts.* 3–30.

Craft-Fairchild, Catherine. *Masquerade and Gender.* University Park: Pennsylvania State University Press. 1993.

Crochunis, Thomas. "Authorial performances in the criticism and theory of Romantic women playwrights." *Women in British Romantic Theatre.* Ed. Burroughs. 223–54.

Cullens, Chris. "Mrs. Robinson and the Masquerade of Womanliness." *Body and Text in the Eighteenth-Century.* Eds. Veronica Kelly and Dorothea von Mucke. Stanford: Stanford University Press. 1994. 266–89.

—— "The 'I' Altered." *Romanticism and Feminism.* Ed. Anne K. Mellor. Bloomington and Indianapolis: Indiana University Press. 1988. 185–207.

Curran, Stuart. "Mary Robinson's *Lyrical Tales* in Context." *Re-Visioning Romanticism: British Women Writers 1776–1837.* Eds. Carol Shiner Wilson and Joel Haefner. Philadelphia: University of Pennsylvania Press. 1994. 17–35.

—— ed. *The Poems of Charlotte Smith.* New York: Oxford University Press, 1993.

Davidoff, Leonore and Catherine Hall. *Family Fortunes: Men and Women of the English Middle Class 1780–1850.* London: Hutchinson. 1987.

DeJean, Joan. *Fictions of Sappho, 1546–1937.* Chicago and London: University of Chicago Press. 1989.

De Montluzin, Emily. *The Anti-Jacobins 1798–1800: The Early Contributors to the Anti Jacobin Review.* Basingstoke: Macmillan – now Palgrave Macmillan. 1988.

Donkin, Ellen. *Getting Into the Act: Women Playwrights in London 1776–1829.* London and New York: Routledge. 1994.

Doody, Margaret. "English Women Novelists and the French Revolution." *La Femme en Angleterre et dans Les Colonies Americaines aux XVII Et XVIIIe Siecles.* Publications de l'universite de Lille III. 1975.

—— "Deserts, Ruins and Troubled Waters: Female Dreams in Fiction and the Development of the Gothic Novel." *Genre* 10. 1977. 529–72.

Ellis, Frank. *Sentimental Comedy: Theory & Practice.* Cambridge: Cambridge University Press. 1991.

Ellis, Markman. *The Politics of Sensibility.* Cambridge: Cambridge University Press. 1996.

Erdman, David. V. *Commerce des Lumieres: John Oswald and the British in Paris, 1790–1793.* Columbia: University of Missouri Press. 1986.

Eze, Emmanuel Chukwudi. *Race and the Enlightenment.* Cambridge, MA. and Oxford: Blackwell. 1997.

Ezell, Margaret. *Writing Women's Literary History.* Baltimore and London: Johns Hopkins University Press. 1993.

Fairer, David. "Chatterton's Poetic Afterlife, 1770–1794: A Context for Coleridge's *Monody.*" *Thomas Chatterton and Romantic Culture.* Ed. Nick Groom. Basingstoke: Macmillan – now Palgrave Macmillan. 1999. 228–51.

Favret, Mary. *Romantic Correspondence*. Cambridge: Cambridge University Press. 1993.

Feldman, Paula. "Women Poets and Anonymity in the Romantic Era." *New Literary History* 33 (2002). 279–89.

Fergus, Jan and Janice Farrar Thaddeus. "Women, Publishers and Money, 1790–1820." *Studies in Eighteenth-Century Culture*. Vol. 17. Eds. John Yolton and Leslie Eileen Brown. East Lansing, Michigan: Colleagues Press. 1987. 191–207.

Fletcher, Loraine. *Charlotte Smith: A Critical Biography*. New York: St. Martin's Press – now Palgrave Macmillan. 1998.

Fraistat, Neil and Susan S. Lanser. Introduction. Helen Maria Williams, *Letters Written in France*. Peterborough, Ontario: Broadview Press. 2001. 9–50.

Frazer, Nancy. "Rethinking the Public Sphere: A Contribution to the Critique of Actually Existing Democracy", *Habermas and the Public Sphere*, ed. Craig Calhoun. Cambridge, MA: MIT Press. 1992. 109–42.

Fulford, Roger. *Samuel Whitbread 1764–1815: A Study in Political Opposition*. London: Macmillan. 1967.

Gilmartin, Kevin. *Writing Against Revolution: Literary Conservatism in Britain 1790–1832*. Cambridge: Cambridge University Press. 2007.

Gleadle, Kathryn and Sarah Richardson, eds. *Women in British Politics, 1760–1860: The Power of the Petticoat*. Basingstoke: Macmillan – now Palgrave Macmillan. 2000.

Goodman, Kevis. *Georgic Modernity and British Romanticism*. Cambridge: Cambridge University Press. 2004.

Goodwin, Albert. *The Friends of Liberty: The English Democratic Movement in the Age of the French Revolution*. Cambridge, MA: Harvard University Press. 1979.

Green, Katherine S. "Mr. Harmony and the Events of January 1793: Elizabeth Inchbald's *Every One Has His Fault*." *Theatre Journal* 56:1 (2004). 47–62.

Grenby, M.O. *The Anti-Jacobin Novel: British Conservatism and the French Revolution*. Cambridge: Cambridge University Press. 2001.

—— "Introduction." *The Banished Man. The Works of Charlotte Smith*. 14 vols. London: Pickering and Chatto. 2005–2007. Vol. 7. xix–xxxiii.

Griffin, Robert J. *Wordsworth's Pope*. Cambridge: Cambridge University Press. 1995.

—— "Anonymity and Authorship." *New Literary History* 30 (1999). 877–95.

Guest, Harriet. *Small Change: Women, Learning and Patriotism 1750–1810*. Chicago: University of Chicago Press. 2000.

—— "Suspicious Minds: Spies and Surveillance in Charlotte Smith's Novels of the 1790s". *Land, Nation and Culture, 1740–1840: Thinking the Republic of Taste*, eds. David Simpson, Nigel Leask and Peter de Bolla. Basingstoke: Palgrave Macmillan. 2005. 169–87.

Habermas, Jürgen. *The Structural Transformation of the Public Sphere*. Trans. Thomas Burger. Cambridge, MA: MIT Press. 1989.

Haggerty, George. "Female Abjection in Inchbald's *A Simple Story*." *Studies in English Literature* 36:3 (1996). 655–72.

Hampsher-Monk, Iain., ed. *The Impact of the French Revolution: Texts from Britain in the 1790s*. Cambridge: Cambridge University Press. 2005.

Heinzelman, Kurt. "Roman Georgic in the Georgian Age: A Theory of Romantic Genre." *Texas Studies in Literature and Language* 33:2 (1991). 182–214.

Hoagwood, Terence. "Elizabeth Inchbald, Joanna Baillie, and Revolutionary Representation in the 'Romantic' Period." *Rebellious Hearts*. Eds. Craciun and Lokke. 293–316.

Hunt, Lynn. "The Many Bodies of Marie Antoinette: Political Pornography and the Problem of the Feminine in the French Revolution." *Eroticism and the Body*

Politic. Ed. Hunt. Baltimore and London: Johns Hopkins University Press. 1991. 108–30.

Introduction. Richard Polwhele. *The Unsex'd Females.* etext.lib.virginia.edu/britpo/unsex/unsex.html

Janowitz, Anne. *Women Romantic Poets: Anna Barbauld and Mary Robinson.* London: Northcote House. 2004.

Jarrells, Anthony. *Britain's Bloodless Revolutions: 1688 and the Romantic Reform of Literature.* Basingstoke: Palgrave Macmillan. 2005.

Jenkins, Annibel. *I'll Tell You What: The Life of Elizabeth Inchbald.* Lexington: University Press of Kentucky. 2003.

—— *Jane Austen: Women, Politics and the Novel.* Chicago and London: University of Chicago Press. 1988.

Johnson, Claudia. Introduction. Hannah More, *Considerations on Religion and Public Education* and Frances Burney, *Brief Reflections Relative to the Emigrant French Clergy.* The Augustan Reprint Society Publication Number 262. William Andrews Clark Memorial Library. University of California, Los Angeles. 1990. iii–xi.

—— *Equivocal Beings: Politics, Gender and Sentimentality in the 1790s.* Chicago and London: University of Chicago Press. 1995.

Jones, Chris. *Radical Sensibility: Literature and Ideas in the 1790s.* New York and London: Routledge. 1993.

Jones, Vivien. "Placing Jemima: Women Writers of the 1790s and the Eighteenth-Century Prostitution Narrative." *Women's Writing* 4:2 (1997). 201–20.

Keane, Angela. *Women Writers and the English Nation in the 1790s.* Cambridge: Cambridge University Press. 2000.

Keegan, Bridget. "Nostalgic Chatterton: Fictions of Poetic Identity and the Forging of a Self-Taught Tradition." *Thomas Chatterton and Romantic Culture.* Ed. Groom. 210–227.

Kelly, Gary. *The English Jacobin Novel.* Oxford: Clarendon Press. 1976.

—— *English Fiction of the Romantic Period: 1789–1830.* London: Longman. 1989.

—— *Women, Writing, and Revolution 1790–1827.* Oxford: Clarendon Press. 1993.

—— "Women Writers and the French Revolution Debate: Novelizing the Revolution/Revolutionizing the Novel." *Eighteenth-Century Fiction* 6:4 (1994). 369–88.

Kennedy, Deborah. *Helen Maria Williams and the Age of Revolution.* Lewisburg: Bucknell University Press. 2002.

King, James and Charles Ryskamp, eds. *The Letters and Prose Writings of William Cowper. Volume IV: Letters 1792–1799.* Oxford: Clarendon Press. 1984.

Kraft, Elizabeth. Introduction. Charlotte Smith. *The Young Philosopher.* Lexington, Kentucky: University Press of Kentucky. 1999. ix–xxxii.

Labbe, Jacqueline M. *Charlotte Smith: Romanticism, Poetry and the Culture of Gender.* Manchester and New York: Manchester University Press. 2003.

Landes, Joan B. "The Public and the Private Sphere: A Feminist Reconsideration." *Feminists Read Habermas: Gendering the Subject of Discourse.* Ed. Johanna Meehan. New York and London: Routledge. 1995. 91–116.

Lanser, Susan. *Fictions of Authority: Women Writers and Narrative Voice.* Ithaca and London: Cornell University Press. 1992.

Lean, E. Tangye. *The Napoleonists: A Study in Political Disaffection 1760–1960.* London: Oxford University Press. 1970.

Macmillan, Dougald. *Catalogue of the Larpent plays in the Huntington Library.* San Marino: Huntington Library Press. 1939.

Makower, Stanley. *Perdita: A Romance in Biography.* London: Hutchinson and Co. 1908.

Maunu, Leanne. "Home is Where the Heart Is: National Identity and Expatriation in Charlotte Smith's *The Young Philosopher.*" *European Romantic Review* 15:1 (2004). 51–71.

Maurer, Shawn L. Introduction. Elizabeth Inchbald, *Nature and Art*. London: Pickering and Chatto. 1997. xi–xliv.

—— "Masculinity and Morality in Elizabeth Inchbald's Nature and Art." *Women, Revolution, and the Novels of the 1790s.* Ed. Linda Lang-Peralta. East Lansing: Michigan State University Press. 1999. 155–76.

McGann, Jerome. *The Poetics of Sensibility*. Oxford: Clarendon Press. 1996.

Mee, Jon. " 'Reciprocal expressions of kindness': Robert Merry, Della Cruscanism and the limits of sociability." *Romantic Sociability.* Eds. Russell and Tuite. Cambridge: Cambridge University Press. 2002. 104–22.

Mellor, Anne K. "Mary Robinson and the Scripts of Female Sexuality." *Representations of the Self from the Renaissance to Romanticism.* Eds. Patrick Coleman, Jayne Lewis and Jill Kowalik. Cambridge: Cambridge University Press. 2000. 230–59.

—— *Mothers of the Nation: Women's Political Writing in England, 1780–1830.* Bloomington and Indianapolis: Indiana University Press. 2000.

—— "Embodied Cosmopolitanism and the British Romantic Writer." *European Romantic Review* 17:3 (2006). 290–300.

Miller, Judith Davis. "The Politics of Truth and Deception: Charlotte Smith and the French Revolution." *Rebellious Hearts.* Ed. Craciun and Lokke. 337–63.

Murdoch, John. "The Landscape of Labor: Transformations of the Georgic." *Romantic Revolutions: Criticism and Theory.* Ed. Kenneth Johnston, Gilbert Chaitin, Karen Hanson and Herbert Marks. Bloomington and Indianapolis: Indiana University Press.1990. 176–93.

Nachumi, Nora. " 'Those Simple Signs': The Performance of Emotion in Elizabeth Inchbald's *A Simple Story.*" *Eighteenth-Century Fiction* 11:3 (1999). 317–38.

Norton, Rictor. *Gothic Readings: The First Wave, 1764–1840.* London and New York: Leicester University Press. 2000.

O'Quinn, Daniel. "Inchbald's Indies: Domestic and Dramatic Re-Orientations." *European Romantic Review* 9:2 (1998). 217–31.

—— "Scissors and Needles: Inchbald's *Wives As They Were, Maids As They Are* and the Governance of Sexual Exchange." *Theatre Journal* 51:2 (1999). 105–25.

—— "Elizabeth Inchbald's *The Massacre*: Tragedy, Violence and the Network of Political Fantasy." *British Women Playwrights Around 1800.* June 1999. 8 pars. http://www.etang.umontreal.ca/ bwp1800/essays/oquinn_massacre.html

Parker, Jo Alyson. "Complicating *A Simple Story*: Inchbald's Two Versions of Female Power." *Eighteenth-Century Studies* 30:3 (1997) 255–70.

—— "Mary Robinson and the Literary Marketplace." *Romantic Women Writers: Voices and Countervoices.* Eds. Paula R. Feldman and Theresa M. Kelley. Hanover and London: University Press of New England. 1995. 252–68.

Pascoe, Judith. *Romantic Theatricality*. Ithaca and London: Cornell University Press. 1997.

Patterson, Annabel. *Pastoral and Ideology*. Berkeley and Los Angeles: University of California Press. 1987.

Paulson, Ronald. *Representations of Revolution (1789–1820)*. New Haven and London: Yale University Press. 1983.

Peterson, Linda H. "Becoming an Author: Mary Robinson's *Memoirs* and the Origin of the Woman Artist's Autobiography." *Re-Visioning Romanticism.* Eds. Shiner Wilson and Haefner. 36–50.

Philp, Mark. *Godwin's Political Justice*. London: Duckworth. 1986.

—— "Thompson, Godwin and the French Revolution." *History Workshop Journal* 39:1 (1995) 89–101.

Poovey, Mary. *The Proper Lady and the Woman Writer*. Chicago and London: University of Chicago Press. 1984.

Porter, Roy. *Mind-Forg'd Manacles: A History of Madness in England from the Restoration to the Regency*. London: Athlone Press. 1987.

Prins, Yopie. *Victorian Sappho*. Princeton: Princeton University Press. 1999.

Punter, David. *The Literature of Terror*. London: Longman. 1980.

Rogers, Katharine. "Inhibitions on Eighteenth-Century Women Novelists: Elizabeth Inchbald and Charlotte Smith." *Eighteenth-Century Studies* 11 (1977). 63–78.

—— "Romantic Aspirations, Restricted Possibilities: The Novels of Charlotte Smith." *Revisioning Romanticism*. Eds. Shiner Wilson and Haefner. 193–209.

Russell, Gillian. *The Theatres of War: Performance, Politics and Society 1793–1815*. Oxford: Clarendon Press. 1995.

Saint-Amand, Pierre. "Adorning Marie Antoinette." *Eighteenth-Century Life* 15:3 (1991). 19–33.

St Cyres, Viscount. "The Sorrows of Mrs. Smith." *The Cornhill Magazine* XV (1903). 683–96.

Schama, Simon. *Citizens, A Chronicle of the French Revolution*. New York: Vintage Books. 1989.

Scheuermann, Mona. *Her Bread to Earn: Women, Society and Money from Defoe to Austen*. Lexington: University Press of Kentucky. 1993.

Semmel, Stuart. *Napoleon and the British*. New Haven and London: Yale University Press. 2004.

Setzer, Sharon. Introduction. Mary Robinson, *A Letter to the Women of England* and *The Natural Daughter*. Peterborough, Ontario: Broadview Press. 2003. 9–32.

—— "The Dying Game: Crossdressing in Mary Robinson's Walsingham." *Nineteenth-Century Contexts* 22 (2000). 501–20.

Shaffer, Julie A. "*Walsingham*: gender, pain, knowledge." *Women's Writing* 9:1 (2002). 69–85.

Shteir, Anne B. *Cultivating Women, Cultivating Science*. Baltimore and London: Johns Hopkins University Press. 1996.

Smallwood, Angela. "Women Playwrights, Politics and Convention: The Case of Elizabeth Inchbald's 'Seditious' Comedy *Every One Has His Fault*." Conference Paper. *Women's Writing in Britain 1660–1830*. University of Southampton. July 2003.

Spacks, Patricia Meyer. *Desire and Truth: Functions of Plot in Eighteenth-Century Novels*. Chicago and London: University of Chicago Press. 1990.

—— "Novels of the 1790s: Action and Impasse." *The Columbia History of the British Novel*. Ed. John Richetti. New York: Columbia University Press, 1994. 247–74.

Spencer, Jane. *The Rise of the Woman Novelist: From Aphra Behn to Jane Austen*. Oxford: Basil Blackwell. 1986.

Stafford, William. *English Feminists and their Opponents in the 1790s*. Manchester: Manchester University Press. 2002.

—— "Charlotte Smith's 'Literary Business': Income, Patronage and Indigence." *The Age of Johnson: A Scholarly Annual*. 1 (1987). 375–400.

Stanton, Judith Phillips. " 'This New-Found Path Attempting': Women Dramatists in England 1660–1800." *Curtain Calls: British and American Women and the Theatre*

1660–1820. Eds. Mary Anne Schofield and Cecilia Macheski. Athens, Ohio: Ohio University Press. 1991. 325–54.

—— Ed. *The Collected Letters of Charlotte Smith*. Bloomington and Indianapolis: Indiana University Press. 2003.

Staves, Susan. "British Seduced Maidens." *Eighteenth-Century Studies* 14:2 (1980). 109–34.

Taylor, Barbara. *Mary Wollstonecraft and the Feminist Imagination*. Cambridge: Cambridge University Press. 2003.

Thompson, E.P. *The Making of the English Working Class*. New York: Vintage Books. 1966.

Todd, Janet and Marilyn Butler, eds. *The Complete Works of Mary Wollstonecraft, Vol. 7: Contributions to the Analytical Review*. New York: New York University Press. 1989.

Ty, Eleanor. *Unsex'd Revolutionaries: Five Women Novelists of the 1790s*. Toronto and London: University of Toronto Press. 1993.

Watson, Nicola. *Revolution and the Form of the British Novel 1790–1825*. Oxford: Clarendon Press. 1994.

Williams, Raymond. *Keywords: A Vocabulary of Culture and Society*. London: Fontana. 1976.

Zimmerman, Sarah M. *Romanticism, Lyricism and History*. Albany: State University of New York Press. 1999.

Index